"Our most irresistible literary critic.... Much of the fun of reading Mendelsohn is his sense of play, his irreverence and unpredictability, his frank emotional responses.... He forces the [essay] form in directions Francis Bacon never imagined." —*The New York Times Book Review*

"A scrumptious stylist.... He writes better movie criticism than most movie critics, better theatre criticism than most theatre critics and better literary criticism than just about anyone...practically every sentence of this book [is] an eye-opener." —*The Guardian* (UK)

"Mendelsohn is now, and has been for some time, the finest critic alive.... [The essays] proceed from an unparalleled understanding of the Greek and Roman roots of storytelling, which he braids into reviews with a subtlety and patience that is beautiful to behold.... A supremely entertaining book." —*Toronto Star*

"Mendelsohn's work is absolutely vital in both senses of the word—it breaths with an exciting intelligence often absent in similar but stodgier writing, and it should be required reading for anyone interested in dissecting culture." —*The Daily Beast*

"Wide-ranging and absorbing, this new collection of essays from Mendelsohn is a joy from start to finish.... A wonderfully eclectic set of musings on the state of contemporary culture and the enduring riches of classical literature." —*Publishers Weekly* (Starred Review)

"A throwback...to the glorious public intellectuals of former days such as Dwight Macdonald and Robert Warshow.... 'Waiting for the Barbarians' adds up to more than the sum of its parts, evidencing an impressive range, depth and nobility of mind."

T0382799

"No one who these past years has followed the brilliant work of Daniel Mendelsohn in the pages of *The New York Review of Books*, *The New Yorker*, and *The New York Times Book Review* will be surprised by the extraordinary range of interest this splendid collection reveals. What is so remarkable is the consistency of acuity and sympathy which he brings to all his subjects.... He is, it becomes increasingly clear, one of our major critics." —*PEN Art of the Essay Award Citation*

"His essays often have a deft structure, building an essential question that is left hanging. Keep reading... and eventually you'll arrive at the answer. But the pleasure is not in the answer, necessarily—it's in the process." —*National Book Critics Circle Award Citation*

"Mendelsohn brings to his subjects both an attentive eye and a sympathetic mind.... Mixed reviews, in other hands often as dull as ditchwater, become intellectual detective stories, and Mendelsohn provides illuminating, elegant solutions." —*Bookforum*

"*Waiting for the Barbarians* is a demonstration of Mendelsohn's stunning ability to think—not for us but a step ahead of us as readers, pulling out figments, fragments, and philosophies that we might not catch.... Reading Mendelsohn is a bit like lucid dreaming." —*Interview*

"These essays demonstrate what Coleridge called, in a striking phrase, 'the armed vision,' the highly trained critical intellect, powered by real scholarship and warmed by wit and empathy." —*The Denver Post*

"For Mendelsohn, TV is no less powerful or permanent than epic poetry in shaping, or describing, a society. We are what we watch, read and listen to. This may seem like a high-minded approach to pop culture, but Mendelsohn's not above sitting back with a fistful of popcorn.... For the reader, it's exhilarating to join him." —*The Plain Dealer*

Waiting for the Barbarians

Essays from the Classics to Pop Culture

Waiting for the Barbarians

Essays from the Classics to Pop Culture

Daniel Mendelsohn

NEW YORK REVIEW BOOKS

New York

THIS IS A NEW YORK REVIEW BOOK
PUBLISHED BY THE NEW YORK REVIEW OF BOOKS

WAITING FOR THE BARBARIANS:
ESSAYS FROM THE CLASSICS TO POP CULTURE

Published by The New York Review of Books, 435 Hudson Street, Suite 300, New York, NY 10014
www.nyrb.com

Cover design: Evan Johnston

The Library of Congress has catalogued
the hardcover edition of this book as follows:

Mendelsohn, Daniel Adam, 1960–
  Waiting for the barbarians : essays from the classics to pop culture / by
Daniel Mendelsohn.
    p. cm. — (The New York Review collection)
  ISBN 978-1-59017-607-8 (alk. paper)
  1. Canon (Literature) 2. Literature—Appreciation. 3. Popular culture—21st
century. I. Title.
  PN81.M514 2012
  801'.95—dc23
                              2012012240

ISBN 978-1-59017-713-6

Available as an electronic book; ISBN 978-1-59017-609-2

Printed in the United States of America on acid-free paper

3 5 7 9 10 8 6 4 2

Contents

in memory of my father,
multas per gentes et multa per aequora vectus
haec accipe multum manantia fletu

Foreword

DON'T WORRY. ALTHOUGH the title of this book may seem alarmist, there's nothing to be anxious about. At least, that's what the author of the poem from which I borrowed it thought.

In Constantine Cavafy's "Waiting for the Barbarians," the representatives of a very grand and sophisticated culture, unnamed but apparently Rome, assemble at the city gate in great state, from the emperor to his various officials, awaiting the arrival of envoys from the (also unnamed) "barbarians." The city has fallen into an anticipatory stupor: the senators sit around making no laws, and the orators fall silent, having tactfully absented themselves. (The barbarians are "bored by eloquence and public speaking.") They all wait from early morning until evening, fidgeting with their embroidered scarlet togas, their amethysts and emeralds, until it becomes clear that the barbarians aren't going to come. Only in the final line of the poem does Cavafy give the proceedings an unexpected twist: the emperor and the rest, you learn, are actually looking forward to the barbarians' arrival. "Perhaps these people," the narrator sighs in the last line, "were a solution of a sort."

So the poem is about confounded expectations in more ways than one. There's the disappointed anticipation of the waiting emperor and his people, of course, but even more, perhaps, there are the oddly thwarted expectations of the reader of the poem, which have been set up by that sonorous, portentous, and now-famous title. Detached from its context, the phrase "waiting for the barbarians," which has been used as everything from the title of a novel by J. M. Coetzee to the name of a chic men's clothing store in Paris, seems to be about the plight of a precious civilization perilously under siege by the crude forces of barbarity. And yet Cavafy himself clearly saw it differently. A note he wrote in 1904, the year he published the poem, indicates that for him it was "not at all opposed to my optimistic notion"—that it represented, indeed, "an episode in the progress toward the good."

Why, you wonder, should the imminent advent of the barbarians suggest positive progress? Here it's important to remember a bit of biography. Cavafy had come of age in the late nineteenth century, the era of the flowery and highly perfumed Decadents, and only when he was around forty—the time he wrote "Waiting for the Barbarians"—did he set about stripping his work of all derivative artifice, transforming himself into an idiosyncratic modernist. So the poem may well be a parable about artistic growth—the unexpectedly complex and even, potentially, fruitful interaction between old cultures and new, between (we might say) high and low; about the way that what's established and classic is always being refreshed by new energies that, at the time they make themselves felt, probably seem barbaric to some. As Cavafy knew well—he was, after all, a specialist in the marginal moments of ancient history, the era in which Greece yielded to Rome, when paganism met Christianity, when antiquity made its long and gentle slide into the early Middle Ages—there rarely are any real "barbarians." What others might see as declines and falls look, when seen from the bird's-eye vantage point of history, more like shifts, adaptations, reorganizations.

The meeting of the ancient and the contemporary worlds is one theme that connects the twenty-four essays in this collection. Some of the pieces here are dedicated to the classics themselves: for instance, an essay on a new translation of the *Iliad*, collected in the section called "Classica" (a rubric I owe to my longtime flea-marketing companion Bob Gottlieb, who thus christened a vast category of household knickknacks). And a number of them are concerned with the "waiting for the barbarians" phenomenon: they consider the ways in which the present, and especially popular culture, has wrestled, sometimes successfully and sometimes not, with the past. Julie Taymor's *Spider-Man* musical tried and failed to adapt ancient myths of metamorphosis to modern comic-book sensibilities; it's interesting to think why the two genres don't really mix. Jonathan Littell's *The Kindly Ones* owes a major debt to Aeschylus' *Oresteia*. No fewer than three significant novels published in 2010 took classical myths as their starting points, and their adaptations, as always, tell us as much about the present as they do about the past.

But by far most of these essays are concerned with contemporary popular culture and its products: television, movies, plays, novels, memoirs. Nearly all were first published over the past five years—since 2007, that is, when the manuscript for my first collection was submitted. (The remaining handful, with one exception, were all published within the past ten.) A recurring theme in that collection, *How Beautiful It Is and How Easily It Can Be Broken*, was the effect of the September 11 attacks on pop culture in the first half of the first decade of the new century. It's now clear to me that in the second half of that decade (and since), I've been preoccupied with what I think of as the "reality problem": how the extraordinary blurring between reality and artifice that has been made possible by new technologies makes itself felt not only in our entertainments—the way we create and experience movies (*Avatar*) and Broadway shows (*Spider-Man*, again)—but in the way we think about, and conduct, our lives. Certainly one side effect of the ongoing erosion of the boundary between the inner and the outer self, itself made possible by new technologies and media that allow us to be private in public (smartphones, iPods, blogs, Facebook, etc.), is a profound alteration in our sense of what is truth and what is fiction: readers of a good deal of contemporary writing must ponder the difference between (as one memoirist has put it) "real reality" and "my reality." (This is the subject of my *New Yorker* essay about the memoir craze, "But Enough About Me.") These various erosions have broad and fascinating ramifications. Not the least of these is the way we think about, and re-create, the historical past in our various entertainments: *Mad Men*, novels, *Titanic*, autobiography. The reality problem is, I think, the preeminent cultural event of our day, and references to it crop up more than once here.

The present volume is organized in four sections, each representing a special interest of mine. The title of the first, "Spectacles," shows traces of the career I had embarked on before I started writing and reviewing: as a graduate student in classics, I was particularly interested in Greek tragedy, specifically in the relationship between public theatrical displays and the life of the wider society, its social and political values. Then comes "Classica" (thanks, Bob!); then "Creative Writing," containing a number of pieces on novelists and poets, both contemporary and "classic." Some of these are well known, and what I have to say about them (*The Charterhouse of Parma*, for instance) very likely amounts to a statement about what my standards for the novel or for poetry might be; for others, such as the novels of Fontane or *Sepharad*, the underappreciated masterpiece by the contemporary Spanish novelist Antonio Muñoz Molina, I am happy to advocate. Finally, there is "Private Lives." As someone who has published two memoiristic books myself, I'm keenly interested in how private life ends up represented on the page; the essays in this section ponder that vexed question in various ways.

All of these pieces were written for periodicals, and nearly all appear here more or less as they did when first published. The only cases in which the versions here are substantially different are the essay on Edmund White's memoir, which here takes the form it had before I made a last-minute (and, I now see, unhelpful) structural change; and the piece on Jonathan Franzen's autobiographical essays, which appeared in print at half the length of the original draft. (My fault: I wrote too much for the assigned space.) As for the rest, I have, for the most part, refrained from editing them, apart from a few cases of smoothing out and sharpening; they are, in the end, pieces of journalism, and as such reflect the moment in which they were written.

As any working writer knows, the large part of what's successful in a piece of writing is the work of the editor. This collection owes its existence in particular to the three editors whom I've been enormously lucky to work with over years: Bob Silvers at *The New York Review of Books*, a figure who needs neither an introduction nor my accolades, and to whom in many ways I owe my career; the indefatigable Leo Carey at *The New Yorker*, by now a great friend; and, in many ways hovering over all these pieces although he only actually edited one, Charles McGrath, with whom I worked so often at *The New York Times Book Review* and who, you might say, has been my Chiron. He was particularly great about helping me think through this book and what should be in it. It goes without saying, once again, that Bob Gottlieb has had an enormous influence on nearly everything I've written from the start, a debt I doubt I'll ever be able to repay (among so many).

The person who got all this into book form (following the welcome suggestion by Rea Hederman) is Michael Shae at New York Review Books, whose patience, good sense, and generosity toward me, during an especially trying time, made this collection possible. Lydia Wills shepherded it through with her usual grace and common sense. To all of them, as Bob S. would say, "great thanks"!

I. SPECTACLES

THE WIZARD

TWO HUGELY POPULAR mashups—homemade videos that humorously juxtapose material from different sources—currently making the rounds on the Internet seek to ridicule James Cameron's visually ravishing and ideologically awkward new blockbuster, *Avatar*. In one, the portentous voice-over from the trailer for Disney's Oscar-winning animated feature *Pocahontas* (1995) has been seamlessly laid over footage from *Avatar*, in which, as in *Pocahontas*, a confrontation between dark-skinned native peoples and white-skinned invaders intent on commercial exploitation is leavened by an intercultural love story. "But though their worlds were very different . . . their destinies were one," the plummy voice of the narrator intones, interrupted by the sound of a Powhatan saying, "These pale visitors are strange to us!"

The other mashup reverses the joke. Here, dialogue from *Avatar*—a futuristic fantasy in which a crippled ex-Marine is given a second chance at life on a strange new world called Pandora, and there falls in love with a native girl, a complication that confuses his allegiances—has been just as seamlessly laid over bits of *Pocahontas*.

In one, we see an animated image of Captain John Smith's ship after it makes its fateful landing at Jamestown, while we hear the voice of a character in *Avatar*—a tough Marine colonel as he welcomes some new recruits to Pandora—sardonically quoting a bit of movie dialogue that has become an iconic expression of all kinds of cultural displacement. "Ladies and gentlemen," he bellows, "you are not in Kansas anymore!"

The satirical bite of the mashups is directed at what has been seen as the highly derivative, if not outright plagiaristic, nature of *Avatar's* plot, characters, and themes; themes that do, in many ways, seem like sci-fi updatings of the ones you find in *Pocahontas*. In the film, the ex-Marine, Jake Sully—wounded in a war in Venezuela and now a paraplegic—begins as the confused servant of two masters. On the one hand, he is ostensibly assisting in a high-tech experiment in which human subjects, laid out in sarcophagus-like pods loaded with wires that monitor their brain waves, remotely operate laboratory-grown "avatars" of the indigenous anthropoids, nine-foot-tall, cyan-colored, nature-loving forest-dwellers called Na'vi. All this technology is meant to help the well-intentioned scientists to integrate and, ultimately, negotiate with the Na'vi in order to achieve a diplomatic solution to a pesky colonial problem: their local habitation, which takes the form of an enormous tree-hive, happens to sit on top of a rich deposit of a valuable mineral that the humans have come to Pandora to mine.

The problem is that Jake's other master—for whom he is, at first, secretly working, infiltrating the Na'vi with an eye to gathering strategic reconnaissance—is the mercenary army of Marines employed by the mysterious "Company" that's mining the precious mineral. (Anonymous, exploitive corporations are a leitmotif in the movies of this director.) It's clear from the start that both the Company and the Marines are itching to eschew diplomacy for a more violent and permanent solution to the Na'vi problem. The dramatic arc of the movie traces Jake's shift in consciousness as he gradually comes to appreciate Na'vi culture, with its deep, organic connection to nature (and—the inevitable romantic subplot—as he comes to adore a lovely Na'vi princess bearing the Egyptian-sounding name of Neytiri). Eventually, Jake goes over to their side, leading the native people in a climactic, extremely violent uprising against their thuggish oppressors.

So far, it would seem, so politically correct. And yet most of the criticisms that have been leveled at the film since its premiere are, in fact, aimed at the nature of its politics rather than at the originality (or lack thereof) of its vision. Many critics have lambasted Cameron's film for what they see as the patronizing, if not racist, overtones of its representation of the "primitive" Na'vi; the underlying hypocrisy of a celebration of nature on the part of a special-effects-laden Hollywood blockbuster (to say nothing of the film's polemic against technology and corporate greed); and the way it betrays what David Brooks, in a *New York Times* Op-Ed column, derided as the movie's "White Messiah" complex:

> It rests on the stereotype that white people are rationalist and technocratic while colonial victims are spiritual and athletic. It rests on the assumption that nonwhites need the White Messiah to lead their crusades. It rests on the assumption that illiteracy is the path to grace. It also creates a sort of two-edged cultural imperialism. Natives can either have their history shaped by cruel imperialists or benevolent ones, but either way, they are going to be supporting actors in our journey to self-admiration.

Criticisms such as Brooks's are not to be dismissed—not least because the ugly complex he identifies is one that has consistently marred Hollywood representations of cultural confrontation from the earliest westerns to the more recent products of a supposedly more enlightened age. (One of the many earnest movies to which *Avatar* has been derisively compared by its detractors is the 1990 Kevin Costner epic *Dances with Wolves*, in which a Civil War hero similarly goes native, leading the Indian tribes against his former compatriots.) What's striking is that so many critiques of *Avatar*'s political shortcomings often go out of their way to elide or belittle the movie's overwhelming successes as a work of cinema—its enormous visual power, the thrilling imaginative originality, the excitingly effective use of the 3-D technology that seems bound to change permanently the nature of cinematic experience henceforth—as if to acknowledge how dazzling it is would be an admission of critical weakness.

An extreme example of this is to be found in a searching critique posted by the critic Caleb Crain on his blog:

> Of course you don't really believe it. You know objectively that you're watching a series of highly skilled, highly labor-intensive computer simulations. But if you agree to suspend disbelief, then you agree to try to feel that Pandora is a second, improved nature, and that the Na'vi are "digital natives," to repurpose in a literal way a phrase that depends on the same piece of ideological deception.

But our "objective knowledge" about the mechanisms that produce theatrical illusion is beside the point. To witness a critic working so hard not to surrender disbelief—the aim, after all, of drama since its inception—is, in a way, to realize how powerful the mechanisms that seek to produce that surrender really are. (A notable exception to the trend of critical resistance was the *New Yorker* review by David Denby, which began, "Avatar is the most beautiful film I've seen in years.") As it happens, the movie that haunts *Avatar*—one that Cameron has often acknowledged as his favorite film—is one that takes the form of a fable about the difference (and sometimes traffic) between fantasy and reality; a movie whose dramatic climax centers on the moment when the protagonist understands that visually overwhelming and indeed politically manipulative illusions can be the product of "highly skilled, highly labor-intensive simulations" (a fact that does not, however, detract from the characters', and from our, appreciation of the aesthetic and moral uses and benefits of fantasy, of illusion). That movie is, in fact, the one the Marine colonel quotes: *The Wizard of Oz*. Consideration of it is, to my mind, crucial to an understanding not only of the aesthetic aims and dramatic structure of *Avatar* but of a great and disturbing failure that has not been discussed as fervently or as often as its overtly political blind spots have been. This failure is, in certain ways, the culmination of a process that began with the first of Cameron's films, all of which can be seen as avatars of his beloved model, whose themes they continually rework: the scary and often violent confrontation between human and alien civilizations, the dreadful allure of the monstrous, the yearning, by us humans, for transcendence: of the places, the cultures, the very bodies that define us.

———

Humanity and human life have never held much attraction for Cameron; if anything, you can say that in all his movies there is a yearning to leave the flesh of *Homo sapiens* behind for something stronger and tougher. The movie that made his name and established him as a major writer-director of blockbuster successes, *The Terminator* (1984), is ostensibly about the poignant conflict between the human race and a race of sentient, human-hating machines that create a lethal new weapon: a cyborg,—"part man, part machine... fully armored, very tough. But outside it's living human tissue. Flesh, hair, blood...." The plot, which essentially consists of a number of elaborately staged chase sequences, concerns the attempts by one of these, famously played by Arnold Schwarzenegger—an actor notorious for his fleshly armor as well as for his rather mechanical acting—who returns to the present from a post-apocalyptic future in order to assassinate a woman called Sarah Connor: we are told that she will one day give birth to the boy who, when he grows up, is destined to lead a successful human uprising against the machine overlords.

But whatever lip service it pays to the resilience of the human spirit, etc., the film cannot hide its more profound admiration for the resilience of the apparently indestructible cyborg. As the story evolves, this creature loses ever-increasing amounts of its human envelope in various encounters with the woman and her protectors—an eye here, a limb there—and is stripped, eventually, of all human characteristics. By the end, it emerges out of an explosion as a titanium skeleton, hell-bent on pure destruction. In an interview with *The New Yorker* that appeared just before the release of *Avatar*, Cameron recalled that the inspiration for the movie, which he says came to him in a dream, was this sole image: "a chrome skeleton emerging out of a fire." Everything else came later.

It would be hard to claim that Cameron—who has managed to wring clanking and false performances from fine actors like Kate Winslet, Leonardo DiCaprio, Billy Zane (*Titanic*), and Mary Elizabeth Mastrantonio (*The Abyss*)—is an actor's director; his films' emotional energy, and certainly their visual interest, lie in their awed appreciation of what machines (and inhuman creatures) can do, from the seemingly unkillable cyborgs of the *Terminator* movies to the unstoppable alien monster queen of *Aliens* to the deep-sea diving capsules and remote-controlled robots featured in *Titanic* and *The Abyss*. The performances that work in his films, significantly, are either those of mediocre actors like Schwarzenegger who actually play machines or good actors playing tight-lipped, emotionally shut-down characters, like Sigourney Weaver in *Aliens* (1986), which Cameron wrote and directed.

The Terminator had a dark sense of humor about our relationship to technology, an issue that is at the core, in its way, of *Avatar*. In one memorably disturbing scene, a woman can't hear her boyfriend being beaten to death by the Terminator because she's listening to loud pop music with her headphones on; in another, we—and the Terminator—overhear a crucial message on Sarah Connor's answering machine, which greets callers with the sly announcement: "Ha ha, I fooled you, you're talking to a machine. But that's OK, machines need love too." The joke is that they don't—and that's their advantage. It's no accident that by the end of *Terminator 2: Judgment Day*, Cameron's hit 1991 sequel to the original, Sarah Connor has become rather machinelike herself—pointedly, even cruelly suppressing maternal feelings for the child she has borne, strenuously working out, hardening her body, arming herself to the teeth with an eye-popping arsenal of handguns and automatic weapons.

The fascination with the seeming invincibility of sophisticated mechanical objects, and an accompanying desire to slough off human flesh and replace it with metal (and a celebration of flesh so taut it may as well be metal: Cameron's camera loves to linger on the tightly muscled bodies, male and female, of the soldiers so often featured in his violent films), is a recurrent theme in the techno-blockbusters that cemented the director's reputation in the late 1980s and throughout the 1990s. *Aliens* famously ends with Weaver's character, Ellen Ripley, battling the dragonish alien monster queen after strapping herself into a giant forklift-like machine whose enormous pincers she mechanically controls by maneuvering her own slender arms—a technology that puts the puny human, finally, on a par with her gigantic, razor-toothed, acid-bleeding adversary.

This kind of exaggerated mechanical body gear, which endows people with machinelike strength and power, is a recurrent prop in Cameron's films. It's crucial in *Aliens* and it pops up again in his 1989 submarine fantasy *The Abyss*, which imagines an encounter between a deep-sea oil-drilling team and an ethereally beautiful, bioluminescent species of marine aliens. Even in *Titanic* (1997), the clunky "human interest" subplot, about a doomed romance between a feisty Main Line nymphet and a free-spirited artist in third class, cannot compete with the swooning representation of machines—the ship itself, the whirring turbines and purring hydraulics—and, later, with the awful, methodical disintegration of those mechanical elements. There are a lot of glittering modern-day gadgets, too: the famous disaster story is intercut with scenes of present-day dives to the great wreck, during which human operators remotely manipulate treasure-hunting drones by means of sympathetic arm movements.

A violent variation on the same mechanical bodysuits reappears, memorably, in *Avatar*, which culminates in a scene of bloody single combat between a Na'vi warrior and the evil Marine colonel, who has strapped himself into one such machine. If anything, the recurrent motif of humans inserting themselves into mechanical contraptions in order to enjoy superhuman powers reaches its fullest, most sophisticated expression in the new movie, whose characters can literally become other, superhuman beings by hooking themselves up to elaborate machines. All this seems to bear out the underlying truth of a joke that Linda Hamilton, the actress who played Sarah Connor in the *Terminator* movies, told about her first, unhappy interactions with the director (whom she later married and divorced): "That man is definitely on the side of the machines."

The awed appreciation for superhuman powers—and an understandable desire by human weaklings to lay claim to them, in times of great duress—that recur in Cameron's work before *Avatar* surely betrays a lingering trace of his formative encounter with *The Wizard of Oz*. That movie famously shows us a helpless twelve-year-old, set loose in a strange world inhabited by scary monsters and powerful aliens, discovering her own hitherto unknown powers—and learning, in the end, that certain supposedly supernatural powers are produced by knowing how to maneuver the right gears and levers.

Another inheritance from that visually revolutionary work, of course, is Cameron's taste for plots that have to do with encounters between humans and aliens of one sort or another. *Avatar* would seem to be the most obvious manifestation of this particular debt by Cameron to his favorite film. Apart from a number of explicit allusions to *Oz*—the line about not being in Kansas anymore, a corporate stooge's sneering reference to the Na'vi as "blue monkeys," which recalls the blue-tinged flying monkeys of the 1939 movie—the encounter between the human world and the world of the Na'vi is imbued with a sense of thrilled visual amazement that deliberately evokes a similar experience provided by the Hollywood classic. In the latter, Dorothy's life in Kansas was filmed in black and white; only when she awakes in Oz does the film move into dazzling three-strip Technicolor. In *Avatar*, Cameron quotes this famous gesture. Jake Sully's world, the world of the humans—the interior of the marine transports and fighters, the hangars and meeting rooms, the labs of the scientists and the offices of the nameless corporation—is filmed in a drably monotonous palette of grays and blues (the latter being a favorite color of this director, who uses it often to represent a bleak future); the world of the Na'vi, in contrast, is one of staggering color and ravishing light.

The colors, apart from the opulent greens of the Na'vis' jungle homeland, tend to be lusciously "feminine" on the flora: violet, mauve, delicate peaches and yellows. They grow stronger on the fauna, a series of brilliantly imagined creatures among which, persuasively, certain morphologies recur. (Crests, say, and hammerheads.) All, the plants and animals both, share one trait that clearly owes much to Cameron's lifelong passion for marine exploration, and that provides *Avatar* with much of its visual delight: bioluminescence. As the characters tread on plants or trees, the latter light up delicately, for a moment; the ritually important Tree of Souls looks like a weeping willow made of fiber-optic cables. It's a wonderful conceit that had me literally gasping with pleasure the first time I saw the movie.

This visual ravishment—which is the principal experience of the movie and which is, too, enhanced by the surprisingly subtle use of 3-D technology (there are gratifyingly few shots of objects projecting into the audience's field; you just feel that you're sharing the same plane as the creatures in the movie)—is part of a strategy intended to make us admire the Na'vi. Not surprisingly, given all this natural synergy and beauty, the native people, as we are told again and again, enjoy a special bond with all those colorful creatures and, more generally, with the ecosystem, to which they have given the name Eywa. (Cameron, apparently as much a stickler for linguistic as for biological verisimilitude, had a professor at the University of Southern California work up a functional Na'vi language.)

This, in turn, is part of the film's earnest, apparently anticolonial, anticapitalist, antitechnology message. These creatures, rather sentimentally modeled on popular notions of Native American and African tribes, are presented as being wholly in tune with nature—as preagricultural hunter-gatherers who subsist on the flesh of the animals they kill by means of their remarkable skill at archery. When they do make a kill, they solemnly apologize to the victims: "All energy is borrowed and one day you have to give it back," Neytiri rather officiously informs the avatar-Jake when he makes his first kill. They stand, therefore, in stark contrast to the movie's humans (the "sky-people"), with their heavy, rumbling, roaring copters and tractors and immense, belching, grinding mining-machines—the representatives of destructive "technology" who have, we are told, "killed their mother": which is to say, destroyed their own planet.

All this would be well and good enough, in its genially eco-friendly, *Pocahontas*-esque way, but for the fact that Cameron is the wrong man to be making a film celebrating the virtues of pretechnological societies. As, indeed, he has no intention of doing here. For as the admiring scientists—led by a chain-smoking, tough-talking woman called Grace Augustine, played by Sigourney Weaver (the chain-smoking is an in-joke: *Aliens'* Ripley had the same bad habit)—protest to the trigger-happy Marines, Na'vi civilization is in fact technologically sophisticated: by means of a pistil-tipped appendage, wittily described by Caleb Crain as a kind of USB cable, which plugs into similar appendages on both plants and animals, they can commune not only with other creatures but with what constitutes a planetwide version of a technology with which we today are very preoccupied. "Don't you get it?" an exasperated Dr. Augustine shouts at the corporate and military yahoos who clearly intend to blow all the Na'vi to kingdom come. "It's a network—a global network!" She goes on to describe how, by means of the pistil-thing, the Na'vi can upload and download memories, information, and so forth—and can even communicate with their dead. (One such upload to Eywa herself, transmitted through the Tree of Souls by Jake's avatar, will, in the end, help lead the Na'vi and their furry friends to victory over the human exploiters. This, of course, is the *Dances with Wolves* paradigm.)

And so, even as it looks like it's celebrating nature, *Avatar* is really a valentine to the digital technology that makes so many of its effects possible. Here the film, for all its richly imagined and dazzlingly depicted beauties, runs into deep and revealing trouble. As we know by now, Cameron's real attraction, as a writer and a director, has always been to the technologies that turn humans into superhumans. However "primitive" they have seemed to some critics, the Na'vi— with their uniformly superb, sleekly blue-gleaming physiques, their weirdly infallible surefootedness, their organic connector cables, their ability to upload and download consciousness itself—are the ultimate expression of his career-long striving to make flesh mechanical. The problem here is not a patronizingly clichéd representation of an ostensibly primitive people; the problem is the movie's intellectually incoherent portrayal of its tribal heroes as both admirably precivilized and admirably hypercivilized, as atechnological and highly technologized.

Avatar's desire to have its ideological cake and eat it too suggests something deeply unself-aware and disturbingly unresolved within Cameron himself. And how could it not? He is, after all, a Hollywood giant who insists on seeing himself as a regular Joe, a man with what he called, in the *New Yorker* interview, a "blue-collar sensibility"; more to the point, he is a director whose hugely successful mass entertainments cost hundreds of millions of dollars obligingly provided by deep-pocketed corporations—a "company" man, whether he knows it or not. And these shows depend for their effects—none more than *Avatar*—on the most sophisticated technologies available, even as that director tells himself that the technology that is the sine qua non of his technique isn't as important as people think; that, in fact, what makes *Avatar* special is the "human interest" story, particularly the love story between Jake and Neytiri:

> Too much is being said about the technology of this film. Quite frankly, I don't give a rat's ass how a film is made. It's an *emotional* story. It's a *love* story. They're not expecting that. The sci-fi/fantasy fans see the trailer and they think, Cool—battles, robots. What you really need to get to is, Oh, it's *that* [a love story], too.

But of course, when you see *Avatar*, what overwhelms you is what the technology accomplishes—not only the battles and robots, to be fair, but all the other marvelous stuff, the often overwhelmingly beautiful images of a place that exists somewhere over the rainbow.

Even beyond the incoherence that mars *Avatar* and hopelessly confuses whatever it thinks its message may be, there is a larger flaw here—one that's connected to Cameron's ambivalence about the relationship between technology and humanity; one that also brings you back, in the end, to *The Wizard of Oz*; one that is less political than ethical.

If it's right to see the movie as the culmination of Cameron's lifelong progress toward embracing a dazzling, superior Otherness—in a word, toward *Oz*—what strikes you, in the end, is how radically it differs, in one significant detail, from its model. Like the 1939 classic, the 2009 film ends with a scene of awakening. By the end, the Na'vi (under Jake's leadership) have triumphed, but the human Jake, operating his avatar from within his computerized pod, has been fatally hurt. His dying body is brought back to the Tree of Souls where, in a ceremony of the greatest holiness, the consciousness of the human Jake will be transferred, finally and permanently, into his Na'vi avatar. (Technology at its best, surely.) In the closing moments of the film the camera lingers suspensefully on the motionless face of avatar-Jake; suddenly, the large, feline eyes pop open, and then the screen goes black. We leave the theater secure in the knowledge that the rite has been successful, that the avatar-Jake will live. (And that there will be sequels.)

This moment of waking is, structurally, a crucial one; at the very beginning of the film, during Jake's introductory voice-over, the crippled man has poignantly described the liberating but ultimately deceptive dreams of flying that he often has: "I start having these dreams of flying . . . sooner or later, though, you always have to wake up." The final image of the redeemed and healed Jake waking up to his new Na'vi life is clearly meant, then, to be a triumphant rewriting of that sour acknowledgment.

But the implications of this awakening—in a character that Cameron himself described as an unconscious rewriting of *The Wizard of Oz*'s Dorothy ("it was, in some ways, like Dorothy's journey")—are not only different from but opposite to the implications of Dorothy's climactic wakening. When Dorothy wakes up, it's to the drab, black-and-white reality of the gritty Kansas existence with which she had been so dissatisfied at the beginning of her remarkable journey into fantasy, into vibrant color; what she famously learns from that exposure to radical otherness is, in fact, that "there's no place like home." Which is to say, when she wakes up—equipped, to be sure (as she was not before) with all that she has learned from her remarkable odyssey, not the least of which is a strong new awareness of her own human abilities—she wakes up to the realities, and the responsibilities, of the human world she'd temporarily escaped from. The triumphant conclusion of *Avatar*, by contrast, takes the form of a permanent abandonment of the gray world of *Homo sapiens*—which, as Dorothy learns, may contain its own hidden marvels—for the Technicolor, over-the-rainbow fantasy world into which its hero has accidentally strayed.

This represents something new in Cameron's work, something you can't help thinking is significant. In the director's films of the 1980s and 1990s, in the *Terminator* films or in *Aliens*, in the misbegotten *Abyss*, and even, in its way, in *Titanic*—just before the advent of cell phones and iPhones, of reality TV and virtual socializing, and, indeed, of mashups, of this new moment in which each of us can inhabit what you might call a private reality—the encounters with radical otherness or with extremes of violence and disaster always concluded, however awkwardly in some cases, with a moment of quiet, a return to the reassuring familiarity of life as most of us know it. By contrast, the message of the new movie, his most popular thus far, the highest-grossing film in history, is—like the message of so much else in mass culture just now—that "reality" is dispensable altogether; or, at the very least, is whatever you care to make of it, provided you have the right gadgets. In this fantasy of a lusciously colorful trip over the rainbow, you don't have to wake up. "There's no place like home" has become "there's no need for home." Whatever its futuristic setting, and whatever its debt to the past, *Avatar* is very much a movie for our time.

—*The New York Review of Books*, March 25, 2010

TRUTH FORCE AT THE MET

GOOD PEOPLE DO not, generally speaking, make good subjects for operas. Like the Greek tragedies that the sixteenth-century Venetian inventors of opera sought to re-create, Western musical drama has tended to be preoccupied with the darker extremes of human emotions: excessive passion and wild jealousy, smoldering resentment and implacable rage. These, after all, are the emotions that spark the kinds of actions—adultery, betrayal, revenge, murder—that make for gripping drama. Unpleasant as they may be in real life, such actions are essential to the Western idea of theater itself, in which the very notion of plot is deeply connected to difficulties, problems, disasters. Aristotle, in his *Poetics*, refers to plot as a knot tied by the author out of the manifold strands representing competing wills or desires or ideologies (he calls it *dêsis*, a "binding up"); an ugly and worrisome knot that will, in due course, ultimately come undone in a climactic moment of loosening or release of tension (the *lysis*, or "undoing")—a concept that survives in our term "dénouement."

There can, that is to say, be no theater unless bad things happen, unless there are terrible problems, insoluble knots; without them, there would be nothing for the characters to do. That "doing" gives us the very word by which we refer to what happens on stage: "drama" comes from the Greek *drân*, "to do" or "to act." When we go to the theater, we want to see characters *doing* things. Bad things, preferably.

The inherent dramatic interest of badness helps explain the abiding fascination exerted by bad, or at the very least tormented, characters. In opera as in spoken drama, our attention tends to be focused either on the outright villains—the figures who engineer the bad things that make drama dramatic—or on those characters whose ostensible goodwill is complicated by other qualities, either dark or excessive, that create the titanic dilemmas with which they must struggle so interestingly. But in characters who are saintly—who are without the overweening ambitions that fuel so many plots, who approach life's crises reasonably rather than passionately, who want to be helpful rather than to prevail—we have little interest. For Antigone, with her outsized loyalties and inflexible righteousness, for Carmen, with her transgressive seductiveness and fatal independent streak, we feel an abiding interest—even, though we might not like to admit it, allegiance; but does anyone really want to see a play about Ismene, or sit through an opera about Micaela? Could you even write such a play or opera? What would an opera that contemplates a blameless protagonist look like? (As opposed to an opera about a protagonist whose goodness is, among other things, the refractive lens to examine a villain's badness: *Billy Budd*, say.)

One answer to that question can be found in the reaction of a distinguished musician to a new work that was first presented at the Metropolitan Opera in 1976. The subject of this work was, ostensibly, the physicist and humanitarian Albert Einstein, which is one reason why a good deal of the opera consisted of the soloists and chorus intoning sequences of numbers that happen to correspond to the beats in the score—just one of the things more or less having to do with the violin-playing Einstein, a figure who famously united math and music, to which the text and music allude. (The first words you hear are "Two...Eight...Two-Three-Four...Two-Three ...Two-Three-Four...Five-Six-Seven...," a rehearsal of mathematical elements that, by the end of the work, will lead to a booming representation of another bit of science you might associate with Einstein: nuclear Armageddon.)

Because the hypnotic repetitions of the text reflected the innovative nature of the music, which itself consisted of large and small series of repeated motifs (the composer, who dislikes the term "minimalism," prefers to talk about "music with repetitive structures"), the initial response of some in the audience was precisely the reaction you'd expect to a work that, instead of the linear progression from *dêsis* to *lysis* that is the sine qua non of Western drama, indulged so extravagantly in cyclical repetitions and incremental additions and subtractions. The flutist Ransom Wilson has recalled his state of mind as a member of the audience:

> At first I was bored—*very* bored. The music seemed to have no direction, almost giving the impression of a gigantic phonograph with a stuck needle. I was first irritated and then angry that I'd been taken in by this crazy composer who obviously doted on repetition. I thought of leaving.

The crazy composer in question was Philip Glass, whose career-making *Einstein on the Beach*, a collaboration with the stage director Robert Wilson, may be said to have represented the climax of a linear progression of his own: the abandonment of astringent academic Serialism for the eminently tonal, harmonically accessible music of his maturity; of his Second Viennese School roots for the creative possibilities he was exposed to when he worked, as a young man in Paris, with Ravi Shankar—a stint that was followed by six months of travel and study in India and North Africa. Which is to say, an abandonment, at least in some sense, of the West for the East. Indeed, it's striking that many of those who were in the audience that night in 1976, and during subsequent performances of *Einstein*, talked about their experience of the work as a kind of mystical conversion of a vaguely Eastern nature. Ransom Wilson went on to describe the effect of those many repetitions, so boring at first, as "an amazing transformation":

> Then, with no conscious awareness, I crossed a threshold and found that the music was touching me, carrying me with it. I began to perceive within it a whole world where change happens so slowly and carefully that each new harmony or rhythmic addition or subtraction seemed monumental.

In his review of *Einstein* for *The New Yorker*, Andrew Porter commented on a similarly transformative aspect of the experience of listening to *Einstein*:

> A listener to his music usually reaches a point, quite early on, of rebellion at the needle-stuck-in-the-groove quality, but a minute or two later he realizes that the needle has not stuck; something has happened.

Whatever happened in this work, it wasn't the kind of happening—the "doing"—that got done in traditional drama, the troubled Western arc from knotting to loosening. Instead, Glass's music drama was "doing" something in a rather more Eastern mode—as if the mantric repetitions of the music were a kind of meditative medium (as they can indeed be, in Eastern religions) for achieving a kind of spiritual heightening: not an ideal position from which to witness Medea's infanticide or Peter Grimes's anguish, perhaps, but surely an appropriate state from which to contemplate other, purer characters. (Oliver Messiaen understood this too, as his own rather hypnotic, meditative *Saint Francis of Assisi* demonstrates.) *Einstein* would, in fact, be the first element of what turned out to be a trilogy of Glass operas about saintly men—the other two being *Satyagraha* (1980), about Mohandas Gandhi's evolution into a champion of nonviolent political resistance, and *Akhnaten* (1983), about the Egyptian pharaoh who attempted to establish monotheistic worship.

What's striking in the case of all three is the composer's evident understanding that the traditional resources of Western drama, with its complication-driven plots, were inadequate to representing his subject, which was human goodness. (When he and Wilson first got together, in the 1970s, to discuss doing an opera about a famous man, Wilson suggested Hitler—an ostentatiously more "dramatic" figure—but Glass countered with Einstein.) "In the past, theater has always been bound by literature," Glass, who identifies himself as a man of the theater above all—"I'd rather write an opera than a string quartet"—has justly observed. "*Einstein on the Beach* is not. There is no plot." For, as we know, good men don't tend to generate "plot."

Not least because it is about an Indian, one whose modus operandi was, you could say, to keep repeating small and ostensibly modest acts—nothing violent, nothing "dramatic"—in the service of a great and good goal, Glass's Gandhi opera, *Satyagraha*, may well be the most effectively achieved of his three musical portraits for the stage; in it, form and content are perfectly aligned. In a coproduction with the English National Opera that premiered at the Met in April 2008 —an occasion long overdue in a house whose last experience of the composer was the bloated and (truly) boring *The Voyage*, a work that owed its existence, you felt, to little more than the conceit that its premiere was meant to coincide with the 1992 quinquecentennial of the European discovery of America—the connection between Gandhi's story and the opera's form was perfected by a breathtakingly beautiful and deeply intelligent staging that, unlike certain other of its recent productions, bears out the "new" Met's commitment to the theatrical aspect of serious music drama.

However nonlinear the traditions to which this work owes its modalities, the structure of *Satyagraha* is rigorously organized and deeply meaningful. The opera (whose title means "truth force," the term Gandhi coined during his years in South Africa as a way of referring to the nonviolent protest he championed) is divided into three acts; in one way or another, all of what takes place in those three acts sheds light on the process by which he went from being a fairly timid and conventional Indian lawyer under the Raj to the man who would free India from British rule. That process unfolded, as does the action of this opera, during the twenty-one years, between 1893 and 1914, that Gandhi spent in South Africa agitating for Indian civil rights: the preparation, of course, for the great struggle to come.

The first two acts have three scenes each; the last consists of one long, varied scene. Merely the names of those three acts suggest a kind of shorthand biography of the noble man at the heart of this contemplative work. Each is named for a historical figure closely associated with Gandhi: Act I for Leo Tolstoy, whose *The Kingdom of God Is Within You* (1893), Gandhi said, "overwhelmed" him and led to his first discovery of the doctrine of nonviolence and love; Act II for the Bengali writer and anti-Raj activist Rabindranath Tagore, Gandhi's near contemporary and Asia's first Nobel laureate, with whom Gandhi had a respectful but sometimes contentious relation-ship; and Act III for Martin Luther King Jr., who owed his under-standing of nonviolent political protest to Gandhi. ("Christ gave us the goals and Mahatma Gandhi the tactics.") These three large acts suggest, moreover, a kind of loose chronological frame for what takes place on stage during the opera (you find yourself avoiding the word "action"), since they clearly suggest a movement from Gandhi's past intellectual debt to his present political milieu to his future legacy. In each act of the present production, an actor costumed as the epony-mous figure can be seen on an elevated niche at the back of the stage.

Within the acts themselves historical chronology is beside the point—an aspect of the work that has, no doubt, been responsible for the lazy assertions by many reviewers that *Satyagraha* has no narra-tive structure at all, as if chronological sequence was the only struc-ture there is. ("Mr. Glass...was not interested in fashioning a cogent narrative": thus Anthony Tommasini in *The New York Times*.) Rather, the progression of the three scenes in each of the first two acts repre-sents a discernible and suggestive (and cogent) thematic progress. In each of the first scenes we witness a harrowing representation of armed conflict: a mythic battle in Act I, in which Krishna exhorts a young hero to fight despite his momentary lapse of confidence; in Act II, an ugly confrontation between Gandhi and a band of white hoo-ligans in 1896, on his return to South Africa from India. The second scene in each act depicts a peaceful episode in which we get to see at work the creative energies of the communal movements Gandhi founded. In Act I, it's a scene in which we see people building dwell-ings in 1910 at Tolstoy Farm, the commune he founded outside of Johannesburg; in Act II, we see people working on his highly influen-tial newspaper, *Indian Opinion*, in 1906.

The third scene in each act climactically represents a nonviolent but forceful act of political resistance. Act I ends with "The Vow," a stylized depiction of the September 1906 protest resolution taken by Gandhi and three thousand followers after the passage of the notorious Black Act, which sought to limit Indians' movements by mandating identity cards and fingerprinting for all Indian residents. "Protest," which ends the second act, shows the outcome of that earlier vow: although Gandhi and his followers had gained concessions from the British following their 1906 resolution, the British reneged on their part of the deal, and to protest this treachery Gandhi and thousands of his followers burned their government ID cards in public.

So each act stages a kind of equation: to the violent confrontation of the first scene, Gandhi opposed the peaceable cooperative efforts shown in the second scene; the product of the reaction between those two incompatible modes owed, as the third scene suggests, a little bit to both: a new kind of "war," a nonviolent conflict that was as forceful as what you saw in scene 1 but as peaceable as what you witnessed in scene 2.

All three strands twine together to create a strong and extremely moving climax in the third act, in which elements of all three kinds of scenes— armed conflict, harmonious cooperation, the triumph of Gandhi's new vision—come together in a representation of Gandhi's 1913 New Castle March, an enormous and enormously successful mass protest against yet another piece of political treachery on the part of the British. (This was the triumphant climax of Gandhi's South African activism.) Here, the principles of *satyagraha* are seen enacted on the stage. By this point we have seen Gandhi reacting to the news of the British betrayal (his head is bowed in grief); Act III includes a tableau of solidarity as his *satyagrahis* mourn with him (they walk back and forth across the stage, unspooling hundreds of yards of shimmery, glassy tape: an arresting, symbolic enactment of their oppression), and ends with a scene of nonviolent resistance, as

Gandhi's supporters are removed, one by one, by soldiers with whom they refuse to struggle. Eventually, Gandhi is left alone on stage to sing a final aria.

And just what is he singing? Another aspect of Glass's antitheatrical theater is how he dispenses with the usual means of indicating what's going on—not least, dialogue. None of the words uttered by the various characters—Gandhi; his longtime wife, Kasturbai; his secretary Miss Schlesen; a couple of Indian coworkers, Mrs. Naidoo and Parsi Rustomji; a European co-worker called Kallenbach; and Mrs. Alexander, the police chief's wife who, during the first scene of Act II, rescues him from the ugly mob at the dock, brandishing her parasol like some mighty weapon—take the form of "dialogue" in any recognizable sense. Instead, Glass and his librettist, the novelist Constance DeJong, have provided fairly perfunctory directions about the historical background, setting, and staging for each of the seven scenes in the opera, clearly meant as guidelines for the stage director and designer, as for instance this set of instructions for the second scene of Act II—the scene in which we get to see *Indian Opinion* being produced:

> Setting: 5 P.M. (orange burning sun). Part of communal residence that houses *Indian Opinion*. Large, working press sits center stage. Blue grass field.
>
> Staging: Farm residents set up, issue and distribute *Indian Opinion*. Gandhi, appearing late in the scene, inspects their activity in the printing process. All exit, leaving press to run alone during 3-minute orchestra tutti.
>
> Kallenbach and Miss Schlesen, joined by principals.

What the characters are actually uttering as this scene progresses— what, in fact, all the characters are uttering all the time throughout the various scenes—are passages from the *Bhaghavad Gita*, a text that had tremendous spiritual and aesthetic importance for Gandhi, and in which he found special significance for his life's work. Naturally, this choice on the creators' part may strike you as strange—the *Times* critic found "radical" what he referred to as "the complete separation of sung text from dramatic action, such as it is"—but the gesture is wholly of a piece with the larger project of *Satyagraha*, which everywhere forestalls our expectations of what should take place in an opera house.

It is, in any case, inaccurate to characterize the *Bhaghavad Gita* texts as "completely separate" from the action: if you actually take the trouble to read the libretto, you can see that the Sanskrit texts have been chosen with great care. What the workers in the *Indian Opinion* scene are saying as they fold and pass along great sheets of newspaper is a highly poetic expression of what they are, in fact, doing: "Therefore, perform unceasingly the works that must be done, for the man detached who labors on to the highest must win through." When Mrs. Alexander berates the mob that attacks Gandhi as he returns to South Africa, she angrily decries "the devilish folk" in whom "there is no purity, no morality, no truth. So they say the world has not a law nor order, nor a lord." In the current Met production, no translation has been provided of the entire libretto, but as the production design incorporates projected portions of the sung texts, audience members get the gist of the necessary texts in each scene.

If, indeed, what *Satyagraha* aims at, in both its text and its music, is a kind of meditative state of spiritual elevation that allows us to think clearly about Gandhi's goodness and its effects, rather than to get wrapped up in his "drama," the use of these incantatory texts only enhances our sense that we're participating in a kind of exalting ritual, rather than spending a couple of hours at the theater. Many

New Yorkers I know, opera lovers, balked at the idea of "sitting through four hours of Sanskrit"; but those same people would happily sit through a Te Deum (or bar mitzvah) while understanding little of the text. It's when you see *Satyagraha* as a symbolic action that you can begin to appreciate it.

In an interesting comment he made apropos of another of his historical operas, Glass explained that he wants us to have that kind of experience—one, that is to say, which, unlike traditional theater, does not intend to ape reality, but which creates its own, new kind of reality:

> I've never felt that "reality" was well served in an opera house. And I think this is even more true when the subject of the opera is based on historical events. Surely those with a taste for historical facts and documentation would be better served in libraries where academic research is presumably reliable and readily available. The opera house is the arena of poetry par excellence, where the normal rules of historical research need not be applied and where, in the world of artistic imagination, a different kind of truth can be discovered.

Satyagraha may be the strongest of his portrait operas precisely because its meticulously manipulated poetic text hovers at the midpoint between abstraction, on the one hand (a quality perhaps too heavily in evidence in *Einstein*, with its sometimes dauntingly abstruse metaphorical allusions to things Einsteinian—the toy trains he enjoyed as a child, for instance), and concreteness, a too-obvious connection to the events on the stage, on the other. (The latter is a failing of *Akhnaten*, which relies on a clunky framing device—a modern-day tour guide explaining the ruins of the idealistic pharaoh's crumbled city—to make plain the connections between its ideas and its action.) That mediation between the abstract and the real is, of course, a quality of religious rituals, one powerfully evoked by *Satyagraha* in particular.

———

This rigorous, ingeniously assembled spiritual work received an ideal production at the Met. The relatively young director, Phelim McDermott, and the designer, Julian Crouch, are partners in an innovative production company in England called Improbable, and they seem to have a taste for the irreverent. (They're responsible for the Off-Broadway "junk opera," *Shockheaded Peter*.) But it would be hard to think of a greater reverence than the one they have shown Glass and DeJong's large and significant theater piece. They have clearly thought through not only the text and music but also the life of Gandhi himself, and for that reason virtually every image, every gesture that you see in this *Satyagraha* seems positively to resonate with significance.

Most striking is the way in which, as a homage to Gandhi's own reverence for humble people and humble objects, almost the entire visual world of their staging is organized around two homely objects: pieces of paper and sticks. That they could make magic out of these things became evident very early on. In the scene of the mythical battle with which the work begins ("The Kuru Field of Justice": titles projected onto the semicircular corrugated wall that was the production's only permanent decor told you where you were in each scene), you saw at first two large groups, representing the opposing armies—and, by extension, the Indians and whites of the present-day conflict—one holding a bunch of baskets and the other holding a bunch of newspapers.

As the conflict got underway, however, these groups (who turned out to be members of the puppeteer group, Skills Ensemble, that Mc-Dermott and Crouch work with) started doing things with their bits of paper and humble baskets, twisting the former into rolls, manipulating the latter into clusters; and before you knew it, the paper had coalesced into a gigantic, vaguely arachnid monster, reaching nearly to the top of the proscenium, doing battle with an equally towering knightlike figure made entirely of baskets. The great battle announced by Krishna was symbolized by these artfully constructed champions, who fell to pieces suggestively after the musical climax, hinting at the futility of all armed conflict.

The procession of carefully paralleled scenes in Acts I and II presented many such astonishing and inventive tableaux; and yet what was so gratifying was that the eye-popping visual effects enhanced, rather than competed with, the message the text and the music were sending. Among other things, nearly all of the significant onstage action took the form of either accretions or removals of material objects—things being built up, things being stripped down—which suggests a theatrical analogue to the way in which Glass's music achieves its effects, too.

Hence the Tolstoy Farm scene ingeniously conveyed the pleasure of cooperative labor, as the men and women manipulating bits of corrugated material back and forth across the stage were seen, suddenly, to be assembling one large dwelling place. The first scene of Act II, in which Gandhi is attacked by the mob, made use of a number of gigantic, leering papier-mâché puppet heads that marched around on sticks and stilts and clustered over the cowering Gandhi, indicating the force of European hatred for the Indian's project. (Gandhi himself, at one point early in this scene, seemed to be represented by an endearingly awkward bird puppet, which evoked with curious accuracy his stick-legged, avian walk.)

Perhaps the most stunning example of subtle and ongoing trans-formations was to be found in the *Indian Opinion* scene. It began simply enough with a group of people kneeling on the floor passing impossibly long, continuous sheets of uncut newspaper along to one another; at a certain point these sheets were made to undulate hori-zontally across the width of the stage, creating an image of hypnotic power. Later, the sheets were bunched like ribbons and made into a kind of cape that trailed for a moment from Gandhi's shoulder blades. A crucial cut was then made at the center of the bunch, creat-ing streamers that were subsequently hooked to pulleys and wheeled heavenward, creating at that point a number of enormous streamers that hung down and—the final, heart-stopping climax—onto which vertically written texts in Sanskrit, Gujarati, and Roman characters were projected, sliding down the streamers like rainwater on a win-dowpane. This brilliantly inventive use of humble paper and charac-ters made you feel powerfully—and quite rightly—the pleasure and beauty of words themselves: the greatest weapon in Gandhi's arsenal.

Many elements here, both large and small, reminded you that al-though Glass's historical work isn't bound by conventions of tradi-tional chronology, *Satyagraha* as a whole does chart Gandhi's evolution—the trajectory that is alluded to, however delicately, by the titles of the three acts. The use of costumes was subtle but crucial. We first see Gandhi lying on the ground before the Kuru Field of Justice scene, a tableau that alludes to a notorious incident that oc-curred soon after his arrival in South Africa, when the young lawyer, holding a first-class rail ticket, was physically pushed from a train onto the platform, a moment that marked the beginning of his out-rage against racial injustice. At this point he is wearing the proper, dowdy black-and-white getup of the Victorian lawyer, the frock coat and the well-shined shoes. As the opera progresses he gradually, almost imperceptibly sheds more and more of these clothes, so that by the end he's the Gandhi you recognize: the slender, stork-like figure in the white loincloth. Also wonderfully effective were the costumes in the scene when Mrs. Alexander rescues Gandhi: lurid, vaudeville colors and horizontal stripes for the bigoted Europeans, with Mrs. Alexander and Gandhi in dazzling white, as if to suggest their moral likeness despite their ethnic and national difference.

Acts of disrobing have, indeed, an extraordinary power in this staging. At the end of the battle scene in Act I you know that Gandhi has the support of the chorus because suddenly they take off their shoes and line them up, dozens of them, downstage—a first step, you're meant to feel, in the process of self-revision, and perhaps self-humbling, necessary to appreciate *satyagraha*, to understand the necessity of abjuring violence in favor of a new kind of conflict. This symbolic gesture is amplified in the "Vow" scene at the end of that act, when the assembled supporters of Gandhi's resolution to fight the British racial law start removing their outer garments and then hang them on hangers that have been lowered from the ceiling. When the dozens of frock coats and ladies' coats and shawls and veils suddenly float toward the ceiling, it somehow becomes a moment of deep emotion—it's a stage picture that gets across the potential beauty in self-abnegation, the exaltation that lies in the abandonment of the "I" for the "we." "Let a man feel hatred for no being...done with thoughts of 'I' and 'mine,'" goes one line from the *Bhaghavad Gita* cited here.

Humble objects and small gestures, repeated over and over, sometimes altered, sometimes enlarged: it would be hard to think of a better way to represent, theatrically, not only what Philip Glass has done in his score for *Satyagraha* but what Gandhi himself was doing in eschewing violent "action" and championing the telling gesture as the foundation of his political philosophy. The sense that you get—

because McDermott and Crouch's production wants you to get it—that this philosophy derives from a higher source is something that the production, like the work itself, underscores at every level. Its spare but elevated abstractions, the inventive use and reuse of ordinary objects as exalted symbols, have something of the hieratic about them. It feels like a mystery play.

That sense was, if anything, only heightened in the last scene, in which all of the elements of both the text and the production cohere beautifully. After the New Castle marchers have been removed by the soldiers, Act III ("King") concludes with Gandhi alone, downstage. Upstage, throughout the latter part of the act, a black man playing Martin Luther King Jr. has been standing atop a lofty podium, silently and in slow motion pantomiming King's famous gestures as he gave the "I Have a Dream" speech. (He's facing away from the audience, as if addressing a crowd in the far distance.) The notion of Gandhi communing with his latter-day avatar is perfectly conveyed by the *Bhagavad Gita* text that Gandhi sings at this moment: "The Lord said, I have passed through many a birth and many have you. I know them all but you do not." These and the other sacral lines are sung to a single, ethereal musical figure: an ascending scale of eight notes, in the Phrygian mode, repeated thirty times and yet never quite the same from repetition to repetition. (Once again in this piece, repetition is gripping rather than boring.)

As this goes on, the flats obscuring the back of the stage float away, revealing an expanse of improbably blue, celestial sky; the clouds that had scudded thickly across it while King was giving his speech suddenly evaporate, leaving a clear space. (Another suggestive image.) One white, rather fluffy cloud remains, and slowly, unexpectedly, this cloud starts to morph into an image of a group of Gandhi's followers. This is exactly per Glass's stage direction: "Gandhi, standing down stage, turns, looking toward platform where King reappears and a moment later Satyagraha army appears behind him, up in the starry, night sky." Seated in serried rows like people posing for one of those Victorian group photos, the image is characterized by a stiffness meant, perhaps, to remind you of this specific moment in history to which Gandhi did, after all, belong.

And then something wonderful happens. Raising their forearms in a formal yet warm gesture—of greeting? of farewell? I couldn't make it out—they wave right at you as you sit in the audience. At that moment I burst into tears. Perhaps because it seemed so much like a gesture of benediction, I felt as if something real had actually happened in the auditorium—that I had been blessed, maybe. Made out of insignificant things and yet achieving a large effect that exceeded, finally, the boundaries of the theater, this marvelous work made you feel that it had *done* something. And what is that, if not drama?

—*The New York Review of Books,* June 12, 2008

WHY SHE FELL

THE TRANSFORMATION OF humans into monsters or animals is a standard feature of two great genres: classical myth and American comic books. As those of us know who spent our childhoods and teenage years greedily hoarding the latter, such transformations are only occasionally effected by a mere change of costume. Batman, for instance (introduced in 1939), is an ordinary *Homo sapiens* who simply dons his bat-like hood and cape when he wants to battle evildoers; his extraordinary powers are the fruit of disciplined intellectual and physical training. More often—and more excitingly—the metamorphoses occur at the genetic level. The Incredible Hulk, who debuted in 1962, is a hypertrophied Hercules-like giant, the Mr. Hyde aspect of an otherwise mild-mannered scientist named Bruce Banner, created during a laboratory accident involving gamma rays. Wolverine, one of the X-Men, who sports lupine traits following his transformations, belongs to a despised race of "mutants" with remarkable powers. (The comic-book series, now reincarnated as a hugely popular film franchise, debuted in 1963.)

Perhaps most famously of all, the crime-fighting Spider-Man—the character was introduced in 1962 and got his own comic series the following year—is really just an ordinary teenager from Queens named Peter Parker who undergoes a kind of human-arachnid hybridization after being bitten by a radioactive spider during a class trip to a science fair. It can be no accident that popular narratives involving gamma rays, mutants, and radioactivity should have gripped the imagination of young people in the early 1960s, when the Cold War—and with it the seemingly constant threat of nuclear catastrophe—was at its height.

Two millennia before the Cuban missile crisis, the popular fascination with metamorphosis was already firmly in place. The gods of Greek myth regularly transform themselves, abandoning their everyday humanoid shapes for those of animals—often (if not always wholly explicably) for the purposes of seducing mortal girls: Zeus ravishes Europa in the form of a bull, Leda in the shape of a swan, and, in one odd variant, his own daughter Persephone in the shape of a snake. But the gods clearly enjoy transforming humans, too. Hence, for instance, the story of Actaeon, a young hunter who offends the virgin goddess Artemis and is turned into a stag that is then torn to pieces by his own hunting dogs—the hunter become the victim, in other words. Myth is rich in such cruel inversions. Actaeon's first cousin Pentheus, the ill-fated king of Thebes, is similarly torn to pieces in a horrific "hunt" after his own mother, in the grip of Dionysiac frenzy, mistakes him for a young bull calf—an episode dramatized at the end of Euripides' *Bacchae*, a play that ends, curiously, with a final and literal transformation: that of Pentheus' perhaps insufficiently religious grandfather, Cadmus, into a snake. A closing prophecy informs us that the old man, having taken the form of a serpent, will lead an army of bacchants throughout Greece, destroying the altars of the old gods and establishing the worship of Dionysus.

These by no means atypical examples from classical myth and drama suggest a crucial difference between the ancient and modern models of human-to-animal metamorphosis. For today's audiences, such transformations are liberating—literally "empowering"—whereas for the ancients, they were, more often than not, humiliations, punishments for inappropriate or overweening behavior.

One of the most famous examples of this moralizing strain in ancient tales of shape-shifting is the comparatively late myth (there are no traces of it in the extant Greek material of the Classical Age) of Arachne, the girl who ended up a spider. The story is suavely retold by Ovid in his *Metamorphoses*—an entire verse epic devoted to tales of human transformations, completed when Jesus Christ was a boy of eight or so. In the Roman poet's version, Arachne is distinguished by her marvelous artistic talent at the loom and with the embroidery needle—a gift she rather dangerously refuses to credit to Athena, whom she goes so far as to challenge to a contest. Both females furiously weave their tapestries, which are described at considerable length. Athena's, unsurprisingly, features mythic scenes of mortal arrogance punished by the gods (who transform the offending humans into trees, or mountains, or birds), while Arachne's, just as pointedly, features mythic scenes of divine duplicity—among which are featured Jupiter's seductions of Leda, Europa, and Persephone. Offended by her rival's work, Athena strikes Arachne with her shuttle; in her great shame, the girl hangs herself, but is turned by the goddess into a spider, destined forevermore to "ply her ancient art of weaving."

As it happens, a recent work for the popular theater puts both Spider-Man and Arachne on the same stage. I am referring to Julie Taymor's ill-fated musical *Spider-Man: Turn Off the Dark*, a work that has, *Titanic*-like, already assumed the proportions—and, more importantly, the moral suggestiveness—of myth. Its costs ran upward of a

staggering $65 million (a record for the Broadway theater); its pre-
views—as of April 2011 the show had still not opened, after five
months of performances—were plagued by legal headaches, increasingly bitter squabbling among the artistic principals, and a number
of horrific accidents resulting from the director's Daedalus-like ambitions to make young men fly; and its confidence was dented by crushingly negative reviews from critics who decided they couldn't wait
any longer for the official opening, which was constantly being delayed to make time for improvements that, it seemed, couldn't possibly improve things enough to make a difference.

The whole sodden mess may be said to have sunk, finally, when in
early March the producers fired Taymor. Long the creative force behind the show, Taymor both wrote the book and directed what must
have seemed, early on, like the culminating moment in a long and
distinguished career as a director of serious theater, opera, oratorio,
and film—and of more popular entertainments that, in her nimble
hands, were able to transcend the prefab, corporate aesthetic of the
Disney Corporation (*The Lion King*). After Taymor was fired, it was
announced that *Spider-Man* would close for three months, during
which period it would undergo an extensive retooling at the hands of
the commercially savvy director Philip William McKinley, whose
successes include stints at the Ringling Brothers Circus. In November
2011, she sued the producers; a countersuit followed, triggering nasty
revelations on both sides. (The retooled show has been a box office hit.)

As with the story of Actaeon, there was the unmistakable noise of
baying in the air when Taymor went down; after all these centuries,
it seems that we still find it hard to resist what looks like a story of
hubris finally brought low. As innumerable critics have by now made
clear, pretty much everything was wrong with the show—the incoherent, metastasizing plot (which grafts some Greek mythic material
onto the iconic comic-book narrative of Spidey's career); the banal

music and risible lyrics (by the pop stars Bono and The Edge of U2); and, not least, a series of breathtakingly gratuitous and overcooked production numbers that made "Springtime for Hitler" look like *Die Winterreise.* One such number featured a monstrous female spider being shod with expensive shoes.

But these are merely symptoms. If Taymor's show is a failure, it fails for interesting reasons—as it were, for genetic reasons. For the show itself is a grotesque hybrid. At the heart of the *Spider-Man* disaster is the essential incompatibility of those two visions of physical transformation—the ancient and the modern, the redemptive and the punitive, visions that Taymor tried, heroically but futilely, to reconcile. As happens so often in both myth and comic books, the attempt to fuse two species resulted in the creation of a monster.

In fact, very little about *Spider-Man*—the original comic or, for that matter, its reincarnation as a series of enormously successful blockbuster films directed by Sam Raimi and released throughout the first decade of the 2000s—suggests an ideal vehicle for Taymor's talents.

What made Spider-Man unusual among superheroes when he debuted wasn't so much the arachnid powers he derived from the radioactive spider—an ability to jump great distances, cling to surfaces, and shoot a weblike material from his wrists: not even comparable to, say, Superman's powers—but his very ordinariness. Bullied at school, worried about girls and money, fussing at and fussed at by his foster parents, the kindly Aunt May and Uncle Ben, Peter Parker is a regular lower-middle-class Joe with pretty average teenager problems. (Batman, by contrast, is really a millionaire playboy named Bruce Wayne who lives alone in a mansion with a British butler and a young ward—a lifestyle that, to the original Depression-era audience, must have seemed as unimaginable as that of a bat.) Given the narrowness of Peter's horizon of expectations, it's small wonder that he makes petty use of his newfound powers at first: retaliating at school and making some money as a novelty act.

It's precisely as a typical teenager that Peter makes a fatal error that effects the greatest transformation in him—not physical but ethical. For in a moment of affected coolness, he allows a petty thief to escape—the very criminal who will go on to rob and murder his Uncle Ben. It's Ben's last words to his nephew, at the end of the original comic-book issue—"With great power there must also come— great responsibility"—that finally gives Spidey a moral mission. Much of the ongoing drama of the *Spider-Man* comic books turns on the tension between the teenager's frustrations and the superhero's lofty goals.

It's not hard to see how all this made *Spider-Man* popular among teenage comic-book readers in the 1960s, that decade of the teenager. Indeed, the series marked the beginning of what the comic-book historian Paul Kupperberg, in his 2007 book *The Creation of Spider-Man*, called a "revolution"—a newfound interest on the part of comic-book creators in emphasizing the protagonist's "everyday problems" rather than the glamour of being a superhero. Indeed, unlike Superman and Batman, who are both adored by the press, to say nothing of the civil authorities, Spider-Man instantly becomes the object of the scornful wrath of the powerful newspaper editor for whom Peter works as a photographer, and who tries to expose Spider-Man as a villain. The emphasis on Spidey's ordinary humanness explains why this series, as opposed to a number of other superhero comics, is laden with what Kupperberg calls "heavy doses of soap-opera and elements of melodrama."

One melodramatic element is the striking leitmotif of Peter's guilty conscience. He feels responsible for the death of Uncle Ben; later, anguishingly, it turns out that one of his archenemies, the Green Goblin, is in fact the father of his best friend, Harry Osborn. (The elder Osborn is an industrialist tycoon who turns mad and bad when a lab experiment goes awry.) In a plotline from the early 1970s, Spider-Man is again responsible for the death of a loved one: a girl-friend dies from the "whiplash effect" that results when his webbing suddenly stops her fall from a building. He eventually goes back to an on-again, off-again love interest, Mary Jane Watson, whom he marries in the late 1980s.

This superhero's humdrum background and tormented (but not *too* tormented) psyche are at the heart of a curiously Everyman appeal that has managed to persist through nearly five decades. Not two weeks after the September 11 attacks, Marvel Comics announced that the disaster would be treated in an upcoming *Spider-Man* series, since the angst-ridden hero from the outer boroughs was, in the words of a writer then working on the strip, "best suited" to grappling with the real-life New York crisis (many of whose victims were, as it happens, from the same socioeconomic background). It's noteworthy, in light of this, that the producers of the recent series of Hollywood adaptations chose the actor Tobey Maguire—elf-faced, funky, a bit unprepossessing—to play Peter, rather than some square-jawed hunk.

In *Spider-Man: Turn Off the Dark* (the title, like pretty much everything else about the show, leaves you scratching your head—turn off the *dark?*), Taymor retained most of these familiar, ordinary elements. There's the Queens row-house existence (very cleverly evoked in Act I by means of a succession of panels, painted comic-book style, that open to show the exteriors in ever-closer perspective as the actors walk near them, as if they're getting closer, and which finally open to reveal the interiors); the humble aunt and uncle; the accident at the science fair and Mr. Osborn's botched experiment, both scenes rendered with a vulgar indulgence in gadgety details. There are the battles with the amusingly Day-Glo Green Goblin (staged, as we all know by now, in midair, thanks to immensely costly flying technology) and the tentative romance with the redheaded Mary Jane—here, the victim of abuse at the hands of a hard-drinking father (an added element of gritty "ordinariness"). There's the bullying and the self-doubt and the guilt. Even the comic-book aesthetic has been retained, often ingeniously: in a couple of crucial fight scenes, little cutouts representing dialogue balloons—"KRAAAAK!" "BLAM!"—are waved around on sticks.

So to some extent, the new musical draws on both the comic book and the popular movies. The question is what appeal this material could have had for Taymor, an artist who has admitted to having no feel for what an interviewer called "American popular arts." Her own adolescence was both privileged—she grew up in a Boston suburb, the daughter of a gynecologist—and anything but all-American: she was working in the theater already as a teenager, went to Paris at sixteen to study mime with Jacques Lecoq, stopped in the Netherlands to observe Henk Boerwinkel's puppet theater, and spent four years in East Asia studying local theatrical and ritual traditions and creating her first works.

In 1998, soon after her terrifically inventive Broadway staging of *The Lion King* had brought her widespread recognition of a kind not generally enjoyed by directors who devote themselves, as she had done till that point, to staging Carlo Gozzi fantasies, *Titus Andronicus*, and Stravinsky's *Oedipus Rex*, the director was interviewed by Richard Schechner, a professor of theater and editor of *The Drama Review*. (The interview was published in John Bell's *Puppets, Masks, and Performing Objects*.) During the interview, Schechner asked whether Taymor felt an affinity for what he called "American traditions of performing objects—stuff like the Macy's parade, the Disney and other theme parks." "I never liked those things," Taymor replied. "Not even as a kid. I think I always felt that that kind of thing was just goofy, literally. The roundness of everything—the aesthetic of it—never appealed to me. . . . I've never seen the Macy's parade."

To the roundness of the pop-culture aesthetic—and, perhaps, the accompanying flatness, the literalness of the pat "messages" favored by so many pop narratives—Taymor has, by contrast, always preferred the suggestive symbolic forms of what, in a videotaped interview about her 1992 production of the Stravinsky *Oedipus Rex* in Japan, she's called "mythic, archetypal stories": folkloric and traditional narratives whose large and abstract formal patterns offer the interpreter plenty of room to maneuver, not least since the plots are already well known. ("It's all about interpretation," she has said. "If you do *Hamlet*, we all know *Hamlet* . . . it's all about how you tell a story, not 'is the story new.'") Looking over the landscape of her work, it's hard not to think that the intersection of action and abstractions—what, in describing her use of Herbert Blau's "ideographs" in staging, she has called "essences . . . the most essential two, three brush strokes"—is where Taymor thrives: communal rituals (the basis of some of her early work in Indonesia), religious rites (one early piece she did, on her return to New York from East Asia, was a staging of the Passover Haggadah at the Public Theater for Elizabeth Swados), even the "ritual" of psychoanalysis. She once worked with a psychoanalyst to create masks of psychological archetypes: the overbearing mother, the benevolent patriarch, the bully, the victim.

That it is the formal, the stylized, the extreme that give Taymor's imagination room to expand has been evident from the start. It was obvious in her acclaimed 1994 staging (adapted for film in 1999) of

Titus Andronicus, a work whose extremity, which scares away many directors, inspired some of Taymor's most beautiful and imaginative designs and stagings. (Her 2010 film version of *The Tempest*, by contrast, was curiously slack—not least, you suspect, because so much of it is filmed outdoors on a pretty island. Taymor doesn't know what to do with natural space; she likes the artificial confines imposed by the stage.) And it was clear in one of her first large New York successes, in 1989: an admirable stage adaptation of *Juan Darién*, a story by the Uruguayan writer Horacio Quiroga. The story has the elements of the myths and folktales that Taymor enjoys, while providing the ethical element that, for her, is a crucial part of what theater and ritual do ("It reasserts your place in your own culture"). In it, a jaguar cub is turned, by the force of a grieving mother's compassion, into a boy—and then retransformed, by the power of the neighbors' cruelty and fear, into a beast. Among other things, *Juan Darién* was an early instance, along with the Gozzi plays, of Taymor's fascination with human–animal metamorphosis. And indeed, with metamorphosis in general, not least as an item in the actor's toolbox. "You should be able to transform your body," Taymor has said, recalling the lessons she learned from mime. "That part of Lecoq's work was amazing to me."

So you can see how, when the discussions about a *Spider-Man* musical began nearly ten years ago, the narrative about a boy transformed into a beast might have tempted Taymor—might have led her to overcome her natural distaste for American pop culture. But the fit wasn't really right. For as we know, the *Spider-Man* narrative belongs to a genre in which the metamorphoses are as often as not fortuitous, plot devices invented to give the superheroes the powers that make them worth reading about in the first place; as such, they tend to lack the abstract intellectual and ethical pointedness you get in the mythic transformations of classical narratives (and *Juan Darién*)—which is of course precisely the kind of material suited to Taymor, with her penchant for teasing out the spiritual and social implications of ritual and myth.

And so Taymor, in a clear sign of her frustration with her source material—what is, in the end, just a tale of adolescent angst—made a series of radical additions to the conventional plot. These, not accidentally, take the form of elaborate Greek mythic (and tragic) elements. First, there is an awkward framing device, consisting of—the badness of the pun is, alas, typical—a "Geek Chorus": a group of high school kids familiar, as it turns out, with Ovid, who seem to be "writing" the Spider-Man comic as the play unfolds ("He has to go through a hero's trial"). And then, disastrously—in part because it overloads the action with two major villains who seem to have nothing to do with each other—Taymor has added a new story line involving Ovid's Arachne herself. The poor girl appears in this version as a kind of artiste-vamp ("My illusions—I'm the only real artist working today!") assisted by a troupe of spider-maidens who, in one of the most vulgar numbers staged in recent years, shoe all eight of their mistress's feet with an array of what seem to be Jimmy Choos and Manolo Blahniks. Arachne here gets tangled up in a knotty and ultimately incomprehensible plot having to do with her thwarted love for Peter Parker and, eventually, the frustrated revenge she takes on New York City.

Unsurprisingly, these Greek elements were the first to be jettisoned by Taymor's replacement. But for Taymor, all this—what she called "tying this story back to mythology"—was the point: "the main thing the [*Spider-Man*] movies haven't done, which is something I really wanted to do. It's something you can do in the theater—go into this absolutely dreamlike mythic place, out of time, between reality and dream world." What she says about theater is certainly true, and is borne out in the single scene in *Spider-Man* that is imbued with great beauty and real theatrical magic. When the spider-maidens make their entrance, wearing saffron-colored gowns of a vague Greek cut, they're lowered onto the stage from long saffron-colored ribbons, swinging back and forth as they descend; each time they swing forward, a giant spool of the same ribbon unfurls horizontally behind them—and you realize that the entire tableau is a giant act of weaving, completed as their feet touch the ground in front of what has become a glowing saffron fabric.

It's an extraordinary and very Taymor gesture—abstract, symbolic, true to the material (this is, after all, the story of a spinner, a weaver), suggestive rather than clankingly literal, even as it is itself a "tying back" of the story to mythology. It was difficult to believe that the imagination responsible for this delicate and ethereal sequence could have dreamed up the rest of the show—not least the unbearably literal-minded, special-effects-laden parade of super-villains who appear at one point, and who look like they'd been fabricated in the costume shop of a low-budget sci-fi movie. And for all the fuss about how much was spent on the elaborate harnesses that allow Spider-Man and the Green Goblin and Arachne to fly not only above the stage but all over the auditorium, you couldn't help feeling that it was all just an elaborate distraction—something to keep your mind off the emptiness of the drama, such as it was. ("Even though I couldn't follow the plot, it was entertaining to watch," the fifteen-year-old I saw the show with remarked.) Anyway, it looked cheap: the harnesses were large, all too visible, and ungainly.

Looking back at the *Spider-Man* fiasco, it's possible to see the contours of a familiar story: a woman of great talent, tremendous artistic ambition, and then humiliation. In the end, Julie Taymor got her Greek drama. Like a character in some Attic play, she was led by a single-minded passion to betray her truest self and abandon her greatest virtues. These, as her admirers have long recognized and she herself once seemed to know, lie not in elaborate Hollywood special effects that huge amounts of money can buy in order to make the fantastical seem real and persuasive, but in a very old-fashioned kind of magic that doesn't pretend to be "real" at all. Taymor told an interviewer an interesting story once about a wonderful idea you get to see played out in *The Lion King*: her insistence that the puppeteers operating the animal figures not be concealed. She recalls telling Michael Eisner, the Disney chief to whom she was trying to sell this notion:

> Let's just get rid of the masking. Because when you get rid of the masking, then even though the mechanics are apparent, the whole effect is more magical. And this is where theatre has a power over film and television. This is absolutely where its magic works. It's not because it's an illusion and we don't know how it's done. It's because we know *exactly* how it's done.... I've been calling that the "double event" of *The Lion King*. It's not just the story that's being told. It's *how* it's being told.

"How it's being told" is what great directors excel at, and what Taymor herself has done wonderfully well in the past, on a shoestring. ("The most successful stuff is the stuff I've done my whole life, which didn't cost anything.") In *Spider-Man*, by contrast, she spent the huge amounts of money available to her on the "masking"—on making it look like the heroes were flying, on making it all look real. In the end, the metamorphosis that Taymor tried so disastrously to effect in the show was to transform the proscenium into a silver screen—to make a play that was, essentially, a blockbuster movie.

Talk about tragic irony. At the end of the interview she gave to Schechner, Taymor boasted of what she had been able to accomplish "with no budgets," theatrical miracles that "have *more* power because they are so transparent, so simple." Back then, when she gave the interview, in the first flush of her success with *The Lion King*, she seemed to know who she was and what she wanted to do. And, of course, what she'd never dream of doing. "I never had theater producers run after me," she told Schechner. "Some people want to make more Broadway shows out of movies. But Elliot"—Goldenthal, her partner, who composes the music for many of her shows and films—"Elliot and I aren't going to do *Batman: The Musical*."

—*The New York Review of Books*, May 12, 2011

THE DREAM DIRECTOR

ABOUT HALFWAY THROUGH Alexander Sokurov's extraordinary 2002 film *Russian Ark*, a movie that takes the form of a surreal tour of the Hermitage in St. Petersburg, a woman who's holding forth about a certain painting pauses to observe that "there are so many symbols we can only guess about." Indeed. The painting in question, Van Dyck's *Virgin with the Partridges*, is, to be sure, enigmatic. But by the time you've gotten this far into Sokurov's film—with its unchronological tableaux of pre-Revolutionary moments (a glimpse of Nicholas and Alexandra at tea with their children is followed by a ball given by Alexander I), its jarring juxtapositions of imperial grandeur and human crudity (Catherine the Great hurrying away from a lavish private performance because, as she cries out, she must have a "piss"), its unsettling repetitions (one long scene is reprised in toto), and its many surreal gestures (the woman lecturing on Van Dyck happens to be blind)—you can't help thinking that the remark about unfathomable symbols is meant to refer to the film itself. Despite the smoothness of its surface—the result, not least, of the fact that it was shot in one unbroken take, the longest in film history—the movie is nonetheless continuously ruffled by jagged intrusions of elements that are ostensibly inexplicable but clearly, somehow, meaningful. Small wonder that another character in *Russian Ark* stops at one point to ask himself, "Is this a dream?"

Dreams, as it happens, fill the movies of Sokurov. "Last night I had a dream" are the first words spoken in *Mother and Son*, the 1997 feature that made the director's international reputation. (He had begun in the 1970s as a documentarian and then became a disciple of Andrei Tarkovsky, some of whose intensely devotional, meditative style Sokurov absorbed while giving it a secular, psychologizing, oneiric cast.) An almost unbearably intense, virtually wordless study of the final hours of a terminally ill middle-aged woman whose son has come, perhaps a little reluctantly, to be with her, that film begins with a dialogue between the immobile, recumbent mother and the handsome young son about the dreams and nightmares they have both been having. "That means we have the same dreams!" the son concludes. "Yes, we do," the mother exhaustedly responds.

The film's companion piece, the unsettlingly homoerotic *Father and Son* (2003), also begins with a dream—a bad one, in this case: we first hear, and then see, a teenage boy moaning in distress as he gradually wakes from a nightmare in his father's arms. (They are both naked; the nature of the moaning is not, at first, entirely clear.) Later on, the father remarks that his son's dreams "are getting out of hand," a conclusion with which it is hard to disagree, given that the boy nearly kills the father in his dream—a not-too-subtle expression of his submerged yearning to move out of the overprotective father's apartment and start his own life.

"All is like a dream," intones the narrator of *Oriental Elegy* (1996), an eerie, fog-shrouded fantasy about a Japanese island whose denizens, interviewed at length by a narrator, seem to be ghosts. A documentary that Sokurov made the following year, *A Simple Life*, which meticulously records a day in the life of a solitary Japanese woman, a kimono-maker living in a secluded village, cannot help alluding to this favorite motif: "Dear Hiroko," the narrator begins, mysteriously quoting a letter whose provenance is never explained, "last night I had no dreams, but did I sleep or was it already nonexistence?"

And then there is *Russian Ark*, which—as sometimes happens in dreams—constantly and disorientingly worries whether it is dreaming itself. "Is this a dream?" asks the character whom we might call the film's protagonist: Astolphe de Custine, the aristocratic French historian of Russian autocracy at the beginning of the nineteenth century, whose stork-like, black-clad figure somewhat bemusedly leads us through the Hermitage while stopping to chat, now and then, with various passersby: early-nineteenth-century partygoers, late-twentieth-century visitors to the museum, it makes no difference to him as long as he gets to toss off barbed comments about history and politics and art. ("Russians are so talented at copying, because you don't have ideas of your own. Your authorities don't want you to have any.") When the Custine of Sokurov's film, who is rather sentimental about the past—"everyone can see the future but nobody remembers the past," he grumbles at one point—is sternly reminded by the twentieth-century narrator that "monarchy isn't eternal," the marquis playfully replies, "Don't I have the right to dream a little?" To which the narrator, just as playfully but with a certain pointedness too, retorts: "Dream away!"

This tart acknowledgment that there is a gulf between dreams (Custine's, and the film's, willful decision to look only at the imperial past) and reality (that past is irretrievably lost) is an important reminder that Sokurov's dreams are more than soft and "poetic" reveries, pretty pictures meant to evoke pleasant nostalgia. As with dreams, his images and narratives always suggest other, hidden truths: these surfaces invite, even require, interpretation. The way the young man in *Mother and Son* keeps looking at a plume of smoke from a train that keeps mysteriously passing, the way the director constantly bends and stretches certain other images, suggest that the emotions in play here are a good deal more complex, and a good deal darker, than the ideal love that some critics see as the movie's subject.

Sokurov's penchant for turning away from our waking understanding of our lives in favor of the truths that reverie can reveal is even more important for certain of his films that have larger perspectives, and larger ambitions. These films include not only his masterpiece, *Russian Ark*, with its poignant exploration of historical nostalgia, but also *Moloch* (1999), a fantasy that follows Hitler, Eva Braun, and some guests during a day's retreat at Berchtesgaden, and *Taurus* (2001), an eccentrically imaginative reconstruction of Lenin's last days—the first two installments of a planned tetralogy about twentieth-century autocrats, of which *The Sun*, about Hirohito's last day as a god, is the third. (Released abroad in 2005, it had its US premiere only at the end of 2009.) It is the profoundest and aesthetically the most satisfying of his excursions into biography, films in which his preoccupation with dreams serves what may be his real interest: history.

Or, rather, a very specific facet of history. At a showing of *The Sun* at the Berlin Film Festival, Sokurov declared that he is not interested in the "events or the period" when he makes a historical movie. The facts of history are not what he wants to evoke: these correspond to the waking reality for which, in so many films, he has shown little interest.

Instead, he explained—and this is hardly surprising in someone who came of age in the stagnant final days of the Soviet regime—

Sokurov is interested in exploring the gap that opens up between human realities and what he calls the "theater" of ideological performances. He elucidated this notion in Berlin when asked about *Moloch*, a movie whose effectiveness, in great part, derives from the contrasts between the awesome, fortress-like scale of the Berchtesgaden redoubt and the grandiosity of the ceremony that envelops Hitler and his party, on the one hand, and, on the other, the grotesque baseness of "Adi" and Eva's antics—naked gymnastics on the balcony, slapstick kicks in the buttocks, impromptu wrestling matches, etc. "These people, the people of power, turned their lives into theater...subordinated their behavior to rituals and ceremonies," the director said.

Moloch is haunted by this tension between impressive outward show and inner realities. One intimate scene between Eva and Adi begins in his bathroom with Eva noticing some stains on his dress uniform; "they come from the body," the whiny, hypochondriacal Hitler mournfully observes. This telling reference to the difference between bodies and the clothes that cover them inspires the most pointed line in the movie: a moment later, Eva suddenly looks at her lover with disgust and says, "Without an audience, you're no better than a corpse." For Sokurov, a survivor of the Soviet system, to grandiosely enact history—to sacrifice humanity to ideology—is to be emptied of life itself.

Anxieties about role-playing and the tension between public personae and private realities, between the large events that constitute "history" and the rich if often irretrievable humanity beneath them, are at the core of *Russian Ark*, whose extraordinary atmosphere of wistful tenderness—in contrast to the equally extraordinary atmosphere of repellent crudeness that characterizes *Moloch*—results, not least, from the fact that most of its subjects are not the

makers of history but comparatively ordinary people—the anonymous courtiers, the nameless partygoers and dinner guests and stew-
ards and musicians. (When the movie does train its eye on the tsars
and tsaritsas, what we see are their private rather than public faces.)
"Are we supposed to be playing a role?" Custine nervously asks the
cameraman at one point; but the point of *Russian Ark* is to focus,
again, on what lay behind the elaborate roles and enactments that
constituted life at the Winter Palace during the Imperial era.

The film announces this preoccupation from the start. It begins
with a black screen and a voice-over by the never-identified narrator,
who may well be Sokurov; he seems to be regaining consciousness
after some kind of "accident" that, you strongly feel, is meant to refer
to the Revolution and the Soviet period. ("Everyone ran to safety as
best they could.") Then, as an image comes into focus, history yields
to human pleasures: we see a gaggle of well-dressed revelers—it
seems to be the early part of the nineteenth century—looking for a
grand party. As the camera/narrator starts to follow this dashing
group through a series of twisting passageways and staircases and
then into the sumptuous galleries of what had been the Winter Palace, we catch glimpses of another kind of history—one that, as in
Moloch, is not, for the most part, the history we read about in history
books.

Instead, Sokurov's camera glides past and through a series of remarkably staged tableaux, astonishingly overflowing with magnificent period dress, of lost, minor, or forgotten moments, as if to
remind us that most of the history lurking behind the Hermitage and
its collections—and much of the history before "the accident"—was
composed of unremarkable, human moments. Here again, the emphasis is on the contrast between the magnificence of the "theater"
and the smallness of the people required to play their roles. (Some-

times literally: while Catherine watches the ballet, the camera shows us the performers lounging in the wings. That was history, too.) One set piece concerns an opulent diplomatic ceremony in which the Persian ambassador to the court of Nicholas I formally apologizes for the murder of Russian envoys in Tehran ("His Majesty has sent me to erase from memory this event," the Persian prince announces, tellingly). But the camera's attention is focused less on the ceremony than on the courtiers who stand fidgeting and gossiping. "A terrible boredom will set in," Custine sighs as he leaves the reception room to inspect the Sèvres porcelain at the reception that will follow. The boredom was also part of the story.

When there are reminders of what we might call "big historical moments," they are the more powerful for being so fleeting, so subtle. At one point, the narrator enters a room that, he is told, is forbidden, and that is clearly meant to evoke the Great Patriotic War, as Russians call World War II; in it—as a fierce winter storm suddenly rages outside the windows—we see a man in mid-twentieth-century garb making coffins (the room had apparently once been used to make gilded frames for paintings). Later on, we overhear an anxious Empress Alexandra murmuring "I thought I heard shots" to a nun, as she glides down a hallway toward her tea party. As indeed she will, one day.

These vignettes representing official history, as well as the tableaux showing us what we could call unofficial history, are punctuated by the jarringly surreal moments that give the movie its dreamlike quality. A woman on the perilous boundary between middle and old age gesticulates suggestively before a painting of a voluptuous odalisque; that blind woman gives a sensitive account of a number of works of art to a visitor who can see; a pair of handsome modern-day sailors sniff intently at an oil painting after Custine has remarked on its wonderful smell. (Sokurov's camera tends to linger on the faces of pretty young men, as much in his several documentaries about soldiers as in his narrative films. In one eerily memorable scene in *Russian Ark*, Custine looms over a handsome, cowering youth in a corner of a gallery, wordlessly threatening him—with what, it's not quite possible to know.)

Indeed, the two most beautiful images in this movie of so many beautiful images seem to have no apparent meaning at all. In the first, a plump and elderly Catherine II escapes from a stifling room—she's been showing some children how to curtsey—and runs into a snow-covered courtyard; the camera follows her as she runs, with increasing speed, through a path in the snow, her gray satin train trailing behind her, a wordless shot that lasts an uncannily long time. (Sokurov likes to dwell at unnatural length on certain images, a technique that at once induces reverie and focuses attention.) In the second, at the end of the movie, a stream of richly dressed courtiers—the ones from the Persian ceremony, apparently—stream down a magnificent ceremonial double staircase. The river of courtiers, Pushkin among them, keeps swelling, it seems, and the amazed camera, which is following them down the steps, keeps spinning back and up to capture the swirling movement of the people, the stairway itself, this moment.

As these sumptuously attired characters begin to crowd and overwhelm the screen, the camera cuts away to a small, oddly glowing doorway. Beyond it, we see, is not the city of St. Petersburg but a white, icy ocean of some kind. This small moment, at last, explains the film's title: for as we now see, we are indeed aboard an "ark"—a cinematic vessel that has rescued, "as best it could," apparently random moments from history, and that will float forever in an endlessly circling stream of time itself.

If *Russian Ark* offers tantalizing glimpses of people whom history has forgotten, as well as of men and women who seem very small and vulnerable in comparison to the roles they were required to play, then *The Sun* puts Sokurov's special emphases to excellent use as it explores the gap between historical grandiosity and human weakness at a moment in history when that gulf was most glaringly exposed: the day on which Hirohito consented to acknowledge that he was not, in fact, a god.

The film, like *Moloch*, uses the events of one day as the armature on which to build up a subtle account of the disproportion between a man and his historical persona. (*The Sun* also shares *Moloch*'s dour palette of washed-out browns, greens, and grays, in stark contrast to the opulent colors that enrich *Russian Ark*.) When it opens, we find Hirohito, now living in a bunker beneath his palace, at breakfast, being given his day's agenda by his chamberlain. Nothing is left to chance: after his ten o'clock meeting with his military cabinet and his noon visit to his lab (the late emperor, now technically known as Shôwa, was an accomplished marine biologist with a number of scholarly publications to his name), he is informed when he may nap and when he may have time for "private thoughts." This is a man who, it seems, is unable to function on his own, outside of the structure of court life—a point that is wonderfully made toward the end of the film when, as he leaves a meeting with General Mac-Arthur, he confronts for the first time a door that isn't being opened for him. Bemused, he tentatively reaches down, grabs the handle, and opens it himself, something he has clearly never done before.

And like *Moloch*, this film uses an undue focus on the autocrat's body as a means of underscoring the difference between his public persona and his private self. The former is the object of ardent ministrations by everyone but the emperor himself, who seems if anything eager to be a normal human being. Early on, when he wryly remarks to his valet that "the very last Japanese may be myself"—the valet had commented, apropos of a radio report that the Americans are just outside Tokyo, that as long as there is one Japanese left standing the Americans will never set foot in the palace—the servant exclaims in horror that "it is outlandish to assert that the emperor could be human." To which a plaintive Hirohito replies, "But my body is the same as yours." The ordinariness of his body is strongly linked, in the script, to the ordinariness of Hirohito's inner life and emotions: at one point his disgusted observation that his breath lately "has a bad smell and a bad taste" leads seamlessly into the equally unhappy assertion that "no one loves me except for my wife and my older son."

The action of the film, such as it is—Sokurov is never really interested in strong narratives—follows the events that will make the humble truth of the emperor's observation plain even to the most fanatically loyal of his household. Again and again, he shows himself blind to the realities of the historical situation. During his morning military meeting, he responds to what is clearly a crushingly dire report from his minister of the army by quoting a poem written by his grandfather, the emperor Meiji: "Sea to the north and to the south, to the west and to the east / waves whirl up." This the emperor interprets, to the obvious anguish of his perspiring ministers, to mean that "peace on favorable terms to my people is the only peace; let the sea continue to rage." (Hirohito really did recite a poem by Meiji at an imperial conference, but it was clearly pacifist in its implications.)

Later on, clad in a white coat in his laboratory, he delivers an ecstatic monologue about the virtues of the hermit crab—an animal to which he bears an uncanny resemblance: "the crab can cover himself...it lives at shallow depths and doesn't migrate very far"—which leads to a grotesquely self-serving account of the reasons for Japanese military aggression in Asia:

Migration…migration…yes, it never leaves its shores. Migration…Settled. Settled. Distant migration…migration of species
…migration. Emigration! Discrimination! Unfair immigration
laws! I remember…Wake up! I remember about the causes that
brought about the Great Asian War…When the American government forbade Japanese immigration, which occurred in the
State of California in 1924, that discrimination became a serious cause of anger and indignation among our people, and the
military rode this wave of protest.

It is not the last time in the film that the emperor, who seems to grow
smaller and more awkward during his final hours as a god, rather
pathetically attempts to deflect any accountability for his interventions in history. Later on, when he finally meets with a bemused and
condescending MacArthur, he seems to think that his assertion that
he wasn't actually Hitler's "friend" will absolve him of responsibility.
The crab can cover himself.

Hirohito's interest in marine biology provides Sokurov with a fruitful
thematic and visual leitmotif: images of fish glide through the film,
marking its most emotionally and politically significant moments.
    The most striking of these is in a sequence representing a day-
dream the emperor has while resting alone in his study. He's been
leafing through some photo albums: family albums, whose pictures
he tenderly kisses, as well as albums containing photos of Hollywood
stars—one of whom, Charlie Chaplin, he will be compared to later
in the film. Suddenly he has a vision of American bombers morphing
into wiggling, demonic catfish that rain fire on his dominions. (Earlier, before urging the army to continue fighting, Hirohito the biologist observes that the *na-muzu*, or catfish, protects itself by sinking
to the bottom of the water.) Before, his disquisition on hermit crabs

was the vehicle for our appreciation of his historical arrogance; now, only after his beloved fish are conflated with bombers, does the enemy's destructiveness become real to him. This is the moment when he acknowledges defeat. All this inspires Hirohito to attempt a poem of his own, a cliché verse that inadvertently echoes certain sentiments we find in *Russian Ark*: "The spring *sakura* [cherry blossom] and the January snow," begins an early version, "neither lasts long."

The marine motif is present even in the countenance of Hirohito, to whom Sokurov has given a peculiar tic: over and over again he purses his lips and moves them laboriously, soundlessly—the face you'd make if you had to act out "fish out of water" in a game of charades. For he is, indeed, a fish out of water, a man who on this day seems at home neither in the divine nor in the human element.

Another recurrent motif that suggests the devolution of Hirohito from god to man is an embarrassed physicality; Sokurov stages a number of excruciatingly awkward encounters between the emperor and his subordinates. There is the marvelous opening scene with the valet, during which the old man has great trouble buttoning his master's shirt, and an exquisitely anguished scene in which there is tense and prolonged confusion about where to seat the director of a scientific institute who has come at Hirohito's request in order to discuss a question of long-standing interest to the emperor: Could his grandfather Meiji have seen the northern lights, as he once claimed? No, says the scientist, with anguished embarrassment, after which the emperor observes that the poor man probably hasn't eaten all day, and sends him off with a chocolate bar, a gift from the victorious Americans.

The emperor's cluelessness is underscored in two deftly tragicomic scenes with MacArthur, during which the Japanese keeps parrying the American's blunt questions with replies that are either dazzlingly evasive or staggeringly banal:

"What's it like being a living god?"

"I don't know what to tell you. Of course the Emperor's life is not easy. Some of his habits and hobbies are taken skeptically. Take the catfish for example...with whom shall he share his admiration for its perfection?"

There is, too, a splendid scene in which the emperor agrees to have his picture taken by a group of US Army photographers, who react with dismay, and then amusement, to the unprepossessing, Chaplinesque figure in a suit and a fedora who answers to the title of "emperor." They had thought that his chamberlain, magnificently attired in a morning coat and tails, must be this august figure.

And finally, one of the best scenes that Sokurov has ever filmed: the climactic encounter between Hirohito and his wife, the empress Nagako, who has been brought back to Tokyo from her family's refuge in the countryside. (This indulgence was granted Hirohito once he recorded the speech in which he relinquished his divine status.) The two spouses come together in a small room and there ensues a beautifully staged bit of business about the empress's hat, which she has trouble removing and which her physically shy and emotionally awkward husband finally frees of her lacquered hairdo, with some difficulty. The clunky physicality of this business, our awareness of the tension between his human self and the elaborate protocols of behavior of which he has now been stripped and without which he seems helpless to move—the scene concludes with the emperor rather woodenly laying his head on his wife's breast and keeping it there, once again a bit too long—is the final proof of the claim he had made at the beginning of his day: that his body is like everyone else's.

The point is not to defend Hirohito by somehow humanizing him, as some critics have claimed. If anything, *The Sun* makes us all too aware, not for the first time in this director's work, of the catastrophic disproportion between the character of a man and the nature of the role he played in history. Sokurov's eccentrically beautiful and finally overwhelming film concludes by emphasizing that disproportion—one that, in the end, doesn't escape even his own wife. In their final moments together before they run out of the room to see their children—and after being told by the chamberlain, pointedly, that the young man who recorded the emperor's speech has committed hara-kiri—Hirohito delightedly announces to Nagako that he has abandoned his divinity. "Basically, I felt uneasy... not good at all" is the lumpy way he sums up his motivation. To celebrate this moment of "freedom," as he calls it, he recites for her the finished version of the poem he had started earlier in the afternoon:

Snow in winter looks like the sakura *in March.*
Time is indifferent and erases them both.

There is a moment's pause during which, we imagine, the dreamy world of the poem dissolves into a startled awareness of reality. And then the empress asks, "Is that all?"

—*The New York Review of Books*, February 11, 2010

THE MAD MEN ACCOUNT

SINCE THE SUMMER of 2007, when *Mad Men* premiered on the cable channel AMC, the world it purports to depict—a lushly reimagined Madison Avenue in the 1960s, where sleekly suited, chain-smoking, hard-drinking advertising executives dream up ingeniously intuitive campaigns for cigarettes and bras and airlines while effortlessly bedding beautiful young women or whisking their Grace Kelly–lookalike wives off to business trips in Rome—has itself become the object of a kind of madness. I'm not even referring to the critical reception both in the US and abroad, which has been delirious: a recent and not atypical reference in *The Times* of London called it "one of the...best television series of all time," and the show has repeatedly won the Emmy, the Golden Globe, the Screen Actors Guild Award, the Writers Guild of America Award, and the Producers Guild of America Award for Best Drama Series. (A number of its cast members have been nominated in the various acting categories as well.) Rather, the way in which *Mad Men* has seemingly percolated into every corner of the popular culture—the children's show *Sesame Street* introduced a

Mad Men parody, toned down, naturally, for its tender viewers—suggests that its appeal goes far beyond whatever dramatic satisfactions it affords.

At first glance, this appeal seems to have a lot to do with the show's much-discussed visual style—the crisp postwar coolness of dress and decor characteristic of the 1950s and 1960s. *Mad Men* hardly started this fad: for the past decade at least, a taste for the sleek lines of "midcentury Modern" has been evident everywhere from the glossy shelter magazines to your local flea market. But the series has certainly crystallized and given focus to this retro aesthetic. It's not only apartments; consumers themselves want the look. The clothing retailer Banana Republic, in partnership with the show's creators, devised a nationwide window-display campaign evoking the show's distinctive 1960s look and now offers a style guide to help consumers look more like the men and women in the drama; a nail-polish company is currently hawking a *Mad Men*–inspired line of colors. The toy maker Mattel has released dolls based on some of the show's characters. Most intriguingly, to my mind, Brooks Brothers has partnered with the series' costume designer to produce a limited-edition *Mad Men* suit—which is, inevitably, based on a Brooks Brothers design of the 1960s.

Many popular entertainments, of course, capitalize on their appeal by means of marketing tie-ins, but this yearning for *Mad Men* style seems different from the way in which, say, children who are hooked on the *Star Wars* series long to own Darth Vader action dolls. The people who watch *Mad Men* are, after all, grown-ups—most of them between the ages of nineteen and forty-nine. This is to say that most of the people who are so addicted to the show are either younger adults, to whom the series represents, perhaps, an alluring historical fantasy of a time before the present era's seemingly endless prohibitions against pleasures once taken for granted (casual sex, careless eating, excessive drinking, and incessant smoking), or younger baby boomers—people in their forties and early fifties who remember, barely, the show's 1960s setting, attitudes, and look. For either audience, then, the show's style is, essentially, symbolic: it represents fantasies, or memories, of significant potency.

I am dwelling on the deeper, almost irrational reasons for the series' appeal—to which I shall return later, and to which I am not at all immune, having myself been a child in the 1960s—because after watching the fifty-two episodes of *Mad Men* that have aired thus far, I find little else to justify it. We are currently living in a new golden age of television, a medium that has been liberated by cable broadcasting to explore both fantasy and reality with greater frankness and originality than ever before: as witness shows as different as the now-iconic crime dramas *The Sopranos* and *The Wire*, with their darkly glinting, almost Aeschylean moral textures; the philosophically provocative, unexpectedly moving sci-fi hit *Battlestar Galactica*, which among other things is a kind of futuristic retelling of the *Aeneid*; and the perennially underappreciated small-town drama *Friday Night Lights*, which offers, to my mind, the finest representation of middle-class marriage in popular culture.

With these standouts (and there are many more), *Mad Men* shares virtually no significant excellences except its design. The writing is extremely weak, the plotting haphazard and often preposterous, the characterizations shallow and sometimes incoherent; its attitude toward the past is glib and its self-positioning in the present is unattractively smug; the direction is unimaginative.

Worst of all, in a drama that has made loud claims to exploring social and historical "issues," the show is melodramatic rather than dramatic. By this I mean that it proceeds, for the most part, like a soap opera, serially (and often unbelievably) generating, and then rather synthetically resolving (or simply walking away from) various species of extreme personal crises (adulteries, abortions, premarital pregnancies, interracial affairs, alcoholism and drug addiction, etc.), rather than exploring, by means of believable and carefully established conflicts between personality and situation, the contemporary social and cultural phenomena it regards with such fascination: sexism, misogyny, social hypocrisy, racism, the counterculture, and so forth.

That a soap opera decked out in high-end clothes (and concepts) should have received so much acclaim and is taken so seriously reminds you that fads depend as much on the willingness of the public to believe as on the cleverness of the people who invent them; as with many fads that take the form of infatuations with certain moments in the past, the *Mad Men* craze tells us far more about today than it does about yesterday. But just what is it in the world of the show that we want to possess? The clothes and furniture? The wicked behavior? The unpunished crassness? To my mind, it's something else entirely, something unexpected and, in a way, almost touching.

———

Mad Men—the term, according to the show, was coined by admen in the 1950s—centers on the men and women who work at Sterling Cooper, a medium-size ad agency with dreams of getting bigger; when the action begins, in the early 1960s, the men are all either partners or rising young executives, and the women are secretaries and office managers. At the center of this constellation stands the drama's antihero, Don Draper, the firm's brilliantly talented creative director: a man, we learn, who not only sells lies but is one. A flashback that comes at the end of the first season reveals that Don is, in fact, a midwestern hick called Dick Whitman who profited from a moment of wartime confusion in Korea in order to start a new life.

After he is wounded and a comrade—the real Don Draper—is killed, Dick switches their dog tags: the real Don's body goes home to Dick's grieving and not very nice family, while Dick reinvents himself as Don Draper. (In the kind of cultural winking in which the show's creators like to indulge, the small town in which Dick Whitman's family await his body is called "Bunbury," the term that the male leads in Oscar Wilde's *Importance of Being Earnest* use for their double lives.)

This backstory, as rusty and unsubtle a device as it may be, helps establish the pervasive theme of falseness and hypocrisy that the writers find not only in the advertising business itself but in the culture of the 1960s as a whole just before the advent of feminism, the civil rights movement, and the sexual liberation of the 1970s. (In a typical bit of overkill, the writers have made the ingenious adman the son of a prostitute.) The four seasons that have been aired thus far trace the evolution of the larger society even as the secret that lurks behind Don's private life becomes a burden that is increasingly hard to bear. Female employees become more assertive: one secretary, Peggy Olson, who's not as pretty as the others, becomes a copywriter —to the dismay of the office manager, a redheaded bombshell called Joan Holloway, who's a decade older and can't understand why anyone would want to do anything but marry the boss. One of the fabulously hard-drinking executives finally goes into AA. The firm considers the buying power of the "Negro" market for the first time. And so on.

Meanwhile, Don wanders from career triumph to career triumph and from bed to bed, his preternatural understanding of what motivates consumers grotesquely disproportionate to any understanding of his own motives; back home, his gorgeous blond wife, Betty, a former model from the Main Line, is starting to chafe at the domestic bit. All this plays out against some of the key historical events of the time: the Nixon–Kennedy race (Sterling Cooper is doing PR for Nixon), the crash of American Airlines Flight 1 in March 1962 (a character's father is aboard, triggering a crisis of conscience as to whether he should capitalize on his family's tragedy to help land the American Airlines account), and, inevitably, the Kennedy assassination, which ruins the wedding of a partner's spoiled daughter.

As I have already mentioned, the actual stuff of *Mad Men*'s action is, essentially, the stuff of soap opera: abortions, secret pregnancies, extramarital affairs, office romances, and of course dire family secrets; what is supposed to give it its higher cultural resonance is the historical element. When people talk about the show, they talk (if they're not talking about the clothes and furniture) about the special perspective its historical setting creates—the graphic picture that it is able to paint of the attitudes of an earlier time, attitudes likely to make us uncomfortable or outraged today. An unwanted pregnancy, after all, had different implications in 1960 than it does in 2011.

To my mind, the picture is too crude and the artist too pleased with himself. In *Mad Men*, everyone chain-smokes, every executive starts drinking before lunch, every man is a chauvinist pig, every male employee viciously competitive and jealous of his colleagues, every white person a reflexive racist (when not irritatingly patronizing). It's not that you don't know that, say, sexism was rampant in the workplace before the feminist movement; it's just that, on the screen, the endless succession of leering junior execs and crude jokes and abusive behavior all meant to signal "sexism" doesn't work—it's wearying rather than illuminating. People—liberal-minded young people in particular, in my experience—keep talking admiringly about the show's "critique" of the hypocrisies of advertising and the shallowness of consumerism, but simply to show a lot of repellent advertising men acting repellently does not constitute a meaningful critique; it's a lazy one-liner. As I watched the first season, the characters and their milieu were so unrelentingly awful that I kept wondering whether the writers had been trying, unsuccessfully, for a kind of camp—for a tartly tongue-in-cheek send-up of 1960s attitudes. (I found myself wishing that the creators of *Glee* had gotten a stab at this material.) But the creators of *Mad Men* are in deadly earnest. It's as if these forty- and thirty-somethings can't quite believe how *bad* people were back then, and can't resist the impulse to keep showing you.

This impulse might be worth indulging (briefly), but *Mad Men* suffers from a hypocrisy of its own. As the camera glides over Joan's gigantic bust and hourglass hips, as it languorously follows the swirls of cigarette smoke toward the ceiling, as the sound engineers lovingly enhance the clinking of ice in the glass of someone's midday Canadian Club, you can't help thinking that the creators of this show are indulging in a kind of dramatic having your cake and eating it too: even as it invites us to be shocked by what it's showing us—a scene people love to talk about is one in which a hugely pregnant Betty lights up a cigarette in a car—it's also eroticizing what it's showing us. For a drama (or book, or whatever) to invite an audience to feel superior to a less enlightened era, even as it teases the regressive urges behind the behaviors associated with that era, strikes me as the worst possible offense that can be committed in a creative work set in the past: it's simultaneously contemptuous and pandering. Here, it cripples the show's ability to tell us anything of real substance about the world it depicts—let alone to fashion a serious "critique."

Most of the show's flaws can, in fact, be attributed to the way it waves certain flags in your face and leaves things at that, without serious thought about dramatic appropriateness or textured characterization. (The writers don't really want you to think about what Betty might be thinking as she lights up; they just want you to know that she's one of those clueless 1960s mothers who smoked during pregnancy.) The show's creators like to trigger "issue"-related sub-plots by parachuting some new character or event into the action, often an element that has no relation to anything that's come before. Although much has been made of the show's treatment of race, for instance, the "treatment" is usually little more than a lazy allusion—race never really makes anything *happen* in the show. There's a brief subplot at one point about one of the young associates, Paul Kinsey, a Princeton graduate who turns out—how or why, we never learn—to be living with a black supermarket checkout girl in Montclair, New Jersey. A few colleagues express surprise when they meet her at a party, we briefly see the couple heading to a protest march in Mis-sissippi, and that's pretty much it—we never hear from or about her again. Even more bizarre is a truncated story line involving Lane Pryce, the buttoned-up British partner who's been foisted on Sterling Cooper by its newly acquired parent company in London. (You know he's English because he wears waistcoats all the time and uses poly-syllabic words a lot.) Totally out of the blue, this cardboardish char-acter is given a black Playboy bunny girlfriend whom he says he wants to marry, but she's never explained, either: apart from trigger-ing a weird, vaguely sadomasochistic confrontation between Lane and his bigot father (who beats him with a cane and makes him say "Sir"), the affair leaves no trace. It's simply there, and we're supposed to "get" what her presence is about, the way we're supposed to "get" an advertisement in a magazine.

The show's directorial style is static, airless. Scenes tend to be boxed: actors will be arranged within a frame—sitting in a car, at a desk, on a bed—and then they recite their lines, and that's that. Characters seldom enter (or leave) the frame while already engaged in some activity, already talking about something—a useful tech-nique (much used in shows like the old *Law & Order*), which strongly gives the textured sense of the characters' reality, that they exist out-side of the script. As for the acting, it is unexceptional in general and occasionally downright amateurish. (The baby-doll performance of the porcelain-beautiful January Jones, as Mrs. Don Draper, is an embarrassment.) I am not one of those critics who admires the per-formance of Jon Hamm as Don, which seems to me to emblematize the glossy inauthenticity of the show in general. There is a long tradi-tion of American actors who excel at suggesting the unconventional and sometimes unpleasant currents coursing beneath their appealing all-American looks: James Stewart was one; Matt Damon is, now, another. By contrast, you sometimes have the impression that Hamm was hired because he reminds you of advertisements, and after all the show is about advertising—he's a foursquare, square-jawed fellow whose tormented interior we are constantly told about but never re-ally feel. (He looks uncannily like the guy in the old Arrow Shirt ads.) With rare exceptions (notably Robert Morse in an amusing cameo as the eccentric Japanophile partner Bert Cooper), the other actors in this show are "acting the atmosphere," as directors like to say: they're playing "Sixties people" rather than inhabiting this or that character, making him or her specific. Coupled with the fact that most of them are so awful, your sense of the characters as mere types—the loner with a secret, the prep, the philanderer, the bored housewife—short-circuits any possible connection to them. I cared more about what happened to the people in *Friday Night Lights* after one episode than I did for anyone in *Mad Men* after four seasons.

The way that the scene about Lane and his black girlfriend somehow morphs into a scene about an unnatural emotional current between him and his father is typical of another of *Mad Men*'s vices: you often feel that the writers are so pleased with this or that notion that they've forgotten the point they're trying to make. During its first few seasons the show featured a closeted gay character—Sal Romano, the firm's art director. (He, too, wears vests.) At the beginning of the show I thought there was going to be some story line that shed some interesting light on the repressive sexual mores of the time, but apart from a few semicomic suggestions that Sal's wife is frustrated and that he's attracted to one of his younger colleagues—and a moment when Don catches him making out with a bellhop when they're both on a business trip, a revelation that, weirdly, had no repercussions—the little story line that Sal is finally given isn't really about the closet at all. In the end, he is fired after rebuffing the advances of the firm's most important client, a tobacco heir who consequently insists to the partners that Sal be fired. (This character seems to be suffering from what can only be called sudden-onset homosexuality: there's no hint of his being gay until the writers suddenly need this particular subplot.) Naturally the tobacco heir gives a phony reason for his sudden discontent, and the partners, caving in to their big client, do as he says. So in the end it's not a story about gayness in the 1960s, about the closet; it's a story about caving in to power, about business ethics. A lot of the writing has this ad hoc quality.

To my mind, there are only two instances in which the writers of *Mad Men* have dramatized, rather than simply advertised, their chosen themes. One is about the curvy office manager Joan. At one point, she's asked to help vet television scripts for potential conflicts of interest with clients' ads, and finds she's both good at it and intellectually stimulated by it—only to be told, in passing, that the firm has hired a man to do the job. The look on her face when she gets the news—first crushed, then resigned, because after all this is how it goes—is one of the moments of real poignancy in the show. It tells us far more about prefeminist America than all the dirty jokes and gropings the writers have inflicted on us thus far.

And there's a marvelous sequence that comes at the climax of season four, in which Don's secret past creates a real dramatic crisis in the Aristotelian sense: what Don has done, and what he does, and what he is and wants as opposed to what his society is and wants, all come together in a way that feels both inevitable and wrenching. At the beginning of the episode, we learn that Sterling Cooper's biggest client—that tobacco company whose billings essentially keep it running—is about to drop the account; as a result, the agency is in serious danger. Then—luckily, as it would seem—a young executive seems on the verge of bringing in a huge account from North American Aviation, a defense contractor based in California. But the routine Defense Department background check that is mandated for companies doing business with NAA poses a threat to Don, who, as we know, was a deserter from the army.

This situation creates a conflict with an elegantly Sophoclean geometry: the survival of Don's business depends on doing business with NAA, but doing business with NAA threatens Don himself—his personal survival. In the end, Don's sometime rival—a younger colleague who discovered his secret long ago, but has kept it, sometimes grudgingly, and whom Don has bailed out at a crucial moment, too—covers for him, dumping NAA on some pretext. As I watched this gripping episode I realized it was the only time that I had felt drawn into the drama as *drama*—the only time that the writers had created a situation whose structure, rather than its accoutrements or "message," was irresistible.

———

In its glossy, semaphoric style, its tendency to invoke rather than unravel this or that issue, the way it uses a certain visual allure to blind rather than to enlighten, *Mad Men* reminds you of nothing so much as a successful advertisement. Indeed, the great irony of *Mad Men* may be that it functions the way that ads function, rather than the way that serious drama functions: it's suggestive rather than discursive, juxtaposing some potent pictures and words and hoping you'll make the connection. And yet as we know, the best ads tap into deep currents of emotion. As much as I disliked the show, I did find myself persisting. Why?

In the final episode of season one, there's a terrific scene in which Don Draper is pitching a campaign for Kodak's circular slide projector, which he has dubbed the "carousel"—a word, as he rightly intuits, that powerfully evokes childhood pleasures and, if you're lucky, idyllic memories of family togetherness. To make his point, he's stocked the projector he uses in the pitch with photos of his own family—which, as we know, is actually in the process of falling apart, due to his serial adulteries. But even as we know this, we can't help submitting to the allure of the projected image of the strong, handsome man and his smiling, beautiful wife—the ideal, perhaps, that we all secretly carry of our own parents, whatever their lives and marriages may have been.

The tension between the luminous ideal and the unhappy reality is, of course, what the show thinks it's "about"—reminding us, as it so often and so unsubtly does, that, *like advertising itself*, the decade it depicts was often hypocritical, indulging certain images and styles of behavior while knowing them to be false, even unjust. But this shallow aperçu can't explain the profound emotionalism of the scene. In a lengthy *New York Times* article about *Mad Men* that appeared as the show—by then already a phenomenon—was going into its second season, its creator, Matthew Weiner, recalled that he had shown the carousel episode to his own parents, and the story he tells about that occasion suggests where the emotion may originate.

Weiner, it turns out—like his character, Don Draper—used his own family photographs to "stock" the scene: the most poignant image we see as Don clicks through the carousel of photos, a picture of Don and Betty smilingly sharing a hot dog (a casual intimacy that, we know, can now only be a memory), was based on an actual photograph of Weiner's parents sharing a hot dog on their first date. Interestingly, Weiner made a point of telling the reporter who was interviewing him that when he showed the episode to his parents, they didn't even remark on the borrowing—didn't seem to make the connection.

The attentive and attention-hungry child, the heedless grown-up: this pairing, I would argue, is a crucial one in *Mad Men*. The child's-eye perspective is, in fact, one of the strongest and most original elements of the series as a whole. Children in *Mad Men*—not least, Don and Betty's daughter, Sally—often have interesting and unexpected things to say. Perhaps the most intriguing of the children is Glen, the odd little boy who lives down the street from the Drapers, whose mother is a divorcée shunned, at first, by the other couples on the block. Glen has a kind of fetishistic attachment to Betty—at one point, when she's babysitting him, he asks for and receives a lock of her hair—and he occasionally pops up and has weirdly adult conversations with her. ("I'm so sad," the housewife finds herself telling the nine-year-old as she sits in her station wagon in a supermarket parking lot. "I wish I were older," he pointedly replies.) The loaded way in which Glen often simply stares at Betty and the other grown-ups suggested to me that he's a kind of stand-in for Weiner, who had been a writer on *The Sopranos* and, more to the point, was born in 1965—and is, therefore, of an age with the children depicted on the show. That Glen is played by Weiner's son strikingly hints at a very strong series of identifications going on here.

It's only when you realize that the most important "eye"—and "I"—in *Mad Men* belong to the watchful if often uncomprehending children, rather than to the badly behaved and often caricatured adults, that the show's special appeal comes into focus. In the same *Times* article, Weiner tried to describe the impulses that lay at the core of his creation, acknowledging that

> part of the show is trying to figure out—this sounds really in-eloquent—trying to figure out what is the deal with my parents. Am I them? Because you know you are....The truth is it's such a trope to sit around and bash your parents. I don't want it to be like that. They are my inspiration, let's not pretend.

This, more than anything, explains why the greatest part of the audience for *Mad Men* is made up not, as you might have imagined at one point, by people of the generation it depicts—people who were in their twenties and thirties and forties in the 1960s, and are now in their sixties and seventies and eighties—but by viewers in their forties and early fifties today, which is to say of an age with those characters' children. The point of identification is, in the end, not Don but Sally, not Betty but Glen: the watching, hopeful, and so often disillusioned children who would grow up to be this program's audience, watching their younger selves watch their parents screw up.

Hence both the show's serious failings and its strong appeal. If so much of *Mad Men* is curiously opaque, all inexplicable exteriors and posturing, it occurs to you that this is, after all, how the adult world often looks to children; whatever its blankness, that world, as re-created in the show, feels somehow real to those of us who were kids back then. As for the appeal: Who, after all, can resist the fantasy of seeing what your parents were like before you were born, or when you were still little—too little to understand what the deal was with them, something we can only do now, in hindsight? And who, after having that privileged view, would want to dismiss the lives they led and world they inhabited as trivial—as passing fads, moments of madness? Who would still want to bash them, instead of telling them that we know they were bad but now we forgive them?

—*The New York Review of Books,* February 24, 2011

UNSINKABLE

IN THE EARLY 1970s, my Uncle Walter, who wasn't a "real" uncle but had a better intuition about my hobbies and interests than some of my blood relatives did, gave me a thrilling gift: membership in the Titanic Enthusiasts of America. I was only twelve, but already hooked. The magnificence, the pathos, the enthralling chivalry— Benjamin Guggenheim putting on white tie and tails so he could drown "like a gentleman"—and the shaming cowardice, the awful mistakes, the tantalizing "what if"s: for me, there was no better story. I had read whatever books the local public library offered, and had spent some of my allowance on a copy of Walter Lord's indispensable *A Night to Remember.* To this incipient collection Uncle Walter added the precious gift of a biography of Thomas Andrews, the man who designed the ship. (It has always been among the first books I pack when I move.) A little later, when I was in my mid-teens, I toiled for a while on a novel about two fourteen-year-old boys, one a Long Islander like myself, the other a British aristocrat, who meet during the doomed maiden voyage. Needless to say, their budding friendship was sundered by the disaster.

I wasn't the only one who was obsessed—or writing. It may not be true that "the three most written-about subjects of all time are Jesus, the Civil War, and the *Titanic*," as one historian has put it, but it's not much of an exaggeration. Since the early morning of April 15, 1912, when the great liner went to the bottom of the Atlantic Ocean, taking with it five grand pianos, eight thousand dinner forks, an automobile, a fifty-line telephone switchboard, twenty-nine boilers, a jeweled copy of *The Rubáiyát* of Omar Khayyam, and more than fifteen hundred lives, the writing hasn't stopped. First, there were the headlines, which even today can produce an awful thrill. "ALL SAVED FROM TITANIC AFTER COLLISION," the New York *Evening Sun* crowed less than twenty-four hours after the sinking. A day later, brute fact had replaced wishful conjecture: "TITANIC SINKS, 1500 DIE." Then there were the early survivor narratives—a genre that has by now grown to include a book by the descendants of a Lebanese passenger whose trek to America had begun on a camel caravan. There were the poems. For a while, there was such a glut that *The New York Times* was moved to print a warning: "To write about the *Titanic* a poem worth printing requires that the author should have something more than paper, pencil, and a strong feeling that the disaster was a terrible one." Since then, there have been histories, academic studies, polemics by enthusiasts, and novels, numbering in the hundreds. There's even a *Titanic for Dummies*. This centennial month alone will see the publication of nearly three dozen titles.

The books are, so to speak, just the tip of the iceberg. Between 1912 and 1913 more than a hundred songs about the *Titanic* were published. A scant month after the sinking, a one-reel movie called *Saved from the Titanic* was released, featuring Dorothy Gibson, an actress who had been a passenger in first class. It established a formula—a love story wrapped around the real-life catastrophe—that has resurfaced again and again, notably in a 1953 tearjerker starring Barbara Stanwyck and in James Cameron's 1997 blockbuster, which, when it was released, was both the most expensive and the highest-grossing film of all time. (The film was rereleased during the week of the centenary, after an $18 million conversion to 3D.) There have been a host of television treatments: the most recent is a four-part miniseries by Julian Fellowes, the creator of *Downton Abbey*. And that's just the English-language output. German dramatizations include a Nazi propaganda film set aboard the ship—*not* the same movie as the Leni Riefenstahl *Titanic* movie. A French entry, *The Chambermaid on the Titanic* (1997), based on a novel, fleshes out the story with erotic reveries.

The inexhaustible interest suggests that the *Titanic*'s story taps a vein much deeper than the morbid fascination that has attached to other disasters. The explosion of the *Hindenberg*, for instance, and even the torpedoing, just three years after the *Titanic* sank, of the *Lusitania*, another great liner whose passenger list boasted the rich and the famous, were calamities that shocked the world but have failed to generate an obsessive preoccupation. The aura of significance that surrounds the *Titanic*'s fate was the subject of another, belated headline, which appeared in a special publication of the satirical newspaper *The Onion* in 1999, stomping across the page in dire block letters:

WORLD'S LARGEST METAPHOR HITS ICE-BERG

The "news" was accompanied by an archival image of the ship's famous four-funneled profile. The subhead pressed the joke: "TITANIC, REPRESENTATION OF MAN'S HUBRIS, SINKS IN NORTH ATLANTIC. 1,500 DEAD IN SYMBOLIC TRAGEDY."

The Onion's spoof gets to the heart of the matter: unlike other disasters, the *Titanic* seems to be *about* something. But what? For some, it's a parable about the scope, and limits, of technology: a 1997 Broadway musical admonished us that "in every age mankind attempts / to fabricate great works at once / magnificent and impossible." For others, it's a morality tale about class, or a foreshadowing of World War I—the marker of the end of a more innocent era. Academic historians dismiss this notion as mere nostalgia; for them, the disaster is less a historical dividing line than a screen on which early-twentieth-century society projected its anxieties about race, gender, class, and immigration.

All these interpretations are legitimate, even provocative; and yet none, somehow, seems wholly satisfying. If the *Titanic* has gripped our imagination so forcefully for the past century, it must be because of something bigger than any fact of social or political or cultural history. To get to the bottom of why we can't forget it, you have to turn away from the facts and consider the realm to which the *Titanic* and its story properly belong: myth.

———

If the facts are so well known by now that they seem more like memory than history, it's thanks to Walter Lord. More than fifty years after its publication, *A Night to Remember* (1955) remains the definitive account; it has never gone out of print. In just under 150 pages, the author crisply lays out a story that, he rightly intuited, needs no added drama. He begins virtually at the moment of impact. "High in the crow's nest" of the sumptuous new ship—the largest ever built, widely admired for its triple-propeller design, and declared by the press to be "unsinkable"—two lookouts peering out at the unusually calm North Atlantic suddenly sight an iceberg "right ahead." Within a couple of pages, the ship's fate is sealed: Lord gives us the agonizing thirty-seven seconds that elapsed between the sighting and the collision, and then the eerily understated moment of impact, the "faint grinding jar" felt by so many passengers and crew. ("If I had had a brimful glass of water in my hand not a drop would have been spilled," one survivor recalled.) Only then does he fill in what led up to that moment—not least the decision to speed through waters known to be strewn with icebergs—and what followed.

Until Lord's book, what most people had read about the *Titanic* came from the initial news stories, and then, as the years passed, from articles and interviews published on anniversaries of the sinking. Lord was the first writer to put it all together from a more distanced perspective. The unhurried detachment of his account nicely mirrors the odd calm that, according to so many survivors' accounts, long prevailed aboard the stricken liner. "And so it went," Lord wrote. "No bells or sirens, no general alarm." His account has no bells or sirens, either; the catastrophe unfolds almost dreamily. There are the nonchalant reactions of passengers and crew, many of whom felt the sinking ship was a better bet than the tiny lifeboats. ("We are safer here than in that little boat," J. J. Astor declared; he drowned.) There are the oddly revealing decisions: one socialite left his cabin, then went back and, ignoring the $300,000 in stocks and bonds that he had stashed in a tin box, grabbed a good-luck charm and three oranges. There is the growing realization that there weren't enough lifeboats; of those, many were lowered half full. There are the rockets fired off in distress, which one passenger recalled as paling against the dazzling starlight. And then the shattering end, marked by the din of the ship's giant boilers, torn loose from their housings, hurtling downward toward the submerged bows.

There are iconic moments of panache and devotion, and of cowardice. Benjamin Guggenheim really did trade in his life jacket for white tie and tails. Mrs. Isidor Straus really did refuse to leave her husband, a co-owner of Macy's: "Where you go, I go," she was heard to say. Among the songs written after the sinking was one in Yiddish, celebrating the couple's devotion. And—an anecdote that has been repeated in everything from a poison-pen letter sent soon after the sinking to an episode of *Rod Serling's Night Gallery*—a woman in a lifeboat turned out not to be a woman at all. It was just a terrified Irish youth wrapped in a shawl.

Lord had access to many survivors, and the details that had lodged in their memories have the persuasive oddness of truth. One provides an unsettling soundtrack to the dreadful hour and a half between the sinking, at 2:20 in the morning, and the appearance of a rescue ship. Jack Thayer, a teenage passenger from Philadelphia's Main Line, who was one of only a handful of people picked out of the water by lifeboats, later recalled that the sound made by the many hundreds of people flailing in the twenty-eight-degree water, drowning or freezing to death, was like the noise of locusts buzzing in the Pennsylvania countryside on a summer night.

The closest that *A Night to Remember* comes to engineering drama is an account, shrewdly spliced into the larger narrative, of the doings of two ships that would become intimately associated with the disaster. One was the little Cunard liner *Carpathia*, eastbound that night en route from New York to the Mediterranean. Fifty-eight miles away from the *Titanic* when it picked up her first distress calls, it was the only ship to hasten to the big liner's rescue, reversing its course and shutting off heat and hot water in an attempt to maximize fuel efficiency. The other was the *Californian*, a small steamer that had stopped about ten miles from the *Titanic*—unlike the doomed ship, it had heeded the ice warnings—and sat there all through that terrible night, disregarding the *Titanic*'s frantic signaling, by wireless, Morse lamp, and, finally, rockets. Not all of this was as inexplicable as it seems: the *Californian* didn't have a nighttime wireless operator. (All passenger ships were subsequently required by law to have around-the-clock wireless.) But no one has ever sufficiently explained why the *Californian*'s captain, officers, and crew failed to respond to what seemed like obvious signs of distress. The second officer merely thought it strange that a ship would be firing rockets at night. If Lord had been given to large interpretations, he might have seen in the one ship a symbol of the urgent force of human striving and, in the other, the immovable resistance of sheer stupidity.

About halfway through *A Night to Remember*—this is just after the ship has gone under, and an English socialite in a lifeboat turns to her secretary and sighs, "There is your beautiful nightdress gone"—Lord interrupts his narrative for a few pages of musings about what it all means. The themes he finds are characterized by an appealing combination of nostalgia and skepticism. One notion is that the sinking marked "the end of the old days" of nineteenth-century technological confidence, as well as of "noblesse oblige"; another is a sense that people behaved better back then, whether noblesse, steerage, or crew. When one officer was finally picked up from his lifeboat, he carefully stowed the sails and the mast before climbing aboard the rescue ship.

But overshadowing everything is the problem of money and class. The *Titanic*'s story irresistibly reads as a parable about a gilded age in which death was anything but democratic, as was made clear by a notorious statistic: of the men in first class—who paid as much as $4,350 for a one-way fare at a time when the average annual household income in the U.S. was $1,800—the percentage of survivors was roughly the same as that of children in third class. For all his sentimentality about gentlemanly chivalry, Lord doesn't shy away from what the sinking and its aftermath revealed about the era's privileges and prejudices. "Even the passengers' dogs were glamorous," begins a tongue-in-cheek catalog in *A Night to Remember* that includes a Pekingese called Sun Yat-sen—part of the entourage of Henry Harper, of the publishing family, who, Lord laconically reports, had also picked up an Egyptian dragoman during his preembarkation travels, "as a sort of joke." The book traces a damning arc from the special treatment enjoyed by the pets to the way in which third-class passengers were, at the end, "ignored, neglected, forgotten."

Even so, Lord kept his sermonizing to a minimum. His book ends on a grace note: the seventeen-year-old Jack Thayer climbing into a bunk on the *Carpathia*, which saved 706 of the Titanic's 2,223 souls, and falling asleep after swallowing his first-ever glass of brandy. *A Night to Remember* left the love stories, stolen diamonds, handcuffs, axes, and underwater lock-picking to others.

———

One sign of how efficiently Lord did his job is the air of embarrassment that hangs over the latest studies. John Maxtone-Graham, whose fond and thoroughgoing *The Only Way to Cross*, published in 1972, is considered a classic history of the ocean-liner era, interrupts his *Titanic Tragedy: A New Look at the Lost Liner* halfway through in order to admit that he'd spent a long time trying to avoid the subject altogether. John Welshman's *Titanic: The Last Night of a Small Town* aims to "both build upon and challenge 'A Night to Remember.'" His subtitle is a phrase borrowed from Lord's book.

Yet, perhaps surprisingly, there seems to be no shortage of new angles. Because the allegedly unsinkable ship sank, its design and construction, as well as the number and disposition of the lifeboats, have often been the subject of debate. But Maxtone-Graham shifts the technological focus, by pointing up the crucial role of wireless communication. The *Titanic* was one of the first ships in history to issue an SOS. ("Send SOS," the twenty-two-year-old Harold Bride, the *Titanic*'s junior wireless operator, who survived, told the twenty-five-year-old Jack Phillips, the senior officer, who died. "It's the new call, and it may be your last chance to send it.") And the sinking was among the first global news stories to be reported, thanks to wireless radio, more or less simultaneously with the events. One of the early headlines, which appeared as the rescue ship carried survivors to New York—"WATCHERS ANGERED BY CARPATHIA'S SILENCE"—suggests how fast we became accustomed to an accelerating news cycle. The book winningly portrays the wireless boys of a hundred years ago as the computer geeks of their day, from their extreme youth to their strikingly familiar lingo. "WHAT IS THE MATTER WITH U?" came one response to the *Titanic*'s distress call.

In *Titanic: The Last Night of a Small Town*, Welshman works hard to "re-balance" another narrative—the one about privilege. There's a scene in a not at all bad 1979 TV movie about the sinking, *SOS Titanic*, in which a pair of second-class passengers standing on deck observe the struttings of the first-class neighbors to one side and the antics of some steerage passengers on the other. "This is a funny place to be," one of them, an American schoolteacher played by Susan Saint James, remarks to the other, a British schoolmaster with whom she's been flirting. "We're in the middle." Indeed. In his new book, Welshman persuasively argues that narratives about second-class passengers have tended to be neglected, lacking as they do the glamour of first class or the extreme pathos of steerage. Drawing in particular on the published memoirs of a British science master named Lawrence Beasley (he's the character in the TV movie who gets a crush on Susan Saint James), the author shines welcome light on this overlooked corner of *Titanic* history. His technique of providing little biographies of characters in all classes probably tests the limits of the human-interest approach ("the export of butter from Finland was growing rapidly"), but it pays off in some wonderfully idiosyncratic details. Beasley felt an odd "sense of security" once the ship came to a stop, "like standing on a large rock in the middle of the ocean"; another survivor, a boy of nine at the time, realized long after settling with his family in the Midwest that he couldn't bring himself to go to Detroit Tigers games because the noise that greeted home runs reminded him of the cries of the dying.

The impulse to reappraise is not new. The best dissection of *Titanic* mythmaking is Steven Biel's *Down with the Old Canoe: A Cultural History of the Titanic Disaster*, first published in 1996 and now updated for the centenary. Biel, a Harvard historian, showed how the *Titanic*'s story has been made to serve the purposes of everyone from antisuffragettes to the labor movement to Republicans. He argues that, while the sinking was "neither catalyst nor cause," it "did expose and come to represent anxieties about modernity." One of these was race: an assault on one of the wireless operators during the ship's final minutes was blamed on a nonexistent "Negro" crew member. Another was the influx of "new," non-Anglo-Saxon immigrants. Reports by crew members and coverage in the press revealed a prejudice against southern Europeans so pervasive that the Italian ambassador to the United States was moved to make a formal complaint.

Sometimes, the fancy critical frameworks get out of hand: Welshman's eagerness to talk about "the lifeboat as metaphor" seems a bit grotesque, in this case. One reason that the *Titanic* grips the imagination even today is, if anything, that it poses the big, enduring questions we associate with much larger historical events: as Nathaniel Philbrick writes in the introduction to a new edition of Lord's book, "Who will survive?" and "What would I have done?" These hover over Frances Wilson's *How to Survive the Titanic; or, The Sinking of*

J. Bruce Ismay, a biography of one of the most controversial figures in this story: the man who was the managing director of the company that owned the ship. Ismay was widely reviled for having entered a lifeboat rather than going down with his ship; worse, perhaps, it seems to have been he who pressed the *Titanic*'s experienced captain, E.J. Smith, to maintain a relatively high speed even though the ship had been receiving ice warnings.

Twining Ismay's story around a series of reflections on Joseph Conrad's *Lord Jim*, a novel about a ship's mate who abandons his vessel, Wilson at once confirms and undercuts the familiar cartoon of Ismay. To be sure, there are the sense of entitlement and the convenient ethics. "I cannot feel I have done anything wrong and cannot blame myself for the disaster," he wrote to the widow of one drowned passenger. And yet Wilson deftly evokes the often startling emotional complexities beneath. Drawing on an unpublished correspondence, she reveals that, during the voyage, Ismay fell in love with young Jack Thayer's mother, Marian, and paid her epistolary court after the sinking left her a widow. Even here, though, a self-serving coldness prevailed. When Marian asked for help with her insurance claim, Ismay replied, "I am deeply sorry for the loss you have sustained and of course I know any claim you put in would be absolutely right, but you must agree with me that all claims must be dealt with on the same basis now don't you?"

If you were writing a morality play about class privilege, you couldn't do better than to dream up a glamorous ship of fools and load it with everyone from the A-list to immigrants coming to America for a better life. The class issue is, indeed, one major reason the *Titanic* disaster has always been so ripe for dramatization. And yet the way we tell the story often reveals more about us than it does about what happened. If the indignant depictions of the class system in so many *Titanic* dramas coexist uneasily with their adoring depictions of upper-crust privilege, that, too, is part of the appeal: it allows us to demonstrate our liberalism even as we indulge our consumerism. In Cameron's movie, you root for the steerage passenger who improbably pauses, during a last dash for a boat, to make a sardonic comment about the band as it famously played on ("Music to drown by—now I know I'm in first class"), but you're also happy to lounge with Kate Winslet on a sunbathed private promenade deck while a uniformed maid cleans up on her hands and knees after breakfast.

Perhaps not surprisingly, the strongest treatment of this issue was the 1958 film of Lord's book, made in Britain—which is to say, by people who had a better feel for class distinctions than Lord (an American) did, and who were working at a time when the class system was under tremendous strain, and was the object of relentless examination in literature and theater. It says something that the only star in the film (the popular actor Kenneth More) played a comparatively lowly, though heroic, character—Second Officer Herbert Lightoller, who managed to keep thirty men alive while they all stood on an overturned lifeboat. The film, like the book, depends for its effectiveness on a straightforward presentation of information and an accumulation of damning detail. A short scene in which a group of Irish steerage passengers breaks through a metal gate as they make their way to the lifeboats—they suddenly find themselves in the first-class dining room, set for the next morning's breakfast, and at first can barely bring themselves to penetrate this sacred space—tells you more about the class system than Cameron's cruder populism does.

It certainly tells you more than the ham-handed treatment of the subject in the new Julian Fellowes miniseries. In his hugely popular *Downton Abbey*, and in the script for the 2001 Robert Altman film

Gosford Park, Fellowes showed a subtle feel for the ironies of class, but his *Titanic* sinks under the weight of its ideological baggage: the sneering condescension of the first-class passengers is so caricatured that it ends up having no traction. ("We are a political family," a snooty countess observes. "You, I think, have always been in *trade*.") There's even a fugitive Russian anarchist aboard to give free lessons in politics: "Europe was wrong for me." Worse, the production looks cheap: the first-class dining room has the ad hoc fanciness of a high school cafeteria on prom night. This is a *Titanic* drama in which the class outrage feels synthetic and there's no compensatory luxe.

If the underlying theme of all *Titanic* dramatizations has been class, the engine driving the plot has nearly always been romance. Apart from *A Night to Remember*, movies and television have tended to ignore the *Carpathia-Californian* drama, preferring to use the *Titanic* as a lavish backdrop for tragic passions and eleventh-hour lessons about the redemptive value of love. Fellowes takes this to new heights, or perhaps depths: whereas previous adapters of the story have made their star-crossed lovers fictional, he foists an invented upper-class suffragette on an actual first-class passenger, Harry Widener, to whose death Harvard students owe their university library, built as a memorial by Harry's mother. If I were a Widener, I'd sue.

The yoking of romance to the disaster narrative began with *Saved from the Titanic*, the 1912 movie with the weirdly prescient "reality" angle—it's the one that starred an actual survivor. In it, the heroine must overcome her fear of the sea so that her naval officer fiancé can fulfill his duty. The sinking haunts a 1929 British talkie, *Atlantic*, which sets an adulterous affair on a *Titanic*-like liner, and a bizarre 1937 tragicomedy called *History Is Made at Night*, in which Jean Arthur plays a wealthy American who falls for a famous headwaiter (!) played by Charles Boyer, and travels to Europe with him on a liner that hits an iceberg on its maiden voyage.

The actual *Titanic* makes an important appearance in Noël Coward's *Cavalcade*, a big hit on both stage and screen in the early 1930s. But it took another twenty years for Hollywood to inject romantic melodrama into the real-life story. In Jean Negulesco's *Titanic* (1953), Barbara Stanwyck plays Julia Sturges, a midwestern woman unhappily married to a wealthy man (Clifton Webb) from whom she's become estranged while living an empty life of the beau monde—"the same silly calendar year after year...jumping from party to party, from title to title, all the rest of your life," as she says, when explaining why she has absconded with their two children, a marriageable girl and a boy on the verge of adolescence. The arc of the drama traces the husband's evolution from a superficial cad to a self-sacrificing hero; more important, it outlines the couple's trajectory from estrangement to an inevitable last-minute reconciliation that makes them both realize what's really valuable—not money but love.

If the *Titanic* is a vehicle for working out our cultural anxieties, the 1953 film makes it clear that one of those, during the first years of the Cold War, was the question of who the good guys were. "We're Americans and we belong in America," Julia declares. Middle-class Americans, too. You learn that Julia had started out as a "girl who bought her hats out of a Sears, Roebuck catalog"; on board the *Titanic*, her prissy, Europeanized daughter is being wooed by a handsome American undergraduate who pointedly remarks that the "P" on his letter shirt stands for Purdue, not Princeton. Steven Biel's *Down with the Old Canoe* makes a further argument: that the film represents Cold War–era nostalgia for a more manageable kind of apocalypse—not the blinding thermonuclear flash but the slow freeze that left you time to write your own ending.

With its focus on feminine suffering and self-sacrifice, and, especially, in its presentation of an ill-fated romance between the unpretentious young man and the class-bound society girl, the 1953 *Titanic*, which won an Oscar for Best Story and Screenplay, anticipated Cameron's 1997 movie, which won Oscars for just about everything. A lot of the dialogue that Cameron put in the mouth of his frustrated debutante, Rose DeWitt Bukater (Winslet), reminds you of Barbara Stanwyck's lines: "I saw my whole life as if I'd already lived it," Rose recalls, explaining her attraction to a carefree young artist named Jack Dawson (Leonardo DiCaprio). "An endless parade of parties, cotillions...the same mindless chatter." But Cameron gave his film a feminist rather than a patriotic spin. Rose, of a "good" but impoverished Main Line family, is being married off to the loathsome Cal Hockley, who seals their engagement with the gift of a blue diamond that had belonged to Louis XVI. ("We are royalty," he smugly tells her as he drapes the giant rock around her neck.) "It's so unfair," she sighs during a conversation with her odiously snobbish mother, who, in the same scene, is lacing Rose tightly into a corset. "Of course it's unfair," the mother retorts. "We're women." Small wonder that nearly half the female viewers under twenty-five who saw the movie went to see it a second time within two months of its release, and that three quarters of those said that they'd see it again.

Rose isn't the only troubled girl who's being manhandled. Like all ships, the *Titanic* was a "she," and Cameron went to some lengths to push the identification between the ship and the young woman. Both are, to all appearances, "maidens" who are en route to losing their virginity; both are presented as the beautiful objects of men's possessive adoration, intended for the gratification of male egos. "She's the largest moving object ever made by the hand of man in all of history," a smug Ismay boasts to some appreciative tablemates at lunch. Later, as Rose goes in to dinner, one of Cal's fat-cat friends commends him on his fiancée as if she, too, were a prized object: "Congratulations, Hockley—she's splendid!"

Cameron underscored the parallels between the young woman and the liner in other ways. The scene in which Jack holds Rose by the waist as she stands at the prow, arms outstretched, heading into what will be the *Titanic*'s last sunset, has become an iconic moment in American cinema. (And indeed in life: a couple was married in a submersible parked near that very spot.) But far more haunting is the way the image of the speeding prow in this scene morphs, seconds afterward, into a by now equally famous image from real life—the same prow as it looks today, half buried in Atlantic mud under two and a half miles of seawater, drained of color, purpose, and life. In this movie, there's only one other beautiful "she" that is transformed in this way: we see the flushed face of Kate Winslet, as the young Rose on the night she poses nude for Jack, suddenly wither into the wrinkled visage of Gloria Stuart, the actress whom Cameron cannily chose to play Rose in the modern-day sequences of the narrative. Stuart, a star of the 1930s, was less than a generation younger than Dorothy Gibson, the lead in the 1912 film.

When you compare Cameron's movie to its 1953 predecessor, the evolution in attitudes is striking. The emotional climax of the earlier film is marked by Julia Sturges's agonized realization that she belongs with her husband after all; the disaster brings this shattered family back together again. Cameron's picture is about breaking the bonds of family, a point made by means of a clever contrast between its two leading ladies—Rose and the *Titanic*. At the start of the movie, the ship speeds confidently forward while Rose is described as being "trapped" and unable to "break free" (that corset, that mother); by the end, the ship is immobilized, while the girl strikes off on her own, literally and figuratively. After the sinking, she has to abandon the piece of paneling she's climbed onto—and tearfully let go of Jack (now a frozen corpse), which she'd promised never to do—in order to swim for help.

Rose, in other words, saves herself; in the end the *Titanic* is the sacrifice, the price that must be paid for Rose's rebirth as a girl who acts by and for herself. Or, rather, a woman: she memorably makes love to Jack during her journey, and gets to New York (there's a beautiful little scene in which we see her huddled form on the *Carpathia*'s deck as it glides under the Statue of Liberty), while the ship remains a maiden forever. This is another reason we can't get the story out of our heads. If the *Titanic* had sunk on her twenty-seventh voyage, it wouldn't haunt us in the same way. It's the incompleteness that never stops tantalizing us, tempting us to fill in the blanks with more narrative.

―――――

Toward the end of *A Night to Remember*, Walter Lord briefly nodded to "the element of fate" in the story, which teases its audience with a sense at once of inevitability and of how easily things might have turned out differently. It is, he says, like "classic Greek tragedy."

He was right. All the energy spent pondering the class injustices and the romance, the dissertating about the ship's design, size, and luxury, the panegyrics of the heroics, or the denunciations of the cowardice, of the passengers and crew, the tortured debates over the captain's or Ismay's guilt, the hypothetical pirouetting about what the *Californian* might or might not have done, the endless computations of just how many people perished (still never resolved), have distracted from what may, in the end, be the most obvious thing about the *Titanic*'s story: it uncannily replicates the structure and the themes of our most fundamental myths and oldest tragedies. Cameron intuited this, when he made the ship itself both the double and the opposite of his teenaged heroine. Like Iphigenia, the *Titanic* is a beautiful "maiden" sacrificed to the agendas of greedy men eager to set sail; the 46,000-ton liner is just the latest in a long line of lovely girl victims, an archetype of vulnerable femininity that stands at the core of the Western literary tradition.

But the *Titanic* embodies another strain of tragedy. This is the drama of a flawed and self-destructive hero, a protagonist of great achievements and overweening presumption. The ship starts out like Oedipus: admired, idolized, hailed as different, special, exalted. Sophocles' play derives its horrible excitement from a relentless exposition of its protagonist's fall from grace—and from the fact that his confidence and his talents are what prevented him from seeing the looming disaster. Cameron understood this, too. The enormous resources at his disposal enabled him to give us that other hero: the ship itself, re-created in overwhelming detail. The scene in which the liner puts out to sea, the stokers filling the boilers, the steam gauges rising, the *chunk-chunk* of the engines gathering speed as the pistons thrust up and down—culminating in an underwater shot of the triple propellers starting to churn the water—sets up what you could call "the mechanical tragedy." The director knew what the Greeks knew: that there is a profound theatrical pleasure, not totally free of Schadenfreude, in watching something beautiful fall apart.

Either mythic strand, the virgin sacrifice or the grandiose self-destruction, would be enough to rivet our attention: as a culture, we're hard-wired to respond to these narratives. To have them conflated into one story is overpowering. The reason we keep watching Cameron's movie is the same reason we can't stop thinking about the *Titanic* itself: it irresistibly conflates two of the oldest archetypes in literature.

So much about the story, when you think about it, enhances the feeling of being more like an artistic composition than a real-life event. The ship's mythic name—the Titans were a race of superbeings who fought the gods and lost—points up the greatest of all classical tragic themes: hubris punished. ("God himself could not sink this ship.")

Steven Biel reproduces the lyrics of a song sung by South Carolina cotton-mill workers who clearly grasped this: "This great ship was built by man / That is why she could not stand / She could not sink was the cry from one and all / But an iceberg ripped her side / And He cut down all her pride." In real life, too, people seem to have understood the disaster in this ancient way. A rumor that started circulating at the time of the disaster maintained that her sister ship, the *Britannic*, was supposed to have been called the *Gigantic* but was given a less fate-tempting name.

The structure of the *Titanic*'s story has the elegant symmetry of literature, too: in it, you get a doomed hero caught between an energetic savior (the *Carpathia*) and an obtuse villain (the *Californian*). And there's something else that suggests a quality of having been designed as a dramatic spectacle. One big difference between the *Titanic* and other wrecks—the *Lusitania*, say—is the way her story unfolded in real time. Torpedoed by a U-boat in May 1915, the Cunard liner sank in eighteen minutes—too short an interval, in other words, to generate stories. The *Titanic* took two hours and forty minutes to founder after hitting the berg; which is to say, about the time it takes for a big blockbuster to tell a story.

Greek tragic protagonists, classical themes, perfect structure, flawless timing: if you'd made the *Titanic* up, it couldn't get any better. But then, someone did make it up. Perhaps the most unsettling item in the immense inventory of *Titanic* trivia is a novel called *Futility*, by an American writer named Morgan Robertson. It begins with a great ocean liner of innovative triple-screw design, "the largest craft afloat and the greatest of the works of men. . . . Unsinkable—indestructible." Speeding along in dangerous conditions, the ship first hits something on its starboard side ("A slight jar shook the forward end"); later on, there is a terrifying cry of "Ice ahead," and the vessel collides with an iceberg and goes down.

As the title suggests, the themes of this work of fiction are the old ones: the vanity of human striving, divine punishment for overweening confidence in our technological achievement, the futility of human effort in a world ruled by indifferent nature. But the writing comes to life only when Robertson focuses on the mechanical details, as in the scene of the aftermath of the collision:

> Seventy-five thousand tons—dead-weight—rushing through the fog at the rate of fifty feet per second, had hurled itself at an iceberg. . . . She rose out of the sea, higher and higher—until the propellers in the stern were half exposed. . . . The holding-down bolts of twelve boilers and three triple-expansion engines, unintended to hold such weights from a perpendicular flooring, snapped, and down through a maze of ladders, gratings and fore-and-after bulkheads came these giant masses of steel and iron, puncturing the sides of the ship . . . the roar of escaping steam, and the bee-like buzzing of nearly three thousand human voices, raised in agonized screams and callings. . . . A solid, pyramid-like hummock of ice, left to starboard.

Down to the most idiosyncratic detail, all this is familiar: the bee-like buzzing seems like a nod to Jack Thayer's comparison of the sounds of the dying to locusts on a summer night. And yet it couldn't be. Robertson—who gave his fictional ship the name *Titan*—published his book in 1898, fourteen years before the real liner sailed. If the *Titanic* continues to haunt our imagination, it's because we were dreaming her long before the fresh spring afternoon when she turned her bows westward and, for the first time, headed toward the open sea.

—*The New Yorker,* April 16, 2012

11. CLASSICA

BATTLE LINES

FOR SHEER WEIRDNESS, it would be hard to find a passage in the Western canon that can compete with the tenth book of Homer's *Iliad*—the one classicists call the *Doloneia*, "the bit about Dolon." Not the least of the book's oddities is that it's named after a nobody: Dolon is a character whom the poet conjures up merely so that he can kill him off, a few hundred lines later, in literature's nastiest episode of trick-or-treating. There's a nighttime outing, some creepy interrogation, even outlandish costumes.

By this point in the action, we're in the tenth year of the Trojan War, and things are going badly for the invading Greeks. Achilles, the greatest of the allied warriors, has angrily withdrawn from the fighting after being insulted by his loutish commander in chief, Agamemnon; without his help, the fortunes of the coalition forces are at an all-time low—the Greeks are pressed back against the sea, frantically defending their beached ships. A desperate appeal to the sulky Achilles has failed to persuade him to reenter the fray. At their wits' end, the sleepless Greek leaders call a late-night conference and send two able warriors, the ferocious Diomedes and the crafty Odysseus, to spy on the Trojan positions.

After donning some rather unconventional gear (Odysseus, we are told, is wearing a cap decorated with rows of boars' teeth), the two pick their eerie way through piles of corpses left over from the day's battle. Presently they come across Dolon, who happens to be coming from the opposite direction to spy on the Greeks; as if to underscore the savage, animalistic nature of the encounter, Homer gives him a wolf's pelt and a marten-skin hat. The Greeks capture this rather pathetic Trojan—his teeth chatter audibly after he falls into their hands—and tease him for a while, reassuring him that he will come to no harm even as they smoothly extract the information they want. Then, as Dolon begs for his life, Diomedes cuts off his head, which still gibbers away as it rolls in the dust. The pair then make for the camp of some allies of the Trojans, where they kill a handful of sleeping men and steal some fabulous horses.

When I was first studying the *Iliad*, as an undergraduate classics major thirty years ago, the standard interpretation of this episode was that its very grotesqueness was the point. Everything about it—nocturnal violence instead of glittering, daylit contests of arms; stealth instead of open confrontation; animal pelts instead of gleaming bronze armor—inverts the norms of Homeric warfare, as if to suggest just how complete the Greeks' reversal of fortune is: militarily, ethically, morally.

Readers of Stephen Mitchell's fast-paced and very idiosyncratic new translation of the *Iliad* will have to take my word about all this, because Book 10 doesn't appear in it. Mitchell's is the first major English translation of the poem to implement the theories of the eminent British scholar M. L. West, stripping away what West argues are the impure, later additions to the original written text—one such accretion being the whole of Book 10, whose tone and diction aren't quite like those of the rest of the poem. Merely to claim that there *was* an original text of the *Iliad*, definitively set down in writing by the poet who created it, is sensational stuff in the world of classics: for nearly a hundred years, the dominant orthodoxy has been that this greatest of all epics was the oral composition of a series of bards, evolving over centuries before finally being written down. Whatever its flaws—and Mitchell's translation won't suit every taste—this taut new version is likely to reignite controversies about just what the *Iliad* is that go back nearly as far as Homer himself.

The *Iliad* is about precisely what, in the first of its 15,693 lines, it says it's going to be about: the wrath of Achilles. Aristotle, one of the earliest critics to write about the poem, admired the work's narrow focus. In his *Poetics*, Western culture's oldest extant work of literary criticism, written around 335 BC—which is to say nearly half a millennium after the *Iliad* began its long career—the philosopher argued that

> Homer may be said to appear "divinely inspired" above the rest, since he did not attempt to treat the war as a whole.... Instead, taking up just one section, he used many others as episodes...with which he gives his composition diversity.

Although many people know that the *Iliad* is about the Trojan War, it contains very few of the best-known episodes from that greatest of all mythological conflicts. There's no Judgment of Paris, nor do you get the Rape of Helen—the Trojan prince Paris's adulterous abduction of the world's most beautiful woman, which sets in motion the gigantic Greek recovery expedition, led by her brother-in-law, Agamemnon. The poem does not include Achilles' death, from an arrow wound to the heel, nor will you find the Wooden Horse or any of the horrors that took place during the Fall of Troy. A work that contained all those episodes, Aristotle argued, would be "too extensive and impossible to grasp all at once." Instead, Homer cannily focuses on just one episode from the tenth and final year of the war, and emphasizes a single theme: the anger of Achilles.

Why is he so angry? The *Iliad* can't make sense if the reader doesn't grasp a reality that would have been evident to the poem's original audience, but which can sometimes be difficult for modern audiences to get their minds around: that the hero's wrath, and with it the countless deaths he causes, is justified. Like the Trojan War itself, the trouble in the *Iliad* begins with the abduction of a young woman. In the first of the epic's twenty-four books (the sections into which, at some point long after its composition, it was divided), Agamemnon is compelled to return one of his captured slave girls to her father, a priest of Apollo who comes begging for his daughter. (The god, who looks after his own, visits a plague on the Greeks until they comply.) The Greek commander makes up for this loss of property—and of face—by seizing one of Achilles' slave girls. To us, the petty tit-for-tat might savor of the junior high school cafeteria ("*You* get to keep your own prize, yet I am forced / to...sit here, meekly, with nothing?" an incredulous Agamemnon sputters), but for the heroes in Homeric epic the spoils they amass—their quality, quantity, and provenance—are the symbols of their status, the markers of who they are in the world. This is why they fight. As Achilles tartly reminds Agamemnon, "I didn't come here to Troy because of the Trojans. / I have no quarrel with them; they have done me no harm." For this reason, the seizure of the girl is an intolerable affront; as the furious Achilles puts it, it makes him "a nobody."

This is the crux of the poem. For, as Achilles later reminds his fellow Greeks, he has been allowed to choose between a long, insignificant life and a brief, glorious one: if he stays to fight and die in Troy, it is precisely because he doesn't want to be a nobody. Agamemnon's insult makes a mockery of his choice—it empties his short life of what meaning it had. Hence the uncanny, even inhuman rage. (The noun that Homer uses, *mênis*, is otherwise used only of gods; in the Greek, it's the first word of the poem.)

The extent to which the young warrior's world has been turned upside down is reflected in the radical course of action—or, rather, inaction—that he now decides upon. Before, he had fought to prove who he was: now he will demonstrate his worth by *not* fighting. For nearly the entirety of the poem—from Book 1 to Book 20, when he finally reenters the fray—Achilles, the greatest of all warriors, "the best of the Achaeans," never lifts a weapon. He knows that, without him, the Greeks will suffer badly: their suffering, he declares, will be a "compensation." It is a sign of the magnitude of his grievance that he is willing to let his allies die.

And indeed, we are told in the opening lines of the poem that his anger "hurled down to Hades the souls of so many fighters" (as Mitchell renders it, in the nicely strong five-beat line he favors). But Achilles' *mênis* touches Heaven, too: in those same lines the poet adds that it brings to fruition a divine scheme, one we get to see unfolding in the many scenes set on Mount Olympus. By the end of the poem, "the will of Zeus was accomplished." The epic's effortless oscillation between the mortal and immortal planes, between what is apparent and what, to the rest of us, is obscure, its special ability to see both foreground and background, detail and whole with equal clarity and comprehension, underpin its distinctive authority.

Some of the consequences of Achilles' wrath are direct and obvious. The sinking fortunes of the Greeks, tracked in minute detail in the poem's many battle scenes, are occasions to reflect on the horror, and the allure, of bloodshed. The rococo descriptions of the warriors' deaths—Homer has more than sixty ways to say that someone died—remind you that violence in battle could have a different meaning for the Greeks than it does for us. For us, war is an aberration, and we tend to be squeamish about what happens in it; for them, it was a way of life—most Greek city-states were more or less continually at war—and Homer's poem everywhere gives evidence of a kind of connoisseurship of martial violence. These heroes are artisans of death, with skills that we are invited to admire as we would admire the expertise of a potter or a blacksmith. In one memorable scene, Achilles' beloved companion, Patroclus, spears a Trojan through the jaw and pivots the wounded man over his chariot rail "like a fisherman who sits on a jutting boulder / and hauls a tremendous fish up out of the sea / at the end of his line, caught on the bright bronze hook." The contrast between the grisly violence of the battle scenes and such mundane evocations of ordinary life can give the poem a hallucinatory poignancy. Through the carnage, reminders of the peacetime world hover tantalizingly out of reach.

But even as it traces the intense trajectory of Achilles' wrath—which, ultimately, will pit that greatest of the Greek champions against Hector, the prince of the besieged city and the greatest of the Trojans, in a climactic single combat—the *Iliad* simultaneously spirals outward, giving you a picture of everything else that is at stake in this (or any) war story. Just to list the great set pieces—episodes so fully achieved that tradition has given them their own names—is to run through a remarkable variety of subjects, themes, and techniques. The "Catalogue of Ships," in Book 2, is a prodigious history lesson, complete with the names and numbers of every contingent of the Greek fleet; the sheer recitation of it must have been an astonishing tour de force in performance—epic poetry's answer to Cinema-Scope. The "*Teichoscopia*" ("Watching from the Wall"), in Book 3, set atop the walls of Troy, gives us glimpses of Troy's richly civilized society, one character's psychology, and the mechanics of the poem itself. Here Helen, by now the regretful, slightly embarrassed and embarrassing guest of Paris' family ("bitch that I am," she moans), points out to King Priam and his elegant courtiers the various Greeks on the field of battle below, men she knew in her former life. (It may be the end of the war, but it's the beginning of the poem, and Homer has to come up with some way of introducing the main characters.) The "Embassy," in Book 9, in which the Greeks send a trio of chieftains to appeal to Achilles, shows a subtle grasp of psychology and rhetoric.

So the poem grows and grows. There are scenes set in soldier's huts, scenes set in great palaces, scenes of sacrifice, scenes of quiet and mirth. Some scenes are set in the Greek camp, whose grubby inhabitants are separated by ten years of fighting from the habits and institutions of civilized life; others are set in Troy, the preeminent city, with its lofty walls and elegant courtiers and perfumed bedrooms and seemingly inexhaustible wealth, a place that reminds us of what is at stake when countries go to war. There are sex scenes. One of the most charming passages in the poem, in Book 14, describes how Hera dolls herself up and seduces Zeus, a ruse meant to distract him from the fact that one of the pro-Greek gods is violating his order not to interfere with the progress of the war; crocuses and hyacinths sprout and bloom beneath them as they make love. Indeed, the inconsequential quarrels of the gods on Mount Olympus, who can't die in battle and who watch the Trojan War much as we watch football games, seem to mock the dire strife between the men below.

There are scenes of extraordinary domestic intimacy, filled with tender emotions that stand in vivid contrast to Achilles' titanic feelings. Undoubtedly the most famous of these is the one in Book 6 where we get to see Hector, the defender of Troy (his name means something like "the one who holds things together"), returning from the battlefield to spend time with his troubled wife, Andromache. She fears for his safety and begs him to stay out of the fighting—a thing they both know he can't do, not least because with him, as with Achilles, honor is at stake: "It is my place / to be brave and scorn danger and always fight in the front line." What's remarkable is that he goes to that place, knowing full well that "a day will come when the sacred city of Troy / will be devastated, and Priam, and Priam's people." Even though he knows his people and his family will die, what Hector can't bear, he tells his wife, is the thought of her as some Greek's slave,

> *bent over the loom of some stern mistress*
> *or carrying water up from her well—hating it*
> *but having no choice, for harsh fate will press down upon you.*
> *And someone will say, as he sees you toiling and weeping,*
> *"That is the wife of Hector, bravest of all*
> *the Trojans, tamers of horses, when the great war*
> *raged round Troy." And then a fresh grief will flood*
> *your heart....*

The poignancy of this resigned vision of an inevitable future is exceeded, if that's possible, by what comes next: the famous moment when Hector, who is still in his armor, leans over to pick up his young son, and the boy recoils screaming until his father takes off his terrifying helmet. It's unlikely that there will ever be a greater symbol for the way in which war makes us unrecognizable—to others, to ourselves.

But this war will render Achilles unrecognizable, too. The means and the effects of his transformation are what make the *Iliad* the first genuinely tragic narrative in the Western tradition (just as the *Odys-*

sey, with its successful homecoming and climactic marital reunion, is the first comedy). For Achilles' revenge, designed to enhance the reputation he values above all other things, sets in motion a dreadful loss of his own. In Book 16, the tenderhearted Patroclus begs his friend to let him help the Greeks, which he believes he can do by following a clever plan dreamed up by the ostensibly sage old king Nestor: he'll wear Achilles' armor into battle and thus fool the Trojans into thinking the great hero is back in the fight. Achilles consents, while warning his friend not to push too hard: for after all, Patroclus is no Achilles. (You could say that the whole point of the poem is that only Achilles is Achilles.) But Patroclus does get carried away—he, too, is made unrecognizable by war—and ends up challenging Hector, who kills him. The harrowing scenes of grief that follow demonstrate a truth that Achilles grasps too late: his reputation wasn't, after all, the thing he valued most. That the insight is inseparable from the loss is what gives the poem its wrenching grandeur. *Pathei mathos*, Aeschylus wrote in his *Agamemnon*, one of the innumerable texts of later Greek literature that descended from the *Iliad*: we "suffer into knowledge."

The *Iliad* ends as it began, with a desperate parent pleading to get his child back. In the last book of the poem, Priam comes in secret to Achilles' tent to beg for the body of Hector, whom by this point Achilles has slain. The two enemies share a moment of unexpected tenderness, one that suggests that Achilles' capacity for recognizable human emotions has been enlarged: moved by the sight of the courageous old man, he weeps, thinking of his own father back home—the father and the home he'll never see again, because, as we know, he has chosen a short, glorious life. This connection to his already lost past breaks something loose in Achilles. The hero who, before, had been willing to let his own comrades die in order to enhance his honor now breaks bread with the enemy king, treating the old man honorably and giving him, in the end, what he wants. In his introduction to Robert Fagles's 1990 translation of the *Iliad*, by far the preeminent and most popular English rendering of the past generation, the late classicist Bernard Knox, who among other things was an expert on Sophocles, argued that at the beginning of the poem, Achilles is marked by the same "stubborn, passionate devotion to an ideal image of self" that distinguishes tragic heroes such as Antigone and Oedipus; what makes the trajectory of the *Iliad* so moving is that at the end, this stubborn hero starts to turn his attention outward, toward, as Knox puts it, "community." In a culminating oscillation between private and public, the closeup and the sweeping pan, the finale of the poem is divided between the moment of breathtaking intimacy between Achilles and Priam and the grand funeral the Trojans give Hector. Together, the two scenes represent the final, most distant, unimaginable yet inevitable consequences of the wrath of Achilles.

And so, paradoxically, by maintaining its tight Aristotelian grip on its single theme, the *Iliad* manages to suggest the whole range of human action and emotion—of an existence that, unlike that of the gods, has meaning precisely because we, like Achilles, know it will end.

As if to underscore this, Homer puts a picture of human existence into his epic—a literal picture. In Book 18, after Achilles finds himself in need of new armor, Hephaestus, the blacksmith god, forges a shield for him. Homer devotes fully 130 lines to the description of this intricate object. In what is surely the most elaborate bit of repoussé in history, the shield presents images of a city at peace and a city at war, of weddings and a lawsuit, of people dancing and people arming for ambush, of gods and mortals and animals, of pastures and vineyards, of plowing and sheaving. There are scenes that look suspiciously like scenes from the Trojan War itself ("wives / and children were standing upon the wall to defend it / along with the men who were too old to fight now"), and scenes that, like so many of the extended similes in the poem, offer a mirage-like vision of a life that many of the combatants haven't known for too long, a life of feasting and singing and peace. To complete his masterpiece, the god sets a boundary around this teeming scene: "the powerful river of Ocean flowing / ... along its outermost rim."

All of which is to say that when Achilles returns to battle—returns to deal out death—he is armed with a vision of life, at once expansive and movingly intimate, enormously rich but necessarily confined within a boundary that shapes it and gives it coherence. You could say that Western civilization has likewise armed itself, over the bloodstained centuries and millennia, with the *Iliad*—another richly detailed work of art that provides an image of every possible extreme of human experience, a reminder of who we are and who we sometimes strive to be.

It's because the *Iliad* is both so vast and so fundamental that the nature of its text, what stays in and what comes out, is so important.

Most ancient Greeks believed that there was a poet called Homer who wrote down his poems; a notable exception was Josephus, the Jewish historian, who argued that the early Greeks were illiterate (unlike, needless to say, the early Hebrews). The historian Herodotus thought that Homer must have lived around four hundred years before his own time, which is to say around 800 BC. In about 150 BC, a scholar called Aristarchus, the head of the library at Alexandria and the greatest ancient expert on Homer's texts, surmised that the poet had lived about a century and a half after the Trojan War itself—that is, around 1050 BC. It was generally thought that Homer wrote both the *Iliad* (a product of his passionate youth) and the *Odyssey* (the fruit of his wise and humorous old age), but some ancient scholars, called the Separatists, thought the poems were written by two different people. (The history of Homeric scholarship is filled with factions whose names make them sound like the parties in a religious war or the participants at a Freud conference: Separatists and Unitarians, Oralists and Analysts.) No fewer than seven cities in ancient times claimed Homer as a son—the ancient version of "George Washington Slept Here."

The modern history of the controversy begins late in the eighteenth century, when a French scholar discovered a manuscript of the *Iliad* from the tenth century AD that came complete with transcriptions of the marginal notes of ancient commentators (Aristarchus' included). The notes made it clear that those earlier commentators had access to different and sometimes competing versions of the poems. This discovery soon led a German scholar named Friedrich August Wolf to argue that the texts of the *Iliad* and the *Odyssey* that we possess had not been fixed in writing until relatively late. Homer, he argued, couldn't write but had composed a series of ballads (or "lays") that were short enough to be memorized and that were transmitted orally for generations, perhaps by guilds of professional reciters; these were finally assembled, by someone who knew how to write, into the immensely long poems we have today.

Wolf's theory was immediately taken up and expanded by scholars known as Analysts, who combed through the two epics, confidently identifying traces of many poems by many poets. One advantage of this approach was that it explained the many inconsistencies and oddities of the texts, some historical (the poems refer to elements of both Bronze and Iron Age technology) and some linguistic. A notorious example of the latter is the "Embassy" in Book 9, in which the three Greeks supplicate Achilles to return to battle. The problem is that verbs and pronouns used in the scene are of a special type called the "dual," which can be employed only for pairs of things (eyes, legs, oxen, etc.). The presence of the dual was clearly a remnant of an earlier version of the scene, in which only two Greeks were sent to Achilles' tent. The grammatically impossible dual stayed in the text, uncorrected, because there was, really, no author—no one poet overseeing the whole affair. There it remains, like a fossilized inclusion in a slab of polished stone.

The Analysts held sway throughout the nineteenth century. But early in the twentieth an American scholar named Milman Parry had a game-changing insight into one of the most striking features of the Homeric epics: the repeated use of rigidly formulaic epithets—"swift-footed Achilles," say, or "rosy-fingered Dawn." Like everyone else who'd read the poems in Greek, Parry knew that these epithets always fill the same position in whichever line they appear—that they were ready-made metrical placeholders. But, unlike everyone else, Parry had studied the techniques of living epic poets. (He observed and recorded Yugoslav bards in the 1930s.) What he suddenly grasped was that, while the epithets can seem wearyingly repetitive and add nothing substantive to the action of the poems, they do serve the needs of a poet who's composing *while* he recites. If you're improvising and know in advance how a line of verse is going to end—"swift-footed Achilles," say—you can devote your attention to the middle, the part you're actually inventing. (Think about rap, with its insistent, carrying beat and its predictable, if often approximate, end rhymes.)

The "oral theory" about the use of formulas (which could be linked together to create clusters of lines or entire prefabricated scenes) suggested not only how poems of such length were created but also how they might have been transmitted over centuries without being written down. And it also explained away the inconsistencies and repetitions that had troubled the Analysts: each successive bard used whatever traditional material suited him, even as he added and shaped and refined.

This is the orthodoxy that M. L. West has challenged, using the old techniques of the Analysts to demonstrate that hundreds of lines of the canonical text weren't original. But original to what? For the oralists, "original" is a red herring. West's controversial thesis is that there was in fact a Homer (although West calls him "P," for poet) and that this poet actually wrote down a "primal text" of the *Iliad*, revising it over many years. This apparently regressive heresy, set forth in articles, books, and a two-volume edition of the Greek text, has led to bitter exchanges in the pages of scholarly journals, filled with abstruse proofs that, to the uninitiated, might seem like the dialogue in a *Star Trek* episode ("Movable *nu* was already being used in this early period for the sake of preventing hiatus caused by the loss of digamma").

However academic the debate may appear, a lot depends on who's right. For one thing, an *Iliad* without the *Doloneia* is a very different poem from an *Iliad* with one. But what's really at stake is how we think about the whole of the classical tradition. Say West is right, and the *Doloneia* is a later interpolation by another poet: the fact is that Book 10 has been part of the *Iliad* since antiquity, commented on and interpreted for two and a half millennia, and even furnishing the material for a Greek tragedy (the *Rhesus*, attributed to Euripides). In one obvious sense, the *Iliad* is simply the poem that we have possessed all this while.

An imperfect but perhaps helpful analogy is Wikipedia. For the oralists, the text of the *Iliad* is like a wiki: it's the thing as a whole that matters, not only the kernel of text that someone first put up but also the additions, corrections, and deletions made by others over time. You could say that, for these people, "Homer" is the process itself. For West, it's the original kernel that counts—a text that he thinks he has been able to identify because, like someone turning on the edit function in Wikipedia, he can go in and view the accretions, where they are and who made them, and when.

West's proposed emendations to the texts are couched in the meticulous language of classical scholarship, and take the form of suggestions and proposals; perhaps because Mitchell is not a classicist, he is emboldened to cast West's vision in stone. His new translation not only deletes passages that West merely brackets or questions but omits even some passages that West thinks were "expansions" by P himself. For this reason, his *Iliad* is slimmer and leaner than anything we have seen before (and, in the end, destined to be a specialty act).

Most of the time, the elisions are small, and they do eliminate some hiccups. For instance, West brackets a line in Book 13 in which Hector springs down from his chariot, on the not unreasonable grounds that Hector hasn't been riding in a chariot. Sometimes they are larger and will alter your sense of a passage. Here, too, it's not necessarily for the worse. Toward the end of that beautifully intimate moment between Hector and Andromache in Book 6, the wife makes her famous appeal for caution on the part of her husband, whom she memorably describes as being "everything" to her—"my father, my mother, my brother": in the standard text, this poignant address is followed by seven lines in which this Trojan matron suddenly gives her husband advice on the deployment of his troops. Aristarchus thought there was something fishy about these verses, although West suggests that they were an expansion by P: Mitchell omits them.

Mitchell's stripping away takes other, subtler forms. In a translator's note, he cites the now canonical judgment of the Victorian poet and critic Matthew Arnold, who, in an 1861 essay called "On Translating Homer," enumerated what he saw as the four cardinal qualities of Homeric verse: rapidity, plainness of syntax and diction, plainness of thought, and nobility. Homer's Greek is capacious enough that he can achieve all four, but English translators have generally had to choose one or two at the expense of the others. (The sole exception is probably Alexander Pope, whose *Iliad*, set in rhyming couplets and published between 1715 and 1720, is among the greatest translations of any work in any language.) Richmond Lattimore's craggy 1951 translation, which imitates Homer's expansive six-beat line and sticks faithfully to his archaisms ("Odysseus...laid a harsh word upon him"), has nobility but not rapidity; classicists tend to favor it. The Fagles has a gratifying plainness—my students have always preferred it—but doesn't get the grandeur. Other interpreters go their own way. The stark *War Music* of Christopher Logue is more an adaptation than a translation; Stanley Lombardo's 1997 version goes for a tight-lipped, soldierly toughness—a post-Vietnam *Iliad*.

Mitchell certainly gets the rapidity: this *Iliad* is by far the most swift-footed in recent memory, the iambic line driving forward in a way that gives force to the English and nicely suggests the galloping dactyls (*long*-short-short) of Homer's lines. This is especially useful in those many passages in which characters speak with heated emotion—"with wingèd words," to use the famous formulaic epithet. (An astonishing 45 percent of the poem is direct speech.) In Book 1, for instance, Achilles, at the climax of his argument with Agamemnon, rounds on his commander in chief and insults him openly. Here is Lattimore:

> "*You wine sack, with a dog's eyes, with a deer's heart. Never once have you taken courage in your heart to arm with your people for battle.*"

Mitchell's rendering, in a lurching trochaic rhythm, is far more vivid:

> "*Drunkard, dog-face, quivering deer-hearted coward,*
> *you have never dared to arm with your soldiers for battle.*"

Among other things, Mitchell doesn't make the mistake of weakening the first line by carrying it over to the next—an enjambment that isn't in the Greek.

But too often Mitchell's insistence on speed forces him to sacrifice nobility. Precisely because Homer's Greek is an old inheritance—an amalgam of many styles and periods and dialects going back many centuries (no one ever spoke the Greek you read in Homer)—it has a distinctively archaic quality that, paradoxically, never gets in the way of speed. It likely sounded to Greek ears the way the King James Bible does to ours: old-fashioned but so much a part of the language that it never registers as stuffy. Not the least of the tools in Homer's belt are those famous epithets, but for Mitchell, these can obscure what he calls the "meaning": "'Flashing-helmeted Hector,'" he writes, "means no more than 'Hector.'" But "meaning" isn't the point. Part of the way in which the epic legitimizes its ability to talk about so many levels of existence and so many kinds of experience is its style: an ancient authority inheres in that old-time diction, the plushly padded epithets and stately rhythms.

All this, along with many other subtle effects, is gone from Mitchell's *Iliad*, which, in its eagerness to reproduce what Homer says, strips away how he says it. (Mitchell's translation, which he has said took him only two years, is marked by a certain hastiness: he misses many opportunities to render Homer's rich linguistic effects.) It's as if the translator, like the scholar who inspired him, were trying to get at some purer *Iliad*. In this, both men are indulging in a very old habit. In an article called "Homer: The History of an Idea," the American classicist James I. Porter suggests that the very idea that there is a Homer whom we can somehow get back to, if only we work diligently enough, is a cultural fantasy of purity that dates back to ancient times: Homer, he writes, "is, and probably always was...an idea of something that remains permanently lost to culture." But the *Iliad* isn't pure, at least not in that superficial way; its richness, even its stiffness, is part of what makes it large, makes it commanding, makes it great.

The *Iliad* doesn't need to be modernized because the question it raises is a modern—indeed, existentialist—one: How do we fill our short lives with meaning? The August 22, 2011 issue of *Time* featured, on its "Briefing" page, a quote from a grieving mother about her dead son. The mother's name is Jan Brown, and her son, Kevin Houston, a Navy SEAL, was one of thirty-seven soldiers killed in a rocket attack in Afghanistan that summer. What she said about him might shock some people but will sound oddly familiar to anyone who has read the *Iliad*:

> He was born to do this job. If he could do it all over again and have a choice to have it happen the way it did or work at McDonald's and live to be 104? He'd do it all over again.

Whoever Homer was and however he made his poem, the song that he sings still goes on.

—*The New Yorker*, November 7, 2011

IN SEARCH OF SAPPHO

ACCORDING TO A fragment of a Hellenistic elegy called "Loves, or the Beautiful Boys," by a certain Phanocles, after the legendary poet Orpheus was torn to pieces by the women of Thrace, his head and his lyre—the instrument from which lyric poetry derives its name—were borne by the waves to the island of Lesbos, where they were subsequently buried. This geography was hardly casual. By the time Phanocles was writing, in the later 300s BC (the time of Alexander the Great), Lesbos had long been associated with exceptional achievement in the lyric arts. The reputation of a poet called Terpander, for instance, who came from the Lesbian city of Antissa and is listed on an extant monument as the winner of a song competition that occurred in the 670s BC, was such that he was credited—apocryphally, undoubtedly—with having invented the seven-stringed lyre. Two generations later, Arion, another Lesbian poet, served as a kind of artist in residence at the court of the ruler of Corinth, where he was responsible for raising the genre known as dithyramb to new expressive heights. This same Arion, as Herodotus relates, is said to have been rescued by a dolphin after being mugged and thrown overboard by hooligans during a voyage home from Syracuse.

But no Lesbian poets were more famous or influential in antiquity than two who, of Arion's contemporaries, were most renowned for their lyric songs: Alcaeus and Sappho. Both came from the hothouse social milieu of the Lesbian aristocracy, which was known as much for its political intrigues as for its love of pleasure and beauty—a love that in the classical Greek imagination was associated with the slightly decadent cultures that flourished in the coastal cities of Asia Minor, just across a narrow strip of water from Lesbos. The two poets, not surprisingly, seem to have known each other. (There is a fragment of Sappho, quoted by Aristotle, that has often been taken to be a playful dialogue between the two.)

And yet the surviving fragments of their poems bespeak wildly divergent interests. Those of Alcaeus suggest a person, or at least a poetic persona, along the lines of an Elizabethan rake: there are drinking songs, war songs, and quite a few verses, often bitter ones, about the tumultuous political situation in Mytilene, Lesbos's largest city and the two poets' hometown. The first-century-BC scholar and critic Dionysius of Halicarnassus, who taught Greek to Romans, dryly noted that without the meter, certain of Alcaeus' poems read like political speeches. The poems of Sappho, on the other hand, are famously and almost exclusively preoccupied by erotic yearning for young women. The poetess's extraordinary gifts—her reputation a scant century after her death was such that Plato could refer to her as "the Tenth Muse"—may bring to mind the rich lyric tradition of her homeland (and thus suggest why Phanocles had Orpheus end up there), but it is her subject matter that explains why the place-name "Lesbos" has come to have connotations for us that are somewhat different from those it had for Phanocles and his readers.

If the fanciful tale told in "Loves, or the Beautiful Boys" inevitably calls to mind the traditional association of Lesbos with erotic poetry—for Phanocles' poem, as its name suggests, was a catalog of the loves of various gods and heroes for beautiful young boys—its story of the severed head also introduces another element that becomes crucial in any consideration of Sappho's verse: fragments.

The library at Alexandria possessed nine volumes—which is to say, rolled papyrus scrolls—of Sappho's verses; the first book alone contained 1,320 lines. These books were arranged primarily by meter. (The first was a collection of poems composed in the distinctive four-line stanza known as the Sapphic strophe, a complicated and exacting meter later brilliantly adapted by Catullus into Latin; the second featured verses in something called Aeolic dactylic pentameter, composed in two-line stanzas; and so forth.) It is likely that the ninth book was a collection of poems known as epithalamia, songs to be sung during various stages of the wedding ritual; to this book belongs the fragment made famous as the title of J. D. Salinger's book *Raise High the Roof Beam, Carpenters*—the poem written, perhaps, on the occasion of a girl's wedding to a rather tall man. ("The humour," as Sappho's greatest twentieth-century editor, Denys Page, grumpily noted in his definitive 1955 edition of the poems, "not for the last time in the history of weddings, is heavy and flat.") Even if we grant that not every one of the nine books contained as many verses as did the first, the foregoing catalog should suffice to provide an idea of the extent of the original Sapphic corpus.

Of that extensive output, we possess precisely one complete poem. (A second, nearly whole lyric, about the heartache of old age, emerged only in 2004, when two scholars realized that lines from a papyrus in Cologne completed a fragmentary poem that had been published in the 1920s.) Generally referred to as "Fragment 1" in the standard editions of Sappho's works, this seven-stanza lyric, composed in

Sapphic strophes, is a self-deprecatingly humorous request for assistance by the lovelorn Sappho to Aphrodite, goddess of love. ("Come to me now...be my ally.") The reason it has survived, however, has nothing to do with love: the poem was quoted in full by Dionysius of Halicarnassus in an essay on literary composition because he admired its polish and intensity.

It is, indeed, odd to contemporary readers, who are likely to value Sappho for those traits of emotional intensity, self-reflection, and subjective expressiveness that we see as fundamental to lyric poetry, that this most famous of all the ancient lyricists has survived primarily because of what seem to us today to be the dry preoccupations of long-dead pedants. One lovely fragment ("I would not think it right to touch the sky with my two arms") comes to us because it contained a spelling of the Greek word for "sky" that interested the second-century-AD grammarian Herodian in his treatise "On Anomalous Words." (Lest you conclude too hastily that Herodian's interests were overly narrow, it should be noted that his other works included a study of the accentuation of the *Iliad* and *Odyssey*.) Some of the most emotionally stark snippets ("you've forgotten me / or you love some man more than me") or the most tantalizing ("as long as you are willing...") occur in a treatise by Herodian's equally learned father, Apollonius Dyscolus, a book that even in antiquity was unlikely to have been a page-turner: *On Pronouns*.

It's probably safe to say that none of these fragments would arouse a great deal of excitement were it not for two facts: first, that Sappho was a woman, and second—even more, you suspect—that she wrote about desire. The first is a fascinating anomaly, given what we know of the often oppressive grip of Greek patriarchy, even in the comparatively relaxed milieu of the Lesbian elite. (Aristotle remarks that Sappho was honored "even though she was a woman.") The second dovetails with certain ideas we have that are central not only to our understanding of lyric poetry but, indeed, to our conception of the self in general—desire and sexuality being so crucial to our contemporary understanding of personality. With a directness seemingly unmediated by vast stretches of time, Sappho seems to speak to us quite clearly today, no matter what the form our desire takes. "No one who has been in love," the poet and classics scholar Anne Carson wrote at the beginning of *Eros the Bittersweet*, her brilliant and idiosyncratic 1986 study of Greek erotic poetry, "disputes her"—that is, argues with Sappho's definition of eros as "bittersweet," a word that Sappho in fact coined. (The Greek is *glukupikron*, which literally means "sweet-bitter"; the significance of sweetbitter, as opposed to bittersweet, is just one of the many objects of Carson's shimmering investigation.)

Hence our hunger for those paltry fragments. And yet many classics scholars have been wondering whether Sappho's poems meant something wholly different to her and her original audience from what their partial remains mean to us. Some, for instance, believe that those intense expressions of individual subjective yearning were written—as their frequent use of the first-person-plural pronoun has suggested —for performance by large choruses of young girls who sang Sappho's songs at public occasions. We know that such choruses were a fact of cultural life in Archaic Greece, just as we know of choruses of men and boys who sang other formalized songs, such as the dithyramb, at civic festivals (the origin, so Aristotle tells us, of tragedy). This possibility, in turn, raises further questions. How do we read those frequent addresses to Aphrodite if Sappho was not a desire-crazed proto-Romantic but the leader of a *thiasos*, a formal cult association that met to honor the goddess—or even of a school for girls at which she officiated as a kind of headmistress? What if Sappho was the head of one of several informal associations of young women —her poems mention, with amusing tartness, the leaders of rival groups, as far as we can tell—to whose nubile members, preparing for their inevitable destinies in Greek society as brides and then mothers, Sappho's yearning lyrics were meant to provide a kind of emotional instruction? What if, alternatively, the lyrics were meant not to provide a voice to private yearning, or to emphasize in the public eye the desirability of her young female subjects on the occasion of their nuptials (another theory), but to mediate in a yet more subtle fashion between private and public (yet another theory)—to make *eros* manageable by giving it form and voice and a place in society?

The foregoing catalog is intended merely to suggest the range and variety of explanations—given over the years and centuries—of the meaning of Sappho's lyrics, explanations that put Sappho back in her original social and historical setting. True, some of these explanations were undoubtedly motivated by distaste for the possibility that Sappho was homosexual in the way we understand that word. Yet some are sensitive and informed attempts to understand Sappho's verse in a fashion that takes into account what we know of Archaic Greek culture—not only that it was patriarchal, and therefore unlikely to tolerate unbridled expressions of lesbian desire (as we understand it to be, at least), but also that the settings for lyric performance were, like so many other aspects of Greek culture, likely to be much more public than the contemporary poetry-reading audience might imagine.

In fact, the controversy about Sappho and her work has raged since the beginning of modern classical scholarship; the discrepancy between the apparent passion of the words that have been preserved and the pedantic dryness of the contexts in which they survived seems to reflect the two sides of the scholarly debate. In one corner are the scholars for whom the "real" Sappho is the one we seem to recognize, the intensely private singer of unique songs about forbidden desire; in the the other are the classicists who argue that she and her work belong—somehow—to the public world of civic and social practices in a way that is difficult for us today to apprehend. The stakes in this debate are, clearly, more than purely academic. As the classicist Thomas Habinek puts it in his introduction to *Re-Reading Sappho* (1996), a collection of critical essays on the subject:

> The increasing empowerment of women, with the resultant interest in women's history, women's writing, and women's "ways of knowing," has accounted for the focus on Sappho as the first female writer in the Western tradition whose works have survived in any quantity.

An extracurricular investment in Sappho is also evident in the work of queer theorists, and indeed of any number of critics—and their constituencies in the larger world—who wish to claim her as a forebear, one who could lend ancient and powerful cultural authority to marginalized identities.

And yet we know that Sappho has not, in fact, survived "in any quantity." Indeed, one reason that there is no satisfactory way to resolve that controversy about the "real" Sappho and her circle and the "real" meaning of her poems is precisely because so much of the evidence we possess is fragmentary: what we know for certain about Sappho is that she did (or did not?) lead a circle of women who were (or were not?) lesbians in the contemporary sense of that word; that she did compose songs (for public performance? for private delectation?) about young girls (who were students? lovers? disciples? fellow cultists?). And, in what is surely an unproductive circularity, the fragmentary knowledge we use to illuminate Sappho's poems comes from the precious fragments themselves.

One way to deal with the problems that arise from the desperately incomplete state in which we find the Sapphic corpus is to forgo entirely any thought of reconstruction, of interpretation: to take the beautiful fragments, in other words, at face value. The idea that fragments of ancient culture—not only poems but vases and statues as well—can be aesthetically pleasing despite their incompleteness is one that has considerable allure and a distinguished Romantic pedigree ("the pleasure in ruins"); during the past century in particular, we have found a great appeal in the notion that fragments are beautiful *because* they are incomplete. You only have to think of Rilke's famous lyric "Archaic Torso of Apollo" to be reminded of the hold that the notions of incompleteness or fragmentation, and indeed a kind of wholeness-in-fragmentation, had on the twentieth-century artistic imagination, as far back as the beginning of that century. This is, if anything, even more true for our present postmodern imagination, with its obsession with fragmentation, allusiveness, quotation, and reconfiguration of elements of the past. The cultural climate of postmodernism helps to account for the attitudes of Sappho's most recent generation of translators and interpreters: one contemporary classicist, for instance, prefers to see the tattered corpus of Sappho as a Lacanian "body in pieces," and hence forgoes traditional attempts at reconstructing Sappho's work and historical setting in favor of a meditation on "the aesthetics of the fragment"; another has observed that for many critics, the "irony implicit in the fragmentary preservation of poems of yearning and separation serves as a reminder of the inevitable incompleteness of human knowledge and affection."

And yet as alluring and provocative to us today as the notion of "the fragmentary" may be, it must be said that it has no meaningful relation to the presumed object of serious scholarship and translation, which, you would think, ought to be some kind of responsible representation of Sappho herself to the wider world—even if that representation must remain partial and unsatisfying to the world (which, as we know, is often eager to see in her its own reflection). We may not know a great deal about Sappho, but we do know that she wrote whole poems, not fragments. The resemblance between the shattered state of the Sapphic texts and the shattered state of the broken hearts that are sometimes described in those texts is purely coincidental; the use of such resemblance as an element in the criticism of Sappho's work is, ultimately, as sentimental as any of the theories advanced by the Victorian critics of yore.

The contemporary critical penchant for fragmentation invariably colors new translations of the poems themselves. The admirable Stanley Lombardo, a classicist and translator who produced a remarkably fresh and distinctive new version of the *Iliad* in 1997, writes in the preface to his *Sappho: Poems and Fragments* (2002) of the "gaps in the text that often leave us with only these beautiful, isolated limbs." "Beautiful, isolated limbs" brings us back full circle to old Phanocles and that disembodied head of Orpheus, washed up on the shore of Lesbos—a fable that now takes on contemporary overtones, suggesting as it does the way in which poetry can enjoy sentimentalizing and idealizing the fragmentary body (as Rilke would do millennia after Phanocles). And indeed, for Lombardo, the allure of gaps and fragments dictates a philosophy of translation that affects even intact passages: "I sometimes deliberately treat a more or less intact passage as if composed of fragments that reduce to rhythmic phrases. I have made no attempt to follow, although I do sometimes suggest, Sappho's various lyric meters." Here, preference for fragmentation actually erases what is, in fact, recoverable and intact in the original.

The problems inherent in the sentimental "fragmentist" approach to Sappho are even more evident in *If Not, Winter: Fragments of Sappho* (2002), the translation of Sappho's poems, with commentary, by

Anne Carson, who is not only a serious scholar of Greek poetry but also a serious poet whose oeuvre thus far represents, to my mind, the most distinguished, original, and successful adaptation and reconfiguration of classical models produced in the past generation. Mimnermos, an elegiac poet of Sappho's era, is the subject of part of her mosaic-like *Plainwater* (1995); *Autobiography of Red* (1998) is a verse novel that reimagines the myth of Geryon as narrated in the poetry of Stesichorus, a poet of the late seventh and early sixth centuries who was praised by one ancient scholar as being among the most "Homeric" of writers. The Greek lyric genius Simonides of Keos, who wrote the famous epitaph of the Spartans who fell at Thermopylae ("Go tell the Spartans...") meets Paul Celan in the essay *Economy of the Unlost* (1999); Aristotle and the choral lyricist Alkman appear meaningfully in *Men in the Off Hours* (2000).

So Carson comes to Sappho with the tools of both the rigorous scholar and the freewheeling poet. Both personae are to be found here and, as the following passage suggests, sometimes tango uncomfortably with each other. At one point she writes that the absence, the gaps—the lack of what Sappho actually wrote—have become an "exciting" presence:

> When translating texts read from papyri, I have used a single square bracket to give an impression of missing matter, so that] or [indicates destroyed papyrus or the presence of letters not quite legible somewhere in the line. It is not the case that every gap or illegibility is specifically indicated: this would render the page a blizzard of marks and inhibit reading. Brackets are an aesthetic gesture toward the papyrological event rather than an accurate record of it.... Brackets are exciting. Even though you are approaching Sappho in translation, that is no reason you should miss the drama of trying to read a papyrus torn in half

or riddled with holes or smaller than a postage stamp—brackets imply a free space of imaginal adventure.

To get a sense of what such adventures entail, you might look at Carson's translation of the poem known as Fragment 22, a partial line of which lends her new book its title. Here are the first few lines:

>]
>]work
>]face
>]
>]
> if not, winter
>] no pain
>]
>]I bid you sing
> of Gongyla, Abanthis, taking up
> your lyre as (now again) longing
> floats around you . . .

It should be noted that Carson has taken liberties here—slightly greater ones than she warns in her preface that she would. "Gongyla" and "Abanthis," for instance, appear in the Greek text as the headless fragments ". . . gyla" and ". . . anthis"; there is, presumably, only so much drama to which the lay reader may safely be exposed. And she has also neglected to represent the brackets that, in fact, mar the sixth line of the Greek text. (But then, who would buy a book called "]f not, winter["?)

I harp on Carson's selective application of her principles of representation because it seems to me symbolic of the strange waffling that characterizes her new book itself, which, like so much about Sappho, has ended up stranded between the scholarly and the impressionistic—between an attempt to recover something concrete of Sappho's meanings and the desire to make Sappho reflect our own preoccupations. (In this case—as Carson's subtitle, to say nothing of her prefatory remarks, indicates—preoccupations with the beauty and "excitement" of fragments and the fragmentary.) Like Sappho's songs, indeed, Carson's translation raises a difficult question of audience: For whom is this book intended? To the lay eye, at least, *If Not, Winter* presents itself as an authoritative new Sappho: it accounts for every one of the nearly two hundred fragments of which at least one legible word survives, and provides the Greek text, brackets and all, on the page facing each translation. There are, too, notes in back that contain many references to and citations of ancient authors. And yet an intelligent reader not familiar with the controversies raging around Sappho and her work, and trusting in the amplitude of Carson's book, in the scholarly-looking apparatus of notes and Greek citations and, indeed, the Greek on those facing pages, is likely to take away from this new translation, and from what can best be described as the fragments of information to be gleaned from its notes, a picture of the poet and her corpus that is disingenuously taciturn at best and misleading at worst.

There is, to be sure, a great deal to be admired here, not least because as a scholar Carson has special insight into the elaborate rhetorical strategies at play in the few substantial fragments we do have. Perhaps the most famous poem by Sappho—sufficiently influential in antiquity to have been translated by the Roman poet Catullus half a millennium after she composed it—is Fragment 31 in the standard edition, four complete Sapphic stanzas and a single additional line from the fifth, that survive because it was quoted (rightly) in Longinus' treatise *On the Sublime*:

He seems to me equal to gods that man
whoever he is who opposite you
sits and listens close
to your sweet speaking

and lovely laughing—oh it
puts the heart in my chest on wings
for when I look at you, even a moment, no speaking
is left in me

no: tongue breaks and thin
fire is racing under skin
and in eyes no sight and drumming
fills ears

and cold sweat holds me and shaking
grips me all, greener than grass
I am and dead—or almost
I seem to me.

But all is to be dared, because even a person of poverty

The poem ends—a bit maddeningly, appropriately enough—with a fragment: the first line of a next stanza whose contents must, for the present, remain unknown.

Longinus admired the way in which the contradictory symptoms of the lover's passion, as she watches her beloved talk easily to a third party—a man—come together to form a persuasive whole. More contemporary interpreters have admired the way in which it introduces the imagination into lyric utterance for the first time, as the poem

engages in some complex thinking about "seeming"—about perceptions of phenomena both exterior and interior to oneself. The new
translation conveys the real drama of this remarkable lyric, which lies
in the way that the speaker becomes both increasingly aware of, and
yet increasingly detached from, her own body, whose various organs
—eyes, tongue, skin—take on lives of their own. Carson allows us to
hear how the first four stanzas are framed by words of seeming (the
Greek *phainetai*, "he seems," and *phainomai*, "I seem"): her exact
translation places the reader in the slightly echoing inner world of
perception that is the special achievement of the poem, and that is
not well conveyed, for instance, by Stanley Lombardo's "Look at
him...Look at me," which has the unfortunate effect, because of the
implied apostrophe to the reader, of introducing into this work's
much-commented-on perfect triangle (Sappho, the girl, the man) an
extraneous fourth person: the reader.

There are other details in Carson's rendering of Fragment 31 that
show a praiseworthy sensitivity to the original: "puts the heart in
my chest on wings" is a stunning solution for the Greek *eptoaisen*,
a word that conveys both a fearful shuddering and the airborne
intention of beating wings; and "drumming" successfully brings
across the almost onomatopoetic force of the Greek verb *epibro-
meisi*, which Lombardo's "my ears ring" fails to suggest. But the
best and most persuasive aspect of Carson's rendering is to convey
the odd, stilted quality of the Greek when it describes the symptoms
that make Sappho not the subject but the object of the phenomena
she describes: the Greek literally says "Nothing any longer comes
to me to speak," which is brought across much better here than in
Lombardo's "I can't get any words out." It is the poem's complex
play of subject and object, perceiving and suffering, detachment and
involvement, that accounts for its privileged place in the Western

lyric tradition, and this elaborate play is what Carson beautifully renders.

And yet as persuasive as much of the translation is, there are odd lapses and strange inconsistencies. A distinctive aspect of Sappho's verse is that unquantifiable element, voice: in Sappho's case, forthright and plain, however artful the rhetorical strategies may be. Carson admirably re-creates the directness of Sappho's voice, explaining her choices thus:

> In translating I tried to put down all that can be read of each poem in the plainest language I could find, using where possible the same order of words and thoughts as Sappho did. I like to think that, the more I stand out of the way, the more Sappho shows through.

But it isn't clear that to mimic the word order of a highly inflected language like Greek results, in fact, in an "accurate" representation of the words—any more than to postpone the verb to the end of a sentence in a translation from the German would be an accurate or appropriate translation of the German. One result is a certain stiffness in Carson that you don't find in Sappho.

Other lapses seem to be arbitrary. It is strange, given Carson's alertness to the salient gender issues in these poems, that she would choose to translate Fragment 108—at one short line, admittedly not among the most crucial ones—as "O beautiful O graceful one," when the Greek very explicitly provides a noun for those adjectives: *kora*, "girl." On the other hand, it's all too easy to see why Carson has chosen to render the tiny two-word Fragment 38, *optais amme*, as "you burn me." What the Greek says is "you burn us"; the pronoun is plural. As we know—and as Carson acknowledges in her note to this fragment —one reason that Sappho uses the plural is that the poetry was choral in origin; but Carson goes on to say that she's chosen to render this fragment the way she has in order to preserve what she calls its "fragile heat." In other words, she's chosen to sacrifice what the words actually say in order to project an image of Sappho as we want her: the private voice of individual erotic yearning. If the fragment is hot enough to translate, it's hot enough to render accurately—with, of course, the same explanatory note. But then it might not seem so hot, after all.

Indeed some of Carson's choices seem to adhere to a subtle agenda. This is evident particularly in her introduction and notes, which consist of an array of asides about the sources of the fragments, comments on the meaning of the Greek, and general observations that, while often amusing, fail to provide a consistently informative addendum to the fragments laid out in these pages. Much of this is most likely a matter of personal quirkiness in someone who can be rather mandarin. (The author's note at the back of her books famously declares that she "lives in Canada"—and that's it.) Yet it seems to me that, for instance, her account of what she calls the "marks and lacks" in the extant fragments is not wholly free from playing to the prejudices of her likely audience. This serious scholar assumes an air of disdain for the "ancient scholiasts, grammarians, metricians, etc., who want a dab of poetry to decorate some proposition of their own and so adduce *exempla* without context"; she then goes on to cite these *exempla* while dryly chiding those ancient philologues for not giving us more of the precious fragments we want:

> It would be nice to know whether this question comes from a wedding song.... Apollonius Dyskolos is not interested in such matters.... And who is this girl? And why is Sappho praising

her? Chrysippos is not concerned with anything except Sappho's sequence of negative adverbs....Who would not like to know more about this garment? But the curiosity of Pollux is strictly lexical.

Here again, we are confronted, implicitly, with the two poles of the old Sappho debate: on the one side stand the desiccated scholars with their narrow, airless interests, and on the other the sensitive advocates of passionate feeling. There's little doubt about which group Carson's readers are meant to identify with.

But it's surely unjust (although it will just as surely gratify some readers) to deride ancient commentators for not realizing that the poetry they took for granted would eventually vanish, and for merely doing their scholarly jobs; just as it would be unfair for us to expect our contemporary poets to be like second-century Alexandrian scholars with their dry, scholarly concerns. (Concerns, for instance, about the difference between singular and plural pronouns.) Carson's goal of letting Sappho "show through" is an admirable one; less so her presentation of this vexed body of poetry as transparent, as being about what most readers are already likely to assume it's about. "It seems that she knew and loved women as deeply as she did music," she writes in her introduction. "Can we leave the matter there?"

Well, no, we can't. Carson's new book is, in the end, as fragmentary and frustrating as the object of its highly idiosyncratic scrutiny. Like so many other products of the recent school of Sappho commentaries, it leaves us with a strange and unsettling feeling that to some, at least, will be familiar: that there, over there, is a woman of beauty, saying enchanting things to someone; but in our excitement at being in her presence, we can't quite make out her meaning.

—*The New York Review of Books*, August 14, 2003

ARMS AND THE MAN

HISTORY—THE RATIONAL and methodical study of the human past—was invented by a single man just under twenty-five hundred years ago; just under twenty-five years ago, when I was starting a graduate degree in classics, some of us could be pretty condescending about the man who invented it and (we would joke) his penchant for flowered Hawaiian shirts.

The risible figure in question was Herodotus, known since Roman times as the "Father of History." The sobriquet, conferred by Cicero, was intended as a compliment. Herodotus' *Histories*—a chatty, dizzily digressive nine-volume account of the Persian Wars of 490 to 479 BC, in which a wobbly coalition of squabbling Greek city-states twice repulsed the greatest expeditionary force the world had ever seen—represented the first extended prose narrative about a major historical event. (Or, indeed, about virtually anything.) And yet to us graduate students in the mid-1980s the word "father" seemed to reflect something hopelessly parental and passé about Herodotus, and about the sepia-toned "good war" that was his subject. These were, after all, the last years of the Cold War, and the terse, skeptical manner of another Greek historian—Thucydides, who chronicled the Peloponnesian War, between Athens and Sparta, two generations later—seemed far more congenial. To be an admirer of Thucydides' *History*, with its deep cynicism about political, rhetorical, and ideological hypocrisy, with its all too recognizable protagonists (a liberal yet imperialistic democracy and an authoritarian oligarchy, engaged in a war of attrition fought by proxy at the remote fringes of empire) was to advertise yourself as a hardheaded connoisseur of global realpolitik.

Herodotus, by contrast, always seemed a bit of a sucker. Whatever his desire, stated in his preface, to pinpoint the "root cause" of the Persian Wars (the rather abstract word he uses, *aitiē*, savors of contemporary science and philosophy), what you take away from an initial encounter with the *Histories* is not, to put it mildly, a strong sense of methodical rigor. With his garrulous first-person intrusions ("I have now reached a point at which I am compelled to declare an opinion that will cause offense to many people"), his notorious tendency to digress for the sake of the most abstruse detail ("And so the Athenians were the first of the Hellenes to make statues of Hermes with an erect phallus"), his apparently infinite susceptibility to the imaginative flights of tour guides in locales as distant as Egypt ("Women urinate standing up, men sitting down"), reading him was like—well, like having an embarrassing parent along on a family vacation. All you wanted to do was put some distance between yourself and him, loaded down as he was with his guidebooks, the old Brownie camera, the gimcrack souvenirs—and, of course, that flowered polyester shirt.

A major theme of the *Histories* is the way in which time can effect surprising changes in the fortunes and reputations of empires, cities, and men; all the more appropriate, then, that Herodotus' reputation has once again been riding very high. In the academy, his technique, once derided as haphazard, has earned newfound respect, while his popularity among ordinary readers will likely get a boost from the publication of perhaps the most densely annotated, richly illustrated, and user-friendly edition of his *Histories* ever to appear: *The Landmark Herodotus*, edited by Robert B. Strassler and bristling with appendices by a phalanx of experts on everything from the design of Athenian warships to ancient units of liquid measure. (Readers interested in throwing a wine tasting *à la grecque* will be grateful to know that one amphora was equal to a hundred and forty-four *kotyles*.) The underlying cause—the *aitiē*—of both the scholarly and the popular revival is worth wondering about just now. It seems that, since the end of the Cold War and the advent of the Internet (and of a new kind of war), the moment has come, once again, for Herodotus' dazzlingly associative style and, perhaps even more, for his subject: implacable conflict between East and West.

Modern editors, attracted by the epic war story, have been as likely as not to call the work *The Persian Wars*, but Herodotus himself refers to his text simply as the publication of his *historiē*—his "research" or "inquiry." The (to us) familiar-looking word *historiē* would to Herodotus' audience have had a vaguely clinical air, coming, as it did, from the vocabulary of the newborn field of natural science. Not coincidentally, the cradle of this scientific ferment was Ionia, a swath of Greek communities in coastal Asia Minor, just to the north of Halicarnassus, where the historian was born around 484 BC. (He died at about sixty, having spent a number of years, starting in his late thirties, in Athens, a city for which he expressed great admiration.) The word only came to mean "history" in our sense because of the impact of Herodotus' text.

The Greek cities of Ionia were where Herodotus' war story began, too. These thriving settlements, which maintained close ties with their mother cities across the Aegean to the west, began, in the early sixth century BC, to fall under the dominion of the rulers of the Asiatic kingdoms to the east; by the middle of the century, however, those kingdoms were themselves being swallowed up in the seemingly inexorable westward expansion of Persia, led by the charismatic empire-builder Cyrus the Great. The *Histories* begins with a tale that illustrates this process of imperialist digestion: the story of Croesus, the famously wealthy king of Lydia. For Herodotus, Croesus was a satisfyingly pivotal figure, "the first barbarian known to us who subjugated and demanded tribute from some Hellenes" who nonetheless ended up subjugated himself, blinded by his success to the dangers around him. (Before the great battle that cost him his kingdom, he had arrogantly misinterpreted a pronouncement of the Delphic oracle that should have been a warning: "If you attack Persia, you will destroy a great empire." And he did—his own.) The fable-like arc of Croesus' story, from a deceptive and short-lived happiness to a tragic fall arising from smug self-confidence, admirably serves what will turn out to be Herodotus' overarching theme: the seemingly inevitable movement from imperial hubris to catastrophic retribution.

The fall of Croesus, on May 28, 585 BC—we know the date because the battle he lost to Cyrus took place on the day of a solar eclipse that had been predicted by the Ionian scientist Thales of Miletus—marked the beginning of the absorption of the Ionian Greeks into the Persian Empire. Almost a century later, starting in 499, these Greeks began a succession of open rebellions against their Persian overlords; it was this "Ionian Revolt" that triggered what we now call the Persian Wars, the Asian invasions of the Greek mainland in 490 and 480. Some of the rebellious cities had appealed to Athens and Sparta for military aid, and Athens, at least, had responded. Herodotus tells us that the Great King Darius was so infuriated by this that he instructed a servant to repeat to him the injunction "Master, remember the Athenians!" three times whenever he sat down to dinner. Contemporary historians see a different, less personal motive at the root of the war that was to follow: the inevitable, centrifugal logic of imperialist expansion.

Darius' campaign against the Greeks in 490 and, after his death, that of his son Xerxes in 480–479 constituted the largest military undertakings in history up to that point. Herodotus' lavish descriptions of the statistic-shattering preparations—he numbers Xerxes' fighting force at 2,317,610 men, a figure that includes infantry, marines, and camel-riders—are among the most memorable passages of his, or any, history. Like all great storytellers, he takes his sweet time with the details, letting the dread momentum build as he ticks off each stage of the invasion: the gathering of the armies, their slow procession across continents, the rivers drunk dry, the astonishing feats of engineering—bridging the Hellespont, cutting channels through whole peninsulas—that more than live up to his promise, in the preface, to describe *erga thōmasta*, "deeds that inspire wonder." All this, recounted in a tone of epic grandeur that self-consciously recalls Homer, suggests why most Greek cities, confronted with the approaching hordes, readily acceded to Darius' demand for symbolic tokens of submission—"earth and water." (In a nice twist, the defiant Athenians, a great naval power, threw the Persian emissaries into a pit, and the Spartans, a great land force, threw them down a well—earth and water, indeed.)

And yet, for all their might, both Persian expeditions came to grief. The first, under Darius, was plagued by a series of military and natural disasters and finally defeated at the Battle of Marathon, where a overwhelmingly outnumbered coalition of Athenians and Plataeans held the day, losing only 192 men to the Persians' 6,400. (The achievement was such that the Greeks, breaking with their tradition of taking their dead back to their cities, buried them on the battle-field and erected a grave mound over the spot. It can still be seen to-day.) Ten years later, Darius' son Xerxes returned to Greece, having taken over the preparations for an even vaster invasion. Against all odds, the scrappy Greek coalition—this one including ultraconservative Sparta, usually loath to get involved in Panhellenic doings—managed to resist yet again.

It is to this second, far grander conflict that the most famous Herodotean tales of the Persian Wars belong; not for nothing do the names Thermopylae and Salamis still mean something today. In particular, the heroically suicidal stand of the three hundred Spartans—who, backed by only a couple of thousand allied troops, held the pass at Thermopylae against tens of thousands of Persians, long enough for their allies to escape and regroup farther to the south—has continued to resonate. Partly, this has to do with Herodotus' vivid description of the Greeks' feisty insouciance, a quality that all freedom fighters like to be able to claim. When Xerxes demanded that the Greeks turn over their arms, the Spartan king, Leonidas, famously replied, "Come and get them"; on hearing that the Persians were so numerous that their arrows would "blot out the sun," another Spartan quipped that this was good news, as it meant that the Greeks would fight in the shade. "In the shade" is the motto of an armored division in the present-day Greek army.

But the persistent appeal of such scenes, in which the outnumbered Greeks unexpectedly triumph over the masses of Persian invaders, is ultimately less a matter of storytelling than of politics. Although Herodotus is unwilling to be anything but neutral on the relative merits of monarchy, oligarchy, and democracy (in a passage known as the "Debate on Government," he has critical things to say about all three), he structures his presentation of the war as a kind of parable about the conflict between free Western societies and Eastern despotism. (The Persians are associated with motifs of lashing, binding, and punishment.) While he isn't shy about portraying the shortcomings of the fractious Greek city-states and their leaders, all of them, from the luxury-loving Ionians to the dour Spartans, clearly share a desire not to answer to anyone but their own leaders.

Anyone, at any rate, was preferable to the Persian overlord Xerxes, who in Herodotus' narrative is the subject of a magisterial portrait of corrupted power. No one who has read the *Histories* is likely to forget the passage describing the impotent rage of Xerxes when his engineers' first attempt to create a bridge from Asia to Europe across the Hellespont was washed away by a storm: after commanding that the body of water be lashed three hundred times and symbolically fettered (a pair of shackles was tossed in), he chastised the "bitter water" for wronging him, and denounced it as "a turbid and briny river." More practically, he went on to have the project supervisors beheaded.

And yet Herodotus' Xerxes is a character of persuasive complexity, the swaggering cruelty alternating with childish petulance and sudden, sentimental paroxysms of tears, a personality likely to remind contemporary audiences of a whole panoply of dangerous dictators from Nero to Hitler. One of the great, unexpected moments in the *Histories*, evoking the emotional finesse of the best fiction, comes when Xerxes, reviewing the ocean of forces he has assembled for the invasion, suddenly breaks down, "overcome," as he puts it to his uncle Artabanus (who has warned against the enterprise), "by pity as I considered the brevity of human life." Such feeling for human life, in a dictator whose casual indifference to it is made clear throughout the narrative, is a brilliant and persuasive psychological touch. And indeed, the unstable leader of a ruthlessly centralized authoritarian state is a nightmare vision that has plagued the sleep of liberal democracies ever since Herodotus created it.

Gripping and colorful as the invasions and their aftermaths are, the Greco-Persian Wars themselves make up just half of the *Histories*—from the middle of Book 5 to the end of the ninth, and final, book. This strongly suggests that Herodotus' preoccupation was with something larger still.

The first four and a half books of the *Histories* make up the first panel of what is, in fact, a diptych: they provide a leisurely account of the rise of the empire that will fall so spectacularly in the second part. Typically, Herodotus gives you everything you could conceivably want to know about Persia, from the semi-mythical, Oedipus-like childhood of Cyrus (he's condemned to exposure as a baby but returns as a young man, disastrously for those who wanted him to die), to the imperial zenith under Darius, a scant two generations later. (Darius, who had a talent for unglamorous but useful administrative matters—he introduced coined money, a reliable postal system, and the division of the empire into manageable provinces called satrapies—was known as "the shopkeeper.") From book to book, the *Histories* lets you track Persia's expansion, mapped by its conflicts with whomever it is trying to subjugate at the time.

In Book 1 for instance, you get the Massagetae, who were apparently strangers to the use, and abuse, of wine. (The Persians—like Odysseus with the Cyclops—get them drunk and then trounce them.) In Book 2 come the Egyptians, with their architectural immensities, their crocodiles, and their mummified pets, a nation whose curiosities are so numerous that the entire book is devoted to its history, culture, and monuments. In Book 3, the Persians come up against the Ethiopians, who (Herodotus has heard) are the tallest and most beautiful of all peoples, and bury their dead in crystal coffins. In Book 4, we get the mysterious, nomadic Scythians, who cannily use their lack of "civilization" to confound their would-be overlords. (Every time the Persians set up a fortified encampment, the Scythians simply pack up their portable dwellings and leave.) By the time of Darius' reign, Persia had become something that had never been seen before: a multinational empire covering most of the known world, from India in the east to the Aegean Sea in the west and Egypt in the south. The real hero of Herodotus' *Histories*, as grandiose, as admirable yet doomed, as any character you get in Greek tragedy, is Persia itself.

What gives this tale its unforgettable tone and character—what makes the narrative even more leisurely than the subject warrants—are those infamous, looping digressions: the endless asides, ranging in length from one line to an entire book (Egypt), about the flora and fauna, the lands and the customs and cultures, of the various peoples the Persian state tried to absorb. And within these digressions there are further digressions, an infinite regress of fascinating tidbits whose apparent value for "history" may be negligible but whose power to fascinate and charm is as strong today as it so clearly was for the author, whose narrative modus operandi often seems suspiciously like free association. Hence a discussion of Darius' tax-gathering procedures in Book 3 leads to an attempt to calculate the value of Persia's annual tribute, which leads to a discussion of how gold is melted into usable ingots, which leads to an inquiry into where the gold comes from (India), which, in turn (after a brief detour into a discussion of what Herodotus insists is the Indian practice of cannibalism), leads to the revelation of where the Indians gather their gold dust. Which is to say, from piles of sand rich in gold dust, created by a species of—what else?—"huge ants, smaller than dogs but larger than foxes." (In this case, at least, Herodotus' guides weren't necessarily pulling his leg: in 1996, a team of explorers in northern Pakistan discovered that a species of marmot throws up piles of gold-rich earth as it burrows.)

One reason that what often looks like narrative Rorschach is so much fun to read is Herodotus' prose style. Since ancient times, all readers of Herodotus, whatever their complaints about his reliability, have acknowledged him as a master of language. Four centuries after Herodotus died, Cicero wondered rhetorically "what was sweeter than Herodotus." In Herodotus' own time, it's worth remembering, the idea of "beautiful prose" would have been a revolutionary one: the ancient Greeks considered prose so debased in comparison to verse that they didn't even have a word for it until decades after the historian wrote, when they started referring to it simply as *psilos logos*, "naked language," or *pedzos logos*, "walking language" (as opposed to the dancing, or even airborne, language of poetry). Herodotus' remarkable accomplishment was to incorporate, in extended prose narrative, the fluid rhythms familiar from the earlier, oral culture of Homer and Hesiod. The lulling cadences and hypnotically spiraling clauses in each of his sentences—which replicate, on the microcosmic level, the ambling, appetitive nature of the work as a whole—suggest how hard Herodotus worked to bring literary artistry, for the first time, to prose. One twentieth-century translator of the *Histories* put it succinctly: "Herodotus's prose has the flexibility, ease and grace of a man superbly talking."

All the more unfortunate, then, that this and pretty much every other sign of Herodotus' prose style is absent from *The Landmark Herodotus*, whose new translation, by Andrea L. Purvis, is both naked and pedestrian. A revealing example is her translation of the work's Preface, which, as many scholars have observed, cannily appropriates the high-flown language of Homeric epic to a revolutionary new project: to record the fabulous deeds not of gods and legendary heroes but of real men in real historical time. In the original, the entire preface is one long, winding, quasi-poetic sentence, a nice taste of what's to come; and in the still-useful 1858 translation of George Rawlinson (which Lawrence of Arabia thought "respectable"), reproduced in the Everyman's Library edition, this syntax is replicated while faithfully reproducing the rich array of tonal registers:

> These are the researches of Herodotus of Halicarnassus, which he publishes, in the hope of thereby preserving from decay the remembrance of what men have done, and of preventing the great and wonderful actions of the Greeks and the Barbarians from losing their due meed of glory; and withal to put on record what were their grounds of feuds.

"Researches" (rather than the blander "inquiry," one possible alternative) nicely gets the slight whiff of chloroform and lab chemicals that, as it were, still clung to the word *historiē* a full century after the Ionian Enlightenment; perhaps even more importantly, the archaic flavoring of "losing their due meed of glory" brilliantly evokes Herotodus's use of a crucial buzzword of Homeric epic, the adjective *aklea*, "without *kleos*"—*kleos* being the heroic renown for which the heroes at Troy fought and died. In appropriating this word, Herodotus was announcing in a single stroke that the Persian Wars were every bit a match for the Trojan War as a subject of an extended literary work.

Robin Waterfield's 1999 translation for the Oxford World Classics series, by contrast, breaks up the syntax a little but is beautifully sensitive to what you might call the "scientific" flavor of Herodotus's prose in this all-important opening—his invocation of the vocabulary of the Ionian Enlightenment in order to bring intellectual legitimacy to his project:

Here are presented the results of the enquiry carried out by Herodotus of Halicarnassus. The purpose is to prevent the traces of human events from being erased by time, and to preserve the fame of the important and remarkable achievements produced by both Greeks and non-Greeks; among the matters covered is, in particular, the cause of the hostilities between Greeks and non-Greeks.

And here, finally, is Purvis:

Herodotus of Halicarnassus here presents his research so that human events do not fade with time. May the great and wonderful deeds—some brought forth by the Hellenes, others by the barbarians—not go unsung; as well as the causes that led them to make war on each other.

Apart from breaking up Herodotus's one flowing sentence into three clanking parts, the rather vague "may the great and wonderful deeds...not go unsung" is disastrously severed from Herodotus's activity as a researcher; Purvis makes it sound as if the historian is committing the project into the hands of Allah, whereas the point of the original is that his rational inquiry is what's going to "sing" those deeds—his prose is now doing what Homer's poetry once did. This flat-footedness makes itself felt throughout the new text.

But in almost every other way *The Landmark Herodotus* is an ideal package for this multifaceted work. Much thought has been given to easing the reader's journey through the narrative: running heads along the top of each page provide the number of the book, the year and geographical location of the action described, and a brief description of that action ("A few Athenians remain in the Acropolis"). Particularly helpful are notes running down the side of each page, each one comprising a short gloss on the small "chapters" into which Herodotus' text is traditionally divided. Just skimming these is a good way of getting a quick tour of the vast work: "The Persians hate falsehoods and leprosy but revere rivers"; "The Taurians practice human sacrifice with Hellenes and shipwreck survivors"; "The story of Artemisia, and how she cleverly evades pursuit by ramming a friendly ship and sinking it, leading her pursuer to think her a friendly ship or a defector." And *The Landmark Herodotus* not only provides the most thorough array of maps of any edition but is also dense with illustrations and (sometimes rather amateurish) photographs—a lovely thing to have in a work so rich in vivid descriptions of strange lands, objects, and customs. In this edition, Herodotus' description of the Egyptians' fondness for pet cats is paired with a photograph of a neatly embalmed feline.

———

As both a narrator and a stylist, then, Herodotus is supremely sophisticated. A synoptic view of the *Histories* reveals, if anything, that for all the ostensible detours, the first four and a half books of the work—the "Rise of Persia" half—lay a crucial foundation for the reader's experience of the war between Persia and Greece. The latter is not the "real" story that Herodotus has to tell, saddled with a ponderous, if amusing, preamble, but, rather, the carefully prepared culmination of a tale that grows organically from the distant origins of Persia's expansionism to its unimaginable defeat. In the light of this structure, it occurs to you that Herodotus' subject is not simply the improbable Greek victory but, just as much, the foreordained Persian defeat. But why foreordained? What, exactly, did the Persian Empire do wrong?

The answer has less to do with some Greek sense of the inevitability of Western individualism triumphing over Eastern authoritarianism

—an attractive reading to various constituencies at various times— than it does with the scientific milieu out of which Herodotus drew his idea of *historiē*. For Herodotus, the Persian Empire was, literally, "unnatural." He was writing at a moment of great intellectual interest in the difference between what we today (referring to a similarly fraught cultural debate) call "nature versus nurture," and what the Greeks thought of as the tension between *physis*, "nature," and *nomos*, "custom" or "law" or "convention." Like other thinkers of his time, he was particularly interested in the ways in which natural habitat determined cultural conventions: hence the many so-called "ethnographic" digressions. This is why, with certain exceptions, he seems, perhaps surprisingly to us, to view the growth of the Persian Empire as more or less organic, more or less "natural"—at least, until it tries to exceed the natural boundaries of the Asian continent. A fact well known to Greek Civ students is that the word *barbaros*, "barbarian," did not necessarily have the pejorative connotations that it does for us: *barbaroi* were simply people who didn't speak Greek and whose speech sounded, to Greek ears, like *bar-bar-bar*. So it's suggestive that one of the very few times in the *Histories* that Herodotus uses "barbarian" in our sense is when he's describing Xerxes' behavior at the Hellespont. As the classicist James Romm argues, in his lively short study *Herodotus*, for this historian there is something inherently wrong and bad with the idea of trying to bleed over the boundaries of one continent into another. It's no accident that the account of the career of Cyrus, the empire's founder, is filled with pointed references to his heedless treatment of rivers, the most natural of boundaries. Cyrus dies, in fact, after ill-advisedly crossing the river Araxes, considered a boundary between Asia and Europe.

What's wrong with Persia, then, isn't its autocratic form of government but its size, which in the grand cycle of things is doomed one day to be diminished. Early in the *Histories*, Herodotus makes reference to the way in which cities and states rise and fall, suddenly giving an ostensibly natural principle a moralizing twist:

> I shall . . . proceed with the rest of my story recounting cities both lesser and greater, since many of those that were great long ago have become inferior, and some that are great in my own time were inferior before. And so, resting on my knowledge that human prosperity never remains constant, I shall make mention of both without discrimination.

The passage suggests that, both for states and for individuals, a coherent order operates in the universe. In this sense, history turns out to be not so different from that other great Greek invention—tragedy. The debt owed by Herodotus to Athenian tragedy, with its implacable trajectories from grandeur to abjection, has been much commented on by classicists, some of whom even attribute his evolution from a mere notetaker to a grand moralist of human affairs to the years spent in Athens, when he is said to have been a friend of Sophocles. (As one scholar has put it, "Athens was his Damascus.")

Athens itself, of course, was to become the protagonist of one such tragico-historical "plot": during Herodotus' lifetime, the preeminent Greek city-state traveled a Sophoclean road from the heady triumph of the Persian Wars to the onset of the Peloponnesian War, a conflict during which it lost both its political and its moral authority. This is why it's tempting to think, with certain classical historians, that the *Histories* was composed as a kind of friendly warning about the perils of imperial ambition. If the fate of the Persians could be intended as an object lesson for the Athenians, Herodotus' ethical point is much larger than the superiority of the West to the East.

Only a sense of the cosmic scale of Herodotus' moral vision, of the way it grafts the political onto the natural schema, can make sense of that distinctive style, of all the seemingly random detours and diversions—the narrative equivalents of the gimcrack souvenirs and brightly colored guidebooks and the flowered shirts. If you wonder, at the beginning of the story of Persia's rise, whether you really need twenty chapters about the distant origins of the dynasty to which Croesus belongs, think again: that famous story of how Croesus' ancestor Gyges assassinated the rightful king and took the throne (to say nothing of the beautiful queen) provides information that allows you to fit Croesus' miserable ending into the natural scheme of things. His fall, it turns out, is the cosmic payback for his ancestor's crime: "Retribution would come," Herodotus says, quoting the Delphic oracle, "to the fourth descendant of Gyges."

These neat symmetries, you begin to realize, turn up everywhere, as a well-known passage from Book 3 makes clear:

> Divine providence in its wisdom created all creatures that are cowardly and that serve as food for others to reproduce in great numbers so as to assure that some would be left despite the constant consumption of them, while it has made sure that those animals which are brutal and aggressive predators reproduce very few offspring. The hare, for example, is hunted by every kind of beast, bird, and man, and so reproduces prolifically. Of all animals, she is the only one that conceives while she is already pregnant.... But the lioness, since she is the strongest and boldest of animals, gives birth to only one offspring in her entire life, for when she gives birth she expels her womb along with her young.... Likewise, if vipers and the Arabian winged serpents were to live out their natural life spans, humans could not survive at all.

For Herodotus, virtually everything can be assimilated into a kind of natural cycle of checks and balances. (In the case of the vipers and snakes he refers to, the male is killed by the female during copulation, but the male is "avenged" by the fact that the female is killed by her young.) Because his moral theme is universal, and because his historical "plot" involves a world war, Herodotus is trying to give you a picture of the world entire, of how everything in it is, essentially, linked.

"Link," as it happens, is not a bad word to have in mind as you make your way through a text that is at once compellingly linear and disorientingly tangential, in which an information-packed aside can take the form of a three-thousand-word narrative or a one-line summary. It only looks confusing or "digressive" because Herodotus, far from being an old fuddy-duddy, not nearly as sophisticated as (say) Thucydides, was two and a half millennia ahead of the technology that would have ideally suited his mentality and style. It occurs to you, as you read *The Landmark Herodotus*—with its very Herodotean footnotes, maps, charts, and illustrations—that a truly adventurous new edition of the *Histories* would take the digressive bits and turn them into what Herodotus would have done if only they'd existed: hyperlinks.

Then again, Herodotus' work may have presaged another genre altogether. The passage about lions, hares, and vipers reminds you of the other great objection to Herodotus—his unreliability. (For one thing, nearly everything he says about those animals is wrong.) And yet, as you make your way through this amazing document, "accuracy"—or, at least, what we normally think of as scientific or even journalistic accuracy, "the facts"—seems to get less and less important. Did Xerxes really weep when he reviewed his troops? Did the aged, corrupt Hippias, the exiled tyrant of Athens now in the service of Darius, really lose a tooth on the beach at Marathon before the great battle began, a sign that he interpreted (correctly) to mean that he would never take back his homeland? Perhaps not. But that startling closeup, in which the preparations for war focus, with poignant suddenness, on a single hopeless old has-been, has indelible power. Herodotus may not always give us the facts, but he unfailingly supplies something that is just as important in the study of what he calls *ta genomena ex anthrōpōn*, or "things that result from human action": he gives us the truth about the way things tend to work as a whole, in history, civics, personality, and, of course, psychology. ("Most of the visions visiting our dreams tend to be what one is thinking about during the day.")

All of which is to say that while Herodotus may or may not have anticipated hypertext, he certainly anticipated the novel. Or at least one kind of novel. Something about the *Histories*, indeed, feels eerily familiar. Think of a novel, written fifty years after a cataclysmic encounter between Europe and Asia, containing both real and imagined characters, and expressing a grand vision of the way history works in a highly tendentious, but quite plausible, narrative of epic verve and sweep. Add an irresistible antihero eager for a conquest that eludes him precisely because he understands nothing, in the end, about the people he dreams of subduing; a hapless yet winning indigenous population that, almost by accident, successfully resists him; and digressions powerfully evoking the cultures whose fates are at stake in these grand conflicts. Whatever its debt to the Ionian scientists of the sixth century BC and to Athenian tragedy of the fifth, the work that the *Histories* may most remind you of is *War and Peace*.

And so, in the end, the contemporary reader is likely to come away from this ostensibly archaic epic with the sense of something remarkably familiar, even contemporary. That cinematic style, with its breathtaking wide shots expertly alternating with heart-stopping closeups. The daring hybrid genre that integrates into a grand narrative both flights of empathetic fictionalizing and the anxious, footnote-prone self-commentary of the obsessive, perhaps even neurotic amateur scholar. (To many readers, the *Histories* may feel like something David Foster Wallace could have dreamed up.) A postmodern style that continually calls attention to the mechanisms of its own creation and peppers a sprawling narrative with any item of interest, however tangentially related to the subject at hand.

Then there is the story itself. A great power sets its sights on a smaller, strange, and faraway land—an easy target, or so it would seem. Led first by a father and then, a decade later, by his son, this great power invades the lesser country twice. The father, so people say, is a bland and bureaucratic man, far more temperate than the son; and, indeed, it is the second invasion that will seize the imagination of history for many years to come. For although it is far larger and more aggressive than the first, it leads to unexpected disaster. Many commentators ascribe this disaster to the flawed decisions of the son: a man whose bluster competes with, or perhaps covers for, a certain hollowness at the center; a leader who is at once hobbled by personal demons (among which, it seems, is an Oedipal conflict) and given to grandiose gestures, who at best seems incapable of comprehending, and at worst is simply incurious about, how different or foreign his enemy really is. Although he himself is unscathed by the disaster he has wreaked, the fortunes and the reputation of the country he rules are seriously damaged. A great power has stumbled badly, against all expectations.

Except, of course, the expectations of those who have read the *Histories.* If a hundred generations of men, from the Athenians to ourselves, have learned nothing from this work, whose apparent wide-eyed naiveté conceals, in the end, an irresistible vision of the way things always seem to work out, that is their fault and not the author's. As he himself knew so well, time always tells. However silly he may once have looked to some people, Herodotus, it seems, has had the last laugh.

—*The New Yorker*, April 28, 2008

THE STRANGE MUSIC OF HORACE

DAYLIGHT WAS FADING on June 3, 17 BC, when there suddenly ascended into the soft air above the Palatine Hill in Rome the pure and reedy sound of fifty-four young voices singing a most unusual hymn. Anyone in the audience that evening who knew his Greek literature—and you can suppose that many did—would have recognized the syncopated, slightly nervous meter of the song being sung as the one invented and made famous six centuries earlier by the Lesbian poet Sappho, who used it to convey some of her most famous lyrics of erotic yearning. ("That man seems to me to be like a god / who, sitting just across from you, / when you've spoken sweetly / hears you.")

On this particular summer night, however, burning desire was not on the poetic menu. That much became clear as soon as the two choirs of twenty-seven singers—one of boys, one of girls, each corresponding to one of the deities invoked in the hymn—called upon Apollo and Diana, "world's brightness and darkness, worshipped forever," to

> ... *make our young men tractable*
> *and virtuous; to our old, grant peaceful health,*
> *give to the whole race of Romulus glory,*
> *descendants and wealth.*

The singing of this hymn was, in fact, the high point of a magnificent and solemn civic occasion: the *ludi saeculares*, Centennial Games, which the First Citizen, Augustus Caesar (né Octavian), had ordered to be held that year—a celebration of Rome as the capital of the world, meant to commemorate the beginning of a new era, a new *saeculum*, in the affairs of humankind. And why not? Fourteen years earlier, Augustus had defeated Cleopatra and Antony at Actium, thereby establishing, for once and for all, Rome as the single great Mediterranean power and putting a hundred years of civil conflict to an end. Since then, he had been consolidating his power abroad and at home, traveling in the East, legislating ethical and moral reforms. Only now, in the year 17 BC, could Rome and the world—and his own position as de facto emperor—be considered secure enough to announce the beginning of what was clearly a New World Order.

We happen to know an unusual amount about the commissioning and performance of the hymn that was meant to celebrate Augustus' achievement because of the survival of two objects from antiquity: a book and a stone. The book, by Suetonius, the historian and biographer of the emperors, was written about a century and a quarter after the evening in question, and in it the author describes how Augustus "approved so highly" of the works of a certain poet and was so "convinced that they would remain immortal that he bade him to compose...the *Carmen saeculare*." The stone, discovered in 1890 and visible today in the Musée des Thermes, is a chunk of the official catalog of the *ludi saeculares*, and with respect to the hymn it notes that on the third day, after a sacrifice offered on the Palatine Hill, twenty-seven young boys and twenty-seven young girls, still having their mothers and fathers, sang a hymn. And in the same way at the Capitol. The song was composed by Q. Horatius Flaccus.

We know him simply as Horace.

The poem that was sung on that long-ago evening—a Greek lyric expression of Roman civic virtues and imperial ambitions; a patriotic anthem set to the lilting poetic rhythms of erotic yearning; a grand celebration of official and communal values given definitive shape by a private individual, a solitary bard—suggests the strange tensions and seeming contradictions that characterize not only Horace's life and work but also our awkward attitude toward him. He is, on the one hand, the august Augustan: during his lifetime, the emperor's friend as well as Virgil's, moving in the highest social, political, and literary circles, acknowledged as the "performer on Rome's lyre," as he himself boasts; after his death, a figure absolutely central to the Western poetic tradition, having had a particular influence in the Renaissance, after languishing in comparative neglect during the Middle Ages. (He has always been more popular when reason is in vogue.) The sixteenth century in France—Ronsard (who in more than one poem rhymes "grâce" with "Horace"), Du Bellay, Montaigne, "the French Horace"—and the seventeenth and particularly the early eighteenth in England (Addison, Steele, Prior, Pope) would be unthinkable without him.

On the other hand, he is—well, the august Augustan: all that avuncular philosophizing about the fleeting nature of pleasure and the inevitable passage of time, from someone comfortably ensconced in the nests of privilege, comes off, today, as complacent and not terribly original, as even his admirers admit. "Heaven knows," the

American critic Brooks Otis wrote a generation ago, in an essay called, significantly enough, "The Relevance of Horace,"

> there is nothing new about "seizing the day" or relaxing from business or moderating one's desires or being philosophic about the future, but we all do fall into the moods that these clichés suggest and, when we do, find Horace just the man for our purposes. He was in short felicitous in his phrasing and charming in his life-style.

Indeed, Horace's lyric output has been reduced in the mind of the general public to a pair of clichés. One, which everyone knows even without knowing its author, concerns the poetry's content: carpe diem. The other concerns its form—the rigorous structures of which their creator was so proud, those formidably dense verse patterns with the funny names that sound like constellations ("Greater Asclepiad"), which have notoriously been the bane of schoolboys both real and imaginary from Shakespeare's Chiron in *Titus Andronicus* ("O, 'tis a verse in Horace, I know it well, / I read it in a grammar long ago") to the pathetic student in Kipling's short story "Regulus," victimized by a sadistic teacher when called upon to translate Horace's paean to the Punic War hero Regulus in one of the six great "Roman Odes" with which Book III of the *Odes* begins.

Neither the charm nor the felicity, the armchair Epicureanism nor the impregnable formality, suits the current taste. When we think of lyricists, it is Sappho who comes to mind, not Horace, who merely used her seamless meters while leaving the messy erotic stuff alone; we like our exaltation in the content, not the form, of our poetry. And yet Horace's steadfast refusal to provide such exaltation, his stubborn artisanal focus on refinements in technique rather than rawness of emotion, is the key to both the beauties and the difficulties in his greatest work, the *Odes*—to the subtle and fragile emotional textures that are so famously hard to convey, and to the elusive tonal artistry that makes it so famously difficult to translate.

———

Horace was born to a freedman, a former slave, on December 8, 65 BC, in Venusia, a small military colony at the heel of Italy. (In the witty and caustic *Satires* with which, at thirty, he first announced his talent to the world—the Latin title, *Sermones*, means something more like "conversations," or perhaps better "*causeries*"—the poet amusingly recounts his schooldays with the "burly sons of burly centurions.") When he died, on November 27, 8 BC, in Rome, he was buried in a tomb on the Esquiline Hill next to his beloved patron, the fabulously wealthy litterateur and bon vivant Maecenas, the emperor's longtime friend; the emperor himself was his heir.

What happened between Venusia and Rome, between centurions' sons and Augustus himself, explains a great deal. The poet's childhood and early manhood witnessed some of the most traumatic years Europe has ever seen: the death throes of the Roman Republic, with its political and social instabilities, and the proscriptions, executions, and confiscations that attended them. (His shrewd, self-made father was an auctioneer's agent, responsible among other things for the disposition of confiscated properties: it's entirely possible that Horace saw firsthand the emotional trauma inflicted by the era's political violence.) As a university student in Athens, where he wrote quantities of verse in Greek—the education that made his later achievement possible—Horace became involved in the upheavals of his era, joining the cause of the "liberators" Brutus and Cassius after their assassination of Julius Caesar in 44 BC. From the disaster at Philippi, he tells us, he barely escaped with his life. He slunk back to Italy to find his father's property confiscated for veterans of the winning side: an ironic twist of fate for the auctioneer's son. Still, he must have had some wherewithal, for he soon after bought himself a clerical post at the treasury—becoming, into the bargain, the model for many distinguished poets (Housman, his great admirer and translator, and also Cavafy) whose stultifying day jobs seem not to have extinguished the lyric impulse.

Insulated from the decade's volatile politics, he began to move in literary circles. By his late twenties he'd joined the circle of Virgil, which suggests he was already circulating poems by that point; and soon after met Maecenas, who remained an intimate for life. Two books of satires, along with a volume of epodes, scathing iambic verses modeled on the invective poetry of Archaic Greek, were published between 35 and 29 BC. It was around this time that Maecenas presented him with the gift of the Sabine farm about which he would write so lovingly—in fact a quite substantial property that allowed the poet to live henceforth as a kind of country gentleman.

It was in the comfort and security afforded by this munificent gift that Horace undertook an enormous project of a character radically different from that of the spicy, scintillating, gossipy *Sermones* and the often outrageous *Epodes*: the three books of odes, comprising eighty-eight poems, in Greek meters on a wide range of subjects. Their publication in 23 BC made his name. (It was the *Odes*, certainly, and not the *Satires*, that earned him the *Carmen saeculare* commission.) There followed some verse epistles; an additional, fourth book of odes, which Augustus himself "compelled" Horace to write, according to Suetonius; and another epistle on the writing of poetry, which has been enshrined separately as the *Ars poetica*, the "Art of Poetry." His last decade was darkened by the losses of friends and other poets: Virgil, Tibullus, Propertius. In the year 8 BC, Maecenas died, admonishing Augustus on his deathbed to treat Horace as "a second me." He needn't have bothered: a few months later, Horace himself was dead.

Even this brief biography should help to account for much about Horace that irritates today: his ostensible embrace of the Augustan regime, his status as a poet of the establishment, his studied avoidance of ecstasy in favor of a measured appreciation of modest beauties and pleasures. For he had seen, firsthand, the worst that his century had to offer; whatever his reservations about Augustus may have been—and given his youthful politics, he must have had some—the new imperial stability was clearly to be preferred to the kind of violent upheavals he had witnessed. Who could blame him for wanting to spend the rest of the life that he had nearly lost celebrating the virtues of solid pleasures sensibly enjoyed—pleasures that are, in the *Odes* more than anywhere else in his work, both shadowed and heightened by an awareness of the violent energies always threatening to destroy them?

Yet it was not the temperate content but rather the artful form of the *Odes* that was their great distinction—or so at least Horace declared. In the final entry to his third book of odes (the last lyric he ever planned to write, before Augustus asked him to whip up some more), he asserts that his claim to poetic fame would rest on the fact that he was the "first to adapt Aeolian [that is, Greek, the verse forms used by Sappho and Alcaeus] verse to the Italian measure"—the very grafting of Roman onto Greek that would be replicated in the great public hymn that Augustus commissioned to celebrate the new Rome.

Why would an achievement that was, at least superficially, a technical one matter so much—and make Horace's influence on later literature so profound? Roman authors during the last two centuries of the Republic—years marked, among other things, by the annexation of much of the Hellenistic Greek world—were acutely aware of the dominance and authority of the Greek cultural inheritance, which proved at once to be a superb model and an irritating burden. Poetry in particular was a vexed subject. The Greeks had an ancient poetic tradition, rich in its own special diction and forms; by comparison, the Roman tradition was both young and relatively impoverished. Roman poets found it was proving difficult to make Latin sound "poetic" (which is to say, Greek). Latin as a language feels heavier than Greek: unlike Greek it has no articles, a phenomenon that lends Latin a certain chunkiness; unlike Greek, it does not have a number of monosyllabic "particles" that can be sprinkled through lines or sentences to give subtle extra flavor—or to help meet the requirements of meter.

As a result, it was difficult to adapt Latin (so ideal for grave prose utterances) to the fluttery and complex stanzaic meters of Greek lyric verse. Horace dealt with this by altering certain conventions of the Greek models used by Sappho and her peers in ways that made them more suitable vehicles for the gravity of Latin words and rhythms (substituting spondees, for instance, where the Greek called for trochees or iambs, and placing regular caesuras, or breaks, within lines to allow for the greater stateliness of Latin speech). By eliminating the hiccupping effect of Greek meters, he achieved verse forms that for the first time sounded natural in Latin—and indeed exploited the monumental quality of the Latin tongue. It was Nietzsche who most famously put his finger on the special quality of Horatian verse, which took the stone blocks that were Latin words, ungainly and difficult to maneuver, and for the first time made them genuinely beautiful and artful: reading Horace, he said, was like encountering a "mosaic of words, in which every word by sound, by position and by meaning, diffuses its influence to right and left and over the whole."

This lapidary quality is the supreme Horatian achievement, the hallmark of his poetry. He ends his famous Mount Soracte ode ("See how deep stands the gleaming snow on / Soracte") with a description of how a flirtatious girl's lovely laughter betrays her hiding place in the corner of a Roman piazza:

> *nunc et latentis proditor intimo*
> *gratus puellae risus ab angulo...*

Literally, the words mean this:

> *Now / too / of a hiding / betraying / from an intimate*
> *lovely / of a girl / laughter / from a corner*

Any translation into syntactically correct English will shatter the cunning effect of the (syntactically correct) Latin, which is capable of a far more elastic word order. To the Roman eye and ear, the first line creates a terrific anticipation, consisting as it does of a series of adjectives describing nouns we don't encounter until the second line. When we do get there, we realize that the correct relationship between each adjective and its noun is meticulously vertical: hiding / girl, betraying / laughter, intimate / corner. So the lines in fact produce the very phenomenon they describe: a sound, a mysterious sound that you cannot at first identify because its source is deeply hidden (as is the word *angulo*, "corner") in a corner. Every line of every ode by Horace is this dense, this complex.

The problem remained of how to give poems composed in those newly useful meters the kind of intellectual heft that suited Roman sensibilities, molded as they were by immersion in the study of rhetoric, focused as they were on the concrete, on the useful, and expressed in the rolling periods, the long, balanced, complex sentences, that so brilliantly distinguish Latin oratory. Horace's second great technical achievement was to learn to thread complicated and extended ideas through one after the other of the four-line stanzas perfected by Sappho and her peers; in so doing he hit upon an unmistakably poetic way to think like a Roman—and he provided, into the bargain, a tautness, variety, and sinew to lyric utterances that had never been achieved before. The energizing tension between the static "mosaic" quality of his diction, which invites you to pause and admire every word, every stanza individually, and the forward-moving pull of his long arcs of thought is what gives Horatian verse its great distinction.

As it turned out, these stylistic and technical innovations perfectly served a characteristic thematic preoccupation: the relationship between pleasure and pain, between how we would like to live and what life does to us. When you carefully follow the strangely winding thread of Horace's thought from stanza to stanza, you often find yourself arriving at a destination quite different from the one the opening line might have promised. Below I have translated I.22, *Integer vitae*, "Wholesome in life," a classic example of this characteristic Horatian sleight of hand, in which the poet's attention wavers between high Romanness and his charming girlfriend, Lalagê:

> *Wholesome in life, of sin completely free:*
> *that man needs no Moorish spears nor bow*
> *nor quiver pregnant with its poisoned*
>   *arrows, Fuscus,*
>
> *even if he's about to journey through*
> *scorching Sidra, or the inhospitable*
> *Caucasus, or regions that the fabled*
>   *Jhelum laps.*

For instance: a wolf—while in the Sabine woods
I once hymned my Lalagê and wandered, beyond
my usual bounds, free of all cares, unarmed—
    fled from me;

a monstrosity such as neither warlike
Apulia rears among her wide oak forests,
nor Juba's land, the arid wet-nurse of
    lions, breeds.

Place me in benumbed plains where not
a single tree is refreshed by summer's breeze,
that region of the world which mists and harsh
    Heaven oppress;

place me beneath the path of a too-close
sun, in a land denied to human habitation:
still I'll love my sweetly laughing Lalagê,
    sweetly talking.

The poem begins as if it's going to celebrate a certain kind of Roman virtue and gravitas. (It was, indeed, often set to music and performed at funerals in Germany and Scandinavia during the nineteenth century.) And yet a shift occurs at the beginning of the third stanza, which purports to give an example of the principle, articulated in the first two, that the honest man needs no armor but his goodness. With a flourish so grand that it suggests we are not to take this business about virtue all that seriously, Horace posits himself as the exemplar of the heroism he lauds in the opening, all because (another letdown) a wolf once avoided him in a forest.

And just what (another shift) was he doing in the forest, anyway? Singing ditties about his darling if perhaps airheaded girlfriend (her Greek name, Lalagê, is derived from the verb "to chatter"). The final pair of stanzas make us realize that the poem is not, after all, about purity and innocence but rather about desire and poetry. For it is Horace's singing and his loving that will endure, however adverse the conditions; and it occurs to you to wonder whether those conditions might not, after all, include a dour cultural emphasis on wholesomeness and purity.

The sudden swerve in Horace's train of thought, so elegantly limned by his particular technique, can be found in a vast range of the odes on many subjects, both patently political and quietly personal. The penultimate poem of Book I, on Octavian's triumph over Cleopatra, famously begins with a call for the celebratory drinking and footstomping to mark the demise of the "demented queen" (*Nunc est bibendum*, "Now let us drink"), but segues to an unsettling simile that compares the fleeing queen at Actium to a "gentle dove" pursued by a hawk—which is to say, Augustus—and then ends, somewhat disorientingly, with a moving *hommage* to the "fierce" dignity of her desire to "die more nobly," "not to be dragged, some lowly woman, in another's proud triumph."

Such shifts are paralleled by another technique: sudden narrowings in focus from the general to the concrete, which can also subvert the poem's ostensible meaning. In the Mount Soracte ode, Horace's blithe admonishment to a young friend to enjoy love while he can takes a sudden, ferocious force from that closing evocation of the laughter of a young girl flirting in some piazza with a boy who's just snatched a love token from her finger. That flirtation was a plausible enough prospect for Horace's friend, but is, you realize, only a memory now for Horace himself. (And the loaded if taut manner in which the poet describes the girl's finger—*male pertinaci*, "badly resisting"—gives some sense of the economy of expression that further characterizes his "lapidary" diction.)

So too the Regulus ode, which so tortured Kipling's schoolboy, and which ends with a description of the dutiful soldier going off to suffer in war—an action the poet decides, almost as an afterthought, to compare to a man going off to a weekend in the country. In the context of what has preceded it, the sudden invocation of peacetime pleasures is shattering. The progressions and shifts of the poet's thought, as it moves through his meticulously fitted verses, is as unpredictable as the progress of any human experience, or human life, and it is this uncertainty that gives the poems, like the lives, their evanescent tone and fragile beauty.

All this is done with such great authority, and with such wit and panache—each of the first nine odes of Book I, the so-called "Parade odes," is in a different Greek meter; it's the poetic equivalent of the compulsories in a sporting event, designed to show you that he's up to all the technical challenges—that it's easy to forget that nobody had ever done it before. But it made a great posterity possible. That we find it perfectly natural that a poet's project might be to express, in a wide variety of personas, something at once weighty and delicate in simple-looking four-line stanzas—to be formally structured but intellectually and emotionally varied, to be discursive and deeply poetic at the same time about a wide variety of subjects, many of them ostensibly everyday rather than ecstatic—is Horace's legacy to Western poetry.

———

The fiercely disciplined reasonableness of Horace's vision, his insistence on a poetic technique as rigorously thought out and meticulously achieved as the happiness the poems themselves endorse, have long endeared him to other poets more, perhaps, than to the reading public at large. Auden had already put his finger on Horace's appeal in his own, very Horatian ode about the modern "Horatians," sensible but deeply feeling people who know that they

> ... are, for all our polish, of little
>   stature, and, as human lives,
>   compared with authentic martyrs
>
> like Regulus, of no account. We can only
>   do what it seems to us we were made for, look at
>   this world with a happy eye
>   but from a sober perspective.

The word "polish" in the contemporary poem suggests the germ of Horace's appeal, particularly to poets who, as J. D. McClatchy points out in the introduction to *Horace, The Odes*, his 2002 collection of verse renderings of the *Odes* by thirty-five well-known poets, have "put aside their singing robes, once they think of themselves as craftsmen rather than as bards, once they attend the world as a surgery and not a party." It is, indeed, Horace's supreme craftsmanship that has always made him at once "wholly untranslatable," as Brooks Otis declared ("like making ropes out of sand," Harold Mattingly once harrumphed in a book about Roman civilization), and irresistible to centuries of poets, particularly poets in English, from Dryden and Pope to Housman and (to cite the most recent of a spate of new translations of the *Odes*) David Ferry, whose much-praised translation appeared in 1997.

It is perhaps inevitable that every new translation of a great classic, like every new production of a canonical opera, needs some kind of self-justificatory new "take" on the work: in Sidney Alexander's meticulous 1999 translation of the *Odes*, for instance, it was that he was giving us Horace as "the quintessential Italian." In the introduction to his volume, McClatchy announces the distinguishing feature of the collection: "Never before," he writes, "have the leading poets of the day assembled specifically to translate all the odes." He goes on to declare that

> the variety of tone to be heard in these translations matches the mercurial shifts in mood and response the Latin poems themselves exhibit. The pairings of poem and translator were deliberate, and made in the hope of creating interesting juxtapositions. To have an American poet laureate write about political patronage, to have a woman poet write about seduction, an old poet write about the vagaries of age, a Southern poet about the blandishments of the countryside, a gay poet about the strategies of "degeneracy"...these are part of the editorial plot for this new book.

These *Odes* thus stand alongside recent collections of translations of a given classic, parts of which are distributed among different contemporary poets: for instance, Daniel Halpern's *Dante's Inferno: Translations by Twenty Contemporary Poets* or Michael Hoffman and James Lasdun's *After Ovid: New Metamorphoses*.

And yet while you admire McClatchy's impulse to create interesting textures between poet and translator, some of that "editorial plot" sounds a little gimmicky to me. Surely it's enough to want to see how a group of excellent contemporary poets handle Horace, without having to suggest, inter alia, that southerners know more about countrysides than (say) midwesterners or New Englanders do, that women know more about seduction than men, or that gay men are more intimate with "degeneracy" (scare quotes or no) than are others. For my part, I'd be happy with a gay translator who knew Latin as well as he presumably knew degeneracy: Mark Doty, a poet I much admire, seems to think that Horace was (as he says in III.14) a young man during the consulship of someone called "Planco," probably because the words *consule Planco* appear in Horace's text; but that's just because *Planco* is the ablative form of *Plancus*, the consul's actual name. Such glitches would have been easy enough to correct, had the editorial focus been on Romans rather than Americans.

There are, to be sure, many deep pleasures to be had from individual translations you find here. Not least is that of an older poet, who has given to the incomparable Ligurinus ode, which begins with a weary rejection of love but ends in an image of heartbreaking erotic turmoil, just the right shift from bantering faux-Sappho ("So it's war again, Venus, / after all this time?") to the plaintive and poignant yearning of the poem's ending. In these last lines, the translator nicely replicates, with the long and short *i*'s, and with the *m*'s of his "Then why, Ligurinus, why / do my eyes sometimes fill, even spill over?," both the assonant repetitions and yearning alliterative *m*'s and *n*'s of the Latin *sed cur heu, Ligurine, cur / manat rare meas lacrima per genas?* I doubt that such felicities are due simply to the fact that Richard Howard, the translator of this "old age" poem, was born in 1929.

Similarly effective is the contribution of John Hollander, who in all of his translations, including an excellent rendering of the Soracte ode, displays a fine sensitivity in matters of enjambment, both between lines and between stanzas—always of vital importance in this poet, in whom sequences of thought are everything. Dick Davis's *Carmen saeculare*, which I quoted at the beginning of this essay, is appropriately dignified and yet manages, by means of rhymes on alternate lines, to sound like a song, which is precisely what it is. And I liked the elegant way in which Rosanna Warren handles the unenviable assignment of IV.7, *Diffugere nives*, "The snows are fled away," the poem that A. E. Housman famously considered to be the most beautiful in ancient literature and which he himself memorably translated in a way that managed to sound both like Horace and like himself ("The snows are fled away, leaves on the shaws / And grasses in the mead renew their birth..."). Warren has managed to find new growth herself in these lines, unpacking the Latin to create fresh but not strained effects in English that make the poem sound, indeed, like poetry: "All gone, the snow: grass throngs back to the fields, / the trees grow out new hair..."

So McClatchy's Horace has grown out some lovely new hair in which we can all luxuriate. Yet as a representation of the *Odes* as a whole (which, with its facing Latin pages, it is impossible not to take it as, whatever the editor's demurs), the new collection has deep problems, for precisely the reasons the editor proffers in order to authorize the new effort: that Horace's "mercurial shifts in mood and response" justify the wildly different tones and degrees of formality, from free verse to rhymed couplets, on offer here.

It seems to me that this represents a fundamental misunderstanding of Horace's work. Horace's poetic identity lies precisely in the meticulous and masterly way he uses form, form above all, to solve both stylistic and intellectual problems: if he writes a poem in a stanzaic meter, it's because he wants you to feel the delicate rhythm of pausing and moving, pausing and moving, en route to the heart-stopping climax; if he casts it as a series of dense lines (as he does in the envoi to the first three books, III.30, *Exegi monumentum*, "I have raised a monument more lasting than bronze"), it's because he wants you to feel the weight, the monumentality. Whatever his mercurial mood shifts, his absolute control and forceful personality give the poems a profound and unmistakable unity.

Indeed, each ode within the larger groupings (the individual books, and all the books taken together) is arranged with as much "mosaic" precision as are individual words within individual odes. To cite just one example: odes II.2–11 are arranged in pairs of poems treating (roughly) the same subject, one poem in skipping Sapphics, the other in more weighty Alcaics. Part of the pleasure this sequence affords is the undulating shifts in tonality and rhythm between, first, the poems within each pair, and then among the pairs themselves.

Of this Horace, McClatchy's collection can give you no impression whatever. The multiple-translator approach works better for epic, whose narrative momentum helps to thread discrete cantos or books, themselves often fairly weighty and substantial, together; the continuities among lyric poems, carefully organized by their creator into a collection, are more fragile. (A device that better suits both the original work and its contemporary admirers is the one employed in R. Storrs's 1959 Oxford University Press collection of 144 translations of a single ode, I.5: *Ad Pyrrham: A Polyglot Collection of Translations of Horace's Ode to Pyrrha*, a work that actually illuminates the ancient original while showing the variety of choices available to translators.)

And of course some of the approaches on display here work less well than others. Rachel Hadas's use of singsong rhyming couplets in the Regulus ode give it a fatally Gunga Dinish ring; Carl Phillips's decision to cast I.32, a crucial poem that quite self-consciously concerns Horace's formal achievement ("give me a Roman song, / my lyre, though Greek yourself") in loose-limbed free verse that trickles down the page makes it, in a way, far too easy—it deprives you of an essential component of the experience of reading Horatian verse, that of an aesthetic and emotional effect achieved by means of a serious intellectual effort. Horace is hard in Latin, and he should be hard in English. Without the formal rigor, the odes are reduced to little more than their apparent content, which is of course much less than what they're really "about."

So the individual talents of translators are on show here at the expense of Horace himself. You wonder, indeed, just who it is this collection is meant to serve. Certainly it will be of little use to those interested in ancient, as opposed to modern, poets: a major and distressing omission is the utter lack of notes of any kind. As nice as it is to think that the average intelligent reader will be able to make sense of (I have opened the collection to a random page) references to Gyges, Peleus, Magnessian Hippolyte, Oricum, and Chloë, you suspect this is a touch optimistic. The importance of the poems' specific references isn't, as the current collection might suggest (one translation leaves out the proper names altogether, substituting blanks), pedantic: when Horace chides Venus for starting up old battles again in the Ligurinus poem, for instance, it's useful to know that Augustus claimed descent from that untrustworthy deity, and hence that the poem thus slyly questions both the erotic and political compulsions responsible for its own creation. To miss such nuances, easy enough to explain in a sentence or two, is to miss much of Horace's wit, and a lot of his seriousness, too.

The startling failure to offer even simple clarifications that would enhance ordinary readers' appreciation of Horace's deeply constructed meanings suggests again that the real focus here is on the translators; there is, indeed, a whiff of clubbiness about the present collection. (I kept wondering why none of the so-called New Formalists—Timothy Steele, Gjertrud Schnackenberg, Dana Gioia—appears in these pages: their emphasis on formal rigor, and particularly Steele's temperament, with its wry celebrations of emotional restraint, would make them ideal candidates for translating Horace.) That hermetic quality will surely have the unfortunate effect of making Horace more rather than less forbidding to the poetry-reading public. Whatever the pleasures it affords, *Horace, The Odes* isn't, finally, Horace's *Odes*. For the present *saeculum*, at least, their strange music—exotic and plainspoken, Greek and Roman, fluid and lapidary, yearning and complacent, earthy and effete—continues to hover in the air, just out of reach.

—*The New York Review of Books*, May 13, 2004

OSCAR WILDE, CLASSICS SCHOLAR

WHEN ASKED WHAT he intended to do after finishing at Oxford, the young Oscar Wilde—who was already well known not only for his outré persona ("I find it harder and harder every day to live up to my blue china," etc.) but for his brilliant achievements as a classics scholar—made it clear in which direction his ambitions lay. "God knows," the twenty-three-year-old told his great friend David Hunter Blair, who had asked Wilde about his postgraduate plans, and who later fondly recalled the conversation in his 1939 memoir, *In Victorian Days*. "I won't be a dried-up Oxford don, anyhow. I'll be a poet, a writer, a dramatist. Somehow or other I'll be famous, and if not famous, I'll be notorious."

As we know, his prediction would be spectacularly fulfilled. Like a character in one of the Greek tragedies he was able to translate so fluently as a student, his short life followed a spectacular trajectory from fame to infamy, from the heady triumphs of his post-Oxford days, when he was already famous enough to be lampooned by Gilbert and Sullivan in *Patience*, to the dreadful peripeteia of the trials and imprisonment. But to some of those who knew him at the time, Wilde's emphatic rejection of the scholarly life must have come as something of a surprise.

He had, after all, shown a remarkable flair for the classics from the start. At the Portora Royal School, where he'd been sent in the autumn of 1864, just before his tenth birthday, he won the classical medal examination with his extempore translations from Aeschylus' *Agamemnon* (the tragedy he loved above all others) and the Carpenter Prize for his superior performance on the examination on the Greek New Testament. Later, at Trinity College, Dublin, he took a first in his freshman classical exams and went on to win the Berkeley Gold Medal for his paper on a subject that was, perhaps, not without augury: the *Fragmenta comicorum graecorum*, "Fragments of the Greek Comics," the great scholarly edition by the early-nineteenth-century German philologue Augustus Meineke. According to his friend Robert Sherard, he occasionally pawned the medal when he needed money, but managed always to redeem it, keeping it until the end of his life.

After transferring to Magdalen College, Oxford, in the autumn of 1874, Wilde scored highest marks on his entrance exams, and finished by taking a prestigious double first in "Greats," the relatively recent, classics-based curriculum officially known as literae humaniores. Always attentive to his image, he liked to imply that these successes came easily—"He liked to pose as a dilettante trifling with his books," Hunter Blair recalled—but in fact put in "hours of assiduous and laborious reading, often into the small hours of the morning." Whatever his taste for lilies and Sèvres, he was a grind.

Wilde's activities immediately following his departure from Oxford suggest an unwillingness to abandon the domain of "dried-up old dons." While scrounging for ways to keep himself employed, he wrote his old friend George Macmillan, of the publishing family, offering to take on projects that would have daunted full-blown classics scholars twice his age: a new translation of Herodotus, a new edition of Euripides' *Madness of Hercules* and *Phoenician Women*. He applied, unsuccessfully, for an archaeology scholarship; he had a hand in an 1880 production of *Agamemnon* that was attended by Browning and Tennyson.

Because he did indeed end up traveling down the path he announced to Hunter Blair, we can never know what the mature work produced by this "classical" Wilde might have been like—the Wilde who could easily have gone on to do a D.Phil. in classics, Wilde the don, Wilde the important and perhaps revolutionary late-nineteenth-century scholar of Greek literature and society. Of that Wilde, the extant record affords us only a few tantalizing glimpses: a university prize essay, an unsigned review article, journeyman's pieces that nonetheless reveal a characteristic bravura. This partial view has occasionally been enlarged over the years by the publication of fascinating bits of juvenilia ("Hellenism," a fragmentary set of notes about Spartan civilization, was published only in 1979). Now we have *The Women of Homer*, published by the Oscar Wilde Society, a substantial although unfinished paper on Homer's female characters that reminds you once more how strongly Wilde's classical training underpinned the sensibility that would make him so famous.

———

Wilde's copy of the *Nichomachean Ethics*, dated 1877, contains this suggestive gloss on the text: "Man makes his end for himself out of himself: no end is imposed by external considerations, he must realize his true nature, must be what nature orders, so must discover what his nature is." At the time he was beginning his studies, the tradition of secondary and university instruction in the classics did not necessarily encourage a profound examination of what one's "true nature" might be. A great premium was placed on proficiency in the languages. Students were expected to be able to translate passages from the classical languages into English—and from English into Greek and Latin prose and verse. (The author and cleric Mark Pattison, who had attended Oriel College in the 1830s, recalled dreary class hours that students spent "construing, in turns, some twenty lines of a classical text to the tutor, who corrected you when you were wrong.") While still at Trinity, Wilde was asked on one exam to translate a fragment of a text about Odysseus into Elizabethan prose, and then was required to translate selections from Wordsworth, Shakespeare, and Matthew Arnold into Greek. This and other tidbits about the writer's intellectual formation can be found in Thomas Wright's admiring intellectual biography, *Built of Books*, a highly useful survey of what Wilde was reading at every stage of his life. (Wright is one of the editors of *The Women of Homer*.)

Luckily, Wilde, whose linguistic abilities were certainly formidable—years later, a former Portora schoolmate recalled his ability to "grasp the nuances of the various phases of the Greek Middle Voice and of the vagaries of Greek conditional clauses"—was to fall into the hands of the right professors. His Trinity master was the Reverend J. P. Mahaffy, a distinguished classicist who had a special interest in later Greek antiquity, and who was, too, a celebrated wit—a quality that must have appealed to his young student. (Informed that the current tenant of an academic post he coveted was ill, Mahaffy replied, "Nothing trivial, I hope?") In an 1874 book called *Social Life in Greece*, Mahaffy argued for a vision of the Greeks and their civilization as something more than a mausoleum of culture, "mere treasure-houses of roots and forms to be sought out by comparative grammarians." Among other things, he showed a refreshing willingness to dust off contemporary attitudes toward one Hellenic institution that would have had a special if secret resonance for Wilde: homosexuality. "There is no field of enquiry," Mahaffy wrote in *Social Life in Greece*, "where we are so dogmatic in our social prejudices, and so determined by the special circumstances of our age and country."

Mahaffy's advocacy of a living engagement with the civilization of the Mediterranean—still somewhat of a novelty at the time—would land the young Wilde in trouble. In the spring of 1877 he accompanied his former professor on a trip to Italy and Greece; after returning to Oxford several weeks late in the term, Wilde was "rusticated" —forced to leave university for the duration of the term. The irony of being temporarily expelled from his classics curriculum for having immersed himself in the Greek world was not lost on the future master of the epigram, who observed that he "was sent down from Oxford for being the first undergraduate to visit Olympia."

The Oxford that punished the unrepentant Wilde had, in fact, been shaking off the old ways, transformed by the energetic reforms of Benjamin Jowett, Regius Professor of Greek, Master of Balliol, and translator of Plato. It was Jowett who insisted that Greats include important currents in contemporary thought (as a young man he had been devoted to Kant); who saw, indeed, the classics as a natural conduit for modern liberal thought. Instrumental in shifting the emphasis of the curriculum from Roman to Greek authors, he made Plato central to it. Not coincidentally, that philosopher's dialectical method was embodied in the university's intimate one-on-one tutorial system—which, as the scholar Linda Dowling reminds us in *Hellenism and Homosexuality in Victorian England*, her fascinating study of the Victorian passion for high Greek culture, occasionally fomented Platonic passions of a less intellectual variety. The special Platonic emphasis at Oxford was clearly what animated Wilde's later, admiring characterization of the curriculum as one in which "one can be, *simultaneously*, brilliant and unreasonable, speculative and well-informed, creative as well as critical, and write with all the passion of youth about the truths which belong to the august serenity of old age." Here, perhaps, is the root of the characteristically Wildean taste for entwining ostensibly incompatible qualities. His work encompassed, sometimes uneasily, what he saw as his "Gothic" and "Greek" sides, veering between a grandiose Romanticism and an astringent Classicism, the fusty nineteenth-century melodrama of most of his theater and the crisp modernism of his critical thought.

Mahaffy and Jowett weren't the only Hellenists advocating a profoundly engaged approach to the classics during the latter half of the nineteenth century. During Wilde's time at Oxford the literary critic and poet John Addington Symonds was publishing his two-volume *Studies of the Greek Poets* (1873, 1876). While their earnestness and dogged effort at comprehensiveness may have been exhaustingly typical of mid-Victorian criticism, these volumes were particularly celebrated (or derided) for their unusually passionate, personal, and florid style: a style that hinted at a more than purely academic degree of investment in the subject, and suggested, once again, that the Greeks could have more than a "dry as dust" meaning for the present day. Symonds, like Mahaffy, urged his readers to visit the Mediterranean sites in order to be able to feel the still-living connection to ancient civilizations. (He compared Aristophanes to Mozart, and Aeschylus to Walt Whitman and Shakespeare.) In 1874 Symonds published a three-volume collection of travel pieces, *Sketches and Studies in Italy and Greece*.

One secret reason for Symonds's engagement is by now well known. Like certain others of the "Oxford Hellenists" of the mid-nineteenth century—including Walter Pater, another figure whose work Wilde would admire extravagantly—Symonds was a secret homosexual who sought, through readings of the Greek classics, to find both expression for and justification of his own sexual nature. Indeed, Symonds later wrote in his memoirs that he had virtually discovered his sexuality through a reading of Plato's *Phaedrus* and *Symposium*: the night he read their "panegyric of paiderastic love" was "one of the most important of my life." In time, he would go on to write explicitly about Greek homosexuality in *A Problem in Greek Ethics*, a text that was circulated privately for ten years before its eventual publication, in 1883, and is now seen as a foundational document of modern homosexual studies. (His *A Problem in Modern Ethics*, published in 1891, suggests reforms for the antihomosexual laws that would, in time, doom Wilde.)

However flowery his style and whatever lip service he paid to conventional condemnation of "paiderastia," there were those who were able to read between the lines of Symonds's work—especially the lines of the final chapter of the second volume of *Studies of the Greek Poets*, with its controversial defense of Greek rather than Judeo-Christian morals, which he dismissed as "theistic fancies liable to change." (Phyllis Grosskurth's 1964 biography of Symonds retells an amusing anecdote about a "shocked compositor" who, after setting the type of Symonds's book, wrote an outraged letter to the author.) The critic and sometime watercolorist Richard St. John Tyrwhitt fulminated against Symonds's book in a lengthy article that appeared in *The Contemporary Review*, warning that *Studies of the Greek Poets* advocated "the total denial of any moral restraint on any human impulses." As a result of the controversy surrounding the second volume of his study, Symonds reluctantly withdrew his candidacy for the Poetry Chair at Oxford.

Small wonder that Wilde's friend Frank Harris later recalled that Symonds's *Studies of the Greek Poets* was "perpetually" to be seen in Wilde's hands. (His copy of the second volume of that work is

dated May 1876, which is to say immediately after its publication: as
the author of *Built of Books* observes, Wilde must have been hanging
around the bookshop waiting for it to appear.) And all the more interesting, too, that when, during the summer holiday of 1876, the
ambitious undergraduate turned his hand to reviewing Symonds's
latest volume—the text now published as *The Women of Homer*—
the chapter to which he directed his critical attention was not the
scandalous final one, with its implicit defense of male homosexuality.
Instead, Wilde wrote about a chapter in which Symonds treated a
subject that was all too clearly a delicate one for the author, an unhappily married homosexual, as well as to his eager young reader,
another secret homosexual who would marry one day: women.

The Women of Homer now takes its place as the earliest of several
youthful classical writings that amply display a precocious intellectual and critical aplomb. A disjointed mass of notes and paragraphs
that Wilde produced in about 1877 was edited a century later into a
misleadingly finished-looking "essay" called "Hellenism." However
unoriginal this account of Spartan culture often is, it sometimes betrays a shrewd and crisply unsentimental appreciation of the Greeks
and their qualities—such shrewdness and lack of sentimentality being the very qualities that mark the "Greek" facets of Wilde's own
work. Not the least interesting of its assertions is that the Greek city-
states' "selfish feeling of exclusive patriotism, this worship of the
πόλις [*polis*, city-state] as opposed to the πάτρια [*patria*, homeland]"
—the quality with which the nineteenth-century admirers of Rome
typically reproached the squabbling Greeks—was, in fact, the key to
the Greek cultural achievement. It was this "selfishness" that, as
Wilde saw it, saved the Greeks "from the mediocre sameness of

thought and feeling which seems always to exist in the cities of great empires."

In an 1879 essay called "Historical Criticism in Antiquity," composed for the Chancellor's Essay Prize, Wilde strikingly rejected the prevailing Victorian appreciation of the classical texts as exemplars of "serenity and balance" (thus the great Greek scholar E. R. Dodds, on what he called "the orthodox Victorian assumption"), advocating instead what today we would call the decadent strain in Greek culture—what he celebrated as "that refined effeminacy, that overstrained gracefulness of attitude" to be found in the later poets and sculptors. Mahaffy's insistence on the living relevance of the Greeks bore fruit in this essay: Wilde goes on to observe, provocatively but shrewdly, that the late nineteenth century, like the late fifth and the fourth centuries BC (the post-Periclean era, that is), was an age of "style," in implicit opposition to the lofty "substance" of an earlier era. To the severity and gravitas of the high classical tradition, of which Sophocles has always been the supreme representative in dramatic literature, Wilde prefers Euripides, as he does the Hellenistic sculptors and other poets and artists who "prefer music to meaning and melody to reality." Here we detect the first stirrings of an argument about aesthetics and society, the provocative elevation of "style" over "substance," that would find its final form in mature works such as "The Decay of Lying," "The Truth of Masks," and Wilde's critical writings.

At virtually the same moment that he composed the Chancellor's Essay, Wilde contributed to the *Athenaeum* a long, unsigned review of Sir Richard Jebb's entries on Greek history and literature in the *Encyclopaedia Britannica*. The twenty-five-year-old blithely took the professor of Greek at Glasgow to task for either denigrating, or omitting altogether from his article, authors or texts that were unconcerned with "serenity and balance." Among the authors was the notoriously effeminate tragedian Agathon, whom Wilde celebrates as "the aesthetic poet of the Periclean age." Among the texts was a bizarre Hellenistic poem called *Pharmaceutria*, an idyll about a love-maddened witch that, Wilde asserts, "for fiery colour and splendid concentration of passion is only equalled by the 'Attis' of Catullus." The admiring reference to the Roman poem—a lengthy work about a handsome acolyte of the goddess Cybele who castrates himself in a transport of religious fervor—is itself worthy of note. Barely out of university, the young Wilde's taste for extreme gestures, in literature as in life, was plain.

The authority and highly defined taste, the willingness to attack established scholars and to propose startlingly original interpretations that distinguish "Hellenism," the Chancellor's Essay, and the *Athenaeum* article of 1879 are evident in *The Women of Homer*, the review of Symonds's book, which Wilde began when he was not quite twenty-two. It is remarkable, not least, for standing in refreshing contrast to the platitudinous moonings of Symonds himself, who is unable to see the preeminent female characters in Homer—Helen, Penelope, and the maiden Nausicaa—as anything but cartoon figures representing conventional types of femininity.

As a product of the "Aesthetic" era, Symonds is good on certain features of Helen. He gets just right the curious and striking way in which Homer's Helen "is not touched by the passion she inspires, or by the wreck of empires ruined in her cause." (He follows this admirably succinct formulation with an unfortunate lapse into the style that irritated so many reviewers: "always desirable and always delicate, like the sea-foam that floats upon the crests of waves.") But while he is capable of appreciating the *Iliad*'s Helen as the abstract symbol of beauty's sheer force in the world—his evident preoccupation—he has no feel whatever for the subtler Helen of the *Odyssey*, of whom he states, with disastrous obtuseness, that "the character of Helen loses much of its charm and becomes more conventional."

Here Symonds is referring to Helen's appearance in Book 4, in which Odysseus' young son, Telemachus, comes calling on Helen's husband, the Spartan king Menelaus, in order to obtain news of his long-lost father. It would, in fact, be hard to find a more unforgettable and less conventional scene in all of Homer. As Helen and Menelaus regale the awestruck youngster with tales of the war, ostensibly to share memories of Odysseus with the son who never knew him, their exchange suggests, with brilliant subtlety, that this marriage is still riven with tensions long after the wayward Helen has returned home with her husband. (Helen tells a self-serving story in which she seeks to present herself as a kind of pro-Greek spy, stranded behind the Trojan lines; Menelaus pointedly replies with a reminiscence of how Helen once tried to trick the Greeks hiding within the Trojan Horse into betraying their ruse.) Symonds ignores all of this—and, bizarrely, makes nothing of the fact that Helen has drugged her guests' wine with a kind of tranquilizer before the storytelling begins: not at all what you'd call "conventional."

Symonds's reading of Penelope, the long-suffering heroine of the *Odyssey*, is similarly trivializing. For him, the "central point" of Odysseus' wife is "intense love of her home, an almost cat-like attachment to the house." In her famously clever ruse—the nightly unraveling of the shroud she claims to be weaving for her father-in-law—he sees not an impressive canniness but only a pat "parable" about those "who in their weakness do and undo daily what they would fain never do at all." He fails completely to appreciate the climactic ruse by means of which Penelope tricks Odysseus into revealing his identity, which among other things demonstrates that she rivals her husband in cunning, and ends by dismissing the character as "far less fascinating than Helen." He waxes ecstatic only about Nausicaa, the virginal princess who so memorably, and with such aplomb, rescues the shipwrecked Odysseus when he washes up on her island home—"the most perfect maiden, the purest, freshest, lightest-hearted girl of Greek romance." In this appreciation, as in so many of his interpretations of Homer's women, Symonds seems trapped by a mid-Victorian fantasy that says more about his own anxieties about women—about his desire, perhaps, to encase them in manageable caricatures—than it does about the literary characters in question.

Wilde's reaction to Symonds's text reveals the same astringent rigor that characterized his attack on Jebb. He begins with an impatient scholarly complaint, criticizing Symonds's failure to include all the relevant texts in his discussion of Helen (not least, the speech by the classical sophist Isocrates known as the "Encomium of Helen"). What makes Wilde's essay really fascinating, though, are the flashes of his own distinctively sharp and original interpretative acumen.

In his discussion of Helen, Symonds had argued that a lost trilogy about her by Sophocles would have presented her as "a woman whose character deserved the most profound analysis"—an assumption wholly in keeping with the contemporary assessment of that playwright as the master of character. To this Wilde retorts, startlingly but with some justice, that "profound analysis" is not necessarily to be expected of the great Athenian dramatist, at least in the case of *Antigone*: "I hardly think that the drawing of Antigone in the play of that name justifies the expression 'profound analysis.'" And he is right: the Theban princess, while a powerful figure, is not a subtle one. *The Women of Homer* offers a number of such bracing zingers.

By far the most arresting observation that Wilde makes in his response to Symonds's catalog of Homeric women is one concerning Penelope, the character about whom Symonds shows himself to be the least perceptive. Wilde remarks on what he calls an "extremely subtle psychological point" that Homer makes about her personality, one that "shows that Homer had accurately studied the nature of women." Rather than being the placid homebody that Symonds insists she is, Penelope, Wilde understands, is in fact strangely liberated by her famous dilemma: the interminable courtship of her by the suitors during Odysseus' absence awakens and sharpens in her the very qualities that make her an ideal mate for her husband. (Symonds simply finds her acts of cunning irritating: "provocative of anger.") Those twenty years without Odysseus may have been lonely, but by the same token they place Penelope squarely at center stage. "Though his return was the consummation," Wilde writes, with a psychological insight that would be remarkable in someone much older and more experienced than an undergraduate in his early twenties, "yet it was in some way the breaking up of her life; for her occupation was gone."

Homer, if not Symonds, clearly recognizes this, giving Penelope a number of scenes that show that she is in many ways ambivalent about the suitors—whose attentions, the poet hints, she unconsciously enjoys. In Book 19, for instance, Odysseus' queen famously takes the mysterious beggar—actually Odysseus in disguise—into her confidence, telling him about a dream she has had in which a mountain eagle attacks twenty tame geese she has lovingly kept: there is no question that the geese are meant to represent the suitors, and the eagle, Odysseus. With a testiness that reminds you of his notoriously sharp-tongued contemporary, A. E. Housman—another extraordinarily talented, young, homosexual classicist, one who, in contrast to Wilde, pursued scholarship instead of notoriety—Wilde bewails the failure of Symonds and so many other contemporary critics to recognize this conflicted aspect of Penelope's character:

It is entirely misunderstood, however, by Mr Symonds and, indeed, by all other writers I have read. It shows us how great was her longing, how terrible the anguish of her soul, and it makes her final recognition of [Odysseus] doubly impressive.

Wilde's ability to discern, beneath the attitudes imposed on women by society, the sharp and surprising contours of unexpected emotions is what would make *The Importance of Being Earnest* the most original and most artistically successful of his works.

"Entirely misunderstood...by all other writers I have read." The breathtaking self-assurance of this pronouncement suggests why Wilde's long-forgotten text is intriguing, for reasons other than the glimpse it gives us of the road not taken by a significant cultural figure. The confrontation between Wilde and Symonds is, in the end, a confrontation between two eras. In Wilde's dismissal of Symonds and the rest, you can already hear not only the voice of the mature writer, blithely dismissing the intellectual and social conventions of his age, but the voice of an as yet unborn criticism, one particularly willing to question prevailing assumptions about style, canons, and gender. Like the best of his mature work, this juvenile piece seems to leapfrog forward from the late nineteenth to the late twentieth century.

———

Not the least of the twentieth-century phenomena that Wilde so uncannily anticipated was the cult of celebrity; and indeed, soon after deciding against a career as a classicist, he was making his first serious effort at courting international fame. During his 1882 tour of America, he was already showing a shrewd understanding of the uses to which that most Greek of literary forms, the epigram, might be put in the age of the telegram and the newspaper. ("His sayings are telegraphed all over the world," the *Pall Mall Gazette* bemusedly reported of Wilde's American visit.) If he invoked the Greeks at all in his American interviews—as we now know he occasionally did, thanks to *Oscar Wilde in America: The Interviews*, a recent compilation of the interviews that Wilde gave to newspapers and magazines during his year in America—it was to compliment a local poet:

> Whitman is a great writer.... There is more of the Greek residing in him than in any modern poet. His poetry is Homeric in its large pure delight of men and woman, and in the joy the writer has and shows through it all in the sunshine and breeze of outdoor life.

But as we know, it was in Wilde himself more than anyone that the Greek spirit resided. If no one today seriously wishes that Wilde had become an Oxford classics don, it's at least in part because his own "Greekness"—the deep understanding of the rhetorical uses of style, the taste for piquant syllogism, the ever-evolving aversion to sentimentality (which reached its apogee in *Earnest*), and, in the end, the tragic understanding of the meaning of suffering—made itself felt so strongly in the work he produced as a poet, writer, and dramatist.

There is, however, one unwritten text that we might legitimately covet. Reading *The Women of Homer*, it's almost impossible not to wish that we might instead possess a review of the chapter in *Studies of the Greek Poets* that was likely to have had greater personal meaning for him than did Symonds's musings on Homer's women. I refer of course to the scandalous final chapter, with Symonds's coded defense of illicit desire and rejection of conventional morality—the very subjects and positions that Wilde himself would take up so sensationally, to his credit and to his cost. But then, you could say that the whole of Oscar Wilde's life and work soon after he laid aside the unfinished essay—everything he did after abandoning Oxford for London, philology for fame—was a commentary on that unmentioned and unmentionable chapter of Symonds.

—*The New York Review of Books*, November 11, 2010

EPIC ENDEAVORS

TOWARD THE END of John Banville's new novel, *The Infinities*, a more or less contemporary tale over which the Greek gods Zeus and Hermes rather startlingly preside, a snooty character to whom someone is describing an "updated" production of a play about the parents of Hercules declares that he "does not approve of the classics being tampered with": the Greeks, he says, "knew what they were doing, after all." The joke is that the pretentious young man doesn't know what he's talking about. The play in question, *Amphitryon*—whose themes, of adultery, confused identities, and improbable Olympian interventions, are threaded through Banville's novel—isn't Greek at all. Rather, it's an early-nineteenth-century German reworking of late-seventeenth-century French and English rewritings of a second-century-BC tragicomedy written in Latin. And that was just then. In the twentieth century alone, the Amphitryon myth has been adapted by a French novelist, two German playwrights, an opera composer, an anti-Nazi filmmaker, and Cole Porter. Have we ever done anything *but* tamper with the classics?

No one, as it happens, tampered more than the Greeks themselves. Shaped as we are by printed literature, we tend to think about myths the way we think about novels—as narratives whose plots and characters and incidents are fixed, as stories whose shape is as immutable as that of, say, *Anna Karenina*. In the same way that, when we hear someone mention Anna Karenina, we think of the woman whose unhappiness leads her to the underside of a railway carriage, when we hear the Oedipus myth mentioned we think of a particular story about the unlucky man who unwittingly kills his father and marries his mother, and about the awful aftermath of the revelation of incest and parricide—how he blinds and then exiles himself, how she hangs herself over her grotesque marriage bed. If the name Helen of Troy comes up, we think of the adulterous Greek wife whose passion for a handsome houseguest started a world war.

But for the Greeks—whose culture was, even in classical times, still a largely oral one—myth was a great deal more fluid. Not twenty years after Sophocles put on his *Oedipus Tyrannus*—whose huge popularity from ancient times on has crystallized the self-blinding-exile-hanging version of the story—Euripides presented his tragedy *Phoenician Women*, in which Oedipus and Jocasta are still shuffling around the palace long after the revelation of incest and adultery. In the same dramatist's lost *Oedipus,* of which only fragments remain, the Theban king's blindness is not self-inflicted at the climax of the play but the result of an injury inflicted during that initial, fatal encounter with his father. As for Helen of Troy, some people may be startled to learn that she might not have run away with Paris at all— and that, therefore, the decade-long Trojan War, like certain other wars, was based on a fatal hoax. In his play *Helen*, Euripides dramatized a tale that had been in circulation since not long after Homer: in it, the woman whom Paris takes home is just a phantom spun from clouds, while the real Helen, virtuous and loyal, is spirited away to

Egypt. There she weeps for her sullied reputation and mourns her husband, Menelaus, who eventually turns up and rescues her.

To us, brought up on *D'Aulaires' Book of Greek Myths*, all this may seem odd. It's as if Tolstoy's novel were only one of many possible *Anna Karenina*s, and there was a version in which the heroine acts on her final, panicked moment of hesitation, climbs back from underneath the train in the nick of time, and goes home to squabble with Karenin. But the Greeks had no *Book of Greek Myths*; they just kept tampering. They knew what they were doing, after all.

As it happens, Banville's book is one of three recent novels that, to varying degrees, not only "do" the Greeks—his features Greek gods as main characters, while David Malouf's *Ransom* is based on a climactic episode of the *Iliad* and Zack Mason's *The Lost Books of the Odyssey* invents forty-four new chapters for that epic—but, far more interestingly, do the Greek thing: play with the texts of the past in order to create, with varying degrees of success, a literature that is thoroughly of the present.

By far the most profound and successful of these is Malouf's. The novel is a riff on the twenty-fourth (and final) book of the *Iliad*—the book whose climax is the tense and poignant meeting between the Greek hero Achilles and the aged Trojan king Priam, who comes to the Greek camp in order to ransom the body of his fallen son, Hector.

Like Euripides, Malouf has scrutinized the vast fabric of Homer's story, looking for open spaces in the weave to insert his own design; he has found one in the last lines of the epic. Here, during the already extraordinary encounter between the Greek and the Trojan—the two sides have, after all, been killing each other all through the previous twenty-three books—a remarkable thing happens: one of the characters tries to imagine an alternative to the foreordained plot of the poem, to step outside, as it were, his own narrative. Priam and Achilles have been sketching the details of a truce that will give the Trojans time to mourn and bury Hector, and decide that eleven days is sufficient. "On the twelfth," Homer's Priam says, "we'll fight again...if fight we must." That "if we must"—pregnant with the tantalizing, wishful possibility that the two sides might not have to fight anymore, that we can break out of character and create a new history—is the subject of Malouf's subtle and extremely moving novel.

Ransom taps the enormous emotional energies unleashed at the end of Homer's poem, which, in its final book, enacts a great drama of restitution and resolution. At the beginning of the *Iliad*, the Greek commander Agamemnon steals a captured princess, part of the spoils of war, from Achilles. The affront provokes the great warrior to sit out the fighting—until his beloved friend, Patroclus, is killed by Hector. Returning to the field, he kills Hector in single combat and, in an outrageous violation of religious propriety and a severe affront to divine sensibilities, refuses to give back the body for proper burial; instead, he lashes it to his chariot and drags it back and forth before the walls of Troy as the dead man's anguished family and people look on. Offended, the gods intervene, ordering Achilles to relent and Priam to go to the Greek camp and offer Achilles a huge treasure as ransom for the body of his son. It is at this point that Malouf picks up the story.

Priam, whose name, as Malouf reveals in an ingenious bit of flashback, could be taken as meaning "ransom"—as a young prince, he had been a prisoner of war, ultimately ransomed (*priatos*) as a favor to his sister—obeys this divine order, and travels to the Greek camp. His eventual return to Troy with Hector's body (the point at which Malouf's narrative ends) precipitates a great outpouring of lamentation on the part of the Trojans that, we are meant to feel, will serve not only as an appropriately cathartic ending but also as their own funeral lament, since Troy itself will soon fall. Thus the work that begins with a man refusing to give up a body—Agamemnon won't return the captive girl—ends with another man, Achilles, finally agreeing to give up a body that doesn't belong to him, either. The epic travels a great arc from selfishness and ethical rigidity to a magnificent relenting.

The plot of *Ransom* is, for the most part, the plot of Homer's Book 24: Malouf deftly covers Achilles' grief-driven rage, the uncanny epiphany of the divine messenger Iris, which inspires Priam's supplicatory embassy, the trip across the plain to the Greek camp with his herald (where the two old men are accosted by Hermes, who has been sent to protect them while they're in enemy territory), the fraught meeting with Achilles and then the return home in a cart that has exchanged its treasures for a single body. The book's only significant weakness is that Malouf, the novelist focusing on a single book of Homer, has to cover twenty-three books' worth of exposition in a handful of rather breathless and unstylish pages. One great advantage of epic, of course, is the leisure provided by length.

On the surface, at least, these episodes constitute inventive paraphrases of Homer, embroidered with lovely imaginative details that often reanimate some familiar elements of the epic. Homer's Hecuba, the mother of the dead Hector, famously and rather shockingly wishes that she could eat Achilles' liver raw, if she only had the chance; Malouf's Hecuba expresses pretty much the same wish, but with an additional, modern consideration. "I carried him," she hisses at her husband, as the couple discuss Priam's planned mission. "It is *my* flesh that is being tumbled on the stones out there." And this is what Malouf does with the divine appearances that happen so often in Homer: "The air, as in the wake of some other, less physical disturbance, shimmers with a teasing iridescence," muses a drowsy Priam, who in Malouf's novel is a hieratic figure prone to divine visitations when he dozes. "The gods will materialise, jelly-like, out of the radiant vacancy." "Jelly-like" is a wonderful touch, giving this mythic scene a novel concreteness.

"Novel" is, indeed, the operative word here. Ultimately, *Ransom*'s tampering with the *Iliad* is the vehicle for a rich meditation on literary genre—on the difference between Homer's form, the epic, with its encrustations of formulaic language, its strict codes of heroic behavior, and its fated ending, and Malouf's own form, the novel. In *Ransom*, the stiff and glittering ceremonial life by which both Priam and Achilles, in their different ways, are constrained—the former by the trappings of a monarch, the latter by the codes of honor that govern the hero's life and actions—becomes a kind of symbol for epic itself. Here is Malouf's Priam thinking about his long life of ceremony:

> In his own world a man spoke only to give shape to a decision he had come to, or to lay out an argument for or against. To offer thanks to one who had done well, or a reproof, either in anger or gentle regret, to one who had not. To pay a compliment whose decorative phrases, and appeals to vanity or family pride, were fixed and of ancient and approved form.

This is the world of Homer's poems, too, a world governed by conventions that, at the beginning of the novel, neither Priam, in his passive grief, nor Achilles, whose maniacal back-and-forthing before the city walls symbolizes his endless, fruitless rage, knows how to break out of. "This knot we are all tied in" is how Malouf's Priam describes the impasse.

For Malouf, the solution to this epic problem is, in both senses of the word, the novel—a new way of thinking, and a new form for thinking it. In his retelling, Zeus' messenger Iris doesn't order Priam to go to Achilles; rather, she subtly suggests that Priam is free to act as he likes, that things are not foreordained but simply "the way they *are.* Not the way they must be, but the way they have turned out. In a world that is also subject to chance." It is at this moment that Priam has the idea of going to Achilles not as a king but as a father, "to take on the lighter bond of being simply a man"; he suspects, correctly, that Achilles will be just as happy to "break free of the obligation of being always the hero." In a marvelous aside, Priam wonders whether this relaxation of coded behavior may in fact be "the real gift" that he will be bringing to Achilles—the real ransom.

Priam gets to sample his newfound freedom during his journey across the plain to the Greek camp, in a simple cart and with only one humble companion: an episode that is brief enough in Homer, but here opens out into a mini-*Odyssey*, in which the king, for the first and last time in his life, experiences the pleasures of an existence that didn't become the focus of serious literature until the rise of the novel, more than two millennia after Homer: the life of ordinary people. Accompanied, in this version, not by his royal herald Idreus, as in Homer, but by a talkative carter named Somax (an appropriately concrete name: *soma* is the Greek word for body), Priam wiggles his hot toes in cold water, learns how pancakes are made ("The lightness comes from the way the cook flips them over. Very neat and quick you have to be," Somax advises the king of Troy), and sees that the world "of ceremony, of high play" to which he has always belonged is merely "representational . . . and had nothing to do with the actual and immediate." Only during his fateful, novelty-filled and novel journey does he realize that "out here," in the real world—which is to say, in the new narrative space that Malouf's novel invents—"everything was just itself."

The pathos of Malouf's novel, as in that one half-line of Homer's *Iliad*, is that the possibility of a different ending, of a life filled with simple pleasures, is and must always be a fleeting one: the end of *Ransom* includes a terrifying flash-forward to the grotesque murder of the aged Priam at the hands of Achilles' young son, Neoptolemus, during the sack of Troy. But for the duration of this book Malouf's Priam, like his creator, has done something truly novel. "He has stepped into a space that till now was uninhabited and found a way to fill it," he thinks as he drives his son's body home. "Look, he wants to shout, I am still here, but the *I* is different." So is your sense of the possibilities of Homer's story, once you've read Malouf. This is tampering at its very best.

The coda of *Ransom* informs you that Somax, long after the Trojan War is over, goes on telling the tale of Priam's remarkable journey to anyone who will listen—becoming, that is, the first of many bards in a long line that leads to Homer. This preoccupation with how history becomes myth, how stories become epics, is a very Greek one, and lies at the heart of the other Homeric epic, which furnishes the material for Zachary Mason's *The Lost Books of the Odyssey*.

The first adjective in the first line of the 12,109 that make up the *Odyssey* is *polytropos*, which means, in the context, "clever"—literally, "of many turns." Both are apt modifiers for the poem's hero, who is subject to many detours and is also notorious for his intellectual and verbal twistiness—he's the preeminent talker, fibber, and plotter of Greek myth, the man who dreamed up the Trojan Horse and survived his decade-long journey home from Troy by employing an impressive and sometimes disturbing array of lies, disguises, traps, and tricks. If the *Iliad*, set during a war, keeps showing us men's bodies, either in frenzied action or stilled by death, and anxiously wrestles with the values that compel those men to act and to die, the *Odyssey*, set in war's aftermath, can be described as a poem about the mind—a celebration of the intellectual and verbal qualities that we might need to survive in a world uneasily settling back into the forgotten habits of peacetime.

One quality of mind that the *Odyssey* admires extravagantly is the ability to tell a good story. (Whether the story is true or false is a question that preoccupies this poem, which in different ways keeps worrying about what is, in the end, a philosophical question: just how you can know whether something is true—the tale told by a total stranger, the protests of a wife who claims to be faithful.) It's sometimes easy to forget that nearly all the famous adventures we associate with Odysseus—the encounters with the Cyclops, the witch Calypso, Scylla and Charybdis, the Lotus-Eaters—are narrated not by the poem's invisible narrator, the "I" who invokes the Muse in the first line, but by Odysseus himself, about himself. At a certain point in his voyage, he finds himself on an island inhabited by refined, pleasure-loving natives called the Phaeacians, and, one night over dinner, he tells them the story of his homecoming thus far. This takes up four entire books of Homer's poem.

Another way of saying this is that much of the *Odyssey* is a kind of epic performance within the epic, a long flashback in which the poet and the hero are one and the same person. (It is no coincidence that both bards and archers—Odysseus is a renowned bowman, too—need a stringed instrument to perform.) This self-conscious interest in narrative gamesmanship and in the nature of storytelling gives Mason the modishly postmodern theme of his book, the preface of which tells us that the chapters that follow are translations of newly discovered sections of the Odysseus cycle: "forty-four concise variations on Odysseus' story...where the familiar characters are arranged in new tableaux."

So, for example, the first such tableau ("A Sad Revelation") consists of a three-page-long variation on the epic's famous ending: here Odysseus returns home to a Penelope who waited only twelve years, instead of the canonical twenty, before marrying a man who has been courting her. The moment the hero understands what has happened, he tells himself that "this is not Penelope...this is not Ithaca—what he sees before him is a vengeful illusion." Odysseus turns and "flees the tormenting shadows," presumably en route to further wandering. Many of these tiny chapters riff Tennyson's famous idea that Odysseus' long-awaited homecoming and, afterward, life back home end up boring the hero; many, if not most, have the gnomic, abbreviated feel of this one. If Homer's *Odyssey* is expansive, Mason's odysseys are studies in compression, but brevity brings many of them close to triviality: too often the sections end with inconclusive teases ("Also not recorded is whether Odysseus had poisoned the ring or whether he had found the word and it sufficed") or with riddles to which, you suspect, the author himself doesn't have an answer.

Some chapters, however, are extremely inventive and suggestive— "clever" in a good way. "Record of a Game" imagines that the *Iliad* is a text that began as a chess primer:

> The purity of the primer eroded over time—formulaic descriptions were added as *aides-mémoire* (pieces were called swift-moving, versatile, valuable in the middle game, and so forth)....
> By the eighth century BC the instructional character of the primer had largely atrophied and the recitation of the by then baroquely ornamented text had become an end in itself.

A terrific little chapter called "The Book of Winter" similarly thinks both inside and outside the *Odyssey*'s narrative: here, an amnesiac living in a hut at the frozen edges of the world realizes, after reading a book that turns out to be the *Odyssey* ("I wonder what the book was meant to tell me. The allegorical possibilities are many..."), that he is Odysseus—an Odysseus who has managed to pull off his greatest trick yet. For in order to escape the wrath of Poseidon (whose harassment is the reason for Odysseus' long wanderings), he has forgotten who he is and become "no one." As readers of the *Odyssey* know, No One is the false name Odysseus assumes in order to trick the Cyclops: when the Cyclops's neighbors come to help after Odysseus has blinded him, he keeps saying "No One has attacked me," at which point they go away. One way of saying "no one" in classical Greek—*outis*—sounds enough like "Odysseus" to constitute a kind of pun; another way, *mê tis*, is a precise homophone of *mêtis*, the word for intellectual resourcefulness. During his long anonymous homecoming Odysseus has indeed been "no one"—just as he has also always been "the resourceful one."

But these sustained, really ingenious variations on Homeric themes are too few and far between; for the most part, *The Lost Books of the Odyssey* leaves you unsatisfied, like a meal of hors d'oeuvres. As you go through the book, it occurs to you that Mason thinks he's doing what Malouf has managed to do—opening a space in the original epic and finding something new to say. The newness that interests him has to do with what academics call "narrativity." One chapter, entitled "Fragment," consists of a single paragraph:

> Odysseus, finding that his reputation for trickery preceded him, started inventing histories for himself and disseminating them wherever he went. This had the intended effect of clouding perception and distorting expectation, making it easier for him to work as he was wont, and the unexpected effect that one of his lies became, with minor variations, the *Odyssey* of Homer.

The author's suggestion that the *Odyssey* itself is just one reflecting surface in a giant literary hall of mirrors has won the book extravagant praise; it feels like such a contemporary conceit, something out of Borges or Calvino.

The problem is that the narrative conjuring tricks that Mason attempts pale, in both scale and complexity, beside the ones that Homer mastered three millennia ago. The *Odyssey* constantly toys with the possibility that it is just one of a number of alternative epics: at one point, a bard at a feast starts singing a kind of parallel *Iliad*, in which Achilles quarrels not with Agamemnon but with Odysseus. (Some scholars, moreover, have wondered whether the song the Sirens sing is not, in fact, the *Iliad*.) Even more dizzyingly—and troublingly—Homer's poem makes you wonder whether there's any more reason for us to "believe" the stories that Odysseus tells his Phaeacian audience (about the Cyclops, the Lotus-Eaters, and so on) than there is to believe certain other long yarns that he spins. Once he's back in Ithaca, for instance, he poses as a Cretan and tells three notoriously elaborate autobiographical stories, all of which contain elements from what we think of as his "real" life. It's at this point that you start to wonder what words like "real" and "true" mean in a work that is itself a fiction.

Yet playful as the *Odyssey* is, it is always serious. At the heart of its narrative Russian dolls and suggestive punning is a profound, ongoing exploration of identity: What does it mean, after all, if your cleverness, the trick that at once defines you and that you need to stay alive, reduces you to being "no one"? At the end of the *Odyssey*, you get the answers to questions that start forming in the first line, the first word of which is *andra*, "man": to be a man, a human being, wildly inventive and creative but inevitably subject to dreadful forces beyond our control—which is to say, death—is to be something wonderful and, at the same time, nothing. The clever games that the *Odyssey* plays are, in the end, games worth playing. Mason's book is merely jokey—too clever by half.

Both the *Iliad* and the *Odyssey* wrestle with paradoxes of life and death, mortality and immortality. Achilles is willing to die young if

it means winning undying renown; Odysseus will do almost anything to survive his journey, but when he's offered immortality by the
amorous nymph Calypso, he rejects her in favor of returning home to
the aging Penelope—surely the greatest and most moving tribute that
any marriage has ever received in literature. The allure of immortality and the competing rewards of a humble human life are the themes
that animate John Banville's *The Infinities*, which, like the novels by
Malouf and Mason, has things to tell us about the act of adaptation.

The myth that Banville adapts is that of the Theban king Amphitryon (a story that the author already engaged with a decade ago,
when he produced an adaptation of Heinrich von Kleist's *Amphitryon*). In the story, Amphitryon goes off to war and, while he's away,
Zeus assumes his form and seduces his unsuspecting wife, Alcmena.
The confusion of identities leads to often hilarious theatrical and
philosophical complications and, ultimately, to the birth of twin children, one of whom is Hercules. The novel, like its model, not only
toys with genres—it starts out as a deathbed drama and ends with a
surprising deus ex machina—but also wrestles with deeper questions. Chief among these is the paradox that human creativity (and
procreativity) seeks to attain a kind of immortality—"infinity"; and
yet mortality, the knowledge that we are finite, is what gives beauty
and meaning to life. The existence of the Greek gods, "immortal and
ageless," might, you suspect, be pretty boring, in the end.

The title *The Infinities* refers to a revolutionary theory promul-
gated by the novel's main character, an eminent mathematician with
the heavily symbolic name Adam Godley, whose work has somehow
unlocked the key to infinity and made it possible "to write equations
across the many worlds, incorporating their infinities...and therefore all those other dimensions." Not the least of these dimensions is,
it seems, death itself: when the book begins, Godley has suffered a
colossal stroke, and the plot follows his family during what seems

likely to be his last day on earth. There's his much younger, hard-drinking wife, Ursula; his son, also called Adam; his daughter-in-law, Helen, an actress, who, like the mythical Alcmena, is unwittingly carrying on an affair with Zeus; and Godley's tormented daughter, Petra, whose boyfriend is the pretentious know-it-all who doesn't recognize the plot of *Amphitryon* even when he's in it.

The infinities that Banville unleashes have startling and provocative implications. Among other things, you come to realize that the world of the novel is not our own world but one of the parallel possible worlds to which Godley's discovery has provided the key. Here Mary, Queen of Scots triumphed against Elizabeth I, Scandinavia is a Middle East–like political mess plagued by endless wars, and energy is derived from saltwater. And, of course, the Greek gods are real—a nice thought since, as the narrator, who happens to be Hermes, reminds us, "we offer you no salvation of the soul, but no damnation, either." These gods envy humans and yearn for mortality, which they attempt to taste by means of "intercourse" both literal and figurative. Such premises give Banville a useful vehicle for his themes of mortality, creativity, and the possibility of making something truly new in a world that seems increasingly exhausted morally, politically, and spiritually.

And yet the book lacks a certain urgency. As often with this author—not least in his highly overwrought *The Sea*, which won the Man Booker Prize—the conceits, the symbolic names, and the ostentatiously "lyrical" diction are striking, but too often you feel that the author is simply amusing himself, swatting, like a cat at tinsel, at notions that have caught his eye. Somehow, it doesn't add up. (The shocking dramatic climax of *The Sea*—a book in which Banville, or at least the excessively gloomy narrator who has "a fair knowledge of the Greek myths," is already thinking of "the possibility of the gods"—is almost totally inorganic, constructed.) By the end, it's hard not to think that Banville himself has fallen into an error that his fictional Hermes observes in Adam Godley: "the peril of confusing the expression of something with the something itself."

About one thing *The Infinities* is not in the least confused: lurking within it is the sly acknowledgment of a fact that has been clear to authors, if not to mathematicians, since that day, three millennia ago, when a blind itinerant singer tampered with some old heroic lays and turned them into the *Iliad*. Literature, like the universe that Godley reveals, has always been a series of endless tamperings, "an infinity of infinities... all crossing and breaking into each other, all here and invisible, a complex of worlds." However flawed or successful Banville's novel and its fellows may be, the mere existence of these proliferating adaptations points, once again, to the inexhaustible, indeed seemingly infinite potential of the classics themselves.

—*The New Yorker*, April 4, 2010

III. CREATIVE WRITING

AFTER WATERLOO

WHAT NOVEL COULD be so essential that even the dead feel compelled to know what it's about? At the beginning of Jean Giraudoux's *Bella* (1926), the narrator, attending a memorial service for schoolmates who fell in the trenches of World War I, begins to hear the voices of his dead comrades. For the most part, they talk about mundane, soldierly things: the discomforts of war, annoying commanding officers. But the last voice the narrator hears is different—it's the voice of a young man tormented by the thought that he'd never had a chance to read a certain seventy-five-year-old novel. What the dead youth wants is for the narrator to summarize the book "in a word." In a word, because "with the dead, there are no sentences."

The book in question is Stendhal's *Charterhouse of Parma*, an epic and yet intimate tale of political intrigue and erotic frustration, set in the (largely fictionalized) princely court of Parma during the author's own time. Almost since the moment it appeared, in 1839, Stendhal's last completed work of fiction has been considered a masterpiece. Barely a year after the book was published, Balzac praised it in a lengthy review that immediately established the novel's reputation. "One sees perfection in everything" was just one of the laurels Balzac heaped on *Charterhouse*, in what was surely one of the world's great acts of literary generosity. Sixty years after Balzac, André Gide ranked *Charterhouse* among the greatest of all French novels, and one of only two French works that could be counted among the top ten of world literature. (The other was *Les Liaisons Dangereuses*.) The encomia weren't restricted to France—or, for that matter, to Europe. In an 1874 article for *The Nation*, Henry James found *Charterhouse* to be "among the dozen finest novels we possess."

At first glance, the bare bones of Stendhal's story suggest not so much a literary masterpiece as a historical soap opera. The novel recounts the headstrong young Italian aristocrat Fabrice del Dongo's attempt to make a coherent life for himself, first as a soldier in Napoleon's army and then, more cynically, as a prelate in the Roman Catholic Church; the attempts of his beautiful aunt Gina, Duchess of Sanseverina, and her lover, the wily (and married) prime minister, Count Mosca, to help establish Fabrice at court, even as Gina tries to fend off the advances of the repellent (and repellently named) Prince Ranuce-Erneste IV; Fabrice's imprisonment in the dreaded Farnese Tower for the murder of a girlfriend's protector, and his subsequent escape with the help of a very long rope; and his star-crossed but ultimately redemptive love affair with his jailer's beautiful (and, it must be said, rather dull) daughter, Clelia.

So what, exactly, makes all this so indispensible to Giraudoux's soldier? Why, in the words of one contemporary Stendhal scholar, does *Charterhouse* exhale "some incomparable air of which every human being needs absolutely to have taken at least one breath before they die"?

As it happens, we're now almost exactly as far from Giraudoux's novel as Giraudoux's characters were from the publication of Stendhal's; a good time, perhaps, to consider the question raised by that strange scene in *Bella*. More important, the superior new translation of *Charterhouse* by the distinguished American poet and translator Richard Howard makes it possible not only to breathe once again that incomparable air but, as good translations always do, to grasp fully its peculiar qualities, to understand why the experience of reading this work is so famously "rapturous," and why the novel itself continues to be so fresh and sustaining.

"Fresh" is the key word here. On November 4, 1838, Stendhal (the most famous of more than two hundred pseudonyms used by Marie-Henri Beyle, a Grenoble-born career diplomat and lover of all things Italian) sat down at his desk at 8, rue Caumartin in Paris, gave orders that he was not to be disturbed under any circumstances, and began dictating a novel. The manuscript of *Charterhouse* was finished seven weeks later, on the day after Christmas—an impressive feat, when you think that a typical French edition runs to five hundred pages. The swiftness of its composition is reflected in the narrative briskness for which it is so well known—the "gusto, brio, elan, verve, panache" of which Howard is rightly conscious in his translation—and, as even die-hard partisans of the novel would have to admit, in passages where compositional speed clearly took a toll in narrative coherence. ("We have forgotten to mention in its proper place the fact that the duchess had taken a house at Belgirate.")

The idea for the book had actually been rattling around in Stendhal's head for some time. His Roman diaries of the late 1820s are crammed with lengthy references to the convoluted histories of the Italian Renaissance nobility, a favorite subject and the basis for a series of short tales he published in the mid-1830s as *Chroniques italiennes*. The lineaments of *Charterhouse* owe a great deal to a seventeenth-century chronicle of the life of Alessandro Farnese, later Pope Paul

III, that Stendhal came across during the course of his Italian travels. (Farnese, who became pope in 1534, had a beautiful aunt, Vandozza Farnese, the mistress of the cunning Rodrigo Borgia; murdered a young woman's servant; was imprisoned in the Castel Sant'Angelo; escaped by means of a very long rope; and maintained as his mistress a well-born woman called Cleria.) So while the extraordinary speed of the novel's composition can be attributed to an almost supernatural flash of inspiration, it can also be seen as the more natural outcome of a long and deliberate process that had finally achieved fruition.

Like the circumstances of its creation, the finished novel seems at once spontaneous and premeditated. The quick pace of the narrative and the vividness of the characters are balanced throughout by a coolly sardonic assessment of human nature and, in particular, of politics. Stendhal, a lifelong liberal who as an idealistic young man had followed Napoleon into Italy, Austria, and Russia, found himself living at a time of almost unprecedented political cynicism in post-Restoration France. Disgust with the bourgeois complacency of his countrymen played no little part in his admiration for the Italians, whom he considered to be more authentic—"more profound and more susceptible to violent emotions," as he wrote in his diary. To Howard's credit, both the Italian passion and the French worldliness are evident here; but it is the novel's distinctive impetuousness and forward momentum, the qualities that so famously make it such a good read, that are fully captured here, perhaps for the first time, in English. (Howard himself finished the translation in twenty-eight weeks—one week per chapter—a feat only slightly less miraculous than Stendhal's.)

But the appeal of *Charterhouse* is more than just a matter of its urgent, even impatient style ("Here we shall ask permission to pass, without saying a single word about them, over an interval of three years"). It lies, too, in the vibrant characters, who are prey to unruly emotions that will be familiar to contemporary readers. There is, to begin with, the novel's ostensible hero, the impetuous young Fabrice, who as a teenager, when the action begins, disobeys his right-wing father and sneaks off to fight for Napoleon. What is most resonant for contemporary readers isn't Fabrice's starry-eyed idealism—which is, after all, endemic among protagonists of Romantic novels, and which, in any case, is constantly belied by the hard and occasionally farcical realities of lived life (an exhausted and slightly hungover Fabrice sleeps through much of Waterloo)—but the decidedly more modern, and even postmodern, way in which a sense of authenticity keeps eluding him.

This more than anything, you suspect, is what keeps *Charter-house* alive for each generation. Like so many of us, Fabrice is always measuring his life against the poems and novels he has read. (At Waterloo, he thinks of the "fine dreams of sublime and knightly comradeship" he learned from studying Tasso.) With a self-consciousness more typical of the late twentieth than the early nineteenth century, he keeps checking up on himself, as if trying to conform to some hidden master plan for being, or for loving—a plan that, as the novel tragically demonstrates, he is never quite able to follow. No wonder he so often expresses himself in the interrogative: "Had what he'd seen been a battle?... Had this battle been Waterloo?" "Am I such a hypocrite?" "What about a minor affair here in Parma?" One ironic measure of Fabrice's inability to master the art of living as a free man is that he finds true happiness only in the womblike security of his prison cell in the Farnese Tower (as many critics have noted, he's jailed for exactly nine months), from which he is loath to escape after he falls in love with Clelia—an affair, appropriately enough for a character obsessed with astrological signs and prophecies and hidden symbols, that is conducted at first exclusively through hand signals.

Fabrice is hardly the only vivid and oddly contemporary character here; you could easily argue—many have—that the real heroes are his aunt and her lover. Master political and social puppeteers, they are far more complicated and interesting than the young man they spend so much time trying, in vain, to establish in an adult life—even as, with Laclos-like sangfroid, they try to stage-manage some contentment of their own. (Mosca to Gina: "We might find a new and not unaccommodating husband. But first of all, he would have to be extremely advanced in years, for why should you deny me the hope of eventually replacing him?") This is one reason why *Charterhouse* tends to appeal to our maturity, whereas Stendhal's 1830 masterpiece, *The Red and the Black*, with its endlessly striving, morally casual young antihero, appeals to our youth.

Gina, in particular, is one of the great creations of the nineteenth-century novelistic imagination: brilliant, flirtatious, cunning, vulnerable, passionate, extraordinarily self-aware, and yet helplessly the prey of a forbidden passion for her beautiful nephew. We first meet her at the age of thirteen, trying to stifle a giggle at the ragged appearance of a Napoleonic officer who's been billeted in her brother's opulent palace (the Frenchman, Stendhal hints, is Fabrice's natural father), and from that moment we're never quite able to take our eyes off this woman who, despite her exalted social position and the Racinian dilemma she finds herself in, is never less than fully, sometimes comically, human. ("Will you for once behave like a man with a brain?" she writes to an admirer.) Mosca, too, who in the perfect, inevitable geometry of unrequited love hopelessly adores Gina in a way he knows will never be reciprocated, is an intricate creation, complex and conflicted in his public as well as his private life (we're told that this leader of the ultraconservative party started out, like his creator, as a Bonapartist) and the victim of erotic passions that grip him, in Stendhal's vivid locution, "like a cramp."

The novel's headlong narrative momentum, and the refreshingly real emotions of its acutely self-conscious characters, are clearly the work of a man who, like his young hero, rebelled in his youth against his stultifyingly conventional family, a man who wanted to be known as an artist and lover of women. (Stendhal's epitaph, in Italian, which he composed while still in his thirties, reads: "He lived. He wrote. He loved.") But *Charterhouse* is just as much the work of a seasoned diplomat only too familiar with the compromises that adult life imposes. The author's older voice comes through in the fate he chooses for his characters: by the end of the book Fabrice, solitary in the religious retreat to which the book's title refers, has died, still very young, having inadvertently caused the deaths of both Clelia (by now married off to another man) and their illegitimate child, the victims of a harebrained kidnapping plot gone horribly wrong; Gina follows him to the grave not long after. Only Mosca, the sole character who governs his passions successfully, survives.

So, like its creator, the novel is part Fabrice and part Mosca. Or, to put it another way, it contains the best qualities of its contemporary French rivals: it has the headlong plottiness of Balzac, complete with assassinations, forged papers, disguises, and politically motivated self-prostitutions, and also the elaborate, almost glacial self-consciousness of Flaubert. In other words, it's got something for everyone.

None of the English versions of *Charterhouse* currently available is inadequate—least of all that of C.K. Scott-Moncrieff, the great translator of Proust, whose 1925 version was the Modern Library's predecessor to the new edition and is still remarkably readable. But because language itself changes, even the best renderings of any work stop sounding modern after a while; and precisely because of its narrative momentum and the contemporary-seeming predicaments of its characters, *Charterhouse* needs to sound modern. This, Howard's translation does. First and most important, it moves with admirable rapidity, fully conveying what James called the "restlessness" of Stendhal's "superior mind" by means of a number of subtle but quite concrete choices on Howard's part, not least of which is his rendering of French verbs more crisply and colloquially than has been done before. (In the great Waterloo scene, for instance, Stendhal's *sabrer* becomes "cut down," which is better and faster than Margaret Mauldon's long-winded "killed by a saber-cut" in the 1997 Oxford Classics version and yet more natural than Scott-Moncrieff's "sabred.")

Accuracy, however, is never sacrificed; this *Charterhouse* is filled with small and ingenious grace notes that are just right, and that you suspect Howard had a lot of fun working out. When Marshal Ney reprimands a subordinate at Waterloo, he "chews him out"—a rendering that, for once, gives the sense of the French verb *gourmander*, which can mean, as it does here, "to reprimand," while wittily capitalizing, with just the right masticatory note, on its resemblance to "gourmand." (In other renderings this is either under- or overtranslated, from the blah "telling off" in Mauldon to the nonsensically literal "chewing up" in Scott-Moncrieff to the rather overbearingly Julia Childesque "making mincemeat out of" in Margaret Shaw's 1958 Penguin Classics version.) My one reservation concerns Howard's decision to give the Italian versions of the names instead of the French—Fabrizio instead of the text's Fabrice, for instance—which obscures the important narrative conceit that this whole tale is one we're hearing from a Frenchman who has, in turn, heard it from Italians who knew the principals. It is a book about Italians, but one seen through French eyes.

Howard's briskness and wit serve just as well in conveying the other side of *Charterhouse*: the very French manner that Proust referred to as Stendhal's "Voltairean," "eighteenth-century style of irony." At the novel's opening, Stendhal makes a passing but pointed reference to the fate of a group of 150 liberals illegally imprisoned by the conservative faction to which Fabrice's father belongs: "Soon they were deported to the bocche di Cattaro, where, flung into underground caves, humidity and especially lack of bread rendered a summary justice." Earlier translations show how easy it is to flub the small but pointed wit here. Mary Loyd's 1901 version—"where damp and, especially, starvation wreaked prompt and thorough justice"—misses the joke altogether, steamrolling Stendhal's deliciously dry and oblique "lack of bread" and indignantly overtranslating the word that Howard more properly and dryly gives as "rendered."

Howard understands that Stendhal's style is inextricable from his substance—the speed from the passion, the irony from the worldliness—and so he gives you Stendhal's style whole, with no touching up. Reread Howard's translation of the line about the murdered liberals; at first glance you'd think it was the humidity and lack of bread that were flung into the bocche di Cattaro. Rightly, Howard reproduces the feel of Stendhal's French, even at the price of the occasional syntactical clunker. Balzac, hardly the most polished of stylists, complained about Stendhal's sloppy grammar, a fault about which the latter was deliciously unapologetic, preferring as he did a conversational naturalness and ease to the geometric perfections of *le siècle classique*. In the very first entry in his journals, dated April 18, 1801, when the author was eighteen, he makes a mistake, but displays a nonchalance on the subject of grammar that will provide retroactive vindication to anyone who struggled through the pluperfect subjunctive in eleventh grade: "There will be a lot more, because I'm making it a rule not to stand on ceremony and never to erase."

Public ceremonies alternating with private mistakes; battles with banquets; stateliness with speed, epic scope with journalistic detail; loves unrequited and passions disastrously indulged; idealism and cynicism; the giddy heedlessness of self-satisfied youth and the sad wisdoms of old age; the minutes you remember in detail and the three-year chunks you completely forget. The grandeur and the messiness, the magnificence and the mistakes. No wonder Giraudoux's young infantryman felt he had to know *Charterhouse*. What else would the dead want but what you find so much of in this novel— and in this new translation more than ever before—which is, in a word, life?

—*The New York Times Book Review*, August 29, 1999

HEROINE ADDICT

WHATEVER OTHERS MAY have thought of the novels of Theodor Fontane—and the long-standing consensus is that they are, as one scholar of German literature has noted, "the most completely achieved of any written between Goethe and Thomas Mann"—Fontane himself clearly thought that they were pretty unexciting. To his mind, *L'Adultera* (1882), one of the studies of tormented heroines on which his present-day reputation rests, was primarily about "the circumstantial and the scenery." He characterized *The Poggenpuhls* (1896), the story of an aristocratic family frantically maneuvering to extract itself from genteel poverty, as a book that "is not a novel and has no subject-matter." In May 1898, a few months before he died, at the age of seventy-eight, he wrote a letter rather wearily describing *The Stechlin*, the unusually "pudgy" tome (most of his fiction is bracingly short) that was the last work he lived to see published:

An old man dies and two young people get married,—that is just about all that happens in 500 pages. Of complications and solutions, of conflicts of the heart and conflicts in general, of excitement and surprises there is virtually nothing.... Naturally I don't claim that this is the best way of writing a contemporary novel but it is the one that is called for.

Even Fontane's characters are plagued by a certain anxiety about having nothing very exciting to talk about. In *Cécile* (1887), a novel about a good woman trying in vain to bury a bad past, a group of tourists in the Harz Mountains are taken around a medieval castle; unnerved by a visitor's embarrassment that there's not much to look at, the tour guide "rapidly resumed his lecture in the hope of compensating by narrative skill for the lack of visible items of interest."

Compensating by narrative skill for the lack of visible interest is an excellent way to sum up both the strangeness and the beauty of Fontane's fiction. The topography of his plots is, for the most part, as flat and monotonous as the notoriously bland landscape of his Prussian homeland, Brandenburg (about which he lovingly wrote in a multivolume work). Most of *Cécile* is devoted to the excursions and the chitchat of those hapless tourists. There's some gossiping, a half-hearted flirtation, and then everyone goes home to Berlin; the revelation of Cécile's sexually compromised early life arrives agonizingly late in the novel, and the denouement, as often in Fontane, is swift, efficient, and a little surprising. In *Jenny Treibel* (1892), a wry social comedy with darker political overtones, a young woman makes a play for the son of the self-absorbed title character, one of the nouveaux riches bourgeois—a class much loathed by Fontane—who dominated German society after Bismarck unified the nation; after the girl has done a good deal of scheming, her plan simply fizzles out. (Fontane loves to create plots in which the characters' own plots never quite work; for all the Poggenpuhls' agonized machinations, what saves them in the end is a fortuitous event.)

And in *Effi Briest* (1895), considered by many to be Fontane's masterpiece, the suffocating dreariness of the young heroine's provincial existence is brilliantly conveyed precisely because the author isn't afraid to be dreary himself; by the time you've got through a few dozen pages in the Baltic town of Kessin, accompanied by Effi's excruciatingly correct, "frosty as a snowman" husband, you'll feel like breaking down in tears, too. Fontane's taste for withholding action, or at least delaying it improbably, is evident in the novel's most famous feature, a structural gambit of daring subtlety: the frustrated Effi's brief affair with a womanizing officer is never actually described—and is only discovered many years later, when she and her husband have settled comfortably into their marriage. (His pursuit of revenge is thus rendered all the more appalling—an effective vehicle for condemning ludicrous codes of masculine "honor.")

When "excitement and surprises" do occur in a Fontane novel, it's usually when the book is nearly over. The death, or suicide, or marriage, or resignation in the face of overwhelming social or familial pressure is a culminating little bump in the otherwise long, smooth, and highly scenic road. (Fontane features more suicides than any other German writer of his century; even these are characteristically quiet.)

At first glance, it's hard to reconcile the sparseness of Fontane's plots, the way he prefers to linger over what he calls "the circumstantial," with the extravagant emotions his work has provoked in so many critics and writers over the years. (Thomas Mann: "No writer of the past or the present awakens in me the sympathy and gratitude, the unconditional and instinctive delight, the immediate amusement and warmth and satisfaction that I feel in every verse, in every line of one of his letters, in every snatch of his dialogue.") The key lies in his understated narrative style, in his paradoxically powerful "discretion," as some critics have called it: a gift for obliquity, for knowing what to leave out, and above all for letting the reader "overhear" the speech of his characters, rather than paraphrasing it for us—the last being a particularly effective alternative to the psychologizing observations of an omniscient narrator. It is this skill at delineating character through dialogue—one early scholar of Fontane's work calls a scene in *Effi Briest* "the greatest conversation scene in the German novel"—that creates the sense of intimacy that his novels have, the sense that you're in there with his characters: the attractive but somehow desperate wives, yearning for recognition in a society dominated by masculine and military codes; the minor nobles, hardworking seamstresses, and disdained intellectuals trying to keep their dignity in a world destabilized by the materialism and the militarism of Bismarck's Second Reich.

Fontane's courteous technique is ideally suited to a rueful wisdom: he is the great novelist of what you might call dignified defeat. In his fiction, love doesn't triumph over class distinctions (*On Tangled Paths*), individual suffering inevitably yields to hard social and political realities (*The Poggenpuhls*, *Effi Briest*, *Cécile*, *The Stechlin*), and climactic reconciliations don't quite take (*Irretrievable*). It is through his characters' failures, rather than their victories, that Fontane quietly critiques politics and society. This modesty, the preference for suggestive description over ambitious prescription, set Fontane apart from other late-nineteenth-century realists. In an 1883 letter to his daughter—part of the voluminous correspondence that established him as one of the century's great letter writers—he remarked that he would have become a Turgenev or a Zola had he not been far more interested in individuals than in society as a whole.

Long revered on the Continent, Fontane has had a hard time catching on in this country. Although he lived to old age and published extensively from his youth until the time of his death, no major work of his enjoyed a complete English translation until 1964. It may be that, caught between Goethe's protean genius and Mann's fin-de-siècle neu-roticism, Fontane simply isn't what we think of when we think of what a great German author ought to be. (If Mann has the temperament of a patient, Fontane has that of a physician. Ours is an age of patients.) The recent publication of two of his most delicate and beautiful novels will, with any luck, help turn the tide. One is the bittersweet romance *On Tangled Paths*, from 1888, newly translated by Peter James Bow-man and published by Angel Books; the other is a curiously gentle tragedy called *Irretrievable*, first published in 1891, now reissued in the 1964 translation of Douglas Parmée by New York Review Books. Together, they convey the distinctive allure of an author who prided himself above all on his "finesses" and whose two salient traits—a severe reserve and a profound empathy—stemmed from an unusual ability, as Mann put it, to see "at least two sides to everything in life."

Fontane himself was a mass of contradictions—"the kind of man in whom both opinions, the conservative and the reactionary, could ex-ist side by side," as Mann would later observe. He was a product of the middle class and yet attracted to the aristocracy, a German pa-triot who admired England and came to detest Prussian militarism, a writer besotted with the "Romantic-Fantastic" who nonetheless had a natural aptitude for what he called the "factualness" of his-tory, a liberal who spent much of his career working for an ultra-rightist newspaper, a well-known balladeer, a dogged journalist, an admired travel writer, and a prolific military historian whose extraor-dinary talent for writing fiction ripened only late in a life that had many more than two sides.

He was born on the next-to-last day of 1819 in Neuruppin, a mil-itary garrison town northwest of Berlin, to parents descended from

French Huguenots who had fled to Prussia in the seventeenth century. Both his mother and his father, a rather eccentric apothecary, had firsthand experience of the Napoleonic Wars, a national trauma that exercised a hold on the writer's imagination all his life. (His first novel, *Before the Storm*, published in 1878, was a historical epic set during the wars, an attempt at a kind of Prussian *War and Peace*.) From Fontane senior, the future writer received a peculiar but effective education: the father enjoyed reenacting great moments from the wars with his young son. At least some of Fontane's interesting bifurcations, political as well as temperamental, may be attributed to his mismatched parents: his father the *Prinzipienverächter*, the hater of rigid principle, his mother a *Prinzipienreiter*, a stickler for principles.

At sixteen, Fontane finished with his formal education and apprenticed as an apothecary; he ended up working for his father. But his literary tastes and ambitions were already in evidence. He published his first story, about a quasi-incestuous brother–sister relationship, when he was not quite twenty, and in his mid-twenties he began publishing the ballads and verses for which he became well known, inspired by his extensive reading in English and Scottish ballads. (He learned English by reading, and translated *Hamlet* into German when he was in his twenties.) In 1844, he was invited to join a Berlin literary club called Tunnel Over the Spree, and made the first of what would be a number of enthusiastic trips to England. In 1848, that year of political upheaval throughout Europe, he had manned the antigovernment barricades in Berlin, but his relationship to liberal politics, like everything else about him, was far from straightforward. The grandson of a courtier of the Prussian Queen Luise, for whom he maintained a lifelong reverence, and an on-again, off-again admirer of Bismarck, whose speeches he loved to read over breakfast (and whose style he compared, favorably, to Shakespeare's), Fontane had an abiding admiration for the values of the old Prussian nobility, the *Junkertum*: simplicity, honor, and directness. As the scholar Alan Bance has pointed out, these values surface in Fontane's greatest female characters, who often struggle to uphold them against the crassness of men, society, the new Prussian state.

By the time Fontane was thirty, he had decided to abandon the apothecary and embrace a life of writing. In 1850, he married Emilie Rouanet-Kummer, another descendant of French Huguenots, and soon afterward took a job in a government press office. A year later, when the first of the couple's seven children was born—four lived to adulthood—Fontane, eager for some financial stability, queasily accepted a job writing about English affairs for *Die Kreuzzeitung*, a government-run newspaper. ("I sold myself to the reaction for thirty pieces of silver a month," he wrote a friend.) He was in England for several months in 1852, and in 1855 he began a three-year stint there; his job was to plant stories favorable to the Prussian state in the British press. He spent a great deal of time going to the theater and—prompted by his impassioned reading of Walter Scott and Robert Burns, and of English and Scottish ballads, all faddishly popular among Germans in the mid-nineteenth century—taking long walks in the Scottish countryside. These walks partly inspired his splendidly discursive and erudite *Rambles in the March of Brandenburg*, whose combination of sentimental enthusiasm and the amateur's besotted enthusiasm for historical anecdote and geographical and zoological minutiae suggests a kind of Patrick Leigh Fermor *avant la lettre*. (In an affectionate study of Fontane, the historian Gordon A. Craig retraced the author's steps.)

Fontane returned to Berlin in 1859 and, after briefly considering a post at the court of the mad Ludwig II of Bavaria—it's hard to resist wondering what the result of *that* collaboration might have been—set to work on *Rambles*, which occupied him for the next two decades. But this was also the period in which Prussian political and military ambition exploded, culminating in three major wars—against Denmark in 1864, Austria in 1866, and France in 1870—and the unification of Germany under Bismarck and the Hohenzollerns. In the decade between 1866 and 1876 Fontane published three major, exhaustively researched studies, one for each war. Contemptuous of "making books out of books," he conducted extensive interviews and visited various battlefields, sometimes before hostilities ceased; at one point, he was captured by French troops, and Bismarck had to intervene to get him released. (Fontane later wrote a book about the experience.) Despite his historian's admiration for Prussian warcraft, Fontane came to speak out with increasing vigor against the chauvinism, jingoism, and triumphalism that characterized so much contemporary writing about the wars. "The mere glorification of the military," he later wrote, "without moral content and elevated aim, is nauseating." His distaste for the public mania that followed the victory against France eerily anticipates a later efflorescence of German militarism:

> The whole situation works upon me like a colossal vision... one stands and stares and is not sure what to make of it all... always *masses*, inside of which one whirls like an atom, not standing aside and in control but surrendered to the great movement without any will of one's own.

At the end of the 1860s, as he reached his fiftieth birthday, Fontane—inspired, perhaps, by his experience writing the first two war books and thinking about the cultural implications of Germany's recent history—quit his post at the conservative, God-and-country *Kreuzzeitung*. (He waited to submit his resignation until the long-suffering Emilie—who, despite the fact that she wrote out the fair copies of each of his books, never quite believed that he would succeed as a writer—left for a vacation.) Soon afterward, he jumped at the opportunity to replace the recently deceased theater critic for the liberal *Vossische Zeitung*: certainly because of the promise of a regular income but also, undoubtedly, because it provided an outlet for his love of the theater. His criticism—conversational yet informed, often crustily amusing (he once wrote of a production of *Macbeth* that all the roles were played badly except that of the rain, which beat convincingly against the walls of the castle)—further increased his fame. He remained happily in this job for the next twenty years.

Many critics have looked to various aspects of Fontane's life—not least, his French ancestry—for clues to a style that was so fresh, so lifelike: so different, in a word, from that of many of his contemporaries. (The author's relationship to his Frenchness was typically bifurcated: he liked to talk about his "essentially southern-French nature," but also called knowing French "a great virtue, which I do not possess.") But it seems clear that he owed much to his deep love of, and appreciation for, the theater—instilled, you suspect, during those playacting sessions with his father. His distinctive way of letting his characters reveal themselves through monologue and dialogue (or letters, or poems—anything that lets them speak for themselves) betrays an intuitive feel for the theatrical. *Jenny Treibel* opens with the title character, an arriviste with grand dynastic ambitions, bustling into the home of her childhood sweetheart, now a colorful old professor, whose daughter, Corinna, will soon threaten Frau Treibel's plans:

> My dear Corinna, how nicely you know how to do all this and how pretty it is here, so cool and fresh—and the beautiful hyacinths! Of course they don't go very well with these oranges, but that doesn't matter, it looks so nice.... And now, thoughtful as

you are, you're even adjusting a pillow for me! But forgive me, I don't like to sit on the sofa; it's so soft and you always sink in so deeply. I'd rather sit over here in the armchair and look at those dear old faces there.

Fontane's novels are filled with characters who talk and talk and, in so doing, reveal themselves more damningly than an omniscient narrator could. Can you doubt that Frau Treibel and Corinna will clash? Do you doubt who will prevail?

The years of theater criticism, of having to articulate his responses to others' writing, were surely crucial to Fontane's evolution as a novelist, strengthening his sense of his own aesthetic responses, his own powers as a writer and thinker. "I have an unconditional confidence in the rightness of my feeling," he once wrote. "I am wholly free from veneration of names or the cult of literary heroes." An arresting passage in a collection of his critical writings (with the characteristically informal title *Chats on the Theater*) suggests where Fontane's veneration did, in fact, lie. He recalled how he would sometimes go into one of the city's many Gothic churches to clear his head after a matinee. One day, following a particularly unsatisfactory performance of *Iphigenia in Tauris*—one of the neoclassical works that were a staple of bland local productions—he wrote of something that had affected him tremendously: "Hidden behind a pillar, I saw a man crying, which shook me more than three acts of tragedy."

It's a fascinating moment, because the best of Fontane's mature fiction is filled with eerie minor epiphanies that have a powerful effect on a given character—and on the reader. In *Effi Briest*, the apparition in a window of the teenage heroine's twin playmates, at the moment she is to be betrothed to the much older nobleman her mother has chosen for her, seems to symbolize the poignant tension between the girlish "child of nature" and the social role she is still unprepared to play—a tension that ultimately destroys her. In *On Tangled Paths*, the lower-class heroine, a seamstress involved in an impossible love affair, sees a young girl washing pots in the river, a vision that somehow irrefutably conveys to her the fact that there will be no way to flout social conventions.

Such moments represent a crucial facet of Fontane's art. He liked to say that he had a well-developed sense of *Tatsächlichkeit*, "factuality"; for him, the trick of literature was to "transfigure" everyday facts into something elevated, imbued with *Rätsel* and *Halbdunkel*, "mystery" and "twilight." ("A piece of bread...is poetry," he once wrote.) He disdained Turgenev—interestingly, Bismarck's favorite novelist—for failing to transcend *Tatsächlichkeit*, for having merely a "photographic apparatus in eye and soul." In the novels of Fontane, apparitions like the one he beheld in the church that day, essentially theatrical in nature, are instances of "facts" elevated into memorable art.

As he was nearing sixty, Fontane made the extraordinary announcement that he was ready to begin a new career—as a novelist. "I am only at the beginning," he wrote his publisher, Wilhelm Hertz, in 1879, with a touching combination of bravado and trepidation. "There is nothing behind me, everything is ahead, which is both fortune and misfortune at the same time." As it turned out, he had nothing to fear. For the next two decades, he and Emilie lived at 134c Potsdamer Strasse, where he produced the seventeen novels that marked him as a great writer.

It's not surprising that Fontane's first novel was a work of historical fiction: partly the factuality of the past, partly the twilight mystery of literary art. Some readers at the time found *Before the Storm* a disconcertingly becalmed work: the author's languid eavesdropping was, they found, ill suited to a subject that raised expectations of high color and excitement. ("Will they sit down at the table again? Will they go to sleep again?" one of Fontane's many correspondents wrote of the characters in that "silly" book.) It took Fontane a while to find the proper vehicle for his talent for depicting everyday realities imbued with the poetic—ordinary people reaching for (and, as often as not, failing to attain) transcendence. That vehicle, as the literary world soon discovered, was women.

As is the case with certain male writers famous for their female characters—Euripides, Tennessee Williams—women in Fontane's work often represent energies and emotions for which there is no room in the world created by men: the world of realpolitik and bombastic officialdom, of matrimonial hypocrisy and erotic double standards. This is why, as with those other authors, Fontane's women are often both impressively self-aware and memorably broken. "If there is a person who has a passion for women," Fontane confided to some friends in 1894, "and loves them almost twice as much when he encounters their weaknesses and confusions, the whole enchantment of their womanhood in full flight, that person is I." It would be hard to think of a better way to describe the figures on whom the author's reputation as a master of characterization and delicate plotting is based. Such weaknesses and confusions, the feminine enchantment in full flight—in both their comic and their tragic expressions—make *On Tangled Paths* and *Irretrievable* small masterworks.

On Tangled Paths (*Irrungen, Wirrungen* in the original, a rhyme nicely finessed in an earlier translation, entitled *Delusions, Confusions*) has a typically unfussy plot. Lene Nimptsch is a pretty young seamstress (she comes complete with a much put-upon foster mother and chatty, eccentric, but loving neighbors, all painted in amusing Dickensian colors) who's in love with Botho von Rienäcker, a dashing officer from an aristocratic family; he loves her. They spend time together; he teases her foster mother and the neighbors; the couple make an overnight excursion on the Spree. (Readers weren't the only ones outraged by Fontane's unsensationalistic depiction of the casual sexual relationship when the novel was first serialized in a newspaper. "Won't this dreadful whore's tale soon be over?" one of the paper's owners protested.) Eventually—and it takes some time—Botho's mother reminds him that he must marry a suitable girl. This he does, reluctantly at first: she's an airhead and a chatterbox. (Fontane just lets her rattle on.) Lene, for her part, ends up marrying a nice enough man. At the novel's close, both young people have accepted their fates, though not without complex emotions: "Our hearts have room for all sorts of contradictions." That could be Fontane's motto.

So there aren't many visible items of interest. The immense pleasures of the novel lie in the author's coolheaded approach to what, in other hands, could have been a forgettable melodrama. As often in Fontane, the drama is internal, and, at first, internally generated; when the "excitement" happens—in this case, the intervention of Botho's mother (in a letter)—it's just an external correlative to something already present in one or more characters. The love affair in *On Tangled Paths* is shadowed from the start by the practical-minded Lene's unblinking understanding that a romance like theirs cannot last:

One day I'll find you've flown away.... Don't shake your head; it's true, what I say. You love me and you're true to me—at least my love makes me childish and vain enough to imagine it. But fly away you will, I can see that very clearly.... You love me but you're weak-willed. We can't change that. All handsome men are weak-willed, and ruled by a stronger force.... What is it? Well, either it's your mother or people's talk or circumstances. Or maybe all three.

It's a remarkable speech to encounter in the mouth of a young woman in a late-nineteenth-century novel. (It's not surprising that Fontane admired Trollope, another creator of strong-willed females who know what's what.) Botho, as it turns out, *is* weak-willed, and bows to his mother's demands. What saves him, and the novel—it's an element that makes for a more stimulating richness of perspective, and makes it harder to "blame" any given character—is that he is ultimately as realistic as Lene, if rather more prone to self-justification. "Do I mean to marry Lene? No. Have I promised her I would? No. Does she expect it? No. Or will parting be any easier for us if I defer it? No, no, and no again."

Lene suffers less than some of Fontane's women because of her class—because her horizon of expectations is narrower than that of Effi or of Cécile, those unhappy wives of high-ranking husbands. Like them, she's astute about the limitations that the world sets on her ambitions, but the ambitions are more realistic and the limitations more relaxed. The pleasure of *On Tangled Paths* is not the thrill of watching a female character struggle against social convention, as so many great heroines of nineteenth-century literature do, but the perhaps more complicated pleasure of recognizing a character who knows when to give in. Still, a sadness hangs in the air, owing in no small part to the innumerable touches the author employs to build up his subtle but affecting portrait of a young woman who is ignorant but not stupid, romantic but not foolish. (She's the inverse of Emma Bovary—more interesting, too.) At one point, Lene uncomprehendingly examines the English captions on two prints in the room where she's staying with her lover—"Washington Crossing the Delaware" and "The Last Hour at Trafalgar." Fontane takes this casual moment and turns it, wonderfully, into a symbol of why the relationship can't last: "But she could do no more than combine the letters into syllables, and, trivial as the matter was, it nonetheless gave her a pang by bringing home to her the gulf that separated her from Botho." The book is filled with comparable moments of small facts transfigured into something magical.

Irretrievable takes the same elements—an appealing man, charming but weak; a clear-eyed, practical-minded woman, perhaps a little pessimistic; a relationship that can't go anywhere; resignation in the face of life's realities—and, as its stark title suggests, turns it into a tragedy. It's one of Fontane's most idiosyncratic achievements, and certainly one of the finest literary autopsies of a foundering relationship. (The translation reprinted in the New York Review Books edition is more fluent and natural but also more prone to infelicities than a new translation, *No Way Back*, published in 2010 by Angel Books.)

The novel's odd, misty, rather *Pelléas et Mélisande* atmosphere has much to do with its unusual setting. It takes place not in Berlin, or even in Germany proper, but in Copenhagen and in the duchy of Schleswig-Holstein, a territory whose vexed history—it was the subject of a long series of ownership disputes between Denmark and Prussia, finally and forcibly resolved by the Danish War of 1864—serves as a metaphor for the condition of the main characters' marriage. The Schleswig-Holstein question, the British foreign secretary Lord Palmerston once quipped, was so complicated that only three people understood it, of whom one, the Prince Consort, was dead; another, a foreign office clerk, had gone mad; and the third, Palmerston himself, had forgotten the whole thing. There's always a background buzz of politics in Fontane's novels—a geopolitical correlative for the emotional drama.

Unlike the couple in *On Tangled Paths*, this pair have no obvious impediments to happiness. Both are aristocratic, and they have in fact been long and happily married, with two attractive teenage children, all living in a replica of a Greek temple on the Baltic coast. (A good setting for a tragedy.) Count Helmut Holk is charming and has many "likeable qualities," and would, his wife can't help thinking at the beginning of the novel, "certainly be an ideal husband—if he had any ideals at all of his own." The countess, Christine, is beautiful, younger, and a bit too dogmatic and overprincipled, as she herself recognizes. When the author deftly alludes to Christine's attitude toward smoking—something "which the countess did not really allow indoors, although she never forbade it"—you have all the information you need about the passive-aggressiveness that will sink the marriage. In the erosive contest between the two spouses, it's hard not to feel the ghosts of Fontane's quarreling parents, the *Prinzipienverächter* and the *Prinzipienreiter*.

What happens in *Irretrievable*? Not much, on the face of it. What Helmut observes of a poem that he likes is true of this novel, as it is of so many others by Fontane: "There is no real content and it is just a situation and not a poem but that doesn't matter. It has a certain tone and just as the coloring makes a picture ... in the same way the tone makes the poem." Fontane charts the course of the Holks' marital decline in his usual desultory way—there's a slow accumulation of talk and events, and then that climactic fillip. The couple bicker about which schools to send the children to; Helmut, suddenly called upon to fulfill his duty as courtier, goes away to Copenhagen for some weeks, where he flirts inconclusively with his landlady's daughter and, more conclusively, with Ebba ("Eve"), a rather spiky lady-in-waiting to the elderly princess whom they both serve. He doesn't write often enough to Christine; there's a fire in the castle where the princess is holding court (no one gets hurt); in a fit of midlife foolishness, Helmut tells Christine it's all over and proposes to the lady-in-waiting, who then tells him off ("You're always sinning against the most elementary rules of the game"); eventually, he comes home to his wife. The moment of narrative "excitement" takes place five pages from the end of the book. As Helmut's scheming landlady says of her daughter's wayward life, "It's something of a love-story but it's not a proper love-story."

As in *On Tangled Paths*, the pleasure of the novel lies in its subtlety—in this case, a discreet exploration of marital psychology. Here again, trouble starts within and, like a dry rot, eats its way outward. The novel begins with one of Fontane's unemphatic epiphanies: in the course of an ordinary domestic conversation one day, Christine realizes that the terrain of her marriage has, somehow, shifted under her feet. "In spite of having the best of husbands whom she loved as much as he loved her, she yet did not possess that peace for which she longed; in spite of all their love, his easy-going temperament was no longer in harmony with her melancholy." The symbol of the fatal disharmony is Christine's preoccupation with restoring the crumbling family vault. (Fontane's novels are filled with brief but meaningful references to cemeteries, graves, burials, funerals, even funeral wreaths.) From the beginning, there's not much question about who will end up in it.

The haunted perception of imminent emotional failure—which, typically, the more sentimental male character resists at first—colors everything that follows in precisely the way the bad faith of a crumbling relationship poisons even the most innocent exchanges. This phenomenon is, indeed, one that the novel evokes in harrowing detail. "In my correspondence with Christine," Helmut heatedly writes to her brother, who is also his close friend, "I have never been able to strike the right note. As soon as one finds oneself suspected, it is very difficult to maintain the right tone and attitude." And, as in *On Tangled Paths*, Fontane gives us access to the kind of tortured emotional self-justification that unhappy lovers are prone to. Here is Helmut, "interpreting" the fact that he wasn't killed in the fire:

If all my feelings had been wrong all this time, punishment would have overtaken us and Ebba and I would have fallen unconscious and been suffocated and never found our way to safety. And if I understood Christine's last letter properly, she also feels that this will be the best thing for us to do. All those happy days we spent together mustn't be forgotten, of course not...but part we must and I think it is our duty to do so.

Masculine self-delusion masquerading as duty is a favorite target of Fontane's. (Helmut's monologue is a grotesque inversion of Lene's coolly self-aware speech in *On Tangled Paths*.) Here it's precisely the reagent necessary to ignite Christine's dangerous penchant for self-righteousness, with predictable results.

Well, not quite predictable: *Irretrievable* lingers in an unexpected cul-de-sac before it realizes the promise of its title. But even after the couple ostensibly reconcile, there's really nothing left; by the end of this mild yet anguished work, all that remains of the marriage is a lifeless residue of thwarted yearning—"nothing but the *willingness* to be happy." As so often in the fiction of Theodor Fontane, that's not enough to save the characters, but it's a marvelous subject for a novel.

—*The New Yorker,* March 7, 2011

REBEL REBEL

ONE WINTER'S DAY in 1883, aboard a steamer that was returning him from Marseilles to the Arabian port city of Aden, a French coffee trader named Alfred Bardey struck up what he no doubt thought would be a casual conversation with a countryman he'd met on board, a young journalist named Paul Bourde. As Bardey chatted about his trading operation, which was based in Aden, he happened to mention the name of one of his employees—a "tall, pleasant young man who speaks little," as he later described him. To his surprise, Bourde reacted to the name with amazement. This wasn't so much because, by a bizarre coincidence, he had gone to school with Bardey's employee; rather, it was that, like many Frenchmen who kept up with contemporary literature, he had assumed that the young man was dead. To an astonished Bardey, Bourde explained that, twelve years earlier, the tall and taciturn young man had made a "stupefying and precocious" literary début in Paris, only to disappear soon after. Until that moment, for all Bardey or anyone else in his circle knew, this man was simply a clever trader who kept neat books. Today, many think of him as a founder of modern European poetry. His name was Arthur Rimbaud.

What Bardey learned about Rimbaud that day is still what most people know about him. There was, on the one hand, the dazzling, remarkably short-lived career: all of Rimbaud's significant works were most likely composed between 1870, when he was not quite sixteen, and 1874, when he turned twenty. On the other hand, there was the abrupt abandonment of literature in favor of a vagabond life that eventually took him to Aden and then to East Africa, where he remained until just before his death, trading coffee, feathers, and, finally, guns, and making a tidy bundle in the process. The great mystery that continues to haunt and dismay Rimbaud lovers is this "act of renunciation," as Henry Miller put it in his rather loopy 1946 study of Rimbaud, *The Time of the Assassins*—which, Miller asserted, "one is tempted to compare...with the release of the atomic bomb." The over-the-top comparison might well have pleased Rimbaud, who clearly wanted to vaporize his poetic past. When Bardey got back to Aden, bursting with his discovery, he found to his dismay that the former wunderkind refused to talk about his work, dismissing it as "absurd, ridiculous, disgusting."

That Rimbaud's repudiation of poetry was as furious as the outpouring of his talent had once been was typical of a man whose life and work were characterized by violent contradictions. He was a docile, prizewinning schoolboy who wrote "Shit on God" on walls in his hometown; a teenage rebel who mocked small-town conventionality, only to run back to his mother's farm after each emotional crisis; a would-be anarchist who in one poem called for the downfall of "Emperors / Regiments, colonizers, peoples!" and yet spent his adult life as an energetic capitalist operating out of colonial Africa; a poet who liberated French lyric verse from the late nineteenth century's starched themes and corseted forms—and, more importantly, from "the language of common sense," as Paul Valéry put it—and yet who, in his most revolutionary work, admitted to a love of "maudlin pictures,...fairytales, children's storybooks, old operas, inane refrains and artless rhythms."

These paradoxes, and the extraordinarily conflicted feelings of admiration and dismay that Rimbaud's story can evoke, are at the center of a powerful mystique that has seduced readers from Marcel Proust to Patti Smith. It had already begun to fascinate people by the time the poet died, in 1891. (He succumbed, at thirty-seven, to a cancer of the leg, after returning to his mama's house one last time.) To judge from the steady stream of Rimbaldiana that has appeared over the past decade—which includes, most recently, a new translation of *Illuminations*, by the distinguished American poet John Ashbery, and Bruce Duffy's *Disaster Was My God*, a substantial novel that wrestles with the great question of why Rimbaud stopped writing—the allure shows no sign of fading.

Depending on your view of human nature, either everything or nothing about Rimbaud's drab origins explains what came later. He was born in October 1854, in the town of Charleville, near the Belgian border. His father, Frédéric, was an army captain who had fought in Algeria, and his mother, Vitalie Cuif, was a straitlaced daughter of solid farmers; it was later said that nobody could recall ever having seen her smile. To describe the marriage as an unhappy one would probably be to exaggerate, if for no other reason than that Captain Rimbaud was rarely in Charleville; each of the couple's five children was born nine months after one of his brief leaves. When Arthur was five, his father went off to join his regiment and never came back. The memory of the abandonment haunts Rimbaud's work, which often evokes lost childhood happiness, and occasionally seems to refer directly to his family's crisis. ("She, / all black and cold, hurries after the man's departure!") Vitalie, devoutly Catholic, took to calling herself "Widow Rimbaud," and applied herself with grim determination to her children's education.

At school, Rimbaud was a star, regularly acing the daunting prize examinations. (One exam required students to produce a metrically correct Latin poem on the theme "Sancho Panza Addresses His Donkey.") Not long after his fifteenth birthday, he composed "The Orphans' New Year's Gifts," the first poem he published. It's a bit of treacle—two children awaken on New Year's to discover that their mother has died—but it is notable for its thematic preoccupation, the absence of maternal love, and its precocious technical expertise. It is likely that Rimbaud inherited his verbal gifts and intellectual ambition from his father, who, while serving in North Africa, had produced an annotated translation of the Koran and a collection of Arab jokes. Rimbaud, who seems to have retained a romantic view of his father, sent for these texts when he moved to Africa; a formidable linguist, he became fluent in Arabic as well as a number of local dialects and even gave lessons on the Koran to local boys. His mother's glumly concrete practicality ("actions are all that count") stood in stark contrast to these cerebral enthusiasms. It's tempting to see, in the wild divergence between his parents' natures, the origins of Rimbaud's eccentric seesawing between literature and commerce.

Certainly the teen-rebel phase that began when he was around fifteen looks like a reaction to life with Vitalie. This was the period during which he remarked, in a letter to his schoolmate Ernest Delahaye, whose memoirs furnish important information about the poet's early years, that orphans or "wild children" were luckier than he and Delahaye were: "Brand-new, clean, without any principles, and notions—since everything they teach us is false!—and free, free of everything!" The frenetic pursuit of what, in another letter, he called "free freedom" runs like a leitmotif through Rimbaud's life: few poets have walked, run, ridden, or sailed as frequently or as far as he did. Indeed, late in the summer of 1870, a couple of months before his sixteenth birthday, he ran away from Vitalie's dour home and took a train to Paris: the first of many escapes. Since he didn't have enough money for the full fare, he was arrested and jailed on his arrival and, after writing a plaintive letter to a beloved teacher back in Charleville, Georges Izambard—and not, as far as we know, one to his mother—he was bailed out and then slunk back home. The pattern of flight and return would recur up until his final return, a few months before his death.

Two days after the iconoclast's arrival in the capital, France was defeated by Prussia and the Second Empire fell; soon after he got back home, the Paris Commune was established. Stuck in Charleville while great things were happening in the world ("I'm dying, decomposing under the weight of platitude"), the once-model schoolboy let his hair grow long, sat around mocking the passing bourgeoisie, and smoked his clay pipe a lot. The yearning to break away now made itself felt in the poems he was writing. Some of these, as Izambard once put it, could have "the cheek to be charming." (The charm is certainly there in the widely beloved "Bohemian" poems written in the autumn of 1870, when Rimbaud strolled across to Belgium: "Off I would go, with fists into torn pockets pressed....Eh, what fine dreams I had, each one an amorous gest!") But the desire to break out could express itself as well in a kind of literary vandalism. He'd already mocked the poetic conventions of the times (one early poem gives the goddess Venus an ulcer on her anus); to the period of frustrated ennui following his first escape, we owe such poems as "Accroupissements" ("Squattings"), which in elegantly metrical verse describes the effortful bowel movements of a priest, or "Les Assis"

("The Sitters"), which pokes vicious fun at the habitués of the town library where Rimbaud himself spent hours. Occasionally, he stole books.

However illicit the acquisition of those volumes, it reminds you that Rimbaud's restless intellect continued to seethe. As Wyatt Mason points out in a vigorous and sensible introduction to his 2003 translation of the poet's letters, as much as we now like to romanticize Rimbaud as a Dionysian rebel, spontaneously tossing off revolutionary verses, the fact is that he made himself a poet by following a distinctly Apollonian trajectory—"a long, involved, and sober study of the history of poetry."

The combination of adolescent rebellion and poetic precocity yielded, in May 1871, a grand statement of artistic purpose. In two letters, one to Izambard and the other to his friend Paul Demeny, also a poet, Rimbaud set out what he had come to see as his great project. To Izambard he wrote:

> I'm now making myself as scummy as I can. Why? I want to be a poet, and I'm working at turning myself into a *Seer*. You won't understand any of this, and I'm almost incapable of explaining it to you. The idea is to reach the unknown by the derangement of *all the senses*. It involves enormous suffering, but one must be strong and be a born poet. And I've realized that I am a poet. It's really not my fault.

The sixteen-year-old went on to make an assertion that Graham Robb, in his idiosyncratic yet magisterial *Rimbaud: A Biography* (2000), refers to as the "poetic $E=mc^2$": "*Je est un autre*," "I is someone else." The young poet's insight, plain perhaps to us in our post-Freudian age but startling in its time, was that the subjective "I" was a construct, a useful fiction—something he'd deduced from the fact that the mind could observe itself at work, which suggested to him that consciousness itself, far from being straightforward, was faceted. ("I am present at the hatching of my thought.") He suddenly saw that the true subject of a new poetry couldn't be the usual things—landscapes, flowers, pretty girls, sunsets—but, rather, the way those things are refracted through one's own unique mind. "The first study of the man who wishes to be a poet is complete knowledge of himself," he wrote in the letter to Demeny. "He searches his mind, inspects it, tries it out and learns to use it."

In this letter, he tellingly added the adjective "rational" to the phrase "derangement of all the senses"—here again he was more Apollonian than we often think—and further asserted that this project required a new kind of poetic language, in which one sense became indistinguishable from another, sight from touch, hearing from smell: "summing up everything, perfumes, sounds and colors, thought latching on to thought and pulling." In one of his most famous poems, he assigns colors to each vowel: "A black, E white, I red, U green, O blue." Here, as so often, he was following the example of Baudelaire, the great iconoclast of the previous generation and the champion of synesthesia.

"Thought latching on to thought and pulling" is an ideal way to describe the workings of the major poem he produced during this crucial period, "Le Bateau Ivre" ("The Drunken Boat"). The poem is characterized by a formal correctness (it's composed of twenty-five rhymed quatrains of alexandrines, the classic French six-beat line) placed in the service of a destabilizing fantasy—a dream of liberation from correct form. It ostensibly describes the downstream journey of a vessel that has lost its haulers, its rudder, its anchor, wandering to and fro and witnessing bizarre sights en route to nowhere in particular. ("Huge serpents, vermin-plagued, drop down into the mire / With black effluvium from the contorted trees!") But as you make your way through the poem, each stanza seeming at once to latch tightly onto the last and yet move further into imaginative space, it seems to expand into a parable about life and art in which loss of control—of the boat, of the poem itself, of what we think "meaning" in a poem might be—becomes the key to a kind of spiritual and aesthetic redemption:

> *The wash of the green water on my shell of pine,*
> *Sweeter than apples to a child its pungent edge;*
> *It cleansed me of the stains of vomits and blue wine*
> *And carried off with it the rudder and the kedge.*

Here, the two faces of Rimbaud's desire to break out—the charming and the destructive—seamlessly come together, as the desire for consummation melds with a desire for annihilation: "Swollen by acrid love, sagging with drunkenness— / Oh, that my keel might rend and give me to the sea!"

Whatever else it is—and many find its inscrutability insurmountable—"The Drunken Boat" is the work of a poet who has achieved his mature voice. In September 1871, Rimbaud made another bid to escape Charleville. He wrote a letter to Paul Verlaine, who, together with Baudelaire, was one of the few poets whom Rimbaud admired, and enclosed a number of his poems. It was not long before he received the older poet's invitation to come to the great city, expressed in words that proved prophetic: "Come, dear great soul. We await you; we desire you."

The rules of poetry weren't the only things that Rimbaud broke when he arrived in Paris. Among other things—bric-a-brac, dishes, and furniture in the various homes where he was offered hospitality, and where his boorish behavior inevitably led to his eviction—he broke up Verlaine's marriage. The two men apparently became lovers soon after Rimbaud's arrival, embarking on an affair that scandalized Paris and made literary history. Verlaine's brother-in-law, for one, was never taken in by the angelic face and striking pale-blue eyes; he dismissed Rimbaud at once as the "vile, vicious, disgusting, smutty little schoolboy whom everyone is in raptures about."

Between the autumn of 1871 and July 1873, the couple wandered from Paris to Belgium to London and, finally, back to Brussels again, drinking absinthe, smoking hashish, engaging in outrageous public displays of affection (one newspaper article cattily referred to the younger man as "Mlle Rimbaud"), quarreling, and—as Verlaine once boasted—making love "like tigers." They apparently liked to puncture each other with knives, and jointly composed a poem called the "Asshole Sonnet," complete with beautifully wrought, anatomically minute descriptions of that orifice. Many readers and biographers see the couple as what Graham Robb calls "the Adam and Eve of modern homosexuality," but the evidence suggests that, as far as Rimbaud was interested in anyone other than himself, he was interested primarily in women. (Later, in Abyssinia, he lived with a strikingly good-looking local woman; she wore Western clothes and smoked cigarettes, while he wore native costume.) It is hard to escape the feeling that Verlaine, an ugly man whose appearance Rimbaud made cruel jokes about, was a kind of science experiment for the poet—part of his program of "rational derangement of all the senses," his strident adolescent ambition to "reinvent" love, society, poetry. Indeed, for someone who uses the word "love" so often in his poetry, Rimbaud comes off as a cold fish; the tenderer emotions seem hypothetical to him.

Whatever the nature of the relationship, the period of their affair was one of tremendous growth for Rimbaud, whose work was undergoing a dramatic evolution. Entranced, at one point, by the charmingly simple lyrics of eighteenth-century operas, he wrote a number of poems so delicately attenuated, so stripped of descriptiveness, that they seem to have no referent at all. ("I have recovered it. / What? Eternity. / It is the sea / Matched with the sun.") But the tranquillity of the verse was not reflected in everyday life. By the time the pair were living, impoverished, in London (they took to placing desperate ads for their services as French tutors), the relationship had seriously frayed. After a catastrophic scene that ended with Verlaine running off to Belgium, Rimbaud—more terrified of being poor and alone, you suspect, than of losing his lover—joined him in Brussels. There, on July 10, 1873, after yet another drama, the distraught Verlaine, who had been making suicide threats, used a revolver he'd intended for himself to shoot his lover in the arm.

And then, as the French writer Charles Dantzig puts it in a tartly shrewd essay on Rimbaud, "our anarchist called the police." Following an official inquest that included a humiliating medical examination, Verlaine was sentenced to two years in prison. Rimbaud went home to his mother.

This sordid emotional cataclysm surely goes some way toward explaining Rimbaud's desire for a new life: perhaps for the first time, he realized that deranging his and other people's senses could have serious and irreversible consequences. Home at Vitalie's farm, a chastened Rimbaud spent the summer of 1873 hard at work on the text he'd begun earlier that year. This collection of "atrocious stories" in prose, as he described them in a letter to a friend, would become *A Season in Hell*, his best-known work and a founding document of European modernism.

If you were to take Dante's *Inferno*, Dostoyevsky's *Notes from Underground*, a pinch of William Blake, and a healthy dash of Christopher Smart's madhouse masterpiece "Rejoice in the Lamb," throw them into a blender, and hit "purée," you might well find yourself with something like *A Season in Hell*. On one level, it looks like a narrative of abasement and redemption, tracing the story of a Rimbaud-like artist who has wantonly corrupted his childhood innocence ("Once, if I remember well, my life was a feast where all hearts opened and all wines flowed") and, after wallowing in a rehearsal of his sins, seeks a kind of healing. Interlaced with political slogans ("Wealth has always been public property") and grandiose vatic pronouncements ("I am going to unveil all the mysteries"), much of *A Season in Hell* is, as one indulgent critic said of Rimbaud's work, "aggravatingly beautiful and too frequently hermetic." Most interesting are what look suspiciously like verbatim quotes from his life with Verlaine. The older poet appears as a character called "the Foolish Virgin," endlessly bemoaning his involvement with the seductive youth:

> He was hardly more than a child. His mysterious delicacies had seduced me. I forgot all my duty to society, to follow him.... I go where he goes. I have to. And often he flies into a rage at me, *me, the poor soul*. The Demon! He is a demon, you know, *he is not a man*.

Ultimately, *A Season in Hell* is a kaleidoscopic evocation of a man who comes to terms with the limits of the self; a heavy sense of failure, of wrong paths taken, hovers over the vignettes. Even the overweening and narcissistic fantasies of artistic transcendence ("I became a fabulous opera") are reoriented, in the end, toward reality: "I who called myself angel or seer, exempt from all morality, I am returned to the soil with a duty to seek and rough reality to embrace!" It is this understanding—that fantasy and romance must be eschewed—that leads to the famous closing utterance: "One must be absolutely modern."

If *A Season in Hell* is seething, anguished, and dialogic, Rimbaud's next, and final, work speaks with an air of quiet authority and calm. It feels like the writing of someone who's forgiven himself. Rimbaud and Verlaine met one last time, in 1875, when Rimbaud was living in Germany. When he handed his former lover a sheaf of papers to take back to France, they had no title; *Illuminations* is the name under which Verlaine, ever generous to his ungrateful ex, eventually published them. The word was meant to evoke the minute illustrations on old manuscripts, and it's easy to see why. These strange, exquisite prose poems—a "crystalline jumble," as John Ashbery calls them in the preface to his new translation, which, like the work itself, is sometimes willful but often has its own crystal purity—are intensely visual, bringing before your eyes fleeting images that have the oddness, the intensity, and the subterranean logic of dreams. Scholars have long argued over which poem was written first, but it seems clear that *Illuminations* begins in a kind of postapocalyptic calm after the crisis evoked in *A Season in Hell*. The opening gives you a sense of what's in store:

> No sooner had the notion of the Flood regained its composure,
> Than a hare paused among the gorse and trembling bellflowers
> and said its prayer to the rainbow through the spider's web.
> Oh the precious stones that were hiding,—the flowers that
> were already peeking out.

This passage offers some examples of how Ashbery sometimes squeezes too hard. In the original, the notion of the Flood simply "took its seat again," the bellflowers are just "moving," and the flowers don't "peek," they just "look."

Reading this remarkable and, it must be said, often incomprehensible work ("Since then the Moon has heard jackals cheeping in thyme deserts") can be a startling, frustrating, and yet exhilarating experience. Among its more uncanny features is the way it often seems to look ahead to the twentieth century. One vignette suggests the grandiose architecture of Hitler's dream Berlin: "The official acropolis beggars the most colossal conceptions of modern barbarity....With a singular taste for enormity, they have reproduced all the classical marvels of architecture." Another prefigures the visual puzzles of M.C. Escher: "A bizarre pattern of bridges, some of them straight, others convex, still others descending or veering off at angles to the first ones, and these shapes multiplying." Rimbaud, who had found the industrial vigor of London exciting, was never more a seer than he was here.

There is much more—not least, a description, delicate as rice paper, of what may or may not be ideal love. ("It's the friend who's neither ardent nor weak. The friend.") In a final section called "Génie," whose haunting, incantatory rhythms Ashbery renders more precisely and more beautifully than any previous translator, the poet exhorts us to embrace the vaguely Christlike figure of the title—perhaps the same genie who appears in an earlier section, described as holding "the promise of a multiple and complex love":

> He has known us all and loved us all. Let us, on this winter night, from cape to cape, from the tumultuous pole to the castle, from the crowd to the beach, from glance to glance, our strengths and feelings numb, learn to hail him and see him, and send him back, and under the tides and at the summit of snowy deserts, follow his seeing, his breathing, his body, his day.

Ashbery, for whom this translation was clearly a labor of love—there is no shortage of fine English versions—calls this "one of the greatest poems ever written." It was, very probably, the last poetry that Rimbaud ever wrote. He was twenty years old.

Defending the opacity of *Illuminations* in his biography of Rimbaud, Graham Robb writes, "Fortunately, aesthetic pleasure can often be derived from a mere impression of complex thought: Einstein's blackboards, Wittgenstein's propositions, Rimbaud's prose poems." It wouldn't be the first time that someone talked about the Viennese philosopher and the Ardennais poet in the same breath. Bruce Duffy, the author of *Disaster Was My God*, the new fictional reimagining of Rimbaud's life, made his début in 1987 with a novel about Wittgenstein, *The World As I Found It*. Although the new novel treats the entirety of Rimbaud's life—it begins with his sour-faced mother reinterring his body in the Charleville cemetery, ten years after his death, and unfolds as a series of flashbacks—its real preoccupation is, inevitably, the question that continues to haunt admirers of Rimbaud. As Vitalie watches the gravedigger at work, she thinks of the journalists and professors who have come calling over the years, asking, "But why did he stop writing?"

There are many lovely touches in Duffy's novel. Rimbaud at one point sits "like a tongue awaiting Holy Communion"; Vitalie in the graveyard arranges some small bones as if they were silverware on a table. More important, Duffy persuasively penetrates the layers of myth and produces characters who suggest the real people they once were. (I liked the way he refers to the young Rimbaud as "the kid.") By far the most impressive—and, in its way, the most moving—of these characterizations is that of Rimbaud's mother, who here emerges not as the familiar harpy of many biographies but as a figure of almost tragic stature, a woman as tormented as she was tormenting. Duffy has the marvelous idea of making Vitalie the real seer in the family: she hears voices and has prophetic dreams. The notion that Rimbaud somehow owed his visionary poetics to his difficult parent has a nice psychological irony. The central emotional drama of the novel is, in fact, the ongoing war of attrition between the son and the mother, resolved—in the only way possible for these two implacable characters—in the final, very moving lines of the book, which imagine the two finally lying "forever coiled like figures in some heavenly constellation."

More problematic, inevitably, is the representation of Rimbaud himself. The interior of an artist's mind is notoriously difficult to represent on the page. (The gold standard, perhaps, is *The Death of Vergil*, the dense 1945 masterwork by the Austrian writer Hermann Broch, which submits the ancient poet to a Joycean treatment, imagining, in the minutest detail, his thoughts as he lies dying in Brindisi.) Although Duffy has some nice evocations of the boy-poet's "cycloning brain," they feel as if they come from outside the organ in question, rather than from within; too often, the author has to fall back on the ungainly device of interjecting reminders of Rimbaud's greatness. ("What other nineteenth-century writer managed to break through to the twentieth?") This cheerleading gets wearisome—as do some misfired attempts at freshening the period drama with contemporary locutions: "Two-seat fat," "cooties of feeling."

But Duffy gets one thing absolutely right. Toward the end, there's a scene in which the alcoholic Verlaine, accompanied by his prostitute pal Eugénie, consents to give an interview to a journalist who's burning to unravel the mystery that pervades the novel: "how a poet of almost unfathomable abilities could willfully *forget* how to write." At one point, the bustling Eugénie interjects with her own theory: "Rimbaud was simply burned out. A dead volcano. Shot his wad." Verlaine, who seems to be speaking for Duffy here, has a larger insight. "Well," he says, "one big reason, perhaps obvious, is he grew up...the child in him died."

Indeed, the mystery of Rimbaud's renunciation may not be such a mystery after all. The apparently irreconcilable extremes of his thought and behavior are easier to account for when you remember that Rimbaud the poet never reached adulthood: violent oscillations between yearning and contempt, sentimentality and viciousness, are not unheard of in adolescents. (The Surrealist André Breton described Rimbaud as "a veritable god of puberty.") Like J. D. Salinger, another beloved celebrant of youthful turmoil, Rimbaud may simply have found that, as he grew up, the urgency of his subject was gone. There was nothing left to say.

This peculiarly adolescent quality of the poet's life and work, the desire to rebel against whatever milieu he happened to find himself in—the schoolboy against school, the wunderkind against his admiring hosts, the poet against poetry—undoubtedly accounts for his particular appeal to teenagers. (A statistic that Rimbaldians like to cite is that one in five French *lycéens* today claims to identify with the long-dead poet.) A striking feature of many of the translations and biographies of Rimbaud is the seemingly inevitable prefatory remark, on the part of the translator or biographer, about the moment when he or she first discovered the poet. "When I was sixteen, in 1956, I discovered Rimbaud," Edmund White recalls at the start of his nimble *Rimbaud: The Double Life of a Rebel*, by far the best introduction to the poet's life and work; Robb observes early on that "for many readers (including this one), the revelation of Rimbaud's poetry is one of the decisive events of adolescence." Ashbery, too, was sixteen at the moment of impact, as was Patti Smith, the author of what is, perhaps, the most moving testament to the effect that a reading of Rimbaud might have on a hungry young mind. "When I was sixteen, working in a non-union factory in a small South Jersey town," she writes in an introduction to *The Anchor Anthology of French Poetry*, "my salvation and respite from my dismal surroundings was a battered copy of Arthur Rimbaud's *Illuminations*, which I kept in my back pocket." The anthology, she adds, "became the bible of my life."

I suspect that the chances that Rimbaud will become the bible of your life are inversely proportional to the age at which you first discover him. I recently did an informal survey among some well-read acquaintances, and the e-mail I received from a ninety-year-old friend fairly sums up the consensus. "I loved Rimbaud poems when I read the Norman Cameron translations in 1942," she wrote—Cameron's translation, which I have used here, is my favorite, too, among the very few in English that try to reproduce Rimbaud's rhymes—but she added, "I have quite lost what it was that so thrilled me." In 1942, my friend was twenty-one. I was twice that age when I first started to read Rimbaud seriously, and, although I found much that dazzled and impressed me, I couldn't get swept away—couldn't feel those feelings again, the urgency, the orneriness, the rebellion. I don't say this with pride. Time passes, people change; it's just the way things are. On the day before his death, a delirious Rimbaud dictated a letter to the head of an imaginary shipping company, urgently requesting passage to Suez. Sometimes, for whatever reason, you miss the boat.

—*The New Yorker*, August 29, 2011

THE SPANISH TRAGEDY

FOR A SPANISH writer to give the name *Sepharad* to a novel that is largely, if not exclusively, about his native land is a subtle, complicated, and fraught gesture. *Sepharad*, after all, is the Hebrew word for Spain. The origins of the term are unclear. Although it occurs (once) as a place-name in the Hebrew Bible, it's unlikely that it refers there to the Spain we know—indeed, it is uncertain whether it refers there to an actual geography at all or is merely a poetic or symbolic name. Some scholars have argued that the name suggests the colonization of Spain by Jews from Sardis, in Asia Minor; a likelier derivation is from the Aramaic *sephar*, connoting a distant limit or seacoast—an apt enough characterization of the Iberian peninsula in the eyes of the Levantine Jews who are said to have migrated there as early as the sixth century BC.

What is both clear and certain is that whatever Jews inhabited Spain twenty centuries after that first migration—perhaps 200,000 souls altogether, nearly a tenth of the total population at the end of the fifteenth century AD—were expelled from it by the infamous 1492 decree of the Catholic monarchs Ferdinand and Isabella. And yet while to all appearances the edict resulted in a remarkably successful ethnic cleansing—today there are about 14,000 Jews in Spain, all arrivals in the past century or so—we also know that it created not only those real exiles but what we might call internal exiles: secret Jews, *marranos*, who to all appearances had accepted their forced conversion to Catholicism but practiced their native religion secretly.

Either way, the cruelty, intolerance, violence, and shame that the 1492 expulsion is likely to summon to the minds of certain readers today—perhaps European, likely but not necessarily Jewish—could not be any further from the associations that that year has for most Americans, for whom 1492 is nothing more than the celebrated year in which Columbus "discovered" America: a year associated in the national consciousness with pride rather than shame, exploration rather than flight, the possibility of limitless freedoms rather than obliterating ideological oppressions.

Hence to call a novel that is much preoccupied with Spain *Sepharad*—to call a country by the name given to it by the citizens it has rejected and cast out—is to invoke, simultaneously and with considerable deftness, the many linked but often opposite connotations of the year 1492. And indeed, shame and guilt, homelands and exile, ceaseless wanderings and bitter alienations both internal and external, metaphorical and real, are persistent motifs of Antonio Muñoz Molina's remarkable novel—one that turns out to be about a territory far vaster than "Sepharad" itself: Europe, perhaps even the world.

It is useful to mention these thematic considerations early on because *Sepharad*, although intensely pleasurable to read, is an extremely difficult book to describe; without the two organizing rubrics so subtly implied by its ostensibly innocuous title, its coherence can be difficult to grasp. When the book (which was published in Spain, as *Sefarad*, in 2001) came out in a very fine English translation by Margert Sayers Pedersen in 2003, it was greeted, when it was greeted at all, with a kind of bemused but constrained admiration. Because the tales that make up the book are narrated in a muted, even affectless voice (beautifully reproduced by Pedersen), and many are set in totalitarian Germany and Russia—for instance, a fleeting tale of a chance meeting in Estonia between a pro-German Spanish officer and the beautiful Jewish mistress of a Nazi official—it was inevitably compared, unfavorably, to the work of W.G. Sebald. Richard Eder, the reviewer for the daily *New York Times*, wrote that Muñoz Molina's novel "lacks the German's stunning calculus of implication and association, farranging and centered, and the sculptured music of his writing."

And yet, because some of the stories that *Sepharad* seems so selfconsciously to anthologize (the Spanish subtitle is *Una novela de novelas*, "a novel of novels") have nothing to do with that Sebaldian theme and tone, other critics accused it of being too diffuse. One story, for instance, is about the death in an Andalusian town of the aunt of the narrator's wife; another recalls the love affair between a provincial cobbler and a sexually voracious nun. "There is much that is loose, some that is repetitious and a little that is self-indulgent," Eder went on to complain, while in the Sunday *New York Times Book Review* Michael Pye wrote of the presence of "cliché" and jarringly "Day-Glo" elements (the beautiful Jewish mistress, the cobbler and the nymphomaniac nun) and ended by suggesting darkly that "a few lapses are enough to turn such a fine piece of literary mosaic into a quite commonplace book."

It is true that, at first glance, the novel seems diffuse. *Sepharad* consists of a series of seventeen ostensibly discrete narratives of between approximately twenty and thirty pages each, the fragmentary, allusive titles of which, always provided in lowercase letters, convey a sense of the tone of the book as a whole: "wherever the man goes";

"you are..."; "those who wait"; "oh you, who knew so well." Many of these are clearly being narrated by a character whom you are invited to identify with the author himself (he is a youngish Spaniard from the provinces, now a successful writer), although the elaborate artfulness with which the ostensibly real-life stories gathered here come together suggests that the line between fact and fiction has been intentionally blurred.

Indeed, the first of the stories is set in Spain and the last in America, a progress that seems intended to remind us of at least one of the trajectories in which the year 1492 resulted (Columbus's), just as other elements seem designed to remind us of others of those trajectories. The first tale, for instance, entitled "sacristan"—the nickname given to the narrator as a boy by a beloved local figure—is a childhood memory of the Holy Week float in his provincial boyhood town, and of how the local artisan who constructed the float used a mean-spirited, money-grubbing tailor as the model for his Judas, while the tall, good-looking, well-liked cobbler served as the model for "the noble Saint Matthew." We are told that this reviled tailor, the first of many characters in the book who are vilified and rejected by their neighbors, had a "Semitic nose," but this oblique reference to the exiled Jews of Spain, that absent presence, is passed over; our desire to grasp at an animating theme, at this early point, is frustrated. (Not that you care: this story, like all the others, is related with such hypnotizing beauty that it is possible to savor each of these "novels" without feeling the need to think ahead to larger connections. It's no surprise that one of them is called "scheherazade.")

This narrator reappears in many stories, often speaking in the first person to a "you," who is his beloved wife. Bit by bit, we get to know more about him. There is the provincial childhood peopled with colorful characters like Mateo Zapatón, the cobbler, whom at the end of the first tale the narrator, now an adult living in Madrid, encounters

on a busy city street, distracted and made unrecognizable by time—
one of many instances in which we feel that the Spain of the present
cannot, somehow, be connected to the Spain of even the recent past.
There is the touching scene in which the aunt of the narrator's wife
dies; there is a hushed visit to a doctor's office during which the narrator learns that he has a potentially mortal illness. There is the un-
nerving trip to Germany that the narrator takes when he is an
established author, during which he sits at a tea parlor wondering
what the well-dressed, well-coiffed old Germans around him were
doing during World War II.

There is a story, set years earlier, about the narrator's stint, as a
young man, working as a booking agent of some kind in a dreary
office of a cultural promotion agency, where, embarrassed by always
having to reject the entreaties of desperate *artistes*, he takes refuge in
the books he obsessively reads and that, he informs us, are for him
more real than his life. Among these is a volume of Kafka's letters to
his mistress, Milena Jesenska, of which the narrator says that they
"nourished my love for the absent beloved, and for the failed or impossible loves I had learned of through films and books."

Such offices, along with other haunted institutions meant to pro-
mote or preserve Spanish culture—museums, in particular—are a recurrent motif in many of the stories, although here again, it is difficult
at first to see a connection among them all. There is, in that first tale,
a brief mention of a museum in rural Andalusia, where an obscure
"regional association" meets primarily, it seems, to swap old stories; a
longer tale concerns a Spanish cultural agency in Tangier that's run by
an expatriate Hungarian Jew; there is the musty Madrid office where
the young narrator books (or doesn't book) second-rate Bulgarian pia-
nists and South American puppeteers; and, finally, there is a visit to
the vast, architecturally overwrought building that houses the Hispanic Society of America, located in a sad neighborhood of New

York City that is all but deserted when the narrator visits it at the end of the book.

It must be said that certain concrete elements that pointedly reappear throughout these languidly narrated tales can seem designed to frustrate rather than create connections. A description of a seashell invites us to make a connection—but how?—between a scene in a darkened examination room, where a patient gets some bad news about his health from a doctor who's been fondling the seashell, to a strange seaside vacation that ends in a dreamlike encounter between the doctor and an aging, desperately ill Nazi. (While hiking in the hills, the doctor strays close to the perimeter of a fenced-off property and is suddenly accosted by a domestic who begs him to save her employer; once inside the house, the doctor sees that it's full of mementoes of the owner's Nazi past.)

A recurrent character—a cousin of the narrator's wife, a beautiful, high-spirited, chestnut-haired, green-eyed young woman who eventually married and had a child, and died of a drug overdose—reappears fleetingly, never clearly identified but always recognizable, in several of the stories, a ghostly figure who hovers over narratives involving railway travel, wasting illness, addiction, and premature death. The motif of premature death and illness—ostensibly unconnected to the many other premature deaths, in the millions, to which the novel alludes—also persists throughout, particularly in the recurrent glimpses we get of the perennially ill, prematurely dead Kafka.

A pervasive aura of ennui and a disjointedness that competes with persistent but ultimately fleeting leitmotifs is nothing new to Muñoz Molina's work. Although relatively young (he was born in Andalusia in 1950), he has achieved considerable prominence in Spain: he has twice won the National Literary Prize there, along with a number of other distinctions. This hasn't translated into recognition in the US.

As far as I can tell, only two of his many novels have appeared in English: *Winter in Lisbon*, a memory-novel that links disconnected motifs—jazz, the names of cities, a love affair—and *Prince of Shadows*, in which a professional assassin who is weary of the trade tracks down his target during the iciest years of the Cold War. Partly this author's relative obscurity here has to do with a by-now notorious indifference to foreign literature on the part of American readers (and publishers); partly it has to do with the fact that much of his previous output, while taking the ostensibly popular forms of detective and spy novels, is dominated by an atmosphere of benumbed angst and marked by the presence of unusual technical features. (Among these are strange oscillations between first- and third-person narrators, a device that recurs in *Sepharad*.) The presence of that tone and those technical features has been attributed to the fact that Muñoz Molina is an author of *el desencanto* ("disillusionment"), a term used to describe the widespread feeling, following the death of Franco in 1975 and the failure of the Socialists elected in 1982 to fulfill their electoral call for *Cambio*, change, of crucial opportunities lost.*

With its dominating tone of dislocation and the overarching structure of fragmentation, *Sepharad* is, then, in many ways the natural heir to its predecessors in both tone and execution. With a postmodern self-consciousness, the narrator of this novel draws his readers' attention to the nature of the narrative they are reading:

> For two or three years I have flirted with the idea of writing a
> novel, imagined situations and places, like snapshots, or like

---

*I am indebted to Lawrence Rich's *The Narrative of Antonio Muñoz Molina: Self-Conscious Realism and "El Desencanto"* (Peter Lang, 1999) for background on this writer's career.

those posters displayed on large billboards at the entrance to a movie theater....When I didn't have the money to go inside, I would spend hours looking at the photographs outside the theater, not needing to invent a story to fit them together like pieces of a jigsaw puzzle. Each became a mystery, illuminating the others, creating multiple links that I could break or modify at my whim, patterns in which no image nullified the others or gained precedence or lost its uniqueness within the whole.

Sepharad is, of course, the novel that the character hoped to be able to write. Only when we keep in mind the implications of the book's title—the implications of 1492, which create the "patterns" that organize the book's pieces and links—does it become clear how brilliantly he has succeeded.

———

The first and most important pattern is the organizing theme of an ideological oppression that results in terrible conditions of exile, and worse. As many reviewers were quick to notice, the destruction, by totalitarian regimes in Europe and elsewhere, of culture itself and the people who create it—artists, writers, intellectuals, impresarios, politicians, and political activists—is a central motif here, although to be sure it apparently has nothing to do with the private lives of its Spanish characters. The most striking of the "novels" that weave their way through this "novel of novels" are, it turns out, not fictions at all but rather the true stories of a handful of characters who, between them, lived out their lives during the harrowing middle years of the last century—stories that, as Muñoz Molina describes in an author's note at the end of his novel, he culled, with little or no further elaboration, from memoirs and biographies.

There is the story of the flamboyant Willi Münzenberg, Stalin's German-born "impresario of the Comintern" who, with his wife, Babette, eventually fell from favor and was pursued to his death by his former Communist colleagues, who hanged him in a remote wood during the mass flight from France in 1940. There is the bizarre and wrenching tale of Babette's sister, Margarete Buber-Neumann, the wife of the director of Germany's Communist Party in the 1930s, who after first fleeing from Hitler into the welcoming arms of Stalin, and then falling from Stalin's grace along with her husband, Heinz, had the peculiar distinction, in the year 1939, of becoming the victim of not one but two regimes, each ideologically opposed to the other, as the characteristically laconic narration in the story called "copenhagen" relates:

> It took Margarete Buber-Neumann three weeks to travel from Moscow to the Siberian camp where she had been sentenced to serve ten years. When only three had passed, they ordered her onto a train back to Moscow, and she thought she would be set free; the train, however, did not stop in Moscow, it continued west. When finally it stopped at the border station of Brest-Litovsk, the Russian guards told Buber-Neumann to hurry and get her belongings together, because they were in German territory.... [She] understood with horror and infinite fatigue that because she was German, Stalin's guard were handing her over to Hitler's guard, fulfilling an infamous clause in the German-Soviet pact.

In the death camp of Ravensbrück, Buber-Neumann met and befriended the doomed Milena Jesenska, who would sometimes tell her new friend about her dead lover and the bizarre tales he wrote.

The allusion to Jesenska is one of those tenuous threads that connects this true story of twentieth-century oppression to the ostensibly private, Spanish world of the narrator's life story: we recall him, as a young man, in the act of reading *Letters to Milena* in the Spanish cultural bureau. This moment and others like it begin to suggest that none of the seemingly discrete narratives gathered here, the stories of small-town Spain and the stories of refugee or deported Central Europeans, is unconnected to the others. There are, to be sure, a number of stories that patently link Spain to the horrors of the mid-twentieth century, for instance stories from the Spanish civil war: one about the ruined family of a Spanish Communist who ends up in Moscow, another about an idealistic, Germanophile Spaniard who joins Spain's Blue Division to fight along with the Nazis on the Russian front. But these more obvious links between Spain and the European disaster of the 1930s and 1940s aren't the ones of greatest interest in revealing the author's subtle unifying strategies.

For what ultimately connects all of the "novels" here is the spirit of Kafka, the author who more than any of the many other authorial voices that hover over this book—Proust, Herodotus, John le Carré—presides over it in its multifaceted entirety. *Pace* those who beat *Sepharad* over the head with Sebald, there is indeed a "stunning calculus of implication and association, far-ranging and centered" that courses through Muñoz Molina's novel. These implications and associations, admittedly so far-ranging at times as to escape easy detection, derive, ultimately, from an experience shared by all of the book's characters—the dread Kafkaesque experience characterized by the narrator in a passage that, typically, is addressed to an unidentified "you":

And you, what would you do if you knew that at any moment they could come for you, that your name may already be on a typed list of prisoners or future dead, or suspects, or traitors?... They notified Josef K. of his trial, but no one arrested him....

This quintessentially twentieth-century experience of sudden, seemingly arbitrary selection and expulsion is, we begin to see, the link that binds together the novel's Spaniards and Germans, its Communists and Fascists. It is the experience typified by the life of a blond, blue-eyed, fully Austrian (or so he thought), half-Jewish youth called Hans Meyer, who, after being persecuted as a Jew, became the writer Jean Améry after the war. It is the tie that binds Spanish Republican soldiers, *desparecidos* in Uruguay, and leukemia-afflicted writers to Kafka himself, as an extraordinary summarizing passage suggests:

> You look at your watch, cross your legs, open a newspaper in the doctor's office or in a café in Vienna in November 1935, when a news article will drive you out of your routine and out of your country and make you a stranger forever. A guest in a hotel, you woke up one night with a fit of coughing and spat blood. The newspaper tells of the laws of racial purity newly promulgated in Nuremberg, and you read that you are a Jew and destined to extermination. The smiling nurse appears in the doorway of the waiting room and tells you that the doctor is ready to see you. Gregor Samsa awoke one morning and found himself transformed.... The healthy, blond man reading his newspaper in a café in Vienna one Sunday morning, dressed in lederhosen and kneesocks and Tyrolean suspenders, in the eyes of the waiter who has served him so often will soon be as repulsive as the poor Orthodox Jew whom men in brown shirts and red armbands humiliate for sport....

The unifying experience, then, is what it means to be "excluded, expelled, from the community of the normal," as the narrator puts it.

There were critics who appreciated this important motif but were nonetheless leery of its moral implications. "But what can such an equation mean when its terms are so different?" Michael Pye asked in his review; and he then went on to suggest that "without morality all these dark stories are just sensations." But it seems to me that Muñoz Molina's multiplex, honeycombed attempt to depict the very root of evil, to create a picture of mankind's impulse to exclude and oppress that goes beyond the particularities of this or that ideology, should be seen as a profound grappling with a very fundamental moral issue indeed. And his insistence on assimilating to the vignettes of political oppression the experience of the suffering sick, particularly those who to all appearances are normal but who are doomed to pain and likely death (both AIDS and leukemia are invoked), is to my mind an effective means of reminding his readers, by means of an analogy, a suggestive narrative metaphor, of that other class of exiles, not the literal but the metaphorical exiles created by political oppressions, as 1492 taught us: the *marranos*, the internal exiles, cut off from the community of the normal to which they bear the most superficial of resemblances, stigmatized by the presence of an invisible trait for which they can bear no responsibility.

But then, to appreciate the large moral vision of Muñoz Molina's novel, you must return, as he does, to the awkward question raised by its disturbingly allusive title. *Sepharad* ends with a grand and tragic gesture that suggests that willed acts of selection and expulsion (or worse) doom nations, as they do people, to a kind of metaphorical exile, an exile from themselves: the ultimate internal exile. This moving point is made in a finale that links the themes of illness, exile, internal exile, of museums and cultural survivals and nationalisms, and in so doing climactically unites the unsettling multiple significances of the fateful year of 1492.

The final section of the novel is called "sepharad." In it, the narrator finds himself living for a brief time in what he describes as a pleasant, self-imposed "exile" in New York City. His prolonged visit from Spain to the New World might put us in mind of Columbus, of "discovery" and the horizons of new worlds and possibilities; yet the same pleasant visit inevitably brings with it reminders of that other result of 1492. (While in New York, the narrator stumbles across an ancient Sephardic cemetery off Fifth Avenue.) As an expression, perhaps, of both aspects of 1492, the last thing the narrator does is to visit what may well be described as a symbol of Spain itself, of its great imperial culture—a culture that is, now, just another exile abroad: the enormous and neglected Hispanic Society, located in uptown Manhattan, a place to which the bus journey takes so much time that it feels like a voyage of discovery itself.

We have by this point been prepared, in a fashion that is typically complex and subtle, for this strange culminating collocation of the two great results of 1492—America as a refuge and Spain as the oppressor, the expeller, the exiler. Earlier on, we learn that the Mateo Zapatón whom the young narrator idolized is not only the dashing swain of their small town but the adulterous lover of many of the small town's matrons; and indeed the lover of the young nun about whom we heard in a much earlier story. The information is typically disconcerting: hundreds of pages after we first hear about Mateo—whose handsome face, we recall, serves as the model for his namesake, the noble Saint Matthew, in the town's Holy Week float—we are forced to revise our moral picture of this attractive but corrupt character, a fornicator whose sins make him far worse morally, after all, than was the loathed tailor, the model for Judas, whose only sin was to have a Jewish-looking nose (a suggestion that he is the descendant of *marranos*, perhaps). There is a strong implication here that we are meant to think hard about the hypocrisies of the various regimes we've encountered in these tales, regimes that are always eager to assign guilt to certain "others," and then to cut those others out.

The revelation about Mateo Zapatón is made during a conversation that provides the climax of Muñoz Molina's moral argument about the human impulse to cut off and expel. Here the expulsions of 1492 are connected to the exterminations of another, more recent year, which is an anagram of the Columbus year: 1942. For even as he laughingly relates the story of his affair with the bride of Christ, Mateo himself, the shoemaker, seems unaware that his personal hypocrisy may ultimately be related to a larger crime, to which he almost unwittingly refers in a reverie about lost shoes, which, he muses, are

the saddest things in the world because they always made me think of dead people, especially that time of year, in winter, when everyone is off to the olive harvest and I could spend the whole day without seeing a soul. During the war, when I was a little boy, I saw a lot of dead people's shoes. They would shoot someone and leave him lying in a ditch or behind the cemetery, and we kids would go look at the corpses, and I noticed how many had lost their shoes, or I'd find a pair of shoes, or a single shoe, and not know which dead man they belonged to. Once in a newsreel I saw mountains of old shoes in those camps they had in Germany.

And indeed we are, I think, meant to think of Mateo, of the moral costs to Spain of its hypocrisies and sins—it is the symbolic model,

here, of all such regimes and their hypocrisies and sins—in the culminating moments of the book, where the author and his wife wan-
der about the fabulous halls of the Hispanic Society. Here, surrounded
by a staggering collection of every conceivable artifact of Spanish
culture, in what looks to the narrator like "a flea market where all
the testimony and heritage of the past has ended"—artifacts that
themselves remind him of the absent presence, of "Sepharad" ("the
1519 *Amadís de Gaula*, the Bible translated into Spanish by Yom
Tov Arias, the son of Levi Arias, and published in Ferrara in 1513
because it could not be published in Spain")—the narrator and his
wife encounter a female character whom, it suddenly becomes obvious, we have met before. This woman, like the narrator himself, is a
voluntary exile from Spain, someone who has followed that other,
liberating trajectory of 1492; yet because she has been linked, in an
earlier story, to Mateo, a morally compromised character, her presence simultaneously reminds us of what we might call the sinful,
sinning Spain, too. Together this woman and the narrator stare at a
Velázquez painting of a girl who, you realize, with her raven hair and
dark eyes, could be either Spanish or Jewish. Or, of course, both.

   That culminating and poignant confusion, coming as the climax
of a scene that simultaneously puts the reader in mind of exile, escape,
and internal, "hidden" exile, suggests that the price paid for their
relentless persecutions of "others" is, ultimately, the oppressors' own
souls. The descriptions of Spain itself, you realize, are all characterized by a sense of loss, of emptiness; it is only here, in a deserted museum on foreign soil, that we encounter what we think of as the best
of Spain's culture and its history. This, surely, is why the narrator
detects, in the eyes of the haunted, hunted face of that elusive painted
figure—the quintessential Spaniard painted by the quintessential
Spanish painter—"the melancholy of a long exile": a term that, by

this point, clearly refers to Spain itself as well as its Jews. It is a measure of the meticulous and exacting artistry with which Muñoz Molina has constructed his vast and subtle, dreamlike and wrenching book that he has arranged for the word "exile" to be the last, devastating word in a work that is, I think, something of a masterpiece.

—*The New York Review of Books*, May 25, 2006

IN GAY AND CRUMBLING ENGLAND

EARLY ON IN Alan Hollinghurst's big new novel *The Stranger's Child*
—his first in seven years, the eagerly anticipated follow-up to his
Man Booker–winning *The Line of Beauty*—a youngish man stands
gazing at a tomb, thinking about an absent penis. The year is 1926,
and the man, George Sawle, is a married scholar in his early thirties,
to all appearances a moderately distinguished product of the com-
fortable middle classes. The tomb (and the penis) belong to Cecil
Valance, a dashing aristocrat and promising poet who had been
killed in the Great War—and who had been George's lover at
Cambridge.

As George examines the marble effigy atop the grandiose tomb,
commissioned by Cecil's grieving family, he is struck, not without a
certain rueful amusement, by the contrast between the "ideal" and
"standardized" quality of the statue and his private memories of their
"mad sodomitical past" together. This thought inevitably leads to
recollections of certain features that the tomb could not, of course,
depict, and that George nearly can't bring himself to name: "the

celebrated...the celebrated *membrum virile,* unguessed for ever beneath the marble tunic, but once so insistently alive and alert."

There was a time when the *membra virilia* you were likely to encounter in Hollinghurst's novels were neither unnamable nor bashfully hidden away. In 1989, when he was thirty-five, he made an impressive debut with his marvelously rich and deft *The Swimming-Pool Library,* in which a plush style, a formidable culture, and a self-confident avoidance of then-fashionable formal tricks were put in the service of a startlingly direct and unembarrassed treatment of gay desire. The novel, set in the early 1980s, traces the surprisingly entwined lives of two gay men: Will Beckwith, a narcissistic, well-to-do young pleasure-seeker whose ambition is to keep "clear of interference from the demands and misery of other people," and an elderly peer called Charles Nantwich, an old Africa hand with a complicated past who has asked Will to write his biography, and whom Will had met, somewhat comically, while "cottaging"—looking for anonymous sex in a public toilet.

Both of them, it turns out, have a taste for young black men, and the novel is, among many other things, a sophisticated investigation into what you could call the erotic component of colonialism. (Will doesn't realize how patronizing is his admiration for the "happiness and loyalty" he sees in the face of a black youth in a painting.) But its most striking feature, perhaps, was its insistence on highlighting the urgent presence, in so many gay men's lives, of what you could call the less theoretical side of desire. Penises, for instance. In one of the many scenes that take place in the shower of Will's gym—set pieces that highlight his cool connoisseurship of the bodies he intends to have, or has had—a swoony catalog of male members gives you an idea of the way in which Hollinghurst's velvety sentences can smoothly twine around a subject that some literary novelists might find dauntingly rebarbative:

In the rank and file of men showering the cocks and balls took on the air almost of an independent species, exhibited in instructive contrasts. Here was the long, listless penis, there the curt, athletic knob or innocent rosebud of someone scarcely out of school. Carlos's Amerindian giant swung alongside the compact form of a Chinese youth whose tiny brown willy was almost concealed in his wet pubic hair, like an exotic mushroom in a dish of seaweed.

The deliberate elegance of the prose makes a certain point. Style, in Hollinghurst's work, is the great leveler—it brings within the orbit of serious fiction subjects and acts that other writers, even gay writers, might "tastefully" elide.

The tension between the lush style and the gritty subject matter would become a hallmark of Hollinghurst's writing. In his next few novels the unflinching gaze and posh pen were often trained on difficult or even unattractive material and characters. His densely atmospheric second book, *The Folding Star* (1994), focused minutely on the antics of an appallingly unself-aware Briton, now working in Belgium as an English tutor, who develops a Humbert Humbert–like obsession with a seventeen-year-old boy pupil. (A soupçon of ephebophilia runs through these books.) A third, entitled *The Spell* (1998), was a slight, rather self-conscious exercise in what some critics called "Austenian" social comedy—in it, a group of four men of all ages fall in and out of bed with one another in various combinations and with no visible consequences. The novel was bracingly matter-of-fact about the important part played by drugs and casual sex in the social lives of many educated, middle-class, "nice" gay men.

Hollinghurst's most acclaimed work, *The Line of Beauty* (2004), is the story of a young, middle-class gay man's complicated relationship with the family of a wealthy and ambitious Tory politician in the

1980s—a kind of Thatcher-era riff on *Brideshead Revisited*, complete with a deceptively soft-spoken matriarch and wayward patriarch. Here, the author turns his coolly ironic gaze on the way in which its protagonist, who is given the suggestive name Nick Guest, and who begins as a graduate student working on Henry James, is led by his deluded social and erotic ambitions to "cut" his "moral nerves" (as he puts it, in a different context), leaving him with nothing but a "life of valueless excess": cocaine, empty sex, and so on. In all of these books, the willies wag and the anuses wink with gleeful abandon. They are, Hollinghurst rightly insists, an important part of the story.

In the best of his work, the unruly presence of charged and illicit desires in otherwise traditional English landscapes is the vehicle for biting commentary by the author—on social and sexual conventions, on the way in which self-concealment can become self-betrayal, on colonial and imperial hypocrisies. "The English idyll had its secret paragraphs, priapic figures in the trees and bushes," a character in the new book observes; or, as *The Swimming-Pool Library*'s Will Beckwith says of the biography he's thinking of writing, "it's the queer side, though, which would give it its interest."

Indeed, Hollinghurst has Lord Nantwich make the provocative argument that "queerness" is what allows us to read the true story of the past. For him, the behaviors or attitudes of an earlier, closeted era, which to today's gay men and women may seem hopelessly furtive or repressed, had aesthetic and even intellectual advantages:

Oh it was unbelievably sexy—much more so than nowadays. I'm not against Gay Lib and all that, of course... but it has taken a lot of the fun out of it, a lot of the *frisson*. I think the 1880s must have been an ideal time, with brothels full of off-duty soldiers, and luscious young dukes chasing after barrow-boys. Even in the Twenties and Thirties, which were quite wild in their way, it was still kind of underground, we operated on a constantly shifting code, and it was so extraordinarily moving and exciting when that spurt of recognition came, like the flare of a match! No one's ever really written about it....

But Hollinghurst himself writes about it, again and again: in his fiction, the ability to puzzle out codes and achieve meaningful recognitions—and the tragic consequences of the failure to do so—have been a constant preoccupation, strongly inflected by the homoerotic element. In the five novels that he has published over the past twenty-two years, the distinctive knowingness to which gay people often feel privy, the sense of having privileged access to powerful secrets and hidden motivations not visible to other people, is a vital element in a serious literary investigation into knowledge, truth, narrative, and history. That the author's gay protagonists—they tend to be so unattractively self-absorbed that you can't really call them heroes—are revealed to be clueless about everything but their own desires adds a telling irony to his treatment of this subject. In *The Swimming-Pool Library*, Will learns from Nantwich's diaries that the old man had been prosecuted and sent to prison in the 1950s for soliciting an undercover police officer; he also learns, to his horror, that the smoothly ambitious prosecutor who used the case to further his political career was his own grandfather, now Lord Beckwith.

The theme of knowledge, self-knowledge, and secret knowledge often sets in motion penetrating investigations into the nature and meaning of desire, art, politics, and identity. In *The Folding Star*, three ingeniously nested tales of erotic obsession—the gay narrator's yearning for his pupil, a long-dead Symbolist painter's undying passion for his drowned muse, and a Belgian youth's affair with a collaborator during World War II—serve as a vehicle for a meditation on the way that our yearning to "know" one person can make us disastrously ignorant of more momentous realities and truths. (The uncanny likenesses among the three tales further underscore the *Vertigo*-like theme of reduplication; the reader is forced to ponder why we make copies of what we find beautiful.) Hollinghurst elaborates these motifs with an irony that is sometimes amusing and sometimes tragic. The title of *The Line of Beauty* alludes to the S-shaped curve admired by Hogarth, in his 1753 *Analysis of Beauty*, as expressive of liveliness—as opposed to straight or intersecting lines, which according to Hogarth suggest stasis and death. One of the many bitter poignancies in the novel is that the gay aesthetes in the story who pursue "the line of beauty"—the curve recurs with pointed frequency, whether of the shape of a piano at a recital or in the undulations of a black youth's torso and buttocks—are themselves doomed to death.

For all these reasons, the new book comes as something of a surprise. In many ways, *The Stranger's Child*—which is about the way in which the true, gay story behind a poem that Cecil Valance wrote, and which for a time becomes a national favorite, is elided over time—takes up themes and settings the author has visited in the past. Not the least of these, as George Sawle's glum ruminations make clear, is the way in which public, family, and "official" narratives come into conflict with, and often betray, the complicated truths of messy private lives. There is, to be sure, a gay love affair; and the story is set in (among other places) a grand Victorian country house and some charmingly old-fashioned suburban acreage—places that have played an important symbolic part in Hollinghurst's earlier books, which, as this one also does, explore the shifting meaning of Englishness from the last century to the present one. But there is something tame about this effort, in which, indeed, cold marble seems too often to substitute for living flesh. By the time you reach the last of its more than four hundred pages, you wonder whether a certain vital organ is missing.

On one level, *The Stranger's Child* rings some interesting and rather elegiac changes on Hollinghurst's characteristic themes. The book takes its title from a line of Tennyson's *In Memoriam*, a poem that someone recites in the first of its five sections and that suggests its dominant preoccupations: how difficult it is to know the past, and the insufficiency of our attempts to memorialize, indeed to remember.

The year is 1913, and the poem is being read by Cecil Valance, who although still an undergraduate is already on his way to becoming a well-known poet himself; he's written a number of poems about Corley Court, the great Victorian country seat belonging to his family, and several have been published. The recitation occurs halfway through Cecil's weekend stay at Two Acres, the suburban home belonging to the family of his lover George. During the course of the weekend Cecil repeatedly ravishes the swooning George (whose clueless mother, Freda, is merely happy to see that her hitherto shy and friendless child has blossomed at school); but he also flirts with, and makes an aggressive pass at, George's sixteen-year-old sister, the highly impressionable Daphne, a girl already breathing "the air of legend." Cecil's apparent polymorphous perversity gives rise to a series of metastasizing misunderstandings that, over the course of the novel's subsequent sections—the second is set in 1926, the third in 1967, the fourth in 1979, and the coda, fittingly centered on a memorial service, brings us to 2008—come to obscure a truth that, we are told, is of some cultural significance.

For by the end of his stay Cecil has written a poem called "Two Acres" in Daphne's autograph book, which goes on to become a sentimental national favorite for a time after Cecil is killed in the Great War: we're told at one point that Churchill makes much of it, and that it has, as someone remarks, "entered the language." (Cecil is clearly modeled on Rupert Brooke; as with the real-life poet, Cecil's posthumous reputation is the object of a fierce though civilized struggle between his mother and his biographer.) With each new section, each of which is tellingly pegged to a major historical or political event—the General Strike in 1926, the decriminalization of consensual homosexual relations in 1967, and so on—the passage of time further blurs the truth of events the exact nature and motivations of which were already murky when they occurred. Daphne thinks "Two Acres" was a love poem written for her; George believes it was written for him. Their mother thinks it's a poem "about her house." Jonah, the handsome local boy who serves at Two Acres, steals some torn-up pages that are an important clue to the poem's meaning.

And meanwhile, a true gay love story, more profound and more moving than Cecil's lordly toying with George, is taking place right under the Sawles's noses: a slowly stoked passion the secret of which won't be uncovered for nearly a hundred years—by accident, a fortuitous discovery made by someone who, in the novel's last lines, is shown to be too preoccupied with his own amours to give this poignant revelation much thought. (Another recurrence of that favorite theme.) All this is meant to bear out the rueful truth of Tennyson's lines—that the passage of time will inevitably make "A fresh association blow, / And year by year the landscape grow / Familiar to the stranger's child."

In many ways, this sentiment ideally suits Hollinghurst's penchant for playing secret gay histories against "History" with a capital H— and for enlisting allusions to other favorite novels to make his point. This time around, he's riffing on Ian McEwan's *Atonement*, which similarly makes a young girl's misunderstanding about grown-up sexuality the basis for a series of increasingly grave errors.

Daphne's fantasies about Cecil lay the groundwork for the most successful element of the book: a richly layered, subtle, and often witty exploration of the way in which the stories we tell ourselves can occlude (comically or tragically) the real story—how "our" truth ends up obscuring "the" truth, whether in poetry, history, or biography. Or in fiction: it's amusing that, from the start, Daphne is a kind of novelist manqué. When we first meet her, she's already an impressionable fabulist: waiting for her brother George to show up with his glamorous Cambridge friend, she starts to imagine that something dreadful has happened to their train, and glows with self-important pleasure at the thought of spreading the news of an accident: "She... saw herself describing the occasion to someone, many years later, though still without quite deciding what the news had been."

This turns out to be both a prophecy about Daphne and a forecast of the theme of the book itself, which shows how each generation interprets—which is to say, rewrites—"Two Acres" and its history in a way that reflects the assumptions, interests, and preoccupations of the times. (By 2008, the queer theorists have gotten their hands on the poem.) At the center of the deliberately vague narrative is Daphne herself. By 1967, when a young man called Paul Bryant enters the now-elderly woman's orbit—eventually he'll write a controversial tell-all biography of Cecil—he is given to believe not only that "Two Acres" "had been written specifically for her" but that Cecil "wrote pretty well everything for her." (Like Nick Guest in *The Line of Beauty*, Paul is a Charles Ryder character, pressing his long nose against the Palladian windows of his social superiors: a not necessarily attractive type that recurs in Hollinghurst's fiction and for which the author has a peculiar and affecting sympathy.) A dozen years later, when the middle-aged Paul, who turns out to have some secrets of his own and is—an amusing paradox—both a good liar and an intuitive biographer, is interviewing the old lady for his book, she rather desperately continues to suggest that she is central to the Cecil story, despite what is clearly, almost amusingly, a lack of hard evidence in the poems themselves. ("In the poem I'm merely referred to as 'you.'") Paul may be haunted by a "curious feeling of imposture," but everyone in this story turns out to be a bit of a fake.

The difficulty of getting at the meaning of the past has always been on Hollinghurst's mind; here, it often has comic overtones. There's a very funny scene in which Paul, who has managed to track down and interview Jonah Trickett (the pretty servant boy at Two Acres, now an old deaf man living in a council flat), reads the transcripts of his taped conversation with Trickett and finds that his great scoop consists of the following:

> PB: Did George Sawle (*inaudible*)?
> JT: Oh, no, he didn't.
> PB: Really? how interesting!
> JT: Oh, lord, no! (*Cackles*)
> PB: So was Cecil himself at all (*inaudible: fortunate?*)
> JT: Well he could be, yes. Though I don't suppose anybody knows that!
> PB: I'm sure they don't! That's not what you expect! (*giggles*)

Time, as Hollinghurst knows, always giggles at our attempts to get around it.

———

And yet despite its often rich elaborations of this favorite theme, there is a hollowness at the center of this book.

Part of this inevitably has to do with a bold choice that Hollinghurst makes: aside from a couple of lines here and there, we never get to see Cecil's poem—and what we do get indicates, amusingly, that

Cecil would, at best, have become a pretty mediocre minor Georgian poet. Hence the center of all this cultural fuss and narrative cleverness is a cipher, as if to suggest that the past we yearn to recapture is always evanescent, if not indeed substanceless. This notion is reflected in the most interesting technical feature of the book, which is built around a series of narrative "gaps": from one section to the next, people disappear, relationships shift, deaths occur, and it's left to the reader to puzzle out these reshufflings.

But organizing a very long narrative around a blank space, however intriguing a notion, in practice has the curious effect of robbing the book of any real stakes: in the end, it's hard to care that much about whom the poem was addressed to or what the circumstances of its composition were. (By contrast, Hollinghurst's marvelously inventive presentation of Nantwich's diaries in *The Swimming-Pool Library* and of the Symbolist painter's canvases in *The Folding Star* gives those books much of their rich texture and appeal.) And, as often in Hollinghurst—perhaps too often, at this point—there's no character appealing enough that you have any real emotional investment in the proceedings.

What's really missing here is the ornery soul that animated Hollinghurst's earlier works and gave them their satirical texture and bite— the priapic figures dancing at the edges of the traditional landscapes he lovingly evokes. In *The Stranger's Child*, for the first time, the landscape overwhelms the satyrs.

Already in *The Swimming-Pool Library*, you could feel a tension between the author's gritty subversiveness and a certain sentimental nostalgia, "the irresistible elegiac need for the tenderness of an England long past," as Will Beckwith puts it. This conflict is reflected in Will himself, suggestively divided as he is between his subversive passion for pretty boys and his wholly conventional passion for beautiful buildings. By day, he toils away at a grand encyclopedia of architecture, and almost sheepishly admits that "the orders, the dome, the portico, the straight lines and the curved...spoke to me, and meant more to me than they do to some." They clearly mean a lot to Hollinghurst, too: in all of his novels, tender descriptions of buildings and interior-design schemes and artworks have a pointed symbolic function. In particular, the great piles built by prosperous and appetitive Victorians—they crop up in *The Swimming-Pool Library*, *The Spell*, and *The Line of Beauty* as well as in the new novel—seem like reproachful reminders of a more confident era: the gloomy fate of these admittedly often tasteless constructions, torn down, boxed in, callously modernized, cut up into flats, suggests a certain nostalgia for a grander, more aesthetically confident past.

So too in *The Stranger's Child*. We learn—ironically—that even as the reputation of "Two Acres" evolves over time, the two houses associated with the poem—the grand Victorian Corley Court and the more modest but charmingly evocative Two Acres—lapse into decrepitude. This devolution and the emotions it provokes are foreshadowed in the first part, when Daphne, excitedly discussing local landmarks with the newly arrived Cecil and George, exclaims over the "sad fate" of a historic house that has been turned into a school. This, in fact, is what will happen to Corley. We learn that, already in the 1920s, before the house is sold, Cecil's younger brother, Dudley (who ends up marrying Daphne), has had its exuberant Victorian excrescences boxed in and smoothed over. (There is a whiff here of Waugh's *Decline and Fall*, that satirical elegy born of a young author's sentimentality about the past: in it, the chatelaine of a masterpiece of Tudor architecture called King's Thursday transforms it into an angular modernistic structure designed by an architect called Dr. Silenus.) The original architectural details come to light only in 1967, when an overflowing bath in the matron's quarters causes a dropped ceiling to cave in, revealing unguessed riches at which Paul's boy-friend, who teaches in the school, gazes in rapture.

As for Two Acres itself, by the time that Paul locates it in 1979, looking for clues about the past, it's been despoiled—the house divided into apartments, the famous eponymous acreage zoned for "Executive Homes." "There was nothing to see," Paul thinks as he noses around the property, whose significance now lies wholly in the past, and in poetry. The passage of time, as we know from Tennyson's poem, makes everything unrecognizable—our landscapes, our houses, ourselves.

A taste for impressive old buildings is not at all illiberal; but the sentimental element that subtends it makes itself felt in other, more troubling ways in Hollinghurst's fiction. The kind of thing I'm talking about appears already in the first book. At one point, Will Beckwith ruefully acknowledges that his family's social status and country seat are of embarrassingly recent vintage ("how recent and synthetic this nobility was—the house itself bought up cheap after the war, half ruined by use as an officers' training school, and then as a military hospital") and you can't help feeling that it's meant to color our sense of just who the Beckwiths are, in particular the loathsome grandfather. Indeed, the elder Beckwith, an arriviste whose lifestyle is bought—he's merely a life peer, to boot—is pointedly contrasted with the man he ruined, Lord Nantwich, whom we're meant to see as nature's nobleman as well as Debrett's. Nantwich comes complete with an ancient, rather ramshackle London house stuffed with dusty but authentic treasures.

But surely the notion that the bad guys aren't bona fide aristocrats and the good guys are is suspect. Similarly, however delicious the lampoon of the nouveaux riches Thatcherites may be in *The Line of Beauty*, you can't help noticing the unspoken assumptions that lie behind the depictions of many of the vulgar right-wingers in whose company Nick Guest becomes immersed. What, exactly, are we being asked to conclude about the crass "new" England when we learn, of one member of Nick's new circle, that the grand Duchess of Flintshire was once "plain Sharon Feingold"? This awkward and, I'm sure, unconscious inclination on Hollinghurst's part is worth mentioning because it inevitably weakens the force of his larger critique.*

You have to wonder what is being critiqued in the new book. Bad design? "These plans!" the Daphne of 1926 says, when she is mistress of Corley, as she glimpses a glamorous lady decorator's plans to box over its gaudy splendors. "We're not going to know ourselves

---

*It is dismaying, indeed, to see an author of Hollinghurst's sophistication and culture lapsing into the old British literary habit of using Jewish names, and their owners, to mark a falling away from pristine Britishness. Daphne's marital history seems intended to suggest a descending arc: her second, untitled husband is a bisexual painter who is killed in World War II, and her third and final spouse is a certain "Mr. Jacobs," a "nice" small-time manufacturer who did not, apparently, fight in the war. What we know of Sharon Feingold herself suggests a Trollopian caricature: she is the heiress to a vinegar fortune (used by her titled husband to fix up his castle), described as a "thoughtless social dynamo." An equally nineteenth-century touch is that, in *The Line of Beauty*, the money behind the right-wing politician with whom the narrator lives and who is the book's symbol of Thatcher-era moral corruption is a Rothschild-like Jewish banking fortune. In this context it's worth mentioning that in the 1920s section of the book, the irritating photographer assigned to photograph the Valances at home—he refers to the children as "kiddies," and seems intended to represent the distressingly crass "modern" world of publicity and celebrity—is called Jerry Goldblatt. While the encounter between Dudley and Goldblatt may be intended to underscore the former's distasteful prejudices, what I see as the hidden strain of regressiveness in the author's own nostalgia for Old England makes these small details come off badly.

These points, when I made them, in slightly different form, in my original article and then in two letters, provoked a strong reaction, first from Galen Strawson, a philosopher and a friend of Hollinghurst's, and then from the author himself. The full exchanges may be found at www.nybooks.com/articles/archives/2011/dec/08/strangers-child/ and at www.nybooks.com/articles/archives/2012/jan/12/strangers-child-exchange/.

soon." The way in which we can become unrecognizable to ourselves is, as we know, a large theme here. But whereas that destabilizing loss of certainty led, in the earlier books, to a salutary new consciousness—Will Beckwith, for instance, finally learns who he and his family truly are by the end of *The Swimming-Pool Library*—what marks *The Stranger's Child* is a strong nostalgia for the old style of life. More strongly, indeed, than in the previous novels, a palpable aura of regret runs through this book, almost a resistance to the present. I lost count of the number of times that characters mournfully say things like "No one remembered the rememberers."

Something about all this isn't right. While it appeals to a certain taste in popular entertainment, which cannot get enough of "old" England—*Downton Abbey*, most recently, to say nothing of *Upstairs, Downstairs*, the endless succession of Austen and Forster adaptations; a taste that, I suspect, will make *The Stranger's Child* the most popular of Hollinghurst's books yet—this abundant tenderness for an England long past sits ill with the other story that's being told here, however atrophied it is: the subversive gay story, which reminds us of what often lay behind those impressive or charming façades: the class arrogance, the middle-class "niceness" that ruined so many lives. Mrs. Sawle's discovery of Cecil's love letters to George triggers a confrontation so traumatic that George ends up trapped for the rest of his life in an airless marriage to a dour lady academic.

And so there's a strange waffling at the heart of *The Stranger's Child*. I was struck by the author's complicated sympathy for Paul Bryant, who can't decide if he wants to cheat Daphne's family or infiltrate them (he ends up doing both); and wondered whether, like Paul—like many of us gay men over the past generation, with its galvanizing traumas and its great successes, too—Hollinghurst the writer can no longer quite decide who he stands with: the "queer" outsiders or the establishment. With its sepia regrets and wry chuckling over its harmlessly wayward characters, *The Stranger's Child* is not the book you'd have thought this author was likely to end up writing, back in the days of Will Beckwith's long showers at the gym. Like Cecil's tomb, it's "a thoroughly dignified piece of work, in fact magnificently proper," as George admits; but one in which—as he murmurs while gazing at the curiously insufficient marble likeness—you "don't quite feel" you've found the person you once knew.

—*The New York Review of Books*, November 10, 2011

TRANSGRESSION

LIKE ORESTES, THE hero of the Greek tragedy to which its title alludes —and which, according to its author, has from the start provided his novel with its "underlying structure"—*The Kindly Ones* has been both extravagantly blessed and hideously cursed. Published in France in 2006 as *Les Bienveillantes*, it was immediately crowned with the most prestigious critical garlands: not only rapturous reviews but also both the Prix Goncourt and the Grand Prix du Roman de l'Académie Française. It was, too, gilded by an astonishing commercial success, selling more than 700,000 copies in France and commanding enormous advances from foreign publishers (nearly $600,000 for German rights alone, and a reputed seven figures for the US rights). This combination of kudos and euros, together with a subject matter that is, to put it mildly, sensational—the book, which runs to nearly a thousand pages, takes the form of a memoir of an SS officer who, apart from the wartime activities that he recalls in meticulous detail, is also a homosexual matricide who has an incestuous relationship with his twin sister—has had a large part in giving the novel the luster of triumph and excess that accompanies its arrival on foreign shores.

As for the curses, these have been abundant, too—starting in France itself. Claude Lanzmann, whose epic documentary *Shoah* Jonathan Littell has referred to as an inspiration for his book, was not alone there in denouncing what he called the novel's "decor of death," the way in which, as some critics saw it, the book and, perhaps, its author seem to revel in offering graphic details of atrocities.

It comes as no surprise that a book that is preoccupied with giving a persuasive account of what it would be like to be an ostensibly civilized person who ends up doing unimaginably uncivilized things should, for the most part, have been enthusiastically embraced and, to a far lesser extent, vigorously resisted in a country that has such a tortured historic relationship to questions of collaboration and resistance. For the same reason, perhaps, you're not surprised to learn that the most violent criticism of the "monstrous" book's "kitsch" and "pornography of violence" has come from Germany and Israel: the countries, that is to say, of the perpetrators and the victims. The critic of *Die Zeit* bitterly asked why she should

> read a book written by an educated idiot who writes badly, is haunted by sexual perversities and abandoned himself to racist ideology and an archaic belief in fate? I am afraid that I have yet to find the answer.

The answer to that impatient query surely has something to do with the novel's large ambitions, which precisely address the question of why we would be interested in how an educated person could abandon himself to racist ideology, and what the ramifications of that abandonment might look like. Some of these ambitions are brilliantly realized; others much less so. But all of them make Littell's book a serious one, deserving of serious treatment.

The key to these ambitions lies in the complex resonances of the novel's title. *Bienveillantes* is the French rendering of the classical Greek word *eumenides*: the "well-meaning" or "kindly" ones, the ritual appellation rather hopefully used to designate the awful supernatural beings far better known to us as the Erinyes, or Furies. In Aeschylus' *Oresteia*—a work that Littell's novel repeatedly invokes, from the protagonist's casual reference to his closest friend as his "Pylades" to large plot elements, not the least of which is his apparent murder of his mother and her second husband—the hero Orestes is pursued by these awful, slavering, dog-faced creatures, whose province is the punishment of kin murder, after he kills his mother, Clytemnestra, in a divinely ordained retribution for her murder of Orestes' father, Agamemnon. (Clytemnestra killed Agamemnon because he sacrificed their daughter Iphigenia in order to win favorable winds for his fleet's journey to Troy.)

The heart of the trilogy is in fact a competition between the claims of vengeance and the claims of justice: not for nothing does its climax, in the third play, take the form of a trial scene. For *Eumenides* ends with Orestes being acquitted by a newly instituted formal court of law, a result that enrages the Furies, who are finally appeased with a promise that they will henceforth no longer be reviled bogies but incorporated into the life of the Athenian state and given a new home beneath the Acropolis. In accordance with their new, rather domesticated status, their name gets prettified, too: instead of the dreadful Furies they will henceforth be known as the Eumenides, "the kindly ones." And yet it is hard not to feel that this ostensibly happy ending has disturbing overtones: How tame, really, do we think these superficially redubbed Furies will be?

To name a literary work after the third play in Aeschylus' trilogy, then, is to invoke, with extreme self-consciousness, two related themes: one having to do with civilization in general, and the other with human nature. The former concerns justice, its nature and uses: how it is instituted, and then executed, how much it conflicts with, regulates, and possibly appeases the more primitive thirst for vengeance, which it is meant to supersede. The latter concerns the unsettling way in which, beneath even the most pleasant, "kindly" exteriors, dark and potentially violent forces lurk. Neither, needless to say, is restricted to Greek tragedy, or classical civilization; if anything, both are intimately connected to the main preoccupation of Littell's novel, the German program of extermination during World War II.

The Kindly Ones comprises two large structural elements intended to explore these questions. The first is the historical/documentary plot— that is to say, the meticulous chronological re-creation of Maximilien Aue's wartime career from 1941 to 1945, which allows us to track Germany's career, too: from the mass graves in eastern Poland and the Ukraine, following Operation Barbarossa, to Babi Yar and Kiev, to the Caucasus, and thence (after he irritates a senior officer who punishes him by sending him to the front) to the disaster at Stalingrad, then back to Berlin where he becomes a favorite of Himmler and Eichmann; then a stint in Paris which allows him to catch up with friends from his student days, collaborators who, like many of the characters, are real historical figures (Robert Brasillach, Lucien Rebatet); then a posting to Auschwitz in 1943, and finally, the fall of Berlin itself, which finds the Zelig-like Aue in Hitler's bunker. This itinerary allows Aue to be both eyewitness to and participant in the atrocities—and, because this narrator is an educated, reasonable-seeming man, allows the reader some access to the mentality of a perpetrator.

The second structural element is the mythic/sexual: that is, the entirety of the *Oresteia* story, superimposed on the primary narrative and consisting of flashbacks to Aue's earlier life and of events transpiring in the wartime present, which establishes him as a latter-day Orestes. He is obsessed with his soldier father's disappearance at the end of the Great War, and with what he sees as the unforgivable betrayal of his father by his "odious bitch" mother. ("It's as if they had murdered him....What a disgrace! For their shameful desires!") He has an unnatural closeness to his Electra-like twin sister, Una, which turns out to be incestuous. (This is a nod to Chateaubriand's *René*, a Gothic tale of brother-sister incest, one of the many French novels that preside over Littell's text; the sibling-incest theme is also a notorious element in the work of the twelfth century German bard Hartmann von Aue, whose name Littell has borrowed for his hero). He kills, or at least believes he has killed, his mother and her second husband, in a scene closely modeled on Greek myth, including the mother's desperate baring of her breast to her ax-wielding son. He is pursued relentlessly by agents of punishment—in this case, a pair of noirish detectives given the suggestive names of Weser and Clemens. (These were the names of the two Gestapo officers who, in real life, harrassed Victor Klemperer, the German Jew whose diaries, *I Will Bear Witness*, have become an indispensable document for the study of the history of the Holocaust—characterized, you might say, by the same proportion of narrative drama and mundane, meticulous, sometimes tedious detail that you find in Littell's novel.) All this is overlaid with increasingly elaborately narrated sexual fantasies and activities, culminating in an onanistic orgy at his sister's abandoned house as the Russians enter Pomerania.

The surprise—and also a key to understanding the outrage Littell's book has provoked, and the reasons for its successes and its failures—is the way in which these structures are meant to tackle the large themes suggested by his Aeschylean title. For it is, in fact, the historical structure that is meant to shed light on the problem of human nature; while it is the mythic-sexual element—and above all, if I am reading

Littell's complex allusion to a much more recent revision of the Orestes myth correctly, those explicit and even pornographic sexual scenes—that are meant to explore the nature of crime, atrocity, and justice.

———

The conflict between civilization and the ugly energies that civilized institutions seek, and often fail, to contain is a tension that stands at the center of any discussion of the moral implications of the Holocaust—a tension that can be seen reflected at the level of individual psychology, too. For the question of how it could have been possible for a country with Germany's superior cultural achievements to have also created Auschwitz inevitably raises, as well, the related question of how individual Germans (or Poles, or Ukrainians, or Latvians, or Lithuanians, or Frenchmen, and so forth)—who, for the most part, saw themselves as reasonable, normal people, and indeed led normal-looking lives throughout the war, apart from their participation in the crimes—could have perpetrated horrors which, perhaps naively, perhaps self-servingly, we like to refer to as "inhuman."

But in a passage that typifies a provocative aversion to sentiment that is likely to alienate some readers, Littell's protagonist disdains any use of the word "inhuman" when talking about Nazi atrocities. Here, Aue recalls the case of a soldier who, he learns, had originally joined the police force because "it was the only way to be sure I could put food on the table," and had ended up as part of a unit given the horrific task of liquidating hopelessly wounded soldiers—German soldiers—at the collapsing Russian front:

> There was a lot of talk, after the war, in trying to explain what had happened, about inhumanity. But I am sorry, there is no such thing as inhumanity. There is only humanity and more

humanity: and that Döll is a good example. What else was he, Döll, but a good family man who wanted to feed his children, and who obeyed his government, even though in his innermost being he didn't entirely agree?

The singular achievement of Littell's novel is the way in which he brings us uncomfortably close to the thinking of people whose careers took them from police work to euthanasia, and worse. The twist is that while Aue tries to get into the mind of an ordinary, working-class man like Döll, Littell very persuasively illumines the thoughts of Aue himself. And why not? He is a well-educated and indeed sensitive person, musical, literate, cultured, who far from being monstrously indifferent to the crimes he sees perpetrated and that he himself is called on to commit, spends a good deal of time reflecting on the questions of guilt and responsibility that a self-aware person could be expected to entertain. Littell makes a point of having Aue—at least at the beginning, before he collapses into his garish *Götterdämmerung*—refuse to acquit himself of responsibility, the defense that became the notorious byword of the war-crimes trials:

> I am not pleading *Befehlnotstand*, the just-obeying-orders so highly valued by our good German lawyers. What I did, I did with my eyes open, believing that it was my duty and that it had to be done, disagreeable or unpleasant as it may have been. For that is what total war means: there is no such thing as a civilian, and the only difference between the Jewish child gassed or shot and the German child burned alive in an air raid is one of method; both deaths were equally vain....

"My duty and...it had to be done," of course, begs the question of the morality of the duty to Nazi ideology. The character's fierce attachment to the "absolutes" of ideology is meant to be explained by the book's mythic/sexual elements, by that landscape of psycho-sexual aberration: a psychologizing cliché that many critics have dismissed. But I think that there is something to Littell's interest in showing us a picture of ideology in action, of what things look like once ordinary and even thoughtful people begin to help carry out ideologies that may well look appalling to others—Manifest Destiny, Iraq, the West Bank.

It's for this reason that Littell keeps reminding us that Aue himself is disgusted by the overt sadists he encounters, rightly objecting that "the ordinary men that make up the State—especially in unstable times—now there's the real danger. The real danger for mankind is me, is you." Anyone who has studied the Holocaust will recognize the bitter wisdom in this statement; its history is peopled with soldiers and civilians, Germans and Poles and Ukrainians and Dutch and Frenchmen, who went to church on Sunday, worried about their health, took care of their sick wives, fretted about their raises and promotions, slapped their children for lying or cheating, and spent the occasional afternoon shooting Jewish grandmothers and children in the head. While some will denounce Littell's cool-eyed authorial sympathy for Aue as "obscene"—and by "sympathy" I mean simply his attempt to comprehend the character—his project seems infinitely more valuable than the reflexive gesture of writing off all those millions of killers as "monsters" or "inhuman," which allows us too easily to draw a solid line between "them" and "us." The first line of the novel takes the form of Aue's unsettling salutation to his "human brothers": the purpose of the book, one in which it largely succeeds, is to keep alive, however improbably, that troubling sense of kinship.

How Littell accomplishes this aim is worth considering, and brings us to the question of his novel's style and technique—one that has often been raised by his detractors. It is true that at the level of words and sentences, Littell's style is unremarkable, even pedestrian—his translator, Charlotte Mandell, has produced an admirably fluid English version that is more pleasing to read than the French. This novel invariably goes off the tracks when the author strives for writerly effects. Sentences such as "My thoughts fled in all directions, like a school of fish in front of a diver" or "I emerged from the war an empty shell, left with nothing but bitterness and a great shame, like sand crunching in your teeth" are all the more wince-inducing for the success with which Littell so often conveys the drearily everyday chit-chat, the gossip about promotions and orders, of his military milieu.

Indeed, the large success of the book, the way in which Littell draws us into Aue's mental world, has much to do with a striking technique he employs throughout, which is to integrate, with more and more insistence as the novel progresses, scenes of high horror (or scenes in which characters coolly discuss horrific acts or plans) with quotidian, even tedious stretches, conversations about petty military intrigues and official squabbling and so forth that go on and on, thereby weaving together the dreadful and the mundane in an unsettlingly persuasive way—the tedious somehow normalizing the dreadful, and the dreadful seeming to infect the tedious. In one characteristic passage, fairly early on, the topic of conversation among a group of officers yo-yos between extermination policy and the quality of the roast duck with apples and mashed potatoes that they're eating. "'Yes, excellent,' Oberländer approved. 'Is this a specialty of the region?'"

At first these juxtapositions horrify, and you may resent what feels like a striving for shocking effects. But then you get used to them—the sheer length and banality of the "everyday" stretches (of which there are far too many: some readers will give up) numbs you after a while. This is, of course, the point: Littell has written a Holocaust novel that renders evil just as banal as we have so often been told it is—which is to say, not "banal" in the sense of boring or ordinary, but *banalisé*: rendered quotidian, everyday, normal.

Many dozens of pages of such juxtapositions, the murderous politics and the roasted potatoes, prepare Aue (and the reader) for the imperceptible slide down a moral slope that, in Littell's hands, becomes eloquently literal. In one of the scenes that critics have denounced as "pornography of violence," Aue finds himself literally slipping among the dead in the steep gullies at Babi Yar:

> The side of the ravine, where I stood, was too steep for me to climb down, I had to walk back around and come in from the rear. Around the bodies, the sandy earth was soaked with blackish blood; the stream too was black with blood. The horrible smell of excrement was stronger than that of blood, a lot of people defecated as they died; fortunately there was a brisk wind that blew away some of the stench. . . . To reach some of the wounded, you had to walk over bodies, it was terribly slippery, the limp white flesh rolled under my boots, bones snapped treacherously and made me stumble, I sank up to my ankles in mud and blood. It was horrible and it filled me with a rending feeling of disgust, like that night in Spain, in the outhouse with the cockroaches.

Here again, the moral shock comes almost less from the details of the killing field than from that climactic, disorienting juxtaposition of extremity and normality: the unbearable scene of mass murder, a merely unpleasant memory from a vacation in Spain.

By the middle of the novel, the thoughtful anguish that accompanied his earlier exploits—an anguish always quashed, in the end, by Aue's fanatical allegiance to Nazi ideology and war aims, even after the brilliantly evoked catastrophe at Stalingrad, one of the novel's great set pieces—has disappeared:

> In the Ukraine or in the Caucasus, questions of this kind still concerned me, difficulties distressed me and I discussed them seriously, with the feeling that they were a vital issue....The feeling that dominated me now was a vast indifference—not dull, but light and precise. Only my work engaged me.

The work in question, it's worth noting, is his service in the "economic" area, to which he has been assigned after he's noticed by Himmler: "economic," as the war starts turning against the Germans, means trying to squeeze greater efficiency from slave laborers, a task that, because he now has to look at prisoners as workers who need to be fed and clothed and housed, eventually puts Aue in the bizarre position of having to value the lives of the Jews he had been obediently killing before. Here again, Littell's meticulous attention to persuasive details, the petty jockeying for position, the exasperated complaints about efficiency and waste—the way in which, finally, the use of the words "my work" in the sentence "Only my work engaged me" bespeaks moral enormities—make Aue's collapse unnervingly accessible to us.

The success of the novel's first large element (the historical/documentary narrative) in allowing us to grasp the mentality of someone in whom civilized values yield to base acts—in whom the Erinyes triumph over the Eumenides, so to speak—depends on maintaining that accessibility, on our continued sense that Aue is a "human brother." This success is disastrously diminished by the novel's second major structural element, one to which Littell is obviously attached: the overlaying of the *Oresteia* parallel, with its high intellectual allure and literary allusiveness. (It's just the kind of thing that Aue himself would appreciate.) And yet as the novel progresses and the Aeschylean parallels, at first rather submerged (the occasional reference to the disappearance of the warrior father, Aue's intense resentment of his mother's remarriage to a lesser man), become unmistakable (the weird emotional twinning with the sister, the matricide and pursuit by the agents of law and justice), what gets lost is precisely any sense of Aue as a human brother.

For as appalling as the descriptions of actual atrocities are in this book, they pale in comparison to the willfully repellent fantasies that are the atrocities' counterparts on the novel's Oresteian plane. What kind of kinship can the ordinary reader be expected to feel with a character who—apart from those basic "Greek" ingredients of incest, matricide, and homosexuality—becomes increasingly violent, dissociated, and deranged as his tale reaches its spectacularly lurid ending, a narrative climax marked by fantasies such as this one:

> I tried to imagine my sister with her legs covered in liquid, sticky diarrhea, with its abominably sweet smell. The emaciated evacuees of Auschwitz, huddled under their blankets, also had their legs covered in shit, their legs like sticks; the ones who stopped to defecate were executed, they were forced to shit as they walked, like horses. Una covered in shit would have been even more beautiful, solar and pure under the mire that would not have touched her, that would have been incapable of soiling her. Between her stained legs I would have nestled like a newborn starving for milk and love, lost.

Such passages are, to be sure, part of a carefully plotted progression: Germany's disintegration is mirrored in Aue's indulgence in increasingly grotesque sexual activities and fantasies (not least, of coprophagy), as well as by other, external elements of the narrative. Toward the end of the novel, when the Soviets have entered German territory and are making for Berlin, Aue and his "Pylades," also trying to get back to Berlin, take up with a band of nightmarish Aryan orphans who wage brutal guerrilla warfare on Soviet troops, and in the book's final few pages Aue commits his last murders at the zoo: he has, in other words, made a climactic regression first to the infantile and finally to the bestial.

But as much as we may admire these structural touches, the problem, in the end, is that they make it harder and harder—and, finally, impossible—to see Aue as anything but, well, "inhuman," a "monster," precisely the kind of cliché of depravity that so many of this novel's strongest passages successfully resist.

Littell's insistence on developing the motifs of the fantastical, the grotesque, and extreme sexual excess, which grow out of his Orestes theme, is clearly the result of a choice. He himself has carefully planted clues about the meaning, and the justification, of that choice, one that has little to do with the Holocaust per se, or with novelizing history, and everything to do with something very French and very literary.

Exactly halfway through *The Kindly Ones*, Aue finds himself in Paris—this is in 1943, the trip at the end of which he will go to the South and murder his mother—and, while strolling among the stalls of the *bouquinistes*, picks up a volume of essays by Maurice Blanchot (an author whom Littell has studied seriously and who, by a nice coincidence, has been recently translated by Mandell, the translator of *The Kindly Ones*). Inevitably, Aue is very much taken with an essay that he vaguely describes as being about a play by Sartre on the Orestes theme. The volume in question, then, must be Blanchot's 1943 collection *Faux Pas*, which, in a section called "From Anguish to Language," contains the essay "The Myth of Orestes"; the Sartre drama in question is *Les Mouches*, which was first produced in 1943. Aue says little about the essay, apart from paraphrasing its point that Sartre "used the figure of the unfortunate matricide to develop his ideas on man's freedom in crime; Blanchot judged it harshly, and I could only approve." But it will turn out that Aue is seriously misreading Blanchot.

Sartre's play has famous connections to the Occupation and the moral dilemmas of France. In it, Orestes returns home to Argos to find a corrupted city and, indeed, a corrupted cosmos; he learns from Zeus that the gods themselves are unjust, a discovery that renders absurd his, or anyone's, wishful yearnings for a life uncomplicated by moral anguish, indeed for a life in which one could simply be a person like any other person, a "human brother." As in the *Oresteia*, Orestes must kill his mother, although here the act has distinctly twentieth-century meanings that Aeschylus could not have dreamed of, as Blanchot's interpretation of the matricide indicates:

> The meaning of the double murder is that he can only be truly free by the ordeal of an act whose unbearable consequences he accepts and bears.... The hero claims all the responsibility for what he has done; the act belongs to him absolutely; he *is* this act, which is also his existence and his freedom. Yet this freedom is not yet complete. One is not free if one is the only one free, for the fact of freedom is linked to the revelation of existence in the world. Orestes must then not only destroy the law of remorse for himself, but he must abolish it for others and through the unique manifestation of his freedom establish an order from which inner reprisals and the legions of terrifying justice have disappeared.

Here, then, we see the large intellectual aim that the Orestes theme is meant to serve, as mediated by the Blanchot text to which Littell's novel so pointedly refers. Very early in *The Kindly Ones*, Aue makes a point of rejecting the solace offered by traditional moral terms: "I am not talking about remorse, or about guilt. These too exist, no doubt, I don't want to deny it, but I think things are far more complex than that." And indeed Littell, both in interviews and in the text of his novel, has dwelt on the differences between Judeo-Christian morality (with its emphasis on intent and mental attitude, on sin and the possibility of redemption) and the sterner, less sentimental, "forthright" morality he finds in Greek tragedy. ("The Greek attitude is much more forthright," he told *Le Figaro Magazine*. "I say it in the book: when Oedipus kills Laius he doesn't know he's his father, but the gods couldn't care less: you killed your father. He fucks Jocasta, he doesn't know she's his mother, that doesn't change a thing: you're guilty, *basta*.")

But Littell doesn't at all want to suggest that Aue is "beyond morality": quite the contrary, he wants to paint a picture of a character who, just as his actions have placed him beyond the bounds of the moral law, has also put himself beyond the comforts that the traditional concepts of morality and justice afford—like Sartre's Oreste, in Blanchot's interpretation:

> It would be infantile to think that by his fearful murder he has rid himself of everything, that, free of remorse and continuing to want what he did even after having done it, he is finished with his act and outside of its consequences. On the contrary, it is now that he will sound the surprising abyss of horror and naked fear that dogmatic beliefs no longer veil, the abyss of naked, free existence, free of complacent superstitions.... He is free; reconciliation with forgetfulness and repose is no longer permitted him; from now on he can only be associated with despair, with solitude, or with boredom.

It is no accident that the elderly Aue whom we meet at the beginning of the novel, as he starts composing his vast reminiscence, is a man who lives exactly such a life: quiet but empty, desperate, alone, and above all very, very bored.

The passages I have cited above make it clear that rather than disapproving of Sartre's play, as Aue suggests is the case in his brief reference to this essay, Blanchot admired it; and indeed his essay begins by extravagantly praising Sartre's play as being of "exceptional value and meaning." So where is the "harsh judgment" that, Aue claims, Blanchot has made?

The answer to that question provides the key to understanding why Littell's book veers off in the direction of the "pornography" that has disturbed so many critics and readers. For, having set out his case for *Les Mouches* as a study of a man who has "decided to strike a blow at the sacred," Blanchot observes that for the play to work, the blow at the sacred, the "sacrilegious quality," must be excessive, overwhelming; and worries that the

> impression of the sacrilegious is sometimes lacking from the play that it should sustain.... Did [Sartre] not push the abjection that he portrays far enough? Orestes' greatness falls short of impiety against real piety.

And so, rather than using the graphic details of violence and sex simply (and naively) to shock his reader in a superficial way, the violence, the "pornography of violence" even, is consciously evoked, given its baroquely nightmarish details, in order to heighten the "impression of the sacrilegious"—not to somehow defend Aue because he is outside of morality but to show us, horribly, what a life outside of morality looks, feels, sounds, and smells like. The "pornographic" material is not a shallow symbol of Aue's evil (a puritanical reading, if anything); it is, rather, Littell completing Sartre's unfinished task, "pushing the abjection far enough," struggling to show "impiety against real piety"—the "piety," in this case, being our own conventional pruderies and expectations of what a novel about Nazis might look like.

In this sense, *The Kindly Ones* places itself squarely within the tradition of a "literature of transgression," especially the French lineage that descends from the Marquis de Sade and the Comte de Lautréamont to Octave Mirbeau and Georges Bataille. Particularly in the elaborate sexual fantasies, the sex between teenage siblings, the coprophilia and incest themes, it is hard not to feel the influence, above all, of Bataille, to whose signature work, *Histoire de l'Oeil*, in which a violently detached eye becomes a sexual fetish used with great inventiveness, Littell alludes more than once. (There are a number of scenes in which eyes pop out of crushed or exploded heads.) I think that Littell might say that precisely because we are by now inured to representations of Nazi evil in literature and especially in film, he needs to break new taboos in order to make us think about evil, about a life lived in evil and a mind unsentimentally willing, even eager, to accept the ramifications of that choice. Whatever else he has done, Littell has written a novel that really does horrify. Critics who complain that it is unpleasant to read are missing the whole point.

So the "kitsch" is in fact integral to the novel's moralizing projects. And yet, as I have said, the effectiveness of the fantastical, mythic/sexual plane of the novel works against the success of the other large element, the historical/documentary: either Aue is a human brother with whom we can sympathize (by which I mean, accept that he is not simply "inhuman"), or he is a sex-crazed, incestuous, homosexual, matricidal coprophage. But you can't have your *Schwarzwälder Kirschtorte* and eat it, too. This is not to say that the aim of either element is mistaken or illegitimate, as some critics have argued: I don't think they are. (One valid complaint, given Aue's "Greek" morality, his eagerness to acknowledge his responsibility for actions, is that the matricide and murder are committed during a kind of blackout on his part: he isn't conscious of what he's doing, which seems a serious evasion.) But precisely because each element works so well on its own, the novel as a whole falls between two horses.

Still, however badly it may stumble, *The Kindly Ones* brings to mind Blanchot's judgment, one of which Aue enthusiastically approves, about another enormous, hybrid novel: *Moby-Dick*. "This impossible book," the French critic wrote, "[the] written equivalent of the universe . . . presents the ironic quality of an enigma and reveals itself only by the questions it raises." As another *Kindly Ones*—that of Aeschylus—continues to remind us, there exist strange fictional creatures, improbable hybrids whose two sides seem to have little to do with each other, freaks that, however unlikely we are to find them in nature, can give us nightmares that will haunt us long after the show is over.

—*The New York Review of Books*, March 26, 2009

IV. PRIVATE LIVES

BUT ENOUGH ABOUT ME

IN AUGUST 1929, Sigmund Freud scoffed at the notion that he would do anything as crass as write an autobiography. "That is of course quite an impossible suggestion," he wrote to his nephew, who had conveyed an American publisher's suggestion that the great man write his life story. "Outwardly," Freud went on, perhaps a trifle disingenuously, "my life has passed calmly and uneventfully and can be covered by a few dates." Inwardly—and who knew better?—things were a bit more complicated:

> A psychologically complete and honest confession of life, on the other hand, would require so much indiscretion (on my part as well as on that of others) about family, friends, and enemies, most of them still alive, that it is simply out of the question. What makes all autobiographies worthless is, after all, their mendacity.

Freud ended by suggesting that the $5,000 advance that had been offered was a hundredth of the sum necessary to tempt him into such a foolhardy venture.

Unseemly self-exposures, unpalatable betrayals, unavoidable mendacity, a soupçon of meretriciousness: memoir, for much of its modern history, has been the black sheep of the literary family. Like a drunken guest at a wedding, it's constantly mortifying its soberer relatives (philosophy, history, literary fiction)—spilling family secrets, embarrassing old friends, motivated, it would seem, by an overpowering need to be the center of attention. Even when the most distinguished writers and thinkers have turned to autobiography, they have found themselves accused of literary exhibitionism—when they can bring themselves to put on a show at all. When Jean-Jacques Rousseau's *Confessions* appeared, shocking the salons of eighteenth-century Paris with matter-of-fact descriptions of the author's masturbation and masochism, Edmund Burke lamented the "new sort of glory" the eminent *philosophe* was getting "from bringing hardily to light the obscure and vulgar vices, which we know may sometimes be blended with eminent talents." (The complaint sounds eerily familiar today.) When, at the suggestion of her sister, Virginia Woolf started, somewhat reluctantly, to compose an autobiographical "sketch," she found herself, inexplicably at first, thinking of a certain hallway mirror—the scene, as further probing of her memory revealed, of an incestuous assault by her half brother Gerald, an event that her memory had repressed, and about which, in the end, she was unable to write for publication.

As it happens, Woolf, the tentative memoirist, met Freud, who wouldn't dream of writing one, when both were nearing the end of their lives; Woolf's nephew Quentin Bell reported that the psychoanalyst presented the novelist with a narcissus. Whatever Freud may have meant by the gesture, it nicely symbolizes the troubling association between creativity and narcissism, an association that is nowhere as intense as when the creation in question is memoir, a literary form that exposes the author's life without the protective masks afforded by fiction.

Such self-involvement, as Ben Yagoda's fact-packed if not terribly searching book *Memoir: A History* reminds you, is just one of the charges that have been leveled against memoirs and their authors over the centuries, the others being the ones that Freud was so leery of: indiscretion, betrayal, and outright fraud. But it's the ostensible narcissism that has irritated critics the most. A decade and a half ago, the distinguished critic William Gass fulminated against the whole genre in a scathing *Harper's* essay, in which he asked, rhetorically, whether there were "any motives for the enterprise that aren't tainted with conceit or a desire for revenge or a wish for justification? To halo a sinner's head? To puff an ego already inflated past safety?" The outburst came at a moment when a swelling stream of autobiographical writing that had begun in the late 1980s was becoming what Yagoda calls a "flood." By the end of the 1990s, a *New York Observer* review of one writer's first book, a memoir, could open with an uncontroversial reference to "this confessional age, in which memoirs and personal revelations tumble out in unprecedented abundance." (The memoirist in question was me; more on that later.)

By now, the flood feels like a tsunami. Things have got to the point where the best a reviewer can say about a personal narrative is— well, that it's not like a memoir. "This is not a woe-is-me memoir of the sort so much in fashion these days," the book critic of *The Washington Post* wrote recently in an admiring review of Kati Marton's *Enemies of the People*, an account of how the journalist's family suffered under Communist rule in Hungary. But as Yagoda makes clear, confessional memoirs have been irresistible to both writers and readers for a very long time, and, pretty much from the beginning, people have been complaining about the shallowness, the opportunism, the lying, the betrayals, the narcissism. This raises the question of just why the current spate of autobiography feels somehow different, somehow "worse" than ever before: more narcissistic and more disturbing in its implications. It may well be that the answer lies not with the genre—which has, in fact, remained fairly consistent in its aims and its structure for the past millennium and a half or so—but with something that has shifted, profoundly, in the way we think about our selves and our relation to the world around us.

***

It all started late one night in 371 AD, in a dusty North African town miles from anywhere worth going, when a rowdy sixteen-year-old—the offspring of an interfaith marriage, with a history of bad behavior—stole some pears off a neighbor's tree while carousing with some friends. To all appearances, it was a pointless misdemeanor. The thief, as he ruefully recalled some thirty years later, was neither poor nor hungry, and the pears weren't all that appealing, anyway; after a couple of bites, he and the others tossed the whole lot away for some hogs to eat. He stole them, he later realized, simply to be bad. "It was foul, and I loved it," he wrote. "I loved my own undoing."

However trivial the crime and perverse its motivations, this bit of petty larceny had enormous consequences: for the teenager's future, for the history of Christianity and Western philosophy, and for the layout of your local Barnes & Noble superstore. For although the boy eventually straightened himself out, converted to Christianity, and even became a bishop, the man he became was tortured by the thought of this youthful peccadillo. His desire to seek a larger meaning in his troubled past ultimately moved him to write a starkly honest account of his dissolute early years (he is disarmingly frank about his prolific sex life) and of his stumbling progress toward spiritual transcendence—to the climactic moment when, by looking inward with what he calls his "soul's eye," he "saw above that same eye of my soul the immutable light higher than my mind." The man's name was Aurelius Augustinus; we know him as Saint Augustine. His book was called *Confessions*.

As Augustine, a teacher of rhetoric, well knew, there had long been a tradition of biographies of accomplished men—Plutarch's *Lives*, say, written at the end of the first century AD—and of autobiographical accounts of daring military escapades and the like. (Xenophon's *Anabasis*, for instance, written in the fourth century BC, recounts how he and his troops managed to make their way back to safety after getting trapped behind enemy lines deep in what is now Iraq.) But Augustine was the first Western author to make the accomplishment an invisible, internal one, and the journey to salvation a spiritual one. The arc from utter abjection to improbable redemption, at once deeply personal and appealingly universal, is one that writers have returned to—and readers have been insatiable for—ever since. Augustine of Hippo bequeathed to Augusten Burroughs more than just a name.

To be sure, the autobiography as an entertaining record of hair-raising or merely risqué scrapes has also proved resilient, from Benvenuto Cellini's ribald *Autobiography* to Errol Flynn's outrageous *My Wicked, Wicked Ways*. ("I played regularly—or irregularly—with a little girl next door named Nerida," the actor reminisced about his childhood in Australia.) But the memoir's essentially religious DNA, the Augustinian preoccupation with bearing written witness to remarkable inner transformations, remained dominant during the sixteen centuries from the *Confessions* to Burroughs's *Running with Scissors*. Among the earliest vernacular memoirs in the postclassical tradition were so-called "spiritual autobiographies": Saint Teresa of Ávila composed one in Spanish, as did Saint Ignatius

Loyola. A fifteenth-century woman named Margery Kempe, whose autobiographical journey included some rather less exalted matter (not least, how she negotiated a sexless marriage with her avid husband), gave us what is considered to be the first memoir in English.

After the Reformation, the Protestants took up the form, partly in response to the Puritan call for "a narrow examination of thy selfe and the course of thy life," as the sixteenth-century divine William Perkins put it. The memoir as a negative examination of the self, a form in which to showcase our reasons to be, in John Calvin's words, "displeased with ourselves," indelibly marked the Anglophone autobiographical tradition thereafter—as did a certain resultant vaingloriousness about the extent of one's waywardness. The title of John Bunyan's *Grace Abounding to the Chief of Sinners* (1666), a masterpiece of the conversion narrative, is an allusion to an epistle of Paul: "Jesus Christ came into the world to save sinners; of whom I am chief." The emphasis on bearing personal witness to spiritual struggle opened up the memoir to people of all classes ("farriers, tailors, farmers, tinkers, and itinerant preachers," Yagoda points out); the perverse allure of wanting to demonstrate one's unholier-than-thou bona fides culminated in the memoirs of abjection with which we are surrounded today. These include, but are by no means limited to, Kathryn Harrison's memoir *The Kiss* (1998), in which the novelist wrote about her incestuous relationship with her father; Burroughs's best seller *Running with Scissors* (2002), which recounts the Gothic excesses of a childhood and adolescence tormented by abuse, madness, homosexuality, rape (statutory and otherwise), and which ends with its hero leaving the scene of these crimes to become a grown-up in New York City; Toni Bentley's *The Surrender* (2004), about the author's penchant for anal sex; and perhaps most notoriously, James Frey's *A Million Little Pieces* (2003), his (as it turned out) semifictional account of the horrors he endured on the road to recovery from addiction to drugs and alcohol. The flesh, in these tales, is weak, or bruised, or lacerated—Frey's book memorably begins with an image of the blacked-out author coming to in an airplane, his front teeth missing, his cheek split open, his body covered in vomit and urine— but the spirit yearns for, and inevitably receives, absolution.

The crucial moment in the evolution of the suffering-and-redemption memoir from its religious origins to its profane zenith (or nadir) today occurred as the Age of Faith yielded to the Age of Reason. Yagoda rightly emphasizes the importance of Rousseau's *Confessions*—published in 1782, four years after the philosopher's death —for the secular transformation of the genre. (The *Confessions* marked the beginning of a boom in memoir-writing that some found deplorable; by 1827, John Lockhart, the biographer of Sir Walter Scott, could rail against "the mania for this garbage of Confessions, and Recollections, and Reminiscences.") Rousseau's work is striking now less for its frankness, which left little of the memoirist's life to the imagination, than for the way it anticipates the present in its representation of memoir-writing as a kind of therapeutic purge. One of the most interesting passages in the *Confessions* mirrors Augustine's *Confessions* in recounting an ostensibly minor youthful infraction; in Rousseau's case, it was the theft of a bit of ribbon in the house of the family he worked for. Rousseau's crime had more serious immediate repercussions than did Augustine's: when the theft was discovered, he blamed a young woman who worked as a cook in the same household. Forty years later, the only way he could ease his guilt was to write about it:

> This burden, then, has lain unalleviated on my conscience until this very day; and I can safely say that the desire to be in some measure relieved of it has greatly contributed to the decision I have taken to write my confessions.

For better or worse, Rousseau gave impetus to the transformation of "confession" into a public and purely literary gesture. He understood that this secularization was a step "without precedent," as he writes at the beginning of the *Confessions*. In the hands of a great thinker the form could yield profound insights; but few of us are Rousseau. Once the memoir stopped being about God and started being about Man, once "confession" came to mean nothing more than getting a shameful secret off your chest—and, maybe worse, once "redemption" came to mean nothing more than the cozy acceptance offered by other people, many of whom might well share the same secret—it was but a short step to what the *New York Times* book critic Michiko Kakutani recently characterized as the motivating force behind certain other products of the recent "memoir craze": "the belief that confession is therapeutic and therapy is redemptive and redemption somehow equals art."

Virtually at the time that Rousseau was writing, redemption was being redefined on this side of the Atlantic, too. There was, above all, Benjamin Franklin's *Autobiography*, first published in French in 1791, a year after his death. An edifying tale of a resourceful young boy's remarkable victory over poverty, of improbable success achieved and enduring international fame won—written not to alleviate the author of any grave psychological burden but to provide a sensible practical model for others—it gave the familiar Augustinian salvation narrative a distinctly American, materialistic twist. "Fit to be imitated," as Franklin put it, and imitated it was: the banker Thomas Mellon, who read it at the age of fourteen, later described it as "the turning point of my life."

Before Franklin, there had been a strong taste in the Colonies for tales of more literal rescues and escapes—local incarnations of those old adventure memoirs. The seventeenth century saw a number of best-selling accounts by settlers who had been captured by "savages" and later escaped. (These, Yagoda intriguingly suggests, provided the blueprint for the subcategory of contemporary American memoir that includes Patti Hearst's 1982 account of her kidnapping by the Symbionese Liberation Army.) But a hundred years later another, new kind of escape memoir began to emerge, one that combined previous strains—the memoir as a record of dangers overcome, the memoir as a road map of spiritual renewal—while giving them a powerful new political resonance: the slave narrative. Running the gamut from the several reminiscences of Frederick Douglass, which the author revised and republished a number of times between 1845 and 1892, to the 1849 life story of one Henry (Box) Brown, who escaped to freedom by mailing himself by parcel post from Virginia to Philadelphia, these autobiographies by slaves and former slaves are remarkable for being among the first memoirs that were meant to serve as politically meaningful testimony to systemic crimes against an entire people.

As such, they anticipate both in form and in function the numerous memoirs written by survivors of the Holocaust and other government-sponsored genocides of the twentieth century. The earliest of the slave narratives were, in fact, contemporaneous with a vast body of political escape narratives that Yagoda, with his nearly exclusive focus on the Anglophone tradition, nowhere mentions: the memoirs written by those who fled the French Revolution and often landed on distant and improbable shores—one acquaintance of Marie Antoinette's milked cows near Albany—before returning, eventually, to France. In these autobiographies, elements of both witness literature and survival epic are combined.

What the slave narratives, the émigré accounts, and the Holocaust and genocide memoirs have in common is that, in them, the stakes of redemption are much higher than ever before. Now the "soul's eye" that Augustine spoke of was turned outward as well as inward, documenting the suffering self but also, necessarily, recording the tormenting other. The implicit and conditional universality in Augustine's suffering-and-redemption narrative—"This happened to me, and could happen to you, if you did what I did"—became explicit and indicative in the memoir of political suffering: "What happened to me happened to many others." Each of these witness memoirs had to bear an awful burden, standing in for the thousands of memoirs that would never be written. As the "I" became "we," the personal journey that had begun in the fourth century was transformed, by the end of the eighteenth, into a highly political one. The conversation between one's self and God had become a conversation with, and about, the whole world.

As the implications of the memoir have grown in importance, so have the seriousness, and the consequences, of another complaint made about it: what Freud called "mendacity." The need for certain kinds of memoir to be true goes back to Augustine's *Confessions*: if the anguish and the suffering aren't real, there's nothing to redeem, and the whole exercise becomes pointless. It is precisely the redemption memoir's status as a witness to real life that makes the outrage so loud when a memoir is falsified; the outrage tends to be exacerbated when the book in question claims to bear witness to social and political injustice. (By contrast, if Errol Flynn bedded ten more or ten fewer starlets than he claims, you don't feel cheated.) Yagoda, who is at his energetic best when indicting phony memoirs, gleefully recounts how a book called *The Blood Runs Like a River Through My Dreams*—one of three memoirs by a Native American writer called Nasdijj, in which the author rehearses the catalog of sufferings that fueled his resentful rejection of Western ways (fetal alcohol syndrome, migrant life, homelessness, HIV infection)—turned out to have been written by a twice-married white midwesterner whose other literary output includes gay S&M erotica.

The 1999 *Esquire* essay on which *The Blood Runs Like a River Through My Dreams* was based was nominated for a National Magazine Award; the book itself was ecstatically reviewed in the Native American literary press. ("Raw, poignant, poetic, and painful.") The effusiveness of the reception explains, to some extent, the violence of the reactions when such memoirs are revealed as phonies. Beneath it lies, all too clearly, a kind of shame—shame at the ease with which we have been seduced, and at how naked our desire is for certain kinds of narrative, however improbable or tendentious or convenient, to be true.

Indeed, the reactions to phony memoirs often tell us more about the tangled issues of veracity, mendacity, history, and politics than the books themselves do. This was already true of the nineteenth-century slave narrative and the way it was sometimes exploited. One of the most interestingly convoluted cases concerns the publication, in 1836, of a book called *The Slave, or Memoirs of Archy Moore*—a startling account of maltreatment, incest, and revenge told by a light-skinned African-American slave. The fact that it soon became clear that the book was a novel—by a Harvard graduate named Richard Hildreth, a New Englander who, during a stay in the South, had been deeply shocked by the treatment of black slaves—didn't bother some abolitionist reviewers; for them, what mattered was the "terrible truths" from which Moore's fiction had been constructed. In a letter to the Boston *Liberator*, the abolitionist author Lydia Maria Child went as far as to claim that Hildreth's novel was more powerful than an authentic narrative written by a slave called Charles Ball. "The extracts I have seen from Charles Ball are certainly highly interesting," she wrote, "and they have a peculiar interest, because an actual living man tells us what he has seen and experienced; while Archy Moore is a skillful grouping of incidents which, we all know, are constantly happening in the lives of slaves. But it cannot be equal to Archy Moore!"

The story of "Archy Moore" anticipates the present-day willingness to accept, as valid works of social or political witness, autobiographical narratives that turn out to be works of fiction. In the preface that Frey was obliged to add after the extent of his fictionalization in *A Million Little Pieces* created an outcry, he writes, "I hope these revelations will not alter [readers'] faith in the book's central message—that drug addiction and alcoholism can be overcome, and there is always a path to redemption if you fight to find one." After the publication, in 1983, of Rigoberta Menchú's memoir describing government atrocities against indigenous Guatemalans, investigations by a Middlebury College professor and by a reporter for *The New York Times* revealed that some of the incidents in the book hadn't happened the way she described. (Among other things, a brother who Menchú said had died of starvation didn't exist.) Menchú, who won the 1992 Nobel Peace Prize, retorted that her book expressed a "larger truth" about the sufferings of her people. Yagoda reports that one sympathetic Wellesley College professor of Spanish—a modern-day Lydia Maria Child—declared, in *The Chronicle of Higher Education*, that "whether her book is true or not, I don't care."

One of the most interesting defenses of memoirs that turn out to be "enhanced" or downright invented is that they accurately reflect a reality present not in the world itself (as in the cases of "Archy Moore" and Rigoberta Menchú) but in the author's mind. This line of argument raises a question that goes to the heart of our assumptions about literature, about the difference between fiction and nonfiction, and about truth, fiction, and reality itself.

At the beginning of 2008, critical and public irritation with memoirs reached a new peak, during a bewildering onslaught of phony-memoir revelations that were made within weeks of one another. There was *Love and Consequences*, a memoir of inner-city gang life by a mixed-race girl living with black gang members, which had been written by a white woman who had gone to a fancy prep school. And there was *Misha: A Mémoire of the Holocaust Years*, by Misha Defonseca, a Belgian woman who wrote about having survived the Holocaust by wandering around Europe with a pack of friendly wolves, but who turned out (a) not to have left Belgium and (b) not to be Jewish. In a statement published after the scandal broke, Defonseca declared, "The story in the book is mine. It is not the actual reality—it was my reality, my way of surviving." (She added, "The truth is that I have always felt Jewish.")

This justification of a literary fraud on the ground that it is true to the writer's interior world—a world that helps the author "cope" or "survive"—strikingly echoes the self-defense offered by Frey. "People cope with adversity in many different ways," he wrote in his published mea culpa, adding that his mistake had been "writing about the person I created in my mind to help me cope, and not the person who went through the experience." Behind such tortured psychological self-justification lies an aesthetic consideration familiar to anyone who has ever gone fishing: the experience Frey actually went through wasn't nearly as compelling as the one he wrote down. "I wanted the stories in the book to ebb and flow, to have dramatic arcs, to have the tension that all great stories require," he explained.

Such claims add up to a quite valid defense of a certain literary genre, but the genre in question isn't memoir—it's the novel. The novelist, after all, is a writer who has a vivid internal reality that wants expressing; who invents stories with dramatic arcs and tensions that point the reader toward a message; and who imagines himself or herself into the experiences of others in order to populate those stories with psychologically real characters.

The seemingly pervasive inability on the part of both authors and readers to distinguish "their" truth from the objective truth is nothing new in the history of modern literature; it goes right back to issues that were simmering away as both the memoir and the novel were emerging in their contemporary forms, at the turn of the eighteenth century. Yagoda points out the curious fact that Daniel Defoe, the earliest major novelist in the English-language tradition, cast many of his novels as memoirs, thereby complicating a relationship that has remained vexed right up until the present. In 1719, a well-known author called Charles Gildon published a tract demonstrating that a popular book that claimed to be "The Life and Strange Surprizing Adventures" of an English mariner, and that came complete with an editor's note ("neither is there any Appearance of Fiction in it"), was a pack of lies. The mariner in question was Robinson Crusoe, and Gildon was, of course, right; like all novels, it was, in one sense, a pack of lies. And yet like all great novels it expresses something we know to be true.

But the truth we seek from novels is different from the truth we seek from memoirs. Novels, you might say, represent "a truth" about life, whereas memoirs and nonfiction accounts represent "the truth" about specific things that have happened. A generation after Defoe and a generation before Rousseau, the philosopher David Hume was pondering the difference between memoir and fiction—a difference that, ultimately, may have as much to do with readers as it does with writers. Yagoda cites a passage from *A Treatise of Human Nature* (1740) in which Hume compared the experience of a reader of what he called "romance" to that of a reader of "true history":

The latter has a more lively conception of all the incidents. He enters deeper into the concerns of the persons: represents to himself their actions, and characters, and friendships, and enmities: he even goes so far as to form a notion of their features, and air, and person. While the former [the reader of novels], who gives no credit to the testimony of the author, has a more faint and languid conception of all these particulars; and except on account of the style and ingenuity of the composition, can receive little entertainment from it.

By "entertainment," Hume meant intellectual stimulation and illumination—what we have been seeking from memoirs, in one way or another, since Saint Augustine. In this reading, memoir is a genre in which truth value is necessarily of greater importance than are aesthetic values.

Two and a half centuries later, in a reaction to the revelation that Binjamin Wilkomirski's *Fragments*, the 1995 account of the author's experiences as a Latvian Jewish child experiencing the horrors of the Holocaust, was a fiction (the author was a Swiss Gentile whose real name was Bruno Grosjean), a Holocaust survivor named Ruth Klüger suggested that, precisely because it lacks truth value, a fraudulent memoir—particularly a fraudulent account of extreme trauma—could never amount to much more than a kind of perverse aesthetic experience, a trashy entertainment (in the more familiar sense of that word):

When it is revealed as a lie, as a presentation of invented suffering, it deteriorates to kitsch.... However valid it may be that much of this may have happened to other children, with the falling away of the authentic autobiographical aspect and without the guarantee of a living first-person narrator identical with the author, it merely becomes a dramatization that offers no illumination.

When readers defended Frey on the ground that his book, however falsified its "memories" were, had nonetheless (as he had hoped) provided them with the genuine uplift they were looking for, they were really defending fiction: an uplifting entertainment that can tell truths but cannot tell the truth.

A question that Yagoda never really explores is why, now in particular, there seems to be so much blurring between reality and fiction. (He doesn't mention, for instance, the scandals involving fraudulent journalism—Stephen Glass at *The New Republic* and Jayson Blair at *The New York Times*—that erupted in the very period when similar scandals were staining the reputations of memoirists.) The answer to this question suggests why there is something distinctive about the current cycle of memoir proliferation and anti-memoir backlash.

For one thing, reality itself is a term that is rapidly being devalued. Take reality TV: on these shows, "real" people (that is, people who aren't professional actors) are placed in artificial situations—they go on elaborately arranged dates, are abandoned on desert islands, have their ugly apartments redecorated, or are dumped into tanks of worms or scorpions—in order to provoke the "real" emotions that the audience tunes in to witness (disappointment, desire, joy, gratitude, terror, whatever). This craving on the part of audiences for real-life displays of increasingly extreme emotion (over, say, the carefully rehearsed displays of synthetic emotion that are provided to us when we go to the theater or to the movies) surely stems from the rise, in the 1970s, of talk shows whose hosts put ordinary people and their problems in the spotlight: first, Phil Donahue and, later, Sally Jessy Raphael and Montel Williams. Those TV shows helped create and promulgate the wider culture of self-discussion and self-exposure without which the recent flurry of memoir-writing and reading would be unthinkable. More important for the history of the memoir, they created a context for the huge popularity of Oprah Winfrey, who has used her show as a platform for people to tell—or, in the case of authors, to sell—their remarkable life stories; and who has, not coincidentally, fallen prey to more than one fraud. (In addition to Frey, Winfrey promoted what may be the strangest phony-memoir case of all: that of Herman Rosenblat, a Holocaust survivor who embellished his true story of survival in the camps with an invented, sentimental twist—his "angel," a little girl who, he claimed, threw apples to him over the camp's fence.) Winfrey's susceptibility suggests how an immoderate yearning for stories that end satisfyingly—what William Dean Howells once described to Edith Wharton as the American taste for "a tragedy with a happy ending"—makes us vulnerable to frauds and con men peddling pat uplift. As Frey's preface reminds us, the grander the dramatic arc, the likelier the tale is to be a tall one.

Winfrey's—and, by extension, her audiences'—hunger for good stories at any price suggests, among other things, that the trauma-and-redemption memoir, with its strong narrative trajectory and straightforward themes, may be filling a gap created by the gradual displacement of the novel from its once-central position in literary culture. Indeed, shows like Winfrey's, with their insistence on "real" emotions, may themselves have created an audience for whom fictional emotions are bound, in the end, to seem like little more than "dramatization without illumination." If you can watch a real lonely suburban housewife yearning after young hunks on a reality dating show, why bother with Emma Bovary? More significant, the premium placed by these shows on the spontaneous expression of genuine and extreme emotions has justified setups that are all too obviously unreal—in a word, fictional. In a way, not only the spate of memoir hoaxes but the recent proliferation of what Yagoda calls "stuntlike" memoirs—narratives that result from highly improbable stimuli ("One Man's Quest to Wash Dishes in All Fifty States")—arise from a deeper confusion about where reality ends and where make-believe begins.

This awkward blurring of the real and the artificial both parallels and feeds off another significant confusion that characterizes contemporary life: that between private and public. The advent of cell phones has forced millions of people sitting in restaurants, reading on commuter trains, idling in waiting rooms, and attending the theater to become party to the most intimate details of other people's lives—their breakups, the health of their portfolios, their psychotherapeutic progress, their arguments with their bosses or boyfriends or parents. The advent of smartphones and other personal devices that enable us to talk to our friends, listen to our music, read our books, watch our movies, check our stock quotes and departure times, all while walking down a city street, literally allows us to create our own hermetic, private reality while passing through the (increasingly unnoticed) spaces of public life. It may be worth mentioning here that the word "idiot" comes from the Greek *idiotês*, from the word *idios*, "private": an idiot is someone who acts in public as if they were still in private.

This experience of being constantly exposed to other people's lives and life stories is matched only by the inexhaustible eagerness of people to tell their life stories—and not just on the phone. The Internet bears crucial witness to a factor that Yagoda mentions in his discussion of the explosion of memoirs in the seventeenth century, when changes in printing technology and paper production made publication possible on a greater scale than before: the way that advances in media and means of distribution can affect the evolution of the personal narrative. The greatest outpouring of personal narratives in the history of the planet has occurred on the Internet; as soon as there was a cheap and convenient means to do so, people enthusiastically paid to disseminate their autobiographies, commentaries, opinions, and reviews, happily assuming the roles of both author and publisher.

So if we're feeling assaulted or overwhelmed by a proliferation of personal narratives, it's because we are; but the greatest profusion of these life stories isn't to be found in bookstores. If anything, it's hard not to think that a lot of the outrage directed at writers and publishers lately represents a displacement of a large and genuinely new anxiety, about our ability to filter or control the plethora of unreliable narratives coming at us from all directions. In the street or in the blogosphere, there are no editors, no proofreaders, and no fact-checkers—the people at whom we can at least point an accusing finger when the old-fashioned kind of memoir betrays us.

Yagoda's relentless and, it must be said, often amusing focus on the genre's opportunistic low points obscures the fact that there are some very great memoirs. He devotes little space to masterpieces like *The Education of Henry Adams*, and merely mentions the titles of, but never discusses, Mary McCarthy's *Memories of a Catholic Girlhood* and Vladimir Nabokov's sublime *Speak, Memory*—a choice he wants to justify on the ground that his approach is "historical" rather than "aesthetic." This odd tactic—a general study of the novel that failed to celebrate the great ones would give us very little sense of why we read novels—betrays an underlying prejudice of his own. Yagoda seems suspicious of the idea that intimate revelations can have motivations other than exhibitionism or "commercial enterprise."

And yet sometimes memoir may be the only way to cover a subject effectively. Fifteen years ago, I found myself unable to complete a study of contemporary gay culture that I'd contracted to write. The book was meant to be a more or less straightforward examination of the way in which the books, movies, and art that gay people were producing, and the way they partied, shopped, traveled, and dined, reflected gay identity. But the deeper I got into the subject, the harder I found it to isolate just what "gay identity" might be, not least because I and most of the other gay men I knew seemed to be torn between the ostensibly straight identities and values we'd been brought up with (domesticity, stability, commitment, mortgages) and the "queer" habits and behaviors—in particular, the freewheeling, seemingly endless possibilities for unencumbered erotic encounters— made possible in enclaves that were exclusively gay. Because I didn't want to suggest that I somehow stood outside those tensions and instabilities, I felt I had to write, in some part, about myself. This was the book that the reviewer introduced by alluding to "this confessional age."

As for Freud's charge that memoirs are flawed by mendacity, it may be that the culprit here is not really the memoir genre but simply memory itself. The most stimulating section of Yagoda's book is one in which he considers, far too briefly and superficially, the vast scientific literature about memory and how it works. The gist is that a seemingly inborn desire on the part of *Homo sapiens* for coherent narratives, for meaning, often warps the way we remember things. The psychologist F.C. Bartlett, whom Yagoda quotes without discussing his work, once conducted an experiment in which people were told fables into which illogical or non sequitur elements had been introduced; when asked to repeat the tales, they omitted or smoothed over the anomalous bits. More recently, graduate students who were asked to recall what their anxiety level had been before an important examination consistently exaggerated that anxiety. As Yagoda puts it, "That little tale—'I was really worried, but I passed'— would be memoir-worthy. The 'truth'—'I wasn't that worried, and I passed'—would not." In other words, we always manage to turn our memories into good stories—even if those stories aren't quite true.

Anyone who writes a memoir doesn't need psychology experiments to tell him that memories can be partial, or self-serving, or faulty. A few years ago, I was on a plane coming home from Australia, where I'd been interviewing Holocaust survivors for a book I was working on, a personal narrative rather different from my first book: an account of my search to find out exactly what happened to my mother's uncle and his family, who were Polish Jews, during World War II. As I interviewed survivors from the same small town where my great-uncle had not survived, I asked not only about my relatives and what might have happened to them but about the tiniest details of life before, during, and after the war: what they ate for breakfast, who their middle school teachers were, how and where they spent their school holidays.

Both the mad ambition and the poignant inadequacy of those interviews—and perhaps of the whole project of reconstituting the past, anyone's past, from memory—came home to me on the long flight home. I was sitting next to my brother Matt, a photographer, who was shooting portraits of the survivors we were interviewing, and about halfway through the flight some kids toward the back of the plane—a high school choir, I think it was—began singing a 1970s pop song in unison. Matt turned to me with an amused expression. "Remember we sang that in choir?" he asked.

I looked at him in astonishment. "Choir? You weren't even in the choir," I said to him. I'd been the president of the choir, and I knew what I was talking about.

Now it was his turn to be astonished. "Daniel," he said. "I stood *next* to you on the risers during concerts!"

Matt was talking about a shared history from 1978—a comparatively recent past. The people we'd just spent ten days with, struggling to find the keys that would spring the locks of their rusted recollections, had been talking about things that had happened sixty, seventy, even eighty years before. I thought about this, and burst out laughing. Then I went home and wrote the book.

—*The New Yorker*, January 25, 2010

HIS DESIGN FOR LIVING

"EVEN THE YOUNGEST of us will know, in fifty years' time," Kenneth Tynan wrote a little over fifty years ago, "exactly what we mean by 'a very Noël Coward sort of person.'" Tynan himself was just twenty-six when he made this confident pronouncement, and although it's likely that "a very Noël Coward sort of person" doesn't signify a great deal to most twenty-six-year-olds today, perhaps some of them—and certainly most people twice their age—would know precisely what kind of person Tynan was talking about. Witty and amusing, with an epigram on his lips, a cocktail in one perfectly manicured hand, and a lighted cigarette in the other, this person would be impeccably and elegantly dressed, and would always manage to be just as impeccably, and perhaps a trifle theatrically, posed whenever he appeared in public.

He would, in fact, look just like the striking Cecil Beaton portrait of Coward that appears on the cover of Barry Day's rich new collection, *The Letters of Noël Coward*: an image of "the Master" in dramatic profile, natty in a perfectly cut suit, holding a cigarette aloft from his lips as if he were just about to pronounce, or maybe had just pronounced, one of the bons mots for which he and his plays were so famous. It's an image that sums up what most people during the twentieth century thought urbane sophistication looked like. And yet to those who know Coward's life and work well, the amused and amusing persona that he perfected in the 1920s, when he first became famous, was just part of the story—"a nice façade to sit behind," as Coward wrote of a character based on Somerset Maugham in his 1935 play *Point Valaine*, "but a trifle bleak."

Coward himself never succumbed to that bleakness. Although he would come to be known for being (as someone says in his 1930 classic *Private Lives*) "jagged with sophistication," the key to his phenomenal productivity and equally phenomenal emotional stability throughout his life may well have been that he managed to retain the stolid values of the decidedly unsophisticated, lower-middle-class suburb where he was born at (as his given name suggests) Christmastime 1899, the second son of a piano-salesman father and a strong-willed mother who liked to reminisce about her family's once-grander circumstances. Pragmatic, hardworking, admirably without illusions about either his strengths or his defects, generous, unabashedly sentimental and patriotic, he was that rarity among people who achieve dazzling success very early on in life (as he did at the age of twenty-four, with his smash-hit cocaine-addiction melodrama *The Vortex*): someone who managed to withstand, for the most part, the powerful aura of his own public persona.

Hence although Day's meticulous and artfully structured edition of the *Letters* will inevitably be read by those eager to be dazzled by refractions of the jagged sophistication of Coward's busy social life ("I had a tremendous party given for me last night and it was rather fun. George Gershwin played and we all carried on like one o'clock"), its greatest significance may well lie in the extent to which its content demonstrates the qualities—unanticipated, perhaps, by those searching here for "a very Noël Coward sort of person"—of humaneness, tenderness, and a kind of Edwardian sentimentality that, as I argued in a review of the 2002 Broadway revival of *Private Lives*,* both underlie and give emotional texture to the surface cleverness in so much of his work. Coward himself understood the way in which, just below the dazzlingly urbane repartee, there lurked the Teddington native's unerring sense for what ordinary people were interested in: "I know all about my facility for writing adroit swift dialogue and hitting unimportant but popular nails on the head," he wrote to T. E. Lawrence, one of his many illustrious correspondents, in 1931. Indeed, among the greatest pleasures of this collection are those moments when we get to see the scion of Teddington intersect with that "very Noël Coward sort of person." Take, for instance, this 1954 letter to the Lunts about a production of his new musical version of *Lady Windermere's Fan*:

> I have been having a terrible time with *After the Ball*, mainly on account of Mary Ellis's singing voice which, to coin a phrase, sounds like someone fucking the cat. I know that your sense of the urbane, sophisticated Coward wit will appreciate this simile.

Coward very rarely confused himself with "Coward."

Day's edition of the *Letters* will add nothing new to the ample record of Coward's life and work, both of which can be known in tremendous detail at this point: apart from no fewer than three volumes of autobiography and an excellent biography by Sheridan Morley, there are by now memoirs by friends and former lovers, his shrewd and funny *Diaries*, edited by Morley together with Coward's longtime lover, Graham Payn, and numerous editions of the plays and

---

*"Bitter-Sweet," *The New York Review of Books*, June 27, 2002.

songs. (No less than seven of these books were the handiwork of Day himself.) But it is particularly interesting to see the life unfold through the letters, which are inevitably more spontaneous, and written with less of an eye on posterity, than the entries in the *Diaries*, and are certainly less craftily premeditated than the published autobiographies.

One nice continuity through the many years covered here—the first letter dates to 1906, the last to 1970 when Coward received his scandalously delayed knighthood—is provided by the fact that an astonishing number of them were written to the playwright's mother, Violet Veitch Coward, who throughout her long life was the recipient of weekly missives that Coward faithfully wrote to her from wherever he happened to find himself. (She died at ninety-one in 1954, and apart from an occasional lapse into stage-motherishness—"I forgive you for making me so unhappy," she wrote to him during World War II, after he had admonished her for being less than totally patriotic—seems to have been entertainingly sharp-witted herself.) This continuity is admirably enhanced by the manner in which Day has organized Coward's correspondence, woven as it is into a fluid, year-by-year narrative, complete with potted mini-biographies of long-forgotten music-hall stars, novelists, and personalities (and, indeed, photographs of them, which give the whole affair a charming, scrapbook feel), which make of this volume of *Letters* virtually a new biography.

And so Day is able to evoke, with great narrative verve and a gratifying richness of detail, the entire career. There is the apprenticeship in touring companies (*Charley's Aunt*, notably), where he learned his craft and suffered from a terrible separation anxiety which he never quite conquered ("I really ought to have got over being a mother's boy by now, but I never shall!" he wrote to his mother when he was in his late twenties) and, soon after, the relatively few years it took him to find his voice as a playwright and songwriter composing for the musical revues that were so popular at the time.

There are the early career-building trips to New York where he made discoveries that would strongly influence his technique ("The *speed*! Everybody seems to say their lines at such a rate you'd think you wouldn't understand a word—but you do! And then it suddenly struck me—that's the way people actually *talk*"), and that laid the groundwork for many long-lasting friendships recorded here. "I went to see her [Lynn Fontanne's] opening night with her fiancé, an actor called Alfred Lunt and, my dear, a star was born," he wrote Violet in 1921, during his first trip to America. These early letters also provide fascinating glimpses of the precocious youth in the process of turning himself into "Noël Coward." Of a female relation whom he went to visit while touring with his fellow child-actor Esmé Wynne: "Esmé and I sang 'We've been married just one year,' and she was most shocked. I've never met anyone so painfully provincial in all my life." Thus spake Teddington's most famous son.

Not the least of the attractions of Day's approach, particularly in the letters from these early years, is that, unlike many other editors, he will often interrupt the chronological trajectory at a given moment to trace for the reader how this or that relationship would develop over time—with Esmé Wynne, for instance, a friendship that began in the 1910s and stretched into the midcentury, when Coward was a celebrity and she, much to her old costar's amusement, was writing inspirational books with titles like *The Unity of Being*; or, more important, with figures like Jack Wilson, the American Yalie who started out as Coward's lover in the 1920s and ended up, disastrously as Coward realized only too late, as his business manager. These digressions provide context for later correspondence that might otherwise remain obscure.

After the remarkably brief journeyman period came the successes that at first seemed to have caught the young Noël by surprise ("And

when you consider that bright particular star will be me!" he wrote
Violet in 1922. "It's a bit breathless!") but that soon thereafter became almost, as Coward might say, monotonously predictable, first
with *The Vortex* and then, in rapid succession, *Hay Fever* (1924),
Private Lives, the patriotic historical pageant *Cavalcade* (1931), the
ménage-à-trois comedy *Design for Living* (1932)—the list was to go
on and on. And once Coward achieved his fame, the cast of correspondents was anything but "provincial." A major advantage of this
collection is that Day has included numerous letters to Coward as
well as from him, a choice that allows us to gauge the effect that the
theatrical prodigy had in his heyday on people we might not have
thought were fans. In 1928 Virginia Woolf wrote to him that her
heart had "leapt" to find out that the twenty-eight-year-old Coward
had liked *Orlando*—although to her diary she confided that she
hoped to "save him from being as clever as a bag of ferrets & trivial
as a perch of canaries."

That the piano salesman's son had risen to very high heights indeed was made clear during World War II, when Coward (who, despite the fact that he spent much of the war on grueling trips to
entertain the troops, had enemies in various government offices)
made use of his connections to people like Louis Mountbatten in
order to guarantee what he was convinced would be the great success
of his cinematic hymn to the Royal Navy, *In Which We Serve*. As the
Letters make clear, certain higher-ups in the British war effort
thought "Noël Coward," the elegant star, was unsuited to the role of
the Captain, who was based on Mountbatten (who along with his
wife, Edwina, was an old friend from the 1920s); "Dickie's" assiduous intervention got Coward the part. Later on, when a hostile government figure wanted to scuttle the entire project on the grounds
that the film depicted a British warship being sunk, George VI himself quite sensibly intervened on Coward's behalf:

I have read it and think it a very good and appealing way of dealing with the subject. Although the ship is lost, the spirit which animates the Royal Navy is clearly brought out. . . .

Coward was never to get over feeling slighted by the way his hard work during the war was continually misrepresented by the English press—among other things, much was made of a quite innocent tax mistake early on in the war, which gave Churchill grounds for blocking a knighthood. These feelings, along with the devastatingly onerous tax strictures after the war, led this most English of entertainers into tax exile, first in Jamaica and then in Switzerland.

This is not to say that he ever lost his sense of humor, which glints and flashes through virtually every page of Day's collection, from its descriptions of the many exotic places his travels took him—a letter he sent while on a government-sponsored intelligence-gathering trip to Russia before the war describes the country as being "exactly like a whole world composed of the Whitechapel Road on August Bank Holiday"—to the sly signatures he'd append to his letters from Paris, where he worked in 1940 for the British propaganda service: "DREYFUS," say, or "GERMAINE DE STAEL." What's remarkable here is how innocent the humor most often is; Coward's letters are strikingly free of backbiting or bitchiness, and when he sharpens his pen, it's hardly with the intent to kill:

> I went to the first night of John Van Druten's new play... all about a very pretty little actress who had to choose between love and a career. Judging by the way Miss Margaret Sullivan [sic] overplayed it I think she was right to choose love.

So there is much to dazzle here, in just the way we expect from a very Noël Coward sort of person. As the years and pages go by, it's often amusing to see Coward smoothly dealing with the great—in 1938 he writes that he is taking "the [Anthony] Edens and the Gary Coopers out to dinner" after Eden was forced to recite a public apologia for Chamberlain's "Peace in Our Time" (to his credit, Coward had a lifelong loathing of Chamberlain)—and the merely glitzy: "We dined with Mike Todd and Liz [Taylor] who was hung with rubies and diamonds and looked like a pregnant Pagoda." Of particular note is his correspondence with his close friend Marlene Dietrich, particularly during her tortured love affair, during the 1950s, with Yul Brynner—an exchange that sheds sympathetic light not only on Coward's loyalty but on Dietrich as well. "I long so for intelligence and brain food," the worldly star managed to sigh even in the midst of being humiliated by the younger, married Brynner.

Other correspondents inevitably included many stars of screen and stage, some of whom had been given a leg-up by Coward at the start of their careers: John Gielgud got his start as Coward's understudy in *The Vortex*, and Laurence Olivier's first important part was in the original production of *Private Lives* in 1930. There are also crowned heads and presidents—Coward particularly admired Roosevelt, whom he visited at the White House during one of his many trips to the US trying to drum up support for Britain at the beginning of the war ("I shall long to be in the warm friendly atmosphere of your study enjoying your very special cocktails," he wrote to FDR in 1940)—and of course many other writers: Edna Ferber and Alexander Woollcott, Somerset Maugham and Ian Fleming, Daphne Du-Maurier and Edith Sitwell. From the start of his long career as a letter writer, Coward remained unintimidated by such famous names. To Lawrence of Arabia, who had rather officiously headed a letter to Coward with both his alias and his full RAF identification number, the thirty-year-old Coward replied, "Dear 338171 (May I call you 338?)…"

What is striking about this volume of correspondence by the twentieth century's archetype of urbane elegance, however, is the degree to which it's devoted to family and the intimate friends to whom Coward would remain so impressively loyal: his secretary Lorn Lorraine, his great friend Gladys Calthrop, the actress Joyce Carey, the inner circle on whom he liked to heap the improbable nicknames of which he was so fond ("Snig," "Snog," "Poj"). To them particularly he loved to address epistles composed in light verse, a form of which he was a master and which, as his letter home for Christmas 1939 indicates, was not necessarily limited to martinis and cigarette holders:

> *Let us ignore all the slaughter and danger*
> *(Think of the Manger! Remember the Manger!)...*
> *Now as our day of rejoicing begins*
> *(Never mind Poland—Abandon the Finns)*
> *Lift up your voices "Long Live Christianity!"*
> *(Cruelty, sadism, blood and insanity)*

All these letters end with effusive valedictions ("Love and mad mad kisses," "Love, love, love love, love"), and you don't ever feel that it's forced.

If anything, this epistolary portrait of Coward reveals an enviably sane personality strikingly devoid of tics and neuroses, in which a healthy self-respect is nicely balanced by a realism that never curdles into cynicism:

> My philosophy is as simple as ever. I love smoking, drinking, moderate sexual intercourse on a diminishing scale, reading

and writing (not arithmetic). I have a selfless absorption in the well-being and achievements of Noël Coward.

His teasing words about his old friend Esmé Wynne's idealistic writings betray his own informal but deeply felt philosophy, which prized above all the importance of snatching happiness in a world filled with emotional confusion imposed from without and exploding from within—the theme of so much of his work ("I think very few people are completely normal, really, deep down in their private lives...there's no knowing what one might do," Amanda says in *Private Lives*):

> It is my considered opinion that the human race (*soi disant*) is cruel, idiotic, sentimental, predatory, ungrateful, ugly, conceited and egocentric to the last ditch and that the occasional discovery of an isolated exception is as deliciously surprising as finding a sudden brazil nut in what you *know* to be five pounds of vanilla creams. These glorious moments, although not making life actually worth living, perhaps, at least make it pleasanter.

Remarks such as these make you realize that Coward's theatrical work is, essentially, Epicurean in nature—with a capital rather than a lowercase "E," perhaps.

Most impressive are his letters during wartime, which often seem to sum up some essential aspect of the English character as he saw it, a kind of secretly tender sturdiness, a trait that in fact saves so much of his theater from being the brittle drawing-room comedy it is now thought to be. There are traces throughout the correspondence of this deep sentimentality about England, the provenance of which was the Edwardian theaters he grew up in, which makes itself felt in everything from *Cavalcade* to *In Which We Serve* to *Brief Encounter*.

Here he is in the letter in which he admonishes his mother for being too critical of the English leadership (she had written him saying that no one should fight for such incompetent governments):

> I am working for the country itself and the ordinary people that belong to it. If you had been here during some of the bad blitzes and seen what I have seen and if you had been with the Navy as much as I have you would understand better what I mean. The reason that I didn't come back to America was that in this moment of crisis I wanted to be here experiencing what all the people I know and all the millions of people I *don't* know are experiencing. This is because I happen to be English and Scots and I happen to believe and know that, if I ran away and refused to have anything to do with the War and lived comfortably in Hollywood, as so many of my actor friends have done, I should be ashamed to the end of my days. The qualities which have made me a success in life are entirely British.... Everything I've ever written could never have been written by anybody but an Englishman.

Indeed, he was just as self-aware with respect to his strengths and his weaknesses as a writer. As early as his earliest successes he knew perfectly well where the former lay. As his letter to T. E. Lawrence demonstrated, he understood that he was above all an entertainer, and no matter how jagged with sophistication he would get, he was never ashamed of the "popular nails" that he kept hitting on the head with such great accuracy. That he understood there was a flip side to this is already evident in a 1928 letter to the critic St John Ervine: "my imagination doesn't feel strong enough to reach things which have not actually happened to me." (And, more tellingly, "constant repetitions of Parisian coquettes having cocktails at the Ritz bar are apt to become a bore.") Still, as he rather startlingly wrote to his mother in 1926 after one of his plays flopped, he found

> on close reflection that I am as unmoved by failure as I am by success which is a great comfort.... I like *writing* the plays anyhow and if people don't like them that's their loss.

What's remarkable is that you believe it.

Coward's sense of the theater came to seem increasingly old-fashioned as the years passed. After World War II he had greater and greater difficulty creating the kinds of hits that seemed to have flowed so effortlessly in the 1920s and 1930s. His horror of what he thought of as the ugliness of the postwar British theater brought "the Master" into conflict with the new generation of playwrights whose work, as he put it in a diary entry about John Osborne (who eventually warmed up to Coward), was characterized by a "destructive vituperation" that was "too easy." No one would accuse Coward of being a theatrical visionary.

Yet as wrongheaded as his judgments could be, they bear witness to a dogged, almost moving belief in the value of pure entertainment that, even late in life, betrayed an underlying identification with the ordinary men and women who saved up each week for their tickets—the kind of people his parents had been. In a letter from the 1960s addressed to Arnold Wesker, the young author of plays about working-class life such as *The Kitchen*, with whom Coward was to become unexpectedly close in an almost paternal way, the Master indignantly defended the value of the theater as he saw it:

> I, who have earned my living all my life by my creative talents, cannot ever agree with your rather high-flown contempt for

"commercial art." In my experience, which is not inconsiderable, the ordinary run of human beings, regardless of social distinctions, infinitely prefer paying for their amusements and entertainments than having them handed out to them for nothing.... There is nothing disgraceful or contemptible in writing a successful play which a vast number of people are eager and willing to buy tickets for.... Personally I would rather play Bingo every night for a year than pay a return visit to *Waiting for Godot*.... This is not to say that I think *all* your cultural activities will inevitably bore the public, but, judging by the purple and black brochure you sent me, quite a number of them are bound to.

You mustn't be cross with me for holding these very definite views because, if you analyse them, you may find that they are based on common sense rather than cynicism.

The pride that resonates in that first sentence—the artisan's, as it were, rather than the artist's; certainly middle rather than upper class—is hard to miss.

And yet, a fascinating 1965 exchange shows Coward reaching across the generations to the young Harold Pinter after reading *The Homecoming*—twice. "You cheerfully break every rule of the theatre that I was brought up to believe in," the sixty-five-year-old icon of sophistication wrote, "except the cardinal one of never boring for a split-second." Here again, the bottom line was entertainment. And, come to think of it, there may have been more of a connection between Coward and Pinter than meets the eye. As Day reminds us in his comment on this exchange, Coward was the man who insisted that "suggestion is always more interesting than statement"; a line from his own *Shadow Play* (1935) brings Pinter's work powerfully to mind: "Small talk, a lot of small talk with other thoughts going on behind."

"Small talk" is, of course, what Coward has been reduced to by now in the minds of so many readers and theatergoers, for whom "a very Noël Coward sort of person"—brittle and brilliantined, crackling with Roaring Twenties sophistication, sleek in smoking jackets and bristling with cigarette holders—is the only person Coward ever was. In this regard I should say that a few (exceedingly few) editorial choices in this otherwise splendid collection might inadvertently suggest to some readers that its subject is indeed rather "small," rather dated. Among other things, you wish that Day had included more of the correspondence between Coward and his various lovers, which, you can't help thinking, would have shed even more light on Coward the refreshingly humane man. The decision not to publish them seems to stem from a reticence that belongs as much to Day himself as to Coward, who was famously cagey when it came to questions about his private life. "The thread that goes through this life in letters is, indeed, love," Day writes in his introduction; "not the homosexual definition of love that can now not only speak but positively shout its name," he goes on to sniff. These and a few other editorial comments—"One wonders what history will make of the present illiterate e-mail era," he writes, apropos of letter collections—will do little to alleviate the sense that many younger readers already have of Coward as hopelessly dated and beside the point.

But this collection of *Letters* overwhelmingly points to a Coward well worth knowing, particularly for a generation nourished on a notion of celebrity—"well known for being famous and famous for being well known," as Day summarizes it—that the hardworking Coward himself would certainly have despised. Indeed, it is surely wrong for Day to claim that Coward was an "early role model" for this brand of celebrity: Coward became famous for having done something substantial extraordinarily well—that is, writing very successfully for the popular theater. If what he considered to be "entertainment" now seems a little narrow to us, we cannot fault him for that. And if some of the values he championed both in his work and in his life—discretion, a gentle self-awareness, the importance of gaiety (that old-fashioned word) and a forgiving humor as weapons in life's conflicts—seem a little quaint today, those very values allowed him to observe the decline of his moment with a rare equanimity.

Indeed, Coward more than most would have appreciated, now, the wisdom of something that Max Beerbohm wrote to him in 1927 apropos of the "operette" *Bitter Sweet*, a work already nostalgic for the past and one that gave us the line most often used to describe Coward's own gift: "a talent to amuse." "Sentiment," Beerbohm wrote,

> is out of fashion. Yet *Bitter Sweet*, which is nothing if not sentimental, has not been a dead failure. Thus we see that things that are out of fashion do not cease to exist.

—*The New York Review of Books*, January 17, 2008

ON THE TOWN

AT THE BEGINNING of a 1953 *New York Times* review of a memoir by Charles Darwin's granddaughter, Leo Lerman—identified as "contributing editor of *Mademoiselle*," a description that hardly did justice to the thirty-nine-year-old's already significant social and cultural influence in New York City during the midcentury—expatiated on the pleasures of reading other people's autobiographies. "The most delightful thing about reading a book of recollections," he wrote,

> is getting to know the person who is doing the recollecting. When this person also has total recall about at least fifteen other engaging persons, the whole book becomes at least fifteen times as delightful. And when the recollector backward-glances wittily, with love and that nostalgic understanding which permits no mawkishness; when the rememberer of things past writes humorous prose, detailing the long ago, the ensuing document may well be a little masterpiece.

The book in question, entitled *Period Piece*, was hardly the only autobiography that Lerman reviewed for the *Times*. He seemed, if anything, to have taken special pleasure in reading and reviewing memoirs and autobiographies, and he reserved his highest praise for those who are able to conjure the lost past in minute detail—an unsurprising enthusiasm from someone who had a lifelong reverence for Proust. In his review of *Period Piece* he approvingly quotes, verbatim, a list of the fourteen items worn by a female houseguest; elsewhere he praises the "documentary" quality of a memoir by a minor European royalty.

In a piece of literary journalism of which he was particularly proud, a front-page article for *The New York Times Book Review* in 1960 about the newly reissued three-volume edition of Francis Kilvert's journals, Lerman was ecstatic about the way in which the Victorian vicar's keen eye for detail and sense of "wonder" about the world seem to bring him to life before our eyes:

> It is wonderfully reassuring when, out of the vast anonymity of the past, a man who did not fire the world with art or, by a talent for disaster, set it blazing, again puts on his own face, fleshes his bones, sets his blood coursing and, eluding, for a pitiful moment, mortality, walks straight into our lives.

At the time he wrote those words, Lerman was famous less for being an "editor of *Mademoiselle*"—he would go on to become features editor at *Vogue* (where he published Rebecca West, Milan Kundera, and Iris Murdoch), briefly editor in chief of *Vanity Fair*, and, finally, editorial consultant to all of Condé Nast—than for having made himself the center of a kind of a celebrity Who's Who of his age. People like Marlene Dietrich and Maria Callas (his two closest girlfriends), Lincoln Kirstein, Philip Johnson, Carmel Snow, Noël Coward, Edith and Osbert Sitwell, Jacqueline Kennedy Onassis, Indira Gandhi, Henry Kissinger, Lionel and Diana Trilling, Luise Rainer, Truman Capote, Susan Sontag, and many others seemed happy to crowd into his various apartments over the years so that they, too, might be included in the haute and heady fun—happy despite not only the fact that (in the case of his first apartment, on upper Lexington Avenue) there were five flights of stairs but also that the fare often consisted of nothing more glamorous than jug wine and rat cheese.

A sense of what it was they were coming for may now be gleaned from *The Grand Surprise*, a massive and engrossing collection of Lerman's own autobiographical writings. "Writings" is an awkward term, but one that must suffice here. Although Lerman published three books during his lifetime (biographies of Michelangelo and Leonardo, and a hundredth-anniversary commemorative volume about the Metropolitan Museum of Art), he was never able to surmount a plaguing anxiety about writing his memoirs—a book that he had long planned (and was under contract) to write. Equally anguishing was the thought of the grand novelistic *recherche du temps perdu* he had conceived, which, increasingly poignantly, this worshiper of Proust continued throughout his lifetime to claim that he was preparing to compose, long after it was clear that he was incapable of doing so.

The Grand Surprise is a selection from the journals that he kept for more than half a century, from 1941 until eight months before his death, at eighty, in August 1994—they were discovered and transcribed only after his death—as well as from hundreds of letters to his many friends, lovers, and ex-lovers. There are also sharp-eyed "vignettes," as the editor of this volume describes them, recounting this or that episode, some written toward the end of Lerman's life as part of the unfinished memoir, others adapted from eulogies or tributes that he gave, still others inserted into the journal to amplify various entries long after the fact.

These have been ingeniously braided into a persuasive whole by Stephen Pascal (working closely with Gray Foy, Lerman's partner for forty-seven years), who for twelve years served as Lerman's assistant at various Condé Nast postings. As such, *The Grand Surprise*, a compendium of essentially casual records of Lerman's extraordinarily rich life, will have to stand in for the polished literary work he was never able to commit to paper. But then, Lerman himself, who consistently deprecated both his journalism ("the emptiness, the waste") and his journal-keeping ("scribbling"), had always suspected, and indeed predicted, that his life was going to crowd out whatever art he was capable of. "I realize that the novel I have wished to write, I have written. My life is that novel. I have been writing it all my life."

The Grand Surprise certainly possesses the qualities that its author so lavishly praised in other autobiographies. The least significant of these, to my mind, is the one that has drawn so much attention to the book: the glittery ubiquity of what Lerman, in his review of *Period Piece*, called "engaging persons"—the bold-faced names whose presence on every page is bound to suggest that his life amounted to little more than one long soiree. (The front-page *New York Times Book Review* article on the book was called "Life of the Party.") To be sure, Lerman's tenacious adherence to the worlds of theater, glossy magazine publishing, dance (a friend to Balanchine and Kirstein both, he was a regular contributor to *Dance Magazine*), art, music (for years he wrote for *Playbill* and wrote the program notes for the Young People's Concerts at the Philharmonic), fashion, and society ensured that his journal entries would read like a guide to fashionable New York culture from the 1940s straight through to the 1990s. This, along with his knack for quickly making friends with the celebrated and the talented whom he met seemingly every night (Judy Garland in 1954, at the party she threw to celebrate the premiere of *A Star Is Born*: "a warm and loving girl with devastating charm"), makes *The Grand Surprise* a useful resource for those interested, as many now are, in the Manhattan midcentury, with its giddy vitality and its sense (so it seems now) of boundless possibility; a period from which we are now as distant as Lerman was from the gaslight era, which he so fondly romanticized.

But what the journals make clear are the extraordinarily interesting qualities of Lerman himself—the magnet that drew all those famous names over so many years, in combinations and configurations one might have thought unlikely. *The Grand Surprise* features guest lists to some of Lerman's more dazzling parties: one of these, for a New Year's Eve party in 1976, includes both Henry Kissinger and Charles Ludlam. In his review of *Period Piece*, Lerman endorsed "wit" and "humor" in books of recollections, and there is no shortage of either here. Whatever his perceived limitations as a writer, he had an extraordinary gift for the amusing yet devastatingly telling character sketch; in a single sentence, he can memorably capture the supremely talented and the merely well-born. (Princess Margaret in 1965: "She's kind of jazzy and looks like her father struck it good in the female-shoe business.") These are always shrewdest when Lerman is describing performers. A born critic, he had a remarkable feel for the stage and those who trod it—actors, singers, dancers. Joan Sutherland is "a cross between Margaret Dumont and a high school pageant"; Carol Channing's "art" (the scare-quotes are his) was "based on that look of apologetic, hopeful anguish seen on the face of a little girl who has just peed in her pants."

What is remarkable about Lerman's wit is that it is entirely lacking in cattiness—and, perhaps even more remarkably in the case of a gay man immersed in the arts at midcentury, entirely lacking in camp attitudinizing. (Or self-aggrandizement of any kind, something Lerman abhorred in Cecil Beaton's diaries, by which he felt "so embarrassed.") The emotion that pervades these journals is, if anything, the "love and nostalgic understanding" that their author so admired in the recollections of Darwin's granddaughter. This undoubtedly has a great deal to do with his deep and loving connection to his family. Lerman, who was born in 1914 and grew up quite happily in a roiling immigrant Jewish milieu in Harlem—the same milieu that produced the chronically dyspeptic Henry Roth—was more than fortunate in his "Momma" and "Poppa" (the latter a house painter), and indeed in the rest of his exuberant and memorable family, fond and highly colored reminiscences of whom occur increasingly, perhaps unsurprisingly, in the journals as Lerman grows older.

In particular, his family's early and seemingly unquestioning acceptance of his homosexuality—rare for the times, to say the least —seems to have given him an admirably balanced emotional constitution. The journals bear moving witness, from an opening love letter to his first serious lover, the painter Richard Hunter, to its closing tributes to Dietrich and above all to Gray Foy, to relationships both platonic and erotic of impressive depth and longevity. As sophisticated as he was, his feelings were strong, and often disarmingly naked. "*Please do not die*," he wrote, only half jokingly, to his great friend Ruth Yorck in 1951.

And yet there is never a hint of "mawkishness," a quality Lerman abhorred in his *Period Piece* review. If he can be severe with others— "I resent Tennessee [Williams]'s evil, sure masturbation of audiences"; "Martha Graham is the Mae West of the dance"—he is never less than severe with himself, too: a welcome quality in a diarist in general, and particularly in one whose writing extends to such great length. "The surface coruscates," he wrote, in 1945, of his work at *Harper's Bazaar*, "but it is sterile." As if in rueful acknowledgment of the possibility that it was a judgment on his life as well, he went on: "How to live?" The lack of mawkishness, despite the intensity of feeling throughout, owes much to a stringent (and often astringent) self-consciousness, which was itself, it's hard not to feel, deeply indebted to Lerman's lifelong reading and rereading of Proust. A 1972 entry begins, "Having just finished (for the eighth or ninth time) the "Overture" to *A la Récherche* [*sic*], I am overwhelmed...." Lerman identified with the aestheticized self-awareness of Proust not least because he liked to think that, as with Proust, his sensibility was founded on his outsider's sexuality and his outsider's religion: "The richness of being Jewish, the very specialness of being queer—these are two of my foundations."

There are, indeed, episodes in *The Grand Surprise* that uncannily mimic episodes in *À la recherche*. Not the least striking of these is one recounted in a 1972 entry, in which Lerman, attending an art opening, is bewildered to find himself among "an assortment of elderly women who greeted me with joy"—only to realize that they are all old friends from thirty years past, now made unrecognizable by time:

> Only when I somehow unfocused these seamed, other-shaped faces, so confidently presenting themselves for friendly kisses, did I perceive within each quite unfamiliar visage the face of some other person I had once known well. Here were women I had seen or chatted with daily—a *danse macabre*...[they] have become those anonymous old women and men who make up lamenting choruses in verse plays.

This is a re-creation (perhaps conscious but all the more moving if it was unconscious: a testament to the extent to which Lerman had internalized Proust's novel) of the narrator's climactic experience at the Princesse de Guermantes's matinee in *Le Temps retrouvé*.

The title of the present volume is, in fact, an allusion to the object that was, for Lerman, something like the famous madeleine: a magnificent butterfly, called a Camberwell Beauty, that he caught sight of as a child and that aroused in him the intensest desire he'd ever known, and that forever after represented to him the thing he sought in life: a sense of wonder, of the swoony and unexpected possibility of sudden beauty. "Thirty-five or so years later," he wrote in a 1956 journal entry, "I read about this butterfly and discovered that it has another name. Sometimes it is called the Grand Surprise."

And so *The Grand Surprise* exemplifies the qualities that Lerman himself sought out in the autobiographies and life recollections that he—an astonishingly successful autodidact with no more than a high school education—so avidly read: wit, respect for time past, profound feeling, a lack of cheap sentimentality, and above all an abiding sense, when others might have become jaded, of deep "wonder" at the haut monde (as he liked to put it) of art and society to which he had struggled so hard to gain access. This was the quality that Lerman, the Harlem-born Jewish homosexual, responded to so strongly in the diaries of Francis Kilvert, the English clergyman: "Kilvert was radiant with wonder. It was his Golden Fleece, his mighty mite, God given."

What makes *The Grand Surprise* most worth reading for anyone interested in the substance, rather than the coruscating surface, of the times and culture it describes is the scintillant quality of Lerman's critical acumen. To read this book is, as it were, to witness a meteor shower of sparkling and provocative (if, more often than not, casually tossed-off) insights into the dance, theater, film, music, art, and literature of his day, and of the past. Dietrich is "the permanent symbol of beauty's decay"; Barbara Bel Geddes was "very good" as Maggie in the 1955 Broadway production of *Cat on a Hot Tin Roof*, but

Miriam Hopkins would have been "extraordinary"; the "curvaceous line" of the melodies in *Tosca*—he is writing about Callas here—suggest to him that Puccini's music is, in fact, "very Art Nouveau." Often, there are throwaway lines about eccentrically fascinating ideas that you wish he'd spent more time working out: at one point he remarks that he thinks of Emily Dickinson and Lizzie Borden as "identical, actually as one woman. They represent to me the two schools, as do Duse and Bernhardt, of the same art."

It's in the extended reflections on this or that opera or book or performer that Lerman's genius for impressionistically conjuring the qualities of art, or artistic people, is fully revealed. Here he is, in 1972, listening to *Das Rheingold*:

> Wagner made audible the caress. Yet his tensions, even when small by design, are monumental. Listening to Wagner is always like traveling through ranges of mountains, each more overwhelming, through size or beauty or sheer being, than those traversed—the sudden, sweeping vast forests—the shimmer, the sheen, all sunlight fluttering—a vastness of soaring, wings in motion—running, that happens in Wagner constantly—the sound of a single bee enlarged to a magnificent thunder—sense of alarums. In Proust's opening pages, night—hurrying through the night. Certain pages of Proust, Beethoven, and Wagner are linked by this sense of distant hurrying, by carriage, by horse, through night.

Here he is in 1951, after seeing Olivia de Havilland's *Romeo and Juliet* in London, on the character of the Nurse:

> I realized that the Nurse was a wicked, genuinely immoral, lazy woman, and that she is, actually, the Mrs. Danvers who permits

Juliet to undo herself, and even abets her, in what the Nurse must know is a fatal act. This Nurse lives in the moment, is spoiled, lewd.... I have never seen a production which has been staged to present her this way.

Here he is, in 1984, making what seems at first like an improbable, even silly—and yet ultimately persuasive—comparison between Jane Austen and Judith Martin ("Miss Manners," whom Lerman saw as "more Jane Austen than Emily Post"):

How Miss Austen strikes flint on stone, and how sparks fly, sometimes igniting small, astonishing fires, sometimes bursting into conflagration.... The amusement and shock of joy comes from how she views commonsensically, from some sharp eminence. She startles realistically—there's the link with Judith. The view from the same sharp eminence.

And to finish this necessarily too-brief catalog, here he is on his beloved Proust; he's been reading *Jean Santeuil*, in 1955, three years after its posthumous publication:

In *Jean Santeuil*, Proust works with a whitewash brush, in frequently crude strokes and slashes. In *Remembrance*, the brushes used are the finest sable, the most expensive in the world, so sensitive that the fiercest storms are minutely impaled. Here [in *Jean Santeuil*] we move gradually through milky Whistlers of damp fog and starry lights, glowing sharply in the blue-white, skim milk light. This is Proust's sketchbook and should be exhibited with Degas's and Manet's and Saint-Aubin's...

Lerman had some interesting brushes of his own.

Judged by Lerman's own standards for autobiographical recollections, then, the document that was the product of all of his talents—as a man, as a diarist, as a critic—might be considered "a little masterpiece." Yet the question that begins to form itself in your mind quite early on in *The Grand Surprise*, and that hovers, increasingly uneasily, over the otherwise festive, even dazzling goings-on here like (as Lerman might put it) the unwelcome fairy godmother, Carabosse, at Sleeping Beauty's christening, is why a person of such talents, appetites, and ambitions was unable to produce a big masterpiece—the "enormous book I want so much to do," as he described it as early as 1946. If the question lingers, it's primarily because Lerman himself keeps referring to his unwritten masterwork (always "my book"); as late as 1989, as he put it in a glum journal entry, he had "not given up the refuge of that dream." And yet by then, if not indeed much earlier, it was surely obvious that he could not muster himself for the task. Why?

Here again, Lerman's early review of *Period Piece* sheds an interesting light. The review, it must be said, is somewhat top-heavy. Lerman, well known as a raconteur, liked to start off his articles with grand, attention-getting flourishes: "I write of the raptures in reading dictionaries, the pleasures in perusing lexicons, chartularies, enchiridions, omnium gatherums..." one 1957 review begins. But in this piece, as indeed often in his journalistic work, you feel that, once he's inside—once he has your attention—his interest flags. The middles, the parts where he's supposed to be engaging the work at hand, tend to feel scanty and superficial, hazily summarizing rather than incisively exploring the contents which, however trivial they may be, he claimed to find both fascinating and worthy of his "study." (You never do get a real feel for what most of *Period Piece* is like, apart from the fact that the author "takes the reader right back into the Cambridge of her childhood.") This seeming inability to translate his brilliance onto the published page was a flaw of which Lerman himself was ruefully aware: "I say such wonderful things about books and people," he confided to his journal in 1949, just after he'd begun writing and editing for *Mademoiselle*, "and...when I come to write it's all gone."

As you make your way through *The Grand Surprise*, it is hard not to think that the reason that Lerman was incapable of writing the book he had in mind was, in the end, temperamental. "I am very good at creating atmosphere," he wrote in 1966, pondering his inability to complete a book he'd been contracted to write about Sotheby's, "and rather blithe"; elsewhere, more devastatingly, he acknowledges that he lacks a certain kind of "content": "I am decoration, not great art." In the end, his knack for savoring atmosphere wherever he might find it, for finding the next grand surprise, for being, when all is said and done, a connoisseur rather than a creator was what he had to offer.

And offer it he did, in those coruscating flashes; but beyond that, there is a curious lack of engagement with the larger world, the world that was more than sensibility and beauty. *The Grand Surprise* is a document that begins in 1939 and ends in 1993, and yet as you read it you cannot help but be struck by the fact that there is virtually no mention (let alone discussion) of World War II, of the Holocaust, of McCarthyism, of the Stonewall Riots, of Watergate, of the Reagan years—apart from a complaint, apropos of Mrs. Reagan, that "everything save her shoes [was] wrong"—which is to say, most of the history that Lerman lived through. (A significant exception is a brief and touching account of his attending, with Gray Foy, a 1971 protest in Washington against the Vietnam War, which is otherwise unmentioned.) This seeming indifference to the world outside of the glistening bubble he inhabited is noteworthy because it suggests a failure to appreciate the deeper "content" of things—a failure that, in turn, might account for that lack of a certain profounder "content" in Lerman himself, as he himself understood.

That content, in the end, is what art, as opposed to decoration, derives from. It may well be significant that a passage in Proust that Lerman delightedly singles out for praise is one in which the Duchesse de Guermantes talks about decor. But of course, what Proust is also about is decay—the deep, rotted mechanics of the society that had such perfect taste in decor. Of this Lerman, too, was aware; but out of that awareness, he would or could not create anything—not least because he himself (as he also well knew) was part of the mechanism of superficiality, of what he calls "the false, generated gaiety," of the ephemeral, "the mighty for a moment."

It's hard not to wonder whether Lerman's melancholy self-consciousness about his lack of deep content, together with his tormented awareness of his complicity with what he himself saw as an inconsequential industry, was responsible for his lifelong case of writer's block—a block that didn't altogether prevent him from writing, as we well know, but did stop him from committing to a project that he had the vision to understand was serious, but not the nature to undertake. What he couldn't do, finally, was absent himself from the worlds, haute or otherwise, that he'd worked so hard to be part of—to leave the theater or the party and to be alone in the way that writers must, at some point, be alone, to "giv[e] up just existing, just riding on the tide from moment to moment" and "shoulder a burden," as he put it in one anguished 1950 entry. Ten years later, he goes into a depression when, after an Israeli author asks if Lerman is a writer, Gray Foy responds, "Not for some time":

If I had written what I should have written these years, even failing at it—but no one is to blame. I am the only one—having written and published millions of words for some twenty-three or so years and to no deep, abiding avail....What wrongs I have done to such talents as I have (had). What self-indulgence and waste....I lack all discipline. This comes of wanting to be loved and admired and be made much of.

What gives *The Grand Surprise* an undercurrent that is, in the end, almost melancholy is Lerman's understanding that the substance of a real writer's life—"just [to] write it and then rewrite it until it's good"—was something he was temperamentally unsuited for. "What a difficult life that is," he wrote mournfully; it was more pleasant to be loved and admired. In this respect it's worth noting some of the many serious midcentury writers and thinkers who do not appear on Lerman's guest lists: Edmund Wilson, Elizabeth Bishop, Elizabeth Hardwick, Robert Lowell, Meyer Schapiro, Philip Roth, John Updike, Saul Bellow, Hannah Arendt.

You could say, of course, that *The Grand Surprise* itself is the great work that Lerman wanted to produce; but I'm not sure that Lerman, with his rigorous insistence on self-knowledge, would agree. He knew well what character he had and what choices he had made. He may have warned himself, as he did in 1954 leaving a party at Nathan Milstein's, that it wasn't "important" to "enter that world," but enter it he did, as we know; he may have complained, that same year, that Marlene Dietrich's late-night phone calls were "consuming my reading and writing time," but a person whose ambition was to be a writer, rather than a persona, would have hung up the phone long ago. Lerman's tragedy, if it may be called that, one that makes itself felt throughout this remarkable volume, was that he kept private, or never was able to bring off, the work that ought to have been public, while devoting his working life, his public life, his enormous talents to the glossy worlds—parties, magazines—that he knew enough to disdain.

The irony is that today's culture of superficial glitter, of knowingness without any real knowledge, is sustained by the very magazines to which Lerman, however lofty his tastes and talents, devoted his working life. And when you lie down with dogs, even greyhounds and Lhasa apsos, you may well get up with fleas. As I savored every page of his remarkable private writings, I couldn't help noting that nearly every historical, literary, artistic, or biographical allusion had to be footnoted or explained, from Saint-Simon to Sainte-Beuve, from Gustave Moreau to William Hogarth, from Aubrey Beardsley to Ned Rorem—the intimates of Lerman's fervent inner life, now apparently presumed to be wholly unrecognizable to readers at large. These, it's perhaps worth noting, are the very readers on whose behalf the reviewer of Lerman's book, in *The New York Times Book Review*, felt compelled to ask rhetorically, in her own introductory flourish, "Who is Leo Lerman?" Poignantly, Lerman himself anticipated this question. "The mortality of the fashion world," he lamented in 1970. "Who will think of me? No one." Here, as often, he knew how to spot a trend.

—*The New York Review of Books*, August 16, 2007

ZONED OUT

IT'S LIKELY THAT the writer Jonathan Franzen is no less famous today for the really good novel he published in 2001 than for the really bad mistake he made a couple of weeks later. What the ensuing half decade—and, now, *The Discomfort Zone*, a collection of autobiographical essays—have subsequently made clear is that the high qualities that made his literary achievement so worthy are inextricable from the flaws that made his real-life behavior so puzzling.

Precisely a week before the World Trade Center fell (a chronology he has drawn attention to), Franzen published his sweeping novel of middle-American decline, *The Corrections*, a critically lauded best seller that went on to win the National Book Award. As is now well known, fairly early on in the critical and public embrace of Franzen's magnum opus the book was selected for Oprah Winfrey's Book Club: a media apotheosis that, whatever else it means to a writer's career—and just what it does mean was the subject of the ensuing flap between Franzen and Winfrey—is commonly believed to guarantee that nearly a million copies of the writer's book will be sold. (Franzen's publisher was reported to have increased its order from 90,000 to nearly 800,000 copies on learning of the selection; half a million of these, according to Franzen's publicist, were directly attributable to the Oprah Book Club selection.)

So much for the literary achievement. For, as we also know, Franzen—bizarrely, it seemed to most people; self-destructively, to many—turned Oprah down. For one thing, he didn't like the little Oprah Book Club sticker that would henceforth appear on his novel. ("I see this as my book, my creation, and I didn't want that logo of corporate ownership on it," he said.) For another, he was made nervous by the fact that Oprah's audience was largely female. ("I had some hope of actually reaching a male audience.") And then there was the whole high-low thing. Franzen had "cringe[d]" on learning of the selection, he later said, since among Oprah's selections in the past there had been some titles that he characterized as "schmaltzy"; and Franzen, as he himself acknowledged, represented the "high-art literary tradition."

Unsurprisingly, Oprah coolly disinvited Franzen soon after these and similar comments were widely reported in the press. The quiet graciousness of the notice posted on her website stood in devastating contrast to the grandiose self-importance of Franzen's public pronouncements about literature and his place in it. "Jonathan Franzen will not be on *The Oprah Winfrey Show* because he is seemingly uncomfortable and conflicted about being chosen as an Oprah's Book Club selection," the notice read. "It is never my intention to make anyone uncomfortable or cause anyone conflict."

Making people uncomfortable—and describing people who are uncomfortable in their own skin—are what Franzen has always been good at doing in his writing: discomfort, conflict, and a hopeless awkwardness have been his great subjects. That they are now the focus of his new collection raises interesting questions—questions very much on readers' minds these days, when the divide between truth and fiction seems increasingly to be blurred—about the relationship between a writer's real life and his fictional work.

Until now, Franzen's preoccupation with "discomfort" was best showcased in *The Corrections*, a ruthless but not unfeeling dissection of one midwestern family falling apart as its stodgy values were put to the test by the go-go avidity of American culture in the 1990s. (A serviceable summary of the book and its themes, in fact, was the one that appeared on the Oprah website: "*The Corrections* is a grandly entertaining novel for the new century—a comic, tragic masterpiece about a family breaking down in an age of easy fixes.") From the start, it was not hard to see where the novel's appeal lay. Ostensibly the drama of one family, the Lamberts, that lives in a St. Louis–like city called (with a knowing sourness typical of Franzen) "St. Jude," it seemed nonetheless to be about something larger—about the failure of something in the culture as a whole at the turn of the millennium, about the awkward fit between American dreams and American life. From the flat, rather desperate opening sentence ("The madness of an autumn prairie cold front coming through"), the sense of imminent crisis and disintegration seemed to be global as well as local, cultural as well as familial.

And indeed, around his story of the decay of this family's values— a process symbolized first by the physical and then by the mental collapse of the paterfamilias, Alfred, a bitter, emotionally crabbed engineer who starts out with Parkinson's disease and ends with Alzheimer's—the author twined motifs and story lines intended to remind readers that the Lamberts' problems were mirrored on a much larger cultural scale. Hence, for instance, the various characters' attempts to "correct" (the word is used repeatedly, and pointedly, throughout the book) their wayward lives was ironically reflected in one ongoing story line about the popularity of a new, mood-altering wonder drug called Correcktall (the most obvious of the book's "easy fixes"); another leitmotif was a widespread if inchoate anxiety on the part of many characters about an imminent "correction" in the financial markets. It was this entwining, by means of suggestive symbols and artful details, of the broadly social and the narrowly personal themes, the family drama and the drama of national anxiety, that gave *The Corrections* the largeness that made it seem so worthy to critics. It was a big American novel about big American themes.

The intensity and raw emotionality of Franzen's account of these hapless people, awkwardly fumbling with their failure to catch up to the larger culture, is clearly what won over readers (male and female)—and was, just as clearly, what elevated it above his previous fictions. His first novel, *The Twenty-Seventh City*, published in 1988, was a nightmare fantasia on American themes. Its fanciful plot was about—well, a plot: a secret plan by an Indian woman and her henchman to take over the city of St. Louis, where she has, rather bizarrely, managed to get herself appointed chief of police. The conflict between these rather over-the-top aliens—these "others"—and the stolid, solid midwestern businessman who resists the Indians' seductions, and who eventually thwarts the plot, indicates the presence early on of Franzen's preoccupation with Americanness under siege, with the uneasy encounter between traditional values and a world that had gone unrecognizably awry. But the overelaborate and (you kept feeling) overly clever donnée kept getting in the way of a profound engagement with his subject. With its intricate plotting (in every sense) and its curdled, paranoid vision of America in crisis at every level, the novel betrayed its author's debt—one owed by many novelists of his generation—to the work of Don DeLillo, who, as Franzen made clear in an essay he published in *Harper's* in 1996, is something of a hero to him.

Even more DeLilloesque was his second novel, *Strong Motion*, a paranoid fantasy (again) about a young man, awkward, geeky, midwestern, named Louis Holland, who stumbles on, and subsequently attempts to expose, a vast and sinister corporate plot to cover up illegal oil drilling in, of all places, Massachusetts. The drilling has destabilized the area's tectonic plates, which in turn has led to a number of earthquakes. The latter are what the title, in part, refers to; but there are other "strong motions" that the book wants to treat. The corrosive relationship, for instance, between the young hero and his awful mother (horrible, intrusive, overbearing mothers run through Franzen's fiction) and his ineffective, post-hippie father; and the budding romance between him and a prickly, sexually avid young female seismologist, whose allure, it must be said, is difficult for the reader to grasp. (Franzen doesn't seem to like younger women much, either: in both of his first two novels, the younger, sexually active female leads get shot.)

But as you went through *Strong Motion*, it occurred to you that what really preoccupied this clever author was the clever bits: the factoids about seismology, the stuff you don't need other human beings to do. The subplots about relationships come off as an afterthought, as if the author realized (or someone—an editor, say—told him) that the novel needed some emotional interest to succeed. Although *Strong Motion* ends with the awkward Louis—who starts out emotionally frozen, traumatized by his bad parenting—ostensibly understanding what love is all about, you suspect that his creator didn't really think there was anything terribly wrong with him to begin with.

It's only if you've read the first two novels that you can appreciate how great a leap—in artistry but also in maturity—*The Corrections* represented. Many readers enjoy cleverness and narrative gamesmanship; a certain and not necessarily hard-won cynicism and sourness, too. This is why the epigones of DeLillo are popular. But far more readers (presumably the half-million people who trust Oprah's taste enough to go out and buy her selections on faith) want to be entertained by a story about real human beings having real human problems and experiencing real human feelings. The evil cultural aliens and dastardly corporate plots can be amusing, but at the end of the day what many of us want from a large novel are characters more or less recognizably like ourselves: imperfect parents, imperfect children plagued by the kind of awkwardness, self-consciousness, weakness, and failure that you can't write about well if you're too invested in showing off your own cleverness and superiority as a creator; the everyday-life stuff, indeed, that Franzen condescendingly referred to as "schmaltz." This is why his third book hit paydirt: the ingeniousness of the first couple of novels served, for the first time, a broad and humane story about life as most of us know it.

Franzen's behavior during the Oprah flap and its aftermath suggests the precise nature of the awkwardness that seems to lie at the heart of both the author and his work. At the most obvious level, there was the perversity of a working writer saying "No" to the prospect of selling a million copies of his book. It is true that, in the now-famous *Harper's* essay, which he published five years before *The Corrections* came out—a long manifesto decrying the woeful state of the American novel, an attention-getting literary cri de coeur—the young writer had idealistically lamented the fact that today "money, hype, a limo ride to the *Vogue* shoot were the main prize, the consolation for no longer mattering to the culture." Yet however much you may have admired or agreed with the lofty sentiments expressed therein, Franzen's refusal to join Oprah's club in the name of High Art seemed not inauthentic but inconsistent. After all, wasn't being picked by Oprah a sign that the high-art literary tradition *did* matter to the culture? Wasn't having a million people actually *read* the high-art literary work you'd been telling everyone you were going to write for the past five years the solution to the problem of America's dire literary situation?

The title of the *Harper's* essay, when it was first published ten years ago, was "Perchance to Dream" (it's since been severely edited and republished as "Why Bother?" in his 2002 collection, *How to Be Alone*); and as you watched Franzen sabotaging himself, it occurred to you that the allusion to *Hamlet* was apposite. There was something simply ornery, something late-adolescent, something of the perennial graduate student in the snide superiority that lay behind the author's willful rejection of a success so tantalizingly within reach; about the refusal to be in and of the adult world—the world of people who realize that success doesn't necessarily mean selling out, who know that people who are ethically rigorous rarely advertise, with so much energy and so little humor, their own ethical rigor.

Given all that, it was hard not to think that the furious backpedaling that almost immediately followed the Oprah flap came less from the author himself than from his own corporate masters. (His publisher, Farrar, Straus and Giroux, after all, is part of the enormous German media conglomerate Holtzbrinck; apparently Franzen had no qualms about having their logo on his book—nor, despite his published objection to money and hype, did he apparently object to the sizable advance the company had paid him.) Everywhere you turned, suddenly, Franzen was apologizing: on the BBC, in *USA Today*, you name it. And yet in the apologies, as in the refusal itself, something struck you once again as awkward, as not quite right. "To find myself being in the position of giving offense to someone who's a hero—not a hero of mine per se, but a hero in general—I feel bad in a public-spirited way," he told *USA Today*. What lingered was not the alleged remorse (that somehow childlike "I feel bad") but rather the insistence on demurral, the childish withholding that suggested that his heart wasn't in it. "Feel bad in a public-spirited way"—what does that *mean*? And then "Not a hero of *mine*," equally infantile in its gracelessness; the slight pedantry, too, of "per se." Listening to all this, we seemed to be hearing voices that we'd heard in the author's fiction, nowhere more so than in *The Corrections*: the voices of bruised, petulant children and of arrogant, rather clueless grown-ups.

These voices echo throughout Franzen's thin and insubstantial new collection, whose greatest virtue, in the end, may be that the essays collected here clearly identify the real-life sources of the fiction, which is often so strong. The question that arises is: Do we really need to be this intimate with the inspiration for the novels?

The Discomfort Zone advertises itself, in a rather optimistic subtitle, as a "personal history," and was described during its prepublication buildup as a "memoir"—a mischaracterization that further disserves a genre that already suffers from too much approximate thinking and lack of discipline on the part of so many who indulge themselves in it. The fact that four of the six chapters here previously appeared in some form in *The New Yorker* confirms the suspicion that the author merely padded a bunch of preexisting occasional pieces on a variety of subjects in order to produce the kind of lifestory narrative that everyone seems to want to read right now. Around a grab bag of subjects—how Franzen learned German; the *Peanuts* cartoonist Charles Schulz, much admired by the author; bird-watching—he has interwoven episodes from a youth and early manhood that will seem familiar to readers of his fiction and particularly of *The Corrections*: the stultifyingly conventional adolescence in a St. Louis suburb; the earnest, aspirational mother; the stern, anhedonic father. But only half the essays properly count as "personal history": one about the sale of his mother's house (which at one point, in what turns out to be a too-rare humaneness here, the author touchingly describes as her "novel"), another on the unintended effects of some high school pranks, another on the author's pubescent experience of a Christian youth group.

The problem here is not one of structure but of content—and, seriously, of tone. An inevitable danger of memoir is the necessary self-absorption of the writer—one that the best memoirists know how to leaven by means of either self-deprecation or humor, or both. But there's a grimness here, a bitterness, that is not only off-putting in large quantities but spoils the many vignettes in which Franzen seems to want to present himself as a nerd or a loser we can identify with. A wrong note always sounds. There's a narrative about a grade school "homonym bee," in which he recalls, of his youthful self, that he "was very much unaccustomed to considering the interior states of people other than myself"; this no doubt accounts for his apparent lack of feeling, at the time, on learning that his opponent in the bee was killed in a car crash. Such moments remind you a bit of what Franzen sounded like when he was making his apology to Oprah —there's a hard edge here, a sense of resentment masquerading as abjection.

When he widens the focus to include the larger world, the self-absorption can become repellent. It isn't that Franzen isn't intelligent or full of interesting things to say. Like many literate and educated people, he has reasonable, liberal-minded opinions on politics, global affairs, the aftermath of Hurricane Katrina, the Gulf War. But his pronouncements are marred by the smug, graduate-studenty know-it-all-ness that you recall from his behavior in real life, and which you recognize in certain of his characters—Chip Lambert, say, the awful pomo hipster academic antihero of *The Corrections*. If someone were to come up to you and say, as Franzen does here, "It seemed to me that helping Katrina's homeless victims ought to be the government's job, not mine," it would sound a reasonable enough claim to make. But in the mood of relentless solipsism established by these essays, this seems like just one more example of what strikes you, in the end, as a kind of political and aesthetic autism.

Hence, for instance, in the bird-watching essay, around which the author somewhat effortfully twines the tale of his disintegrating first marriage, he recalls how "deploring other people—their lack of perfection—had always been [the] sport" of him and his ex-wife. Elsewhere he observes that not having children was his "first, best line of defense" against the environmental pleading of Al Gore: "The climate would be OK until I died, and as a childless person I had no personal connection to what happened after that." It somehow comes as no surprise that this bird-watching author only starts worrying about the environment when the avian species he has grown so fond of will, like millions of human babies, not survive a climatological catastrophe. When he writes that "what sickened and enraged me were all the other human beings on the planet," you realize it's not mere striving for effect.

———

If these pronouncements seem calculated to offend, I suspect it's because Franzen wanted to be rigorous and ruthless with himself—wanted, that is, to write about the self without recourse to the glib narratives of redemption so characteristic of memoir just now, without romanticizing his faults. To strip away the layers of self-congratulation (to say nothing of flat-out lies) that we so often get in "personal histories," in other words, and to say, in effect, "I am an imperfect person and this is what it looks like to be that imperfect person—to insufficiently love one's fellow man, one's parents, one's spouse, even oneself." This in itself is admirable. Ideally, the memoirist's revelation of himself should seduce readers into a comparable willingness to examine themselves and their lives without vanity, without props. In this way, a literary experience can lead to a profound life experience.

This project is, however, fatally marred in Franzen's nonfiction by a flaw that also characterizes even the best of his fiction: that pervasive peevishness, the fundamental failure of genuine good humor—a quality without which, as every stand-up comedian knows, obsessive self-exposure is tedious rather than entertaining or edifying. There is an almost willful resistance to the amusing, the pleasurable, the beautiful in Franzen's work, a body of writing in which every landscape is a landfill, every season is rainy. (All three of his novels are filled with surreally detailed descriptions of blighted cityscapes: a decaying St. Louis in *The Twenty-Seventh City*, the grimier neighborhoods of Cambridge, Massachusetts, in *Strong Motion*, the annihilating blandness of suburban St. Jude in *The Corrections*.) "There was something dreadful about springtime itself," the author recalls at one point. Oy Vey. This blighted vision—which can have great appeal to readers who like to think of themselves as knowing and sophisticated—owes a good deal to, you might say, art: the debt to the paranoid gloom of DeLillo, the master. But as we now know, it had its roots in the author's real life—the upbringing at the hands of a dour, almost abusively stern father with "fantastic Swedish protestant prejudices" who is now all too clearly revealed as the model of the crabbed Alfred Lambert in *The Corrections*; a father whose reaction to the sight of his child reading a book or playing with friends was the contemptuous exclamation, "One continuous round of pleasure!"

Indeed, a strong impression that you get from *The Discomfort Zone* (the title refers to the heavily symbolic setting on a thermostat that Franzen's parents continually argued over during his growing-up years) is, in fact, an appreciation of the extent to which he seems to have internalized rather than rejected his father's resistance to pleasure, his awful severity and contemptuousness; and a corresponding understanding of the son's embrace of a smarty-pants persona that was, you surmise, the child's response to such psychic squashing. Even his willingness to refuse an immense success, and the showily overprincipled gesture that served as the vehicle for that refusal, turn out to be echoes of the father's life: we learn here that Franzen *père* felt he could no longer make use of a business associate's vacation home because he'd started to do more business with the man's competitor.

The two emotional leitmotifs laid bare in these personal recollections—the cleverness, the contempt—make themselves felt not only in the early novels, *The Twenty-Seventh City* and *Strong Motion*, which had the showy intricacy of science projects but which curiously lacked adult feeling, but, I would say, even in *The Corrections*. In what you now see as a characteristic struggle, the brilliance of the novel's presentation of the tortured dynamics of family life—no one who has read it will forget the devastating portrait of Chip's older brother, Gary, as he slowly loses a desperate marital battle for the affections of his children—seems at war with an often undisguised distaste for the broken, awkward, imperfect characters whom its author evoked so uncannily well. (There's something about the way in which Franzen repeatedly ridicules Enid Lambert's pronunciation of the word "mature"—"matoor"—that's deeply unpleasant.) Great novelists, in the end, summon a magisterial sympathy for their most flawed, even worst characters: think of Balzac and Vautrin, Melville and Ahab, Trollope and Melmotte. There's a bitterness in this novel, the residue of some personal resentment that hasn't been worked out. You realize, after reading the new book, that you were hearing the voice of the author's father.

The problem, to my mind, is that whereas the Franzen's considerable artistry as a shaper of fictions makes Alfred a memorable character whom you enjoy encountering on the page, his shortcomings as a memoirist—the failure of feeling for others, the narrowness of vision, the solipsism—render his real-life father a personage you don't want to spend a lot of time with. This, in the end, goes for Franzen himself. The present day is, we know, mad for memoir, but memoir is a genre that has its own requirements, structures, and standards, and they are not the same as the ones imposed by fiction. Some novelists, even very good ones, should avoid it.

The strange conflict and contradictions of personality that have marked Franzen's life and vein his work, the competition between nerds and bullies, the differences (and similarities) between an artist's life and the art he makes, are themes that occur most memorably, in the new collection, in an essay devoted to the comic strip *Peanuts*—a classic of American culture that, revealingly, Franzen seriously misreads.

The second chapter of *The Discomfort Zone* is ostensibly a paean to the creator of a comic strip that, more than anything else in American popular culture for many decades, celebrated the comic side of discomfort—the sheer, poignant, foolish awkwardness that comes with being human. Unsurprisingly, Franzen clearly relishes the deeply flawed personality of the man who created this beloved cultural icon: Charles Schulz, for all his huge success, was, as Franzen expertly suggests in his essay, a difficult, embittered, resentful man, still seething over perceived insults four decades later. Even more suggestive than the portrait itself is the fact that Franzen so fervently defends this not very nice man—the midwestern offspring of Scandinavian parents, it's worth mentioning—whom he describes, not without disapproval, as "childlike... in the absoluteness of his scruples and inhibitions." To Franzen, the aloof, rigid Schulz is an artistic hero: "To keep choosing art over the comforts of normal life," he writes in a passage reminiscent of the *Harper's* essay, "is the opposite of damaged." Reading this, you can't help wondering who it is he's really defending.

Franzen's insistence on seeing this off-putting personality as a model is, no doubt, what leads him to his startlingly wrongheaded interpretation of the comic strip that is so important to him—a misreading that, because it's about the tensions between awkwardness and grandiosity, human failing and inhuman arrogance, says a great deal about the man and the writer both. "Almost every young person experiences sorrows," he rightly points out at the beginning of his exegesis of the *Peanuts* series. The sentence gives you hope that the geeky child still hiding inside the adult Franzen is going to admit that, like everyone else, he loved *Peanuts* because he, too, identified with the perpetually awkward, perpetually failed, and yet just as perpetually optimistic Charlie Brown. But no: for Franzen—who tells us that, as a child, he "personally enjoyed winning and couldn't see why so much fuss was made about the losers"—the real hero of *Peanuts* is not the "depressive and failure-ridden" Brown but the grandiose beagle, Snoopy. Franzen asserts that "clearly Snoopy" was Schulz's "true alter ego,"

> the protean trickster whose freedom is founded on his confidence that he's lovable at heart, the quick-change artist who, for the sheer joy of it, can become a helicopter or a hockey player or Head Beagle and then again, in a flash, before his virtuosity has a chance to alienate you or diminish you, be the eager little dog who just wants dinner.

The problem here is that Snoopy's self-proclaimed virtuosity does, to no little extent, alienate and diminish: if he's amusing, with his grandiose grudge against the Red Baron (and, as I so vividly recall, the Van Gogh and the spiral staircase he lost when his doghouse burned down), it's precisely because he represents the part of ourselves, the smugness, the avidity, the pomposity, the rank egotism that most of us wouldn't dream of strutting the way that Snoopy does. (He's funny precisely because he does the things you'd never dream of doing.) Franzen, like most of us, is an awkward combination of Charlie and Snoopy; the difference being, or so it seems on reading this new book, that whereas most of us think of ourselves as Charlie with a bit of Snoopy, Franzen—still stuck in the compensatory defenses he perfected as the unhappy child he so vividly sketches here—is, and wants everyone to know that he is, a lot of Snoopy with just a bit of Charlie. For my part, I'll stick with Charlie. Who, after all, would want to spend that much time with a character who's so self-involved that he doesn't realize which species he belongs to?

—*The New York Times Book Review,* October 15, 2006

BOYS WILL BE BOYS

WHEN EDMUND WHITE writes an essay like this one—a consideration of the work of another contemporary author—he often finds a way to include an anecdote that shows that he has some personal connection, some social or even sexual history, with the writer in question. "I first met Chatwin in 1978 in New York," he writes, not untypically, at the beginning of a 1997 essay about Bruce Chatwin for *The Times Literary Supplement*. "Maybe it was the excitement of druggy, sexy New York before AIDS or of the Mapplethorpe connection, but we were still standing seconds after he'd come into my apartment when we started fooling around with each other." Not all of White's encounters with literary eminences, of course, were as steamy as that one—although his latest autobiography, *City Boy: My Life in New York During the 1960s and '70s*, rattles off a *Don Giovanni*-esque list of alleged conquests that includes John Ashbery, Robert Wilson, and Mart Crowley. But the precise nature of the relationship in question isn't really the point. The point, which is made again and again in *Arts and Letters*, the 2004 volume in which the Chatwin essay was collected along with nearly forty other articles, lectures, and occasional pieces, is simply that White was *there*—was part of the scene to which these eminences belonged. What's at stake for him, in writing ostensibly about arts and letters, is the artists and the *lettrés*, the social and personal aspect of literary production, as well as the (merely) aesthetic or abstract.

White was born and raised in Ohio—growing up gay in and around Cincinnati in the 1950s furnished him with the material for the most affecting and effective of his several autobiographical novels, *A Boy's Own Story* (1982)—and it occurs to you, at first, that a lingering consciousness of having been a wide-eyed midwestern immigrant to New York City persists in the way that he repeatedly spotlights the moment when he first made contact with this or that famous writer or musician or artist (even after White had become an eminence himself, as the increasingly impressive settings of these encounters suggest). "When I first met Rorem in the 1970s I had been awed in advance by his legend," he recalls in *City Boy*; "I first met [Foucault] in 1980 in New York when I was a fellow of the New York Institute for the Humanities"; "I first met Grace Paley in Paris, where I was living for many years and where she'd come to a giant feminist powwow." Much to his credit, White—whose penchant for drawing his readers to the self-deprecating or even embarrassing autobiographical detail has something almost aggressive about it; it savors, somehow, of the ritualized eagerness for punishment that is found in S&M, a practice that he wrote about in his 2005 memoir, *My Lives* —is willing to admit that he wasn't always as memorable to his subjects as they so clearly were to him. "I was introduced to him at least ten times," he writes at the beginning of an appreciation of Edwin Denby, "though he never remembered me from one time to another."

But of all the key people White met and of all the significant moments at which he managed to be present (not least, the Stonewall

Riots in June 1969, now seen as the beginning of the modern gay movement), none was as historic as an encounter he had in his early thirties that would have immense importance for his life and work— or rather, for the way it changed his thinking about the relationship between his life and work. In *City Boy*, the author recalls a heated exchange that took place not long after Stonewall between himself and the late scholar and editor Richard Poirier, one of the quietly gay older literary figures of the time in whose reticence about his sexuality White, half a generation younger, saw a kind of hypocrisy. Like so many ambitious young writers newly arrived in New York, White was desperately trying to get some literary recognition; unlike many of those other writers, he was unabashedly living an openly gay life in the city, and had begun to wonder why the life he was leading couldn't be the subject of his writing.

Or indeed, the basis of a whole new kind of writing. During his visit with Poirier, White recalls, the older man was "furious" because White insisted that there was "such a thing as gay fiction, even gay poetry—worse, a gay sensibility!—and that at the very least works by gay people could be read in a special light, to illuminate them." Poirier recoiled from this idea, arguing that White's vision would mean isolating gay writers from the mainstream of a larger literature:

> "But things do change," I said confusedly. "There are always new movements in fiction, aren't there?...Why not have a gay school of fiction? Is there any harm in that? At least it's exciting and new."
>
> "Exciting! But it's a betrayal of every humane idea of literature. Have you never heard of universalism?"

For Poirier and like-minded critics, the "harm" lay in the possibility that, while profoundly gay-themed books such as James Baldwin's

Giovanni's Room could, through their artistic merits, attain transcendent, "universal" appeal for all readers, a literature by and for gay people would be diminishing for the writers and, too, for the readers. But for the young White, the niche represented both an ideological battleground and an interesting opportunity. This is undoubtedly the most important of the many scenes of self-positioning you keep coming across in White's work: a scene that places him at the moment when gay lit—the niche genre of which he himself would become the acknowledged leader—was created.

White has always been interested in people, personalities, and personas—and, I suspect, would argue that his interest goes beyond mere gossip or self-aggrandizement. For the encounters with writers and artists so amply recorded in *City Boy* remind you vividly that every author is also just a man or a woman, every eminence just a person—and that everything is, therefore, specific and personal: the first step on the journey from the personal to the political. In the new memoir he reflects on the sometimes disorienting tension between public personae and private selves:

> I suppose it's always strange to know in the flesh someone who is destined to be "immortal," or at least studied and analyzed long after his death....They were once young, uncertain, had a roll of fat about the waistband, one nostril bigger than the other, a shifty look that gave way to a wise stare....They were breathing, digesting animals as vulnerable to injury as the next creature...

This interest in the concrete and often unattractive details of lived lives is, White implies, not so much a matter of prurience (or, when the unappealing details are about himself, exhibitionism) but part of a literary and, indeed, even political project that has special resonance if your subject happens to be gay people and their lives. "I'd say that gay lives are not like straight lives," he writes at the beginning of "Writing Gay," the manifesto with which *Arts and Letters* begins— a discussion of gay biographies and biographers that serves as a kind of *apologia pro opere suo*. (White is deservedly celebrated, outside the gay literary scene and its readership, for a prizewinning biography of Jean Genet; his brief biography of Arthur Rimbaud is by far the best introduction to that complicated figure's life.) "One must know them intimately from the inside in order to place the right emphasis on the facts."

Why would it be more important to know a gay life (by which he seems to mean emotional and sex life) more intimately than a straight life, in writing about that life? Why—as he suggests in this essay and as his own autobiographies, filled as they are with the minutest details of his sexual and sentimental history, make clear—are sexuality and the details of a writer's sex life as important to emphasize as is, say, an evaluation of the writer's work? In some cases, White observes here, it's simply that straight squeamishness about gay sex lives can result in bald factual errors. He cites as an example the way in which some journalists lambasted the late Michel Foucault for having "knowingly" infected his partners with the HIV virus: but Foucault, White asserts, was an "S&M bottom" (that is, he enjoyed being the passive partner in rough anal sex), and passive-to-active infection was thought to be very rare if not impossible. And anyway, "since he was a friend of mine I can attest that he guessed at his diagnosis only five months before his death."

But for White, there is a far larger issue at stake here. For him, the entire fabric of gay men's lives, socially as well as sexually, is radically different from that of straight people: whereas the contours of a straight life are, according to him, conventional in a way that filters into heterosexual writers' writing ("a straight writer," he startlingly asserts at the end of *City Boy*, is "condemned to show nothing but marriage, divorce, and childbirth"), gay men's lives—characterized by unrestricted sexual play, serial rather than monogamous erotic involvements, and a correspondingly high valuation of friends over erotic partners—don't follow a straightforward (or at least conventionally mainstream) narrative. They therefore merit a different kind of narrative altogether: the gay lit that White helped create.

This is the point of his defense, in "Writing Gay," of *City Poet*, Brad Gooch's 1993 biography of Frank O'Hara—a book, White writes, that was unfairly attacked by critics who complained about Gooch's emphasis on the poet's sex life, at the expense of a corresponding emphasis on his work. "But in fact," White argues,

> O'Hara, the founder of "Personalism," wrote poems to his tricks and had such an active sex life, one might be tempted to say, in order to generate his poems, which are often dedicated to real tricks (who were all also his friends) or imaginary crushes. When Joan Accocela [*sic*] in the *New Yorker* complained that *City Poet* was too "gossipy," she missed the point. O'Hara's grinding social schedule and hundreds of sexual encounters offend people who want his life to be like a straight man's of the same period. If O'Hara had one or two gay marriages and had made his domestic life more important than his friendships, then he would have seemed like a reassuring translation of straight experience into gay terms. But O'Hara's real life was messy and episodic in the retelling, even picaresque... not what we expect in the usual literary biography.

And yet despite its lively allure, this argument is sentimental and unrigorous, built as it is on unexamined assumptions and impressionistic logic. It is not entirely clear, for one thing, what "the usual literary biography" might be, and why White thinks such works can't handle messy or episodic or picaresque lives. (Richard Ellmann's biography of Oscar Wilde seems to have no problem doing just that.) Nor is it clear whether White thinks that straight poets (or whoever) who had messy and irregular lives filled with sexual adventures— there are more than a few—deserve "gossipy" biographies, too. But then, the word "gossipy" does not, in fact, occur in Joan Acocella's long and thoughtful essay on O'Hara; nor indeed did she complain at any point that O'Hara's life wasn't enough "like a straight man's." Although White wants to cast her as a prig, the fact is that she's not shocked at all: if you actually read her piece you can see that she makes the very sensible argument that, given the well-known sexual and romantic excesses of downtown bohemians, both gay and straight, in the 1950s and 1960s, O'Hara's habits were simply not worth noting in the excessive detail in which Gooch's book indulges, at the expense of a full consideration of the poet's work—the thing that makes his life worth writing about in the first place.

Still, despite the wishful arguments and a certain casualness with other people's words (habits that recur in *City Boy*), there can be no doubt about the genuineness of White's impassioned defense of specifically gay writing. He has, indeed, chafed at characterizations of his own work as narrow or small, a criticism that he sees as coded distaste for homosexual writing itself. "When I wrote my Penguin life of Proust," he recalls in "Writing Gay," "I decided to discuss his homosexuality...but I was attacked for this approach in the *New York Times Book Review* and in the *New York Review*." ("How else could I make my book different from the hundreds that had preceded it?" he adds, an aside that, it must be said, makes you wonder what other biographies he had consulted.) He doesn't go into the details of the criticisms in question, but his paraphrases make clear the lineaments of what is, essentially, a political argument. The *Times* critic "took me to task for reducing Proust to his sexuality"; the late Roger Shattuck, in *The New York Review of Books*, "struck a blow for Proust's universality against my supposedly narrowing view."

"Universality" brings us back to "universalism," the word that cropped up in Poirier's critique of White's advocacy of "gay writing" many years before White wrote his Proust biography: you could say that the whole of the author's career has traced an arc from one of these poles to the other. His first couple of novels, *Forgetting Elena* (1975), a witty experiment with a fabulously unreliable narrator, and the plotless but oddly mesmerizing reverie on lost love that is *Nocturnes for the King of Naples* (1978; it might remind you of Marguerite Yourcenar's *Alexis*), were idiosyncratic and coolly stylish, with a pungent whiff of chloroform that betrays the influence of White's idol, Nabokov. *Forgetting Elena* fuses an arch haiku sensibility to a plot involving amnesia, set in a Fire Island–esque colony of excruciatingly status-conscious gay men. It's interesting to speculate how the young White, who was capable of an impressive elegance and was clearly preoccupied, too, with interesting formal questions, would have evolved.

But with *A Boy's Own Story*, although an evocative prettiness remains ("just as each shell held to the ears roars with a different ocean timbre, each of these bodies spoke to me with a different music"), the contours of White's incipient project came into focus— which is to say that "life" overtook "art" as his primary concern. He began to devote himself to the sometimes almost dogged recording of the quality, nature, and substance of gay life and experience that has been at the center of most of his output ever since, in fiction and essay, in biography and memoir. You feel it in the several thinly disguised autobiographical novels (*The Married Man*, for instance, with

its minute re-creation of an illness and death from AIDS) as well as
à clef portrayals—not always flattering—of famous friends such as
Susan Sontag (as in his roman à clef *Caracole*). But it is perhaps most
plain in this author's commitment to gay biography (Proust, Rimbaud, Genet) and, of course, undisguised autobiography: first *My
Lives* (2005), with its detailed descriptions of S&M episodes and unapologetic recollections of rent boys, and, now, *City Boy*.

The virtues and flaws of the latest of White's autobiographies—
the talented gossip's eye for the good story, dragged down by a tendency to dish out payback; a passionate chauvinism on behalf of gay
writers and their writing, hobbled by unsound and approximate
judgments about a larger literary world; a carelessness about the pri-
vacy of other people for the sake of a good anecdote—reflect, in the
end, the strengths and limitations of the relentlessly personal perspective that White advocates.

City Boy is interesting not least because it is a reminiscence about the
period when the gay way of life White sees as so distinctive from
straight life had its brief, dazzling *floruit*: the heady, hedonistic
stretch of time between the Stonewall riots (the event that marked
the beginning of the contemporary gay movement and coincided
with a marked, if uneven, increase in the visibility of gay people and
gay issues in American culture) and the advent, not even fifteen years
later, of AIDS, which would cast a dark shadow on the culture of
unrestrained sexual play. That this short period coincided with
White's literary advent—the tentative and often unsuccessful begin-
nings of which he narrates with an amusing lack of vanity—only
overdetermines the connection he likes to make between life and art.
His literary rise precisely followed the rise of modern gay culture.

There's a point in *City Boy* when White—who, in addition to being a well-known writer, is a well-known teacher who has, admirably, always made time to put himself at the service of the younger generation (most recently, at Princeton)—offers some professorial thoughts about the qualities of good fiction, which, he says, "depends on telling details and an exact and lifelike sequencing of emotions, and on representative if not slavishly mimetic dialogue, and on convincing actions." The best passages in the new memoir (whose arc reminds you at times of *Lost Illusions*, a novel that White mentions) have those qualities. Predictably, White is at his best when reminiscing about the gay sexual culture of the 1960s and 1970s in New York City, with its elaborate codes of conduct and erotic ceremonials as rigid as the Japanese court protocols that first fascinated him years ago, as *Forgetting Elena* made clear. Here he is on the preparations for a typical night out during his Greenwich Village days:

> I'd clean my apartment carefully, change the sheets and towels, put a hand towel under the pillow (the "trick towel" for mopping up the come) along with the tube of lubricant (usually water-soluble K-Y). You might even "douche out"—sometimes, if you were a real "senior girl," with a stainless-steel insertable nozzle attached to the shower. You'd buy eggs and bacon and jam and bread for toast, if you wanted to prove the next morning that you were "marriage material." You'd place an ashtray, cigarettes, and a lighter on the bedside table. You'd lower the lights and stack the record player with suitable mood music (Peggy Lee, not the Stones) before you headed out on the prowl. All this to prove you were "civilized," not just one more voracious two-bit whore. Once you'd landed a man, there was no way to know what he liked to do in bed.

What makes the passage work so well is the deliberately sharp and unexpected contrast that snaps into place with the last sentence, between the meticulous, even maniacal preparations, which attempt to foresee every contingency from raw sex to an affectionate sleepover to "marriage," and the elusive unknowability of the trick himself.

White can be as shrewdly observant of others as he is of his younger self. Many readers of *City Boy* are likely to cherish the louche anecdotes and tales out of school about the famous writer friends whom White acquired (and not infrequently lost) on his way up the literary ladder—Sontag, of course, but also Ashbery ("a hapless, amusing presence"), James Merrill, and his early mentor Richard Howard, one of the many more established figures to whom the young White attached himself and who tried to give him advice and help. In keeping with his own stated interests, White prefers to dilate on the quirky detail, the mannerism of speech or gesture or appearance. (He goes on about Howard's shiny bald pate, not nearly as common in the 1960s as now.) It must be said that the occasional detours into discussions of these writers' work, as opposed to their private lives, feel obligatory and none too profound—they have the vacant chirpiness of blurbs. ("A long, sustained look at the self, at what it might and might not be in these godless days": so White on Ashbery's *Self-Portrait in a Convex Mirror*.)

Significantly, White gossips best about those he knows—or who matter to him—least. One of the most entertaining stretches of *City Boy* occurs during a reminiscence of a trip to Italy, in which White reincarnates his wide-eyed younger self on a visit to the Cipriani pool, ogling the decadent, unhappy, much-married jet-setters—a bit of dishing that sparkles with fun precisely because it has the lightness of touch, the clarity, and the *disinvoltura* that characterize a really good gossip. No one knows this better than White, who clearly sees himself as something of a connoisseur of gossip. In *The Married Man*, the White character, a gay American expat long resident in Paris, returns home and sniffs at the locals' inability to gossip with any savoir faire. "They didn't know how to serve it up. They got bogged down in detail, they introduced too many names, and they never told the end."

And yet he himself commits these very errors when he's overly invested in the people he's gossiping about. When he writes about other writers who were more acclaimed or recognized in those days—he has a long memory for people who, like the playwright Mart Crowley (*The Boys in the Band*) didn't understand his work, or who, like the editor Robert Gottlieb, rejected it—the retributive barbs can seem petty and the anecdotes often feel gratuitous: he includes unflattering stories not only about Sontag herself (with whom White had a violent break after *Caracole* came out in 1985) but about her son, David Rieff. When, contemplating his failed friendship with Sontag, he blithely notes that he "never got to the bottom of my impulse toward treachery, especially toward people who'd helped me and befriended me," what strikes you is not so much the unpleasant admission but the blitheness with which he makes it—and, even more, his unwillingness to use the memoir to explore this trait, to get to the bottom of things instead of skimming the surface. This is what a memoir ought to do.

These personal impulses, and other personal preoccupations, often get in the way of the specificity and attention to detail that White himself advocates as crucial ingredients of good writing. When he describes Greenwich Village streets in the 1970s as being "crowded with kids with long hair and burgundy velvet jeans and mirrored vests and filmy shirts with puffy pirates sleeves," or when he recalls, of a brief stint on the West Coast, that "it seemed to us that everyone in San Francisco were doing yoga and reading Krishnamurti," you don't doubt that it's true, but there's something suspiciously generic about these characterizations—they feel cribbed, and don't have the complex textures of real experience. (Recalling New York City's fiscal crisis in the 1970s, White writes that Gerald Ford "told New York to drop dead"; but of course Ford never said that—White is quoting the famous *Daily News* headline.)

A comparable laziness informs White's larger social or political assessments. Do you really need to be told that midcentury suburban Americans were "sealed off in their offices or cars or houses, no one saw anyone outside his or her circle or had any contact with strangers. Suburbia, television, and the automobile had isolated everyone"? Good memoirs should penetrate beyond such clichés, not repackage them. The book itself is carelessly written, and even more carelessly edited: some characters are introduced twice, and a number of descriptions (of New York City, of his own books, of *The New York Times*, against whom he seems to have a particular animus) are repeated verbatim. And sentences like "Yale and Harvard had been a bit sniffy about anything so louche in which mere writers without degrees were allowed to shape young minds" are likely to inspire a bit of anxiety on behalf of undergraduate writing students at Princeton.

I suspect that White, who can be so precise, allows himself to be this lazy because he is, as it were, preaching to the converted—he's a gay writer writing for a sympathetic, if not wholly gay, audience, and after all "we all know what it was like." The kind of cozy parochialisms to which this kind of assumption leads make for some embarrassing moments in *City Boy*—and, worse, suggest the intellectual and aesthetic limitations imposed by the gay-niche writing and thinking White had championed in his conversation with Poirier. He doesn't like E. M. Forster because of his "closetedness"; he finds nothing "human or feeling" in Dante ("terribly underwritten...nothing vulnerable or hesitant") because the Florentine poet placed his homosexual master, Ser Brunetto, in Hell. Here, White's rose-colored glasses have not so much colored his vision as blinded him: to dismiss the *Inferno*, as he does, as "an unimaginative application of the rules to desires" because it isn't somehow "gay-friendly" is intellectually grotesque—and, anyway, an incorrect reading of the text. It would be hard to find a more poignant passage than the one in which the poet meets his doomed, beloved teacher in Hell.

This reflexive tendency to reduce everything to the dimensions of his preexisting interests and predilections can become wearying in *City Boy*; indeed, it was already wearying to some of White's friends in the years to which this book is devoted. After reporting to Richard Howard that he'd spent much of his first trip to Rome visiting gyms and cruising spots, Howard exclaimed in dismay: "Here you are in the central city of Western culture and you've managed to turn it into some sort of kicky version of Scranton." White's honesty in relating the episode is to his credit; the episode is not. In the best memoirs, a single, minutely recorded life can lead to large insight about the world; *City Boy*, by contrast, makes the world feel small.

———

Howard's remark, and with it thoughts about the size of our lives in relation the size of the world itself, bring you back to Poirier's worries, those many years ago, about the reductive implications of a literature by and for gay people. On the one hand, no one would want a biography of a gay (or Jewish, or black) writer that elided his sexuality (or religion, or race); such a work would and should be dismissed as insufficient. On the other hand, a biography (or, for that matter, a novel or a literary essay) that lost sight of the fact that sex and sexuality (or religion, or race) are, finally, a part but not the whole of our lives—there are other influences, other forces at work that help shape the creative mind, indeed any mind—risks devolving into a pat chauvinism, a kind of cultural boosterism. (At the beginning of his Proust biography, White catalogs writers who have been affected by *À la recherche* in one way or another; after briefly listing Joyce, Beckett, Woolf, Faulkner, Hemingway, Fitzgerald, Genet, and Thomas Mann, he dilates upon Proust's effect on Andrew Holleran, the author of a 1978 novel about gay alienation—a juxtaposition that, while meant to elevate Holleran's standing, does him no favors.) White's bad habits—the lopsided parochialism, the cattiness, the knowing winks that too often substitute for genuine insight—are the defects into which niche-thinking and niche-writing can lead us. Whatever its authentic achievements (those early novels, a number of penetrating meditations on the impact of AIDS on the gay creative community), too much of White's work can be personal in the wrong way.

And yet whatever the later impulse to turn Rome into Scranton, White, like so many writers, started out by dreaming big dreams of the great world. Again and again in *City Boy* he recalls his youthful yearning to be "famous among the top echelons of the cultural elite," to have a "lasting reputation" and "literary celebrity"—a yearning to be known that was so great that for him

> writing was essential to survival. Again, not because I had such beautiful or intense sentiments or because my ideas were so pressing and elevated (I didn't even have many ideas except during the five minutes every day when I took a shower), but because it was the label, writer, that mattered to me most in some primitive, essential way.

This kind of self-exposure becomes all the more moving when, in a startling moment of genuine and unusually acute self-reflection (as opposed to mere self-exposure), White worries that the movement that became the vehicle for his literary renown may have been wrong-headed after all. "I sometimes regret the invention of the category 'gay,'" he startlingly writes at the end of *City Boy*, as he looks back on the history of gay-niche publishing:

> Now all these years later, when "gay literature" has come and gone as a commercial fad and a serious movement, I can see [Poirier's] point. It's true that as a movement it did isolate us—to our advantage initially, though ultimately to our disadvantage. At first it drew the attention of critics and editors to our writing, but in the end (after our books didn't sell) it served to quarantine us into a small, confined space. Before the category of "gay writing" was invented, books with gay content (Vidal's *City and the Pillar*, Baldwin's *Giovanni's Room*, Isherwood's *A Single Man*) were widely reviewed and often became bestsellers. After a label was applied to them they were dismissed as being of special interest only to gay people. They could only preach to the converted.

This is a far cry from the attitude of the young White who had once resentfully criticized Poirier and other gay writers he knew when he was starting out—even the ones who were unabashedly out of the closet, like Merrill and Ashbery—for wanting to assimilate aesthetically, as he saw it: to write for the larger world instead of—well, preaching to the converted, to that small "community [that] we want[ed] to celebrate in novels that would create our identity while also exploring it." Hence although *City Boy*, like many a bildungsroman, ostensibly culminates in a happy attainment of maturity—the young White's successful quest to be a published gay writer—there is another, deeper education that plays out in these pages: the one that culminates in the author's poignant, late-life admission that real literature is, in fact, "universal," that it seeks to dissolve rather than create intellectual and artistic ghettos.

Still, you suspect that White, unabashedly a product of the era he recalls in the new memoir, would be the first to admit that what he has been writing all these years—the ongoing, earnest transcription of gay life and gay lives, of which *City Boy* is but the latest installment—has aimed to fill a niche instead of a universe. What he wanted, after all, was to become celebrated, to have a reputation, to be known as a *writer*, whatever the sentiments and the ideas might be. This he has certainly done. Who would begrudge him the satisfaction that he got what he wanted?

—*The New York Review of Books,* September 30, 2010

THE COLLECTOR

IT IS SOMEHOW appropriate that the voice of deep and anguished ambivalence that speaks at the beginning of *Reborn*, the new volume of Susan Sontag's early journals and notebooks, does not belong to Susan Sontag. Self-doubt was not a quality you generally associated with her. From the moment she burst onto the literary scene nearly fifty years ago, with the publication of the essays subsequently collected as *Against Interpretation*—a cultural-critical Athena, armored with a vast erudition, bristling with epigrams—Sontag exhibited a preternatural self-assurance in matters of art and culture, an unwavering belief in her own judgments and tastes that, as these early private papers now make clear, she possessed already in her early teens. (The first of a projected three volumes of Sontag's journals, this one takes her to the age of thirty; fully one third of it is a record of her teenage years.)

The embarrassment with which *Reborn* begins belongs, rather, to her son, the writer David Rieff, who edited his mother's journals. In a preface, Rieff describes how he uneasily consented to publish this "raw" and "unvarnished" sampling of Sontag's adolescent effusions about life and her early perceptions about art; he shows a marked queasiness about "the literary dangers and moral hazards of such an enterprise." The anxiety stems from two sources. The first was ethical and, so to speak, generic: although his mother, in one of her final illnesses, was anxious for him to know where the journals were kept, there was no indication that Sontag would have wanted the contents of these papers to be made public. "The diaries," Rieff notes, "were written solely for herself.... She had never permitted a line from them to be published, nor, unlike some diarists, did she read from them to friends."

Rieff's second scruple, more personal and more revealing, suggests the reason for the first:

> To say that these diaries are self-revelatory is a drastic understatement.... One of the principal dilemmas in all this has been that, at least in her later life, my mother was not in any way a self-revealing person. In particular, she avoided to the extent that she could, without denying it, any discussion of her own homosexuality or any acknowledgment of her own ambition.

Sexuality and ambition are, of course, the reason that many people read the private journals of public figures; in Sontag's case, the inevitable interest in the raw passions corresponding to "homosexuality" and "ambition" is bound to be particularly strong, because her highly polished public and literary persona seemed designed to quash interest in precisely those two things. On the one hand, there was the famous reticence about her lesbianism, despite the fact that it was, as she awkwardly admitted late in life, an "open secret." On the other, there was the cool Artemis-like glamour (that silver streak), the sense she projected of being the high priestess of High Culture. (A sense heightened by her penchant for gnomic utterances: "In place of a hermeneutics we need an erotics of art"; "New York: all sensuality is converted to sexuality.") All of this conferred upon her an aura of intellectual invulnerability, of an authority that, rather than having been earned or having evolved, she somehow had always possessed complete.

It is unlikely that readers who are motivated by prurience will be satisfied by the strangely scattered document that has resulted from Rieff's editing. (The volume has a jittery, disjointed feel; it isn't clear whether this is how the journals were written or if the published version of them was shaped to accord with Sontag's trademark aphoristic style.) What's fascinating and, in the end, extremely suggestive is that the journals reveal an adolescent and, later, a young woman in whom "ambition"—in this case, an overpowering yearning to be surrounded by and immersed in literature and culture—vastly outweighed, and seems ultimately to have overpowered, "sexuality." That disproportion explains a great deal about the strange career, its achievements and its failures both, of a writer who, as her son wrenchingly writes, "was as uncomfortable with her body as she was serene about her mind." Or for whom, as she herself puts it in the last entry of this journal, "intellectual wanting" was the equal of "sexual wanting."

The erotic element about which Rieff worries in his preface is, indeed, the least memorable part of Sontag's private writings, at least in this first volume. There is, to be sure, a good deal of emoting, particularly in the early entries, which are dominated by the usual sorts of adolescent anxieties. "How easy it would be to convince myself of the plausibility of my parents' life!" she writes in 1947, at the age of fourteen, already showing the impatience with the petit-bourgeois, assimilated Jewish-American background into which she was born, and at which she would never look back—the impatience that would later drive her to Berkeley, then to the University of Chicago, and then to New York, where she lived for the rest of her life. "I am in love with being in love!" she writes the next year, in one of the many girlish effusions about her already precocious erotic life that are sprinkled through the journals. (She understood that she was a lesbian very early on, and started having serious affairs as a teenager.)

Much of the material about the diarist's sentimental life constitutes a fairly typical *Bildungsgeschichte*, the record of a young person's initiation into the mysteries of adulthood. The only real surprise here is that, intriguingly for a woman of her class, culture (provincial: she grew up in Arizona), and era (she was born in 1933), Sontag did not express a great deal of anguish about homosexuality itself. The pain that she records in these pages—the journals chronicle two major lesbian relationships—is the pain that comes with any love affair, but the insights are no more illuminating, finally, than the confidences to be found in any number of such documents, straight or gay. ("Lesson: not to surrender one's heart when it's not wanted.") This is also true of the more explicit ruminations about sex itself, which are both infrequent and wholly conventional. "Fucking vs. being fucked. The deeper experience—more gone—is being fucked."

What you do want—what would, perhaps, be illuminating about Sontag's hitherto hidden emotional life—you don't get, at least in the text that has been published. There is almost no comment whatsoever on a notorious enigma of Sontag's early biography—her engagement, at the age of sixteen, to the sociologist Philip Rieff after a ten-day acquaintance: a decision about which this journal's near-total silence may, in the end, be more eloquent than words. As for the aftermath of that bizarre decision, there is much here about a bad marriage that, *pace* Tolstoy, seems to have been a lot like many other bad marriages, although Sontag can bring to her account of its collapse the same crisp intelligence that would make her criticism so satisfying. "Whoever invented marriage was an ingenious tormentor," she wrote in 1956, after nine years with Rieff. "It is an institution *committed* to the dulling of feelings. The whole point of marriage is repetition. The best it aims for is the creation of strong, mutual dependencies." She left Rieff in 1957.

So the sex is not that good. That leaves ambition. That Sontag—the critic who emerged in the early 1960s as a Wildean champion of style wherever it could be found (camp, Godard, theater, "happenings," science-fiction movies, pornography), even as she brandished a formidable familiarity with the classics of the canon—was completely omnivorous and always hungry for something new, you understood from the work itself. What the early journals reveal, and what ends up, curiously, being far more moving than the material about her emotional life, is the intensity and the scope of a remarkable intellectual ambition that was present from the start: the astonishing avidity for culture, for aesthetic stimulation, that more than anything mark Sontag as a writer and a public figure. (Members of a certain generation of writers can invariably recall the play, or opera, or ballet, or opening, or reading at which they first saw Sontag: she seemed to be everywhere.) At the age of fifteen she already had an unwavering conviction of what she wanted to do and where she needed to be: "I want to write—I want to live in an intellectual atmosphere.... I want to live in a cultural center." And then, later: "I intend to do everything."

Much of *Reborn*—and, according to Rieff's occasional interpolated commentaries, a great deal more of the original documents—consists simply of lists of "everything": books that Sontag was determined to read, movies she had to see, poets and playwrights she had to know. An entry from 1948, when she was fifteen, looks like this:

Gide
Sherwood Anderson
Ludwig Lewisohn
Faulkner
George Moore
Dostoyevsky
Huysmans
Bourget
Arsybashev
Trumbo
Galsworthy
Meredith
poems of Dante, Ariosto, Tasso, Tibullus, Heine, Pushkin,
    Rimbaud, Verlaine, Apollinaire
plays of Synge, O'Neill, Calderon, Shaw, Hellman

In an italicized note to this passage, Rieff indicates that the list goes on for another five pages in the original.

As the years pass and the journal continues, this particular passion, at least, never abates. What strikes you is how you encounter less and less the kind of emotions most people confide to their diaries: tenderness, vulnerability, and so on. One list that's genuinely affecting, because it gives a rare glimpse of precisely that kind of awkward vulnerability, is the one that the young woman drew up before her first trip to Paris in 1957, which reveals how nervously the already deeply Francophile writer studied for her transatlantic debut:

cafe crème—white coffee after dinner
cafe au lait—breakfast coffee
une fine (brandy)
un Pernod (as many Pernods as colas in the US)

It's hard to avoid the impression that the outsized cultural avidity, the literary ambition to which these pages bear witness, seems eventually to have occluded the more tender feelings. Not the least of these was the maternal. It cannot have been easy for Rieff to come across lines such as "I hardly ever dream of David, and don't think of him much. He has made few inroads on my fantasy-life." Most editors aren't called upon for, and don't demonstrate, such probity.

Indeed, there is a strange, sometimes even shocking *froideur* in evidence here about subjects that most of us find hot; it is startling to grasp the extent to which Sontag brought to her own life the chilly assessing gaze that made her such a brilliant critic, such an expert looker. In one passage toward the end of the book (she is in her late twenties) she muses that "sex as a cognitive act would be, practically, a helpful attitude for me to have, to keep my eyes open, my head up—where the point is *not* to show sexual excitement as long as you can. (No pelvic spasms, no hard breathing, no words, etc.)" "Practical" and "helpful" do not, for most of us, belong to the linguistic register that we bring to our understanding of a roll in the hay. And later on Sontag again returns to this wish "to make sex cognitive"— and "to correct the imbalance now."

It isn't at all clear that the balancing act was a great success. If anything, the journals reveal a person for whom, however much she saw herself as a sensualist, the cognitive and the analytical invariably dominated the erotic and the affective. ("Emotionally, I wanted to stay," Sontag wrote of her decision to leave home and family in Los Angeles for Berkeley. "Intellectually, I wanted to leave." She left.) The inevitable triumph of the head over the heart in these pages defies, I think, a description of his mother that Rieff gives in his preface: in speaking of Sontag's extraordinary literary ambition, he compares her to Balzac's Lucien de Rubempré, the hero of *Lost Illusions*, the talented youth who comes from the provinces to find literary fame in

Paris. Rieff goes on to conclude with a summary characterization of Sontag as a "nineteenth-century consciousness"—a judgment, you suspect, that Sontag, with her insatiable avidity for experience and her penchant for the Continental novel as model of the highest form of literary activity, would have welcomed.

And yet when you survey her career with an eye as coolly dispassionate as the one she trained on so many objects, it becomes obvious that, temperamentally, she belonged to another century entirely. Her failure to understand just which century it was accounts for the sense you often get, taking the work as a whole, of aspirations that were at odds with her temperament and her talent; and it explains a great deal about both the strengths and the weaknesses of her work, and about the strange fascination that she exerted.

If you looked closely enough, this uneasy, even riven quality was there from the start, in the breathtakingly authoritative critical pieces with which she made her reputation in the early 1960s. But as would often happen with this remarkable personality, the sheer force and stylishness of her utterances overwhelmed whatever doubts there might have been. The essays in *Against Interpretation* (1961) and in *Styles of Radical Will* (1966) may champion, famously, the need not for "a hermeneutics but an erotics of Art," but what is so striking is that there is not anything very erotic about them; they are, in fact, all hermeneutics. In the criticism, as in the journals, the eros is all from the neck up.

The heat, if anything, tended to be generated by the objects of Sontag's interest, rather than by her investigation of them. The early forays into cultural criticism often derive their power precisely from the tension between the iciness of Sontag's Olympian gaze and the unexpectedly funky, roiling, popular objects at which she levels it: porn, movies, sci-fi, camp. There was a deep pleasure, a thrill even, in seeing how she used a formidably broad and deep learning, and the traditional tools of formal literary analysis, to turn cultural sows' ears into critical silk purses. In demonstrating the deeper cultural significance of phenomena that nobody else had thought to take seriously ("camp is the answer to the problem: how to be a dandy in the age of mass culture... camp taste transcends the nausea of the replica"), she anticipated by a generation the belated adolescence of the American academy—all those Comp Lit and Cultural Studies dissertations, in the late 1980s and early 1990s, on Madonna and Boy George. This willingness to see the value in material disdained by "high" culture—something for which Pauline Kael would later become famous, after Sontag's tastes ossified—was an important and satisfying part of Sontag's rhetorical persona, and went a long way toward giving her the iconoclastic allure that would cling to her for the rest of her life, however conservative her tastes were to become.

And yet this astoundingly gifted interpreter, so naturally skilled at peeling away trivial-seeming exteriors to reveal deeper cultural meanings—skilled, too, at teasing out the significance of surface features to which you might not have given much attention ("people run beautifully in Godard movies")—fought mightily to affect an "aesthetic" disdain for content. Again and again, the essays themselves give the lie to her agenda of devaluing interpretation: even as she appears to swoon over "the untranslatable, sensuous immediacy" of, say, *Last Year in Marienbad*, you can't help noticing that there is not a single sensuous surface that she does not try to translate into something abstract and rarefied, that is not subject to the flashing scalpel of her critical intellect. While this championing of form and especially "style" at the expense of content and "meaning" is hardly original—it's reheated Wilde—what's so striking in Sontag's case is her furious insistence that it be true, her desperate need to believe the rhetorical claim that her own writing subverts.

There is an odd quality of protesting too much to these gestures, to the booming opening salvos against contemporary intellectual culture's "hypertrophy of the intellect at the expense of energy and sensual capability," and of interpretation as "the revenge of the intellect upon art." As you make your way through these exercises in interpretative finesse, with their flourishes of epigrammatic bravura ("the greatest artists attain a sublime neutrality"), you wonder who is taking revenge on whom, exactly. Here again you feel the presence of an underlying conflict: Sontag the natural analyst against Sontag the struggling sensualist. You don't doubt that she genuinely wished to experience works of art purely with the senses and the emotions; but the author of these celebrated essays is quite plainly the grown-up version of the young girl who, at fifteen, declared her preference for "virtuosity...technique, organization...the cruelly realistic comment (Huxley, Rochefoucauld), the mocking caricature." Technique, virtuosity, raillery, cruelty even: all this, capped by the reference to Rochefoucauld, reminds you that, whatever her Balzacian yearnings, Sontag's young tastes were far more in line with French classicism than with Romantic passion.

Sontag's career as a novelist is similarly marked by a strange misapprehension of her own gifts and nature. Everything that makes her an extraordinary critic—the extreme analytical self-consciousness, the way in which she can't help but train the cool and assessing eye on every available object, the thirst for learning all the relevant and arcane details, the inability to resist any opportunity to interpret and to explain—makes her an inept novelist. There's a jarring contrast between the thrilling vividness of her critical writing and the almost total inertness of her fiction. And yet she clung stubbornly to a view of herself as essentially a writer of novels and stories, from her claim in the preface to *Against Interpretation* that her critical essays were largely ancillary to her fiction, helping her to "radically change" her "conception of [her] task as a novelist," to her pronouncement, in a speech she gave on accepting a prize in Germany in 2003, that "I am a storyteller."

Her fiction suggests otherwise, from the strained exercise in Francophilia that was *The Benefactor* in 1963, replete with the kind of archness and striving for effect that so often result when critics aspire to fiction ("he always spoke across the unbesiegeable moat of his own chastity") to *The Volcano Lover*, in 1992, and *In America*, in 2000. In all of these the critic's analytical and self-examining eye dominates, explaining too much, getting in the way. In both *The Volcano Lover*, a kind of intellectual recasting of *That Hamilton Woman*, and *In America*, a highly self-referential fictionalization of the career of the nineteenth-century Polish actress Helena Modjeska, Sontag herself, in the form of a disembodied narrator's voice, hovers intrusively over the story that she claims to want to tell, commenting on the action, distracting your attention from the story by reminding us that this is a Susan Sontag production. "Appalled by the lethal upsurge of nationalist and tribal feelings in my own time," the narrator of *In America* says, apropos of some ruminations about her Polish characters' national history, "I'd spent a good part of three years in besieged Sarajevo." There is no aesthetic reason, nothing in the form or the narrative, for the reader to have this information; Sontag just can't get out of the way. You suspect that this arch carrying on was meant to be justified as a playful, even chicly postmodern device, but Sontag was too solemn and self-serious a writer to get away with such tricks, and the intrusions come off as merely pretentious.

The Sontag that the author of the later fiction seems to think we want is not even Sontag the great critic: it's just "Sontag," the celebrated public figure. Already in *The Volcano Lover*, but particularly in the unbearably labored and self-conscious *In America*, the authorial interventions feel not only self-referential but also self-congratulatory. Even the true believers who felt that *In America* deserved the acclaim it received must have stumbled over passages such as the following one, in which, as the novel opens, the hovering Sontag-narrator explains how she manages to understand the conversation of the Polish characters she mysteriously finds herself observing at the beginning of her tale:

> But I, with my command only of Romance languages (I dabble in German, know the names of twenty kinds of fish in Japanese, have soaked up a splash of Bosnian, and understand barely a word of the language of the country in which this room is to be found), I, as I've said, somehow did manage to understand most of what they were saying.

The command "only" of Romance languages; the pompous advertisement for what we understand to be her sophisticated appreciation of sushi and sashimi—stuff like this, and there is a lot of it, makes you wish that Sontag had hoped more fervently for herself what, as the narrator of *In America*, she "hoped" for her protagonist: that "she hadn't been made less of an artist by high-mindedness. Or by self-regard."

The great irony of her career is that her apparent conviction, derived from her early immersion in nineteenth-century European literature, that to be a significant literary figure you had to be a novelist, paradoxically blinded her to what already made her a significant literary figure. There's a passage in *Regarding the Pain of Others*, a slender critical work published in 2003, in which, making a case about the special rhetorical quality of photography, she observes that "photographs [are] both objective record and personal testimony, both a faithful copy or transcription of an actual moment of reality and an interpretation of that reality—a feat literature has long aspired to, but could never attain in this literal sense." But of course literature does possess a genre that strives to be both objective and personal, an accurate record and a subjective testimony, a representation and an interpretation at the same time, and it's the genre at which Sontag really excelled: criticism. That she could write such a passage—that it never occurred to her to think of her own métier when thinking about what literature could do—is more wrenching than anything she ever wrote in her fiction.

The contrast between the pointed effectiveness and verbal élan of Sontag's critical writing and the bloated grandiosities of her fiction makes it that much more regrettable that, as time passed, the criticism itself seemed to metamorphose, to change direction and tone.

Like Wilde, whose arguments and aphoristic dazzle she appropriated, Sontag achieved considerable fame and authority early on by rebelling against staid, academic, old-fashioned intellectual culture. And like Wilde, she paradoxically used the tools provided by a formidable traditional education (he as a classicist, she as a student of philosophy and a precocious autodidact) to reject the academy, carving out a career for herself instead as a popular literary figure—a move that surely accounts for the cult-like status that she, like Wilde, enjoyed. Both were intellectuals who made good, who achieved glamour in the great world. And yet, once she had made her name with those extraordinarily cunning and excitingly fresh validations of popular American culture, Sontag went on to spend the rest of her career as a tireless cheerleader for the canon, for what she referred to, with telling frequency, as "greatness"—a quality that, strikingly, she seemed increasingly to find only in the works of middle-aged, white, European men.

This is most apparent in the later essays, such as those collected in *Where the Stress Falls* (2001). These pieces were written in the years after she published the last of her significant works of cultural criticism, *Illness as Metaphor* and *AIDS and Its Metaphors*—texts in which she brilliantly brings a calm philological eye to reveal the cultural anxieties and prejudices that lie beneath the overwrought diction of pop epidemiology and professional medicine. The problem with *Where the Stress Falls* is, in fact, that there is not a whole lot of stress in evidence. There is a played-out feel about the book, whose serious critical reflections are increasingly rambling and diffuse, and whose many incidental pieces seem, more than anything, like advertisements for Sontag's status as a cultural icon: answers to French questionnaires about the role of intellectuals, for example, and self-flattering ruminations on being translated. ("You might say I'm obsessed with translations. I think I'm just obsessed with language." What writer isn't?)

This exhaustion is even more marked in the collection that was published after Sontag died, in 2004, called *At the Same Time*, which includes the now-notorious speech in which she seems to have plagiarized her observations about hypertext: the ultimate mark of creative exhaustion. But a critical tendency does emerge. The vast majority of these late and ostensibly critical pieces are encomia to, and sometimes eulogies for, a long list of European (preferably *Mittel-*) men: Victor Serge, W.G. Sebald, Robert Walser, Danilo Kiš, Joseph Brodsky, Witold Gombrowicz, Adam Zagajewski. The essays are curiously shorter and more desultory than the early pieces; there is a restless quality even to the project of praise, which Sontag very early on saw as her specialty. ("I don't, ultimately, care for handing out grades to works of art," she wrote in a later preface to *Against Interpretation*. "I wrote as an enthusiast and a partisan.") Walser, for whom she professes to want to perform her signal service and thereby "bring [him] to the attention of a public that has not yet discovered him," gets a scant two pages, which end with the kind of banal encomium, a blurb really, that you expect from the harried reviewers in the dailies: "a truly wonderful writer."

Compare all this to the forty-two densely packed pages of her thrillingly brilliant 1968 dissection of Godard, for whose reputation she set out to perform a similar service. In that instance Sontag was providing a rigorous and wholly original way of thinking about the complex work of a major young contemporary artist; it was an essay that felt like part of something vital that was happening in the arts. In the Walser piece, by contrast, you get a whiff of Lemon Pledge: she's dusting off a forgotten tchotchke and putting it back on the very high shelf from which it had fallen. The style, too, is diminished, wearied. The surgical gleam and "aphoristic glitter"—Sontag's admiring description of Glenway Wescott's style in *The Pilgrim Hawk*—of the strong youthful pieces come more and more to be replaced here by expressions of anxious concern for the safety of High Culture. "Is literary greatness still possible?" she frets in the slim essay on Sebald.

All this suggests, in the end, a certain melancholy fulfillment of a prophecy that Sontag made in her journals when she was in her early twenties. Not long before her twenty-fourth birthday, she wondered to herself which of two roads she might take, and the question she posed suggests that she understood more, then, about the divided nature of both her gifts and her ambitions—the struggle, not least, between genuine innovation and intelligent adulation—than some of her later pronouncements, and projects, might indicate. The answer, too, was prescient. "To philosophize, or to be a culture-conserver?" she wondered in October 1956. "I had never thought of being anything other than the latter."

Anyway, what had "greatness" come to mean for Sontag? It was, for a start, almost exclusively identified with Europe. In his preface Rieff acknowledges that for his mother "American literature was a suburb of the great literatures of Europe," and he is right: Sontag devoted none of her remarkable interpretative energies to significant American writers, either of an earlier time or of her own. The most effusive of her literary encomia, indeed, often come at the expense of the Anglo-American tradition. "When has one heard in English a voice of such confidence and precision, so direct in its expression of feeling, yet so respectfully devoted to recording 'the real'?" she asks in her piece on Sebald, the last in the string of German novelists whom she exalted—an adulation that started with her life-altering reading of *The Magic Mountain* as a teenager. (In *Reborn* Sontag records her meeting with Mann when she was fourteen and he seventy-two, and both were living in Los Angeles; rather typically, she expresses disappointment that the flesh-and-blood person failed to live up to the books.) And as the list of writers whom Sontag does choose to exalt in collections such as *Where the Stress Falls* also suggests, "greatness" seems to be largely the property of men, and is most likely to be achieved through the writing of novels. And so, in the end, Sontag became a genuine traditionalist—not only a conserver but also, at least in matters of culture, a conservative.

This desire to be associated with greatness of a kind that is, when all is said and done, exceedingly old-fashioned brings you back to the Sontag of the early journals—to the "ambition," to the starry-eyed lover of books who reminds Rieff of Lucien de Rubempré. Lucien's real name is the comically plebeian Chardon, or "thistle": he has to shake the family tree a bit before the surname that he eventually adopts, with its glamorous aristocratic "de," falls out. The desire not merely for self-transformation but for a kind of validation that only an association with the highest echelons of culture can bring is one to which *Reborn* bears ample witness. As his name change indicates, Lucien's aspirations were social as well as artistic; Sontag, to her great credit, was purely intellectual and cultural in her ambitions. Her desire, twice articulated in these pages, to be "reborn" itself testifies to the fervor of her belief that it was necessary to abandon where she came from in order to get where she wanted to be—an impetus that may well never have found an end point, and that itself may have seemed to her a mark of "greatness."

But the obsession with greatness has other implications. There is, you realize, another odd thing about the list of qualities that Sontag associated with literary greatness: it is a list of things that she herself was not. The sense you get here of a profoundly divided identity is, for Rieff, entirely consonant with his mother's taste for transformation, the lifelong effort to "remake herself." Anticipating the questions about self-knowledge and identity that such efforts inevitably raise about people, he hints that what in other people could be seen as embarrassment, a kind of covering up, was in Sontag's case exemplary. Casting her strenuous "jettisoning" of her middle-class, American, Jewish roots ("her social and ethnic context," as he puts it) as a heroic, nineteenth-century, and even somewhat Nietzschean affair—the achievement of a titanic "will"—he cites Fitzgerald on second acts in American lives, a nice way of suggesting that Sontag's increasing dissociation from things American was the most American thing about her.

But this pervasive irresolution and desperate desire for transformation can also be ascribed to another factor, to the other of the two strands that unspool in *Reborn*—not to ambition but to sexuality. In

WAITING FOR THE BARBARIANS

this case, the instability had a marked effect on Sontag's engagement with politics. I am referring to the issue of the writer's homosexuality, which she discussed forthrightly enough in her private musings, but about which she remained curiously reticent even when such reticence was no longer expected of important left-wing intellectuals—indeed, when to come out of the closet would have been an affirmation of a certain kind of cultural bona fides.

It is a measure of the intimidating power of Sontag's mystique that comparatively little has been made over the years of the refusal by this most public of public intellectuals to engage, in her speeches and her essays, with the pressing issues raised particularly by the AIDS crisis and the political and cultural controversies that it generated throughout the 1980s and 1990s. It says something that when Sontag did write about homosexuality, it was in a work of fiction: the now-famous short story "The Way We Live Now," first published in *The New Yorker* in November 1986. (It's a story about men, about male homosexuals and their experience: a suggestive displacement.) Any notion that she might have connected the dots between her sexual nature and her public utterances on power and justice tended to be cast as a vulgar parochialization, a crass infringement upon her citizenship in the wider republic of letters. Rieff, as we know, acknowledged that his mother "avoided to the extent that she could, without denying it, any discussion of her own homosexuality." Much depends on that lawyerly "without denying it." Sontag's passivity in this regard may have been the only feeble thing about her; she was, after all, no stranger to controversy. She herself was almost touchingly forthright about her ambiguity, in remarks she made late in life to the editor of *Out* magazine:

> I grew up in a time when the modus operandi was the "open secret." I'm used to that, and quite OK with it. Intellectually, I

know why I haven't spoken more about my sexuality, but I do wonder if I haven't repressed something there to my detriment. Maybe I could have given comfort to some people if I had dealt with the subject of my private sexuality more, but it's never been my prime mission to give comfort, unless somebody's in drastic need. I'd rather give pleasure, or shake things up.

The passage is wholly typical. Apart from the characteristic tension between the mind ("Intellectually, I know why") and the heart, and a certain awkwardness reflected in the stiffness and the circuitousness of the language ("I do wonder if I haven't repressed something there"), the statement represents yet another triumph of that ferocious intellect at the expense of the realm of feelings. Note the reflexively disdainful dismissal of any possibility that she might have spoken publicly about issues relating to homosexuality as a merely sentimental gesture, a treacly project of "giving comfort."

But as we know, Sontag certainly wasn't above giving comfort to groups that she saw as oppressed, and didn't disdain making large and dramatic public gestures meant to validate the rights, and the humanity, of certain minorities. About the citizens of Bosnia, that province of Mitteleuropa that became one of her intellectual homelands, about Europe and its political outrages, Sontag never ceased to speak, with her usual crispness and a smart, outraged passion. All this was deeply admirable. But finally there was something familiar about the way in which she championed the foreign over the domestic, the idealized identity rather than the core identity. *Intellectually I wanted to go.* As we know, she went; and to be sure, there is a kind of touching grandeur to the famous *folie* of her producing *Waiting for Godot* in Sarajevo under siege, which, whatever else it may have achieved, certainly gave comfort.

My point is not to correct Sontag politically; nor do I want to denigrate the significant positive effects of her political arguments and activities. Everyone, after all, is self-interpreting and self-inventing— writers and artists more than most. Sontag was a true cosmopolitan, and that is an achievement not only of morality but also of imagination. But cosmopolitanism, too, is a set of choices, and Sontag's choices in the realm of politics strikingly resemble her choices in the realm of literature and culture. At a certain point you have to ask why there was this unquenchable need to comfort, this limitless sympathy, for Bosnians but not for lesbians.

In the end, it was Sontag herself who gave us the most useful metaphor for understanding her. The key is to be found in *The Volcano Lover*, a work whose ambivalent seesawing between two crucial centuries, between two irreconcilable worldviews, tells us more than anything else she wrote about the uneasy divisions in Sontag herself.

The novel is an unusual take on a famous story: the love affair between Emma Hamilton and Admiral Nelson. It is told primarily through the eyes of Emma's cuckolded husband, Sir William Hamilton, the great collector of classical antiquities who, as British envoy to the Kingdom of the Two Sicilies, in Naples, had the pick of the splendid works that emerged from the excavations at Pompeii and Herculaneum; these helped to create the great craving for all things classical (and neoclassical) that marked the end of the eighteenth century. A good deal of the book is devoted to brilliant ruminations on the nature and the psychology of collecting, a passion apparently shared by the Sontag-like narrator who, like the narrator of *In America*, hovers obtrusively over the opening of the novel. "I'm seeing," this disembodied voice says, during a visit to what seems to be a flea market,

I'm checking on what's in the world. What's left. What's discarded. What's no longer cherished. What had to be sacrificed. What someone thought might interest someone else...there may be something valuable, there. Not valuable, exactly. But something I would want. Want to rescue. Something that speaks to me. To my longings.

As we know, a taste for "checking on what's in the world," to say nothing of aesthetic rescue missions, constituted a significant part of Sontag's critical project. Hamilton's own characterization of the point of his activities—"To surround oneself with enchanting and stimulating objects, a superfluity of objects, to ensure that the sense will never be unoccupied, nor the faculty of imagination left unexercised"—reminds you even more strongly of the author, with her frenetic desire to be aesthetically stimulated, occupied, exercised. The sense of a strong identification is palpable. Not surprisingly, this novel was the closest to a real literary success that her fiction ever achieved.

The metaphor of the collector is the perfect one for Sontag. Her impressive sympathy for Hamilton, with his great hunger for inanimate objects, explains so much about her—the unbelievable avidity, the impossibility of satiety, the need to possess it all, to know "everything." And it provides, too, another explanation for her incessant promotion, toward the end of her career, of "greatness": like all good collectors, she wanted you to know how precious her objects were, how much they were worth. Small wonder that some of her most intense aesthetic enthusiasms were inspired by collectors: William Hamilton; Walter Benjamin, in his library and in the arcades; Godard. She wrote feelingly about the latter's "hypertrophy of appetite for culture (though often more avid for cultural debris than for museum-consecrated achievements); they proceed by voraciously scavenging in culture, proclaiming that nothing is alien to their art." It would be hard to think of a better description of Sontag herself.

As it proceeds, *The Volcano Lover* moves away from the eighteenth century, from the cool acquisitive gaze of the Enlightenment, to the grand passions of the Romantic century that followed. (The book's coy subtitle is "A Romance.") In the novel, headlong passions are represented by two narrative threads, one "personal" and one "political," that become intertwined. The first is the adulterous love of Nelson and Emma (who abandons, you might say, the love of the old for the love of the new—the elderly Hamilton for the war hero Nelson); the second is an ongoing series of references to the violent revolutions with which the eighteenth century ended—in particular, the brief republican revolution in Naples in 1799, which resulted in the short-lived overthrow of the Bourbon monarchy. Nelson, on orders from London, gave the royalist regime military support, as Hamilton gave diplomatic support. (Emma, for her part, was the bosom friend of the queen, Maria Carolina, sister of Marie Antoinette.) With Nelson's aid, the republic was soon overthrown and the repressive monarchy was reestablished.

But if the novel moves you, it is—as sometimes occurs in Sontag's writing—because of something that happens between the lines. Everything about Hamilton, about the collector, is wonderful: the evocation of what it is like to live a life given to intellectual and aesthetic pursuits, the rich sense that Sontag gives of what it's like to "discover what is beautiful and to share that with others," an activity that Hamilton passionately defends as "also a worthy employment for a life." And yet against all narrative and logical expectation, Sontag ends by wrenching the novel (and the reader's sympathy) away from Hamilton, who, we perceive, will not be the hero. That role, it turns out, is given to a person who comes late on the scene: another historical figure, Eleonora de Fonseca Pimentel, a Neapolitan aristocrat and poet who sided with the republican rebels and was executed by the restored Bourbons as the exhausted century ended, in August 1799. The book ends with her musings at the moment of her death—reflections that comprise a stunning rejection of the character, and indeed the values, that Sontag has so feelingly evoked throughout the book. "Did he ever have an original thought," Pimentel furiously wonders about Hamilton,

> or subject himself to the discipline of writing a poem, or discover or invent something useful to humanity, or burn with zeal for anything except his own pleasures and the privileges annexed to his station? He knew enough to appreciate what the picturesque natives had left, in the way of art and ruins, lying about the ground.

And the novel's last lines make a final overt allusion to Sontag herself, one that suggests that she saw her political engagement as an expression of this "romantic" side:

> Sometimes I had to forget that I was a woman to accomplish the best of which I was capable. Or I would lie to myself about how complicated it is to be a woman. Thus do all women, including the author of this book. But I cannot forgive those who did not care about more than their own glory or well-being. They thought they were civilized. They were despicable. Damn them all.

Anyone who has considered Sontag's career will find that "damn them all" profoundly affecting; it expresses, yet again, her desire to forsake who she was in favor of a romantic dream. *The Volcano Lover* makes it clear that Sontag's sensibility was the eighteenth-century one that she so successfully evoked in the character of Hamilton, whom she ends by damning. And yet this aesthete and accumulator of experience nonetheless yearned all her life—because she was so taught by the kind of novels that she ingested but could not, in the end, ever write—to inhabit the century to which her son touchingly assigns her: the nineteenth, with its grand passions and its Romantic energies. Emotionally, she thought she was the one; intellectually, she was the other. This confusion helps to account for so much about her life and her work: the strange analytical coldness about normal human passions (that desire to make sex "cognitive") and the remarkably hot passion for the stimulation of books, theater, films; the initial embrace of the importance of the daringly new, the avant-garde, the louche and outré, followed by the retreat into the conventional (the historical novel!), the canonical, the established, the "great"; the wobbly relationship between the criticism, which was her calling, and the fiction, which was not.

This lifelong struggle to find a place between these various poles—extremities nicely summed up, in *The Volcano Lover*, during an amusing encounter between Hamilton and Goethe, as "beauty" and "transformation"—gives Sontag a certain novelistic allure of her own. But here again the character whom she calls to mind is a decidedly pre-Romantic figure. In one of the shortest literary essays that she ever wrote, Sontag ruminated on a favorite novel, and her description of its hero suggests a strong affinity between the critic and the character:

With Don Quixote, a hero of excess, the problem is not so much that the books are bad; it is the sheer quantity of his reading. Reading has not merely deformed his imagination; it has kidnapped it. He thinks the world is the inside of a book.... Bookishness makes him, in contrast to Emma Bovary, beyond compromise or corruption. It makes him mad; it makes him profound, heroic, genuinely noble.

Thanks to her son's nervous but rewarding decision, Sontag herself has finally achieved a kind of resolution. For she has made the translation that, you sometimes feel, she had always yearned for and so long awaited. Now others must do the interpreting; she herself, beyond compromise and corruption, no madder than most and more noble, too, has become the text. Infinitely interpretable, she has at last ended up on the inside of a book.

—*The New Republic*, April 15, 2009